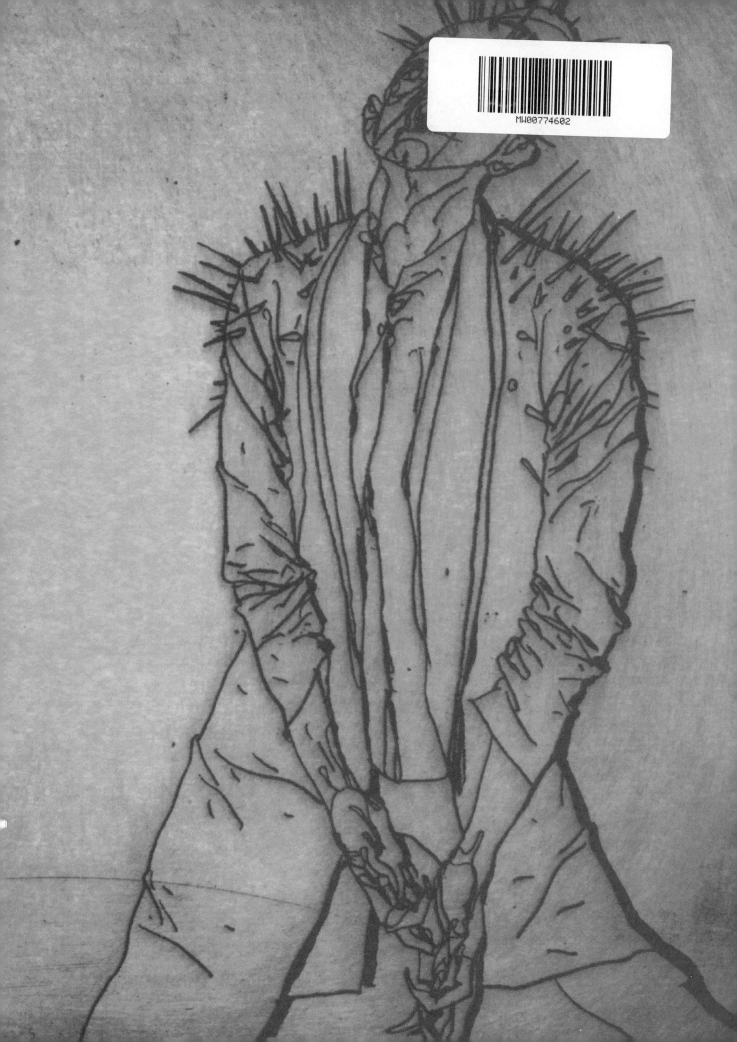

GUIDE TO THE

SABBAT

FAIT ACCOMPLI

By Justin R. Achilli, with W. H. Bourne,
Anne Sullivan Braidwood, Joanne FitzRoy and Jess Heinig

CREDITS

Original Concept, Design and Development: Steven C. Brown and Andrew Greenberg

Updated Concept, Design and Development: Justin R. Achilli

Authors: Justin R. Achilli, W.H. Bourne, Anne Sullivan Braidwood, Joanne FitzRoy, Jess Heinig

Addtional Material: Clayton Oliver

Editor: Carl Bowen

Art Director: Richard Thomas and Lawrence Snelly

Layout & Typesetting: Matt Milberger

Interior Art: Andrew Ritchie, Fred Hooper, Greg Loudon, Jason Felix, Leif Jones, Michael Gaydos, Mike Danza, Ron Spencer, Rebecca Guay, Richard Kane Ferguson, John Estes, Guy Davis, Vince Locke, Mike Huddleston along with Adam Rex, Larry Macdougall, Brian LeBlanc, Darren Frydendall, Matt Roach, John Cobb, Andy Bennett, Paul Lee

End Papers: Phil Hale

Front Cover Art: Bill Sienkiewicz

Front & Back Cover Design: Matt Milberger

735 PARK NORTH BLVD.
SUITE 128
CLARKSTON, GA 30021
USA

WHITE WOLF
GAME STUDIO

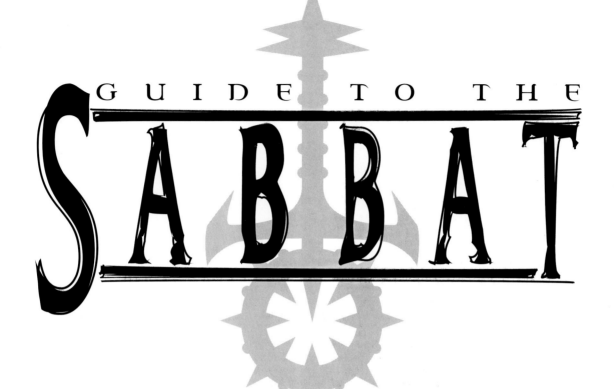

GUIDE TO THE SABBAT

TABLE OF CONTENTS

Smart Money's on Vegas

I love California. The place is crawling with anarchs who don't want the hassle of Camarilla babysitters, so they booted every last one of them. Now, the whole state's overrun with brat-packs of biker and goth Licks. Good place to recruit, let me tell you. They all hang out in gangs, too, so they never have civil words for each other — Ellum and I have been up and down the state a dozen times in as many years, and no one's wised up to us yet. We roll into town, go local and convince a handful of anarchs that, hey, the Sabbat's really where it's at if you want to stick it to the elders.

It doesn't hurt that we're gorgeous, too. People, even vampires, seem to want to trust beautiful folks. Ellum (actually, her name's Lisa Marie, because her dad was a big Elvis fan, but we shortened it to LM, which just changed into Ellum over time) looks like a model off the runway. She always wears this battered straw cowboy hat that makes her look like a junkie, and I guess people just feel safe with her. Initially anyway. I'm tall and thin and just shy of Ellum's attractiveness. That, and I "have a way with people." People trust her; they do what I say.

I slid my fat, black '49 Merc up to the curb in front of Package Store (what an exciting name!). Ellum and I got out and headed into the store. I gave Ellum that "behave" look I always give her before we do, well, anything.

"Hey, Cholly, Ellum and I are headed to Vegas. We need some money."

Charlie, the Asian guy who owns Package Store, looked at me without fondness. I made a Charlie Chan rictus face at him and he opened the register, lifting the till to show me there was no money in it.

"Slow night. We haven't had any sales yet," Charlie told me.

"Oh, Chuck, don't lie to me," I said. "You know I hate it when you lie. It jus' breaks my li'l ole heart."

"Seriously. No one's been in all night except a couple kids who tried to steal some forties of OE."

"Look, you fishhead squint," I stepped up to the counter, pressing my face against the bulletproof glass to look Charlie in the eyes, "just gimme the goddamn money."

The crash startled both of us. Whipping around to face the back of the store, we saw Charlie's wife sprawling halfway out from one of the beer coolers. Ellum looked at me with a smirk. She stood in a pool of blood that gurgled out from Charlie's wife's gut, where the broken glass had cut her almost in two.

"Oops."

Charlie screamed and ran from his little booth, sandals flapping against his feet. He made it about 15 feet before I caught him by the belt and tossed him across the room into one of the coolers near his wife.

"Fucking hell, Ellum, what's the matter with you?" I shouted as I scrambled back to the booth and snatched up all the loose bills Charlie had cleverly stuffed under the register's till drawer. "Now we *have* to go." I didn't care so much about the violence — I see plenty, believe me — as much as I cared about the inconvenience. We'd spent weeks leaning on Charlie, getting him to cough up extortion money and not call the cops afterward. He certainly wasn't going to be too predisposed toward our little scheme anymore.

"Well, shit, Adam, she tried to grab my tits and then she said I was trying to steal her husband...."

"Ellum, she doesn't speak any fucking English! Go get in the damn car!" I pulled the dropsafe from its mooring and yanked the phone cord from the wall. It wouldn't do to have the pigs or an ambulance show up before we were well on our way out.

I spat on the floor as I left, leaving the couple lying in piles of their spilled innards.

"Sorry, Charlie," I laughed. Fuck it. We were headed out of town anyway.

▼   ▼

The Merc needed gas about halfway between San Fran and Vegas, so I pulled in to a roadside station.

I looked over at Ellum, who was just sort of staring out the windshield at the vast flatness surrounding us. I gathered a few of the shadows cast by the buzzing fluorescent lights and wrapped them around her eyes, making her look like Marlene Dietrich on heroin.

I leaned across her and kissed her on the mouth. She bit my tongue and sucked a trickle of blood from me before putting her hand on my hip and pushing me away.

While I was filling up the car, a blue-and-white Bel Air chopdrop pulled into the lot with two guys inside. The driver was the kind of guy who would drive this pedestrian classic: a complete cheeseball who looked like he kicked Brian Setzer's ass and took his clothes, right down to the wallet-on-a-chain. The passenger was a black kid with a shaved head and a leopard-print shirt. He was wearing sunglasses even though it was dark.

"Nice Pontiac," the driver said, getting out. Loser.

"It's a Mercury, and thanks."

"Sorry. On the bottle?"

"Nope. All-natural." Nitrous is for girls.

"Wanna go title-for-title?"

I smiled, not bothering to hide my fangs. "Tell you what, kiddo. You win, you get my car. I win, I get your souls."

He hesitated a second, but then nodded his head. "Whatever, guy."

I blew a kiss to Ellum through the windshield and winked. She knew what was going on.

So I let the rock star beat me. Between you and me, I could have wasted him easily, but I didn't feel like it. Not that way, anyhow.

We both pulled over to the side of the road and climbed out of our cars. The kid was excited with his victory, but I had no intention of turning over my pride and joy.

"Looks like I won, mister." Pretty smarmy for an ignorant soon-to-be-ex-juicebag.

I hit the kid — too hard — and broke his jaw. He looked at me in shock, eyes tearing up, mouth dangling open as a stream of blood and spit poured out.

"I guess you didn't really win, did you?" I smiled.

He turned to run, but Ellum stood in his way. I grabbed him around the waist from behind, pinning his arms to his sides. As I lifted him, a cloud of the desert dust whiffed up. I hammered him face first against the Bel Air's fender, and his head left a dent and a messy streak of blood. Ellum stared at the black guy in the car as she licked a stripe of vitae from the automobile.

He yanked off his idiotic sunglasses, and all I could see of him were his eyes and teeth. It was dark, but he was fooling with something at the dashboard. As it turned out, he had taken a gun from the glovebox. I dropped the unconscious kid and pulled his friend from the car. Ellum snagged the revolver as it flew from his hand.

"Damn, son, you've got some spirit. Trade you, Ellum?" She tossed me the gun as I shoved the guy into her arms. The cylinder was full.

"I know you weren't going to *shoot* me. You just wanted to let me know the gun was there, I bet. So I wouldn't be scared, right?"

He didn't say anything. The guy squirmed in Ellum's grip like a worm on a hook, grunting and gibbering a bit. He was all eyes and teeth again.

"Check this out, my friend."

I stretched out my arm in front of him, pointed the revolver at it and *bang*! Right between whatever those two bones are called.

"Oh, fuck! Ellum, I do believe I've hurt myself!" She just laughed and nibbled the guy's ear a bit. "Think you can take the heat, kiddo?"

Ellum shoved the kid to the ground and pulled his head up a bit so he could see me and his unconscious friend. With her knee in his back and her arm holding his to the ground, he wasn't going anywhere.

"I bet you can."

I stepped on his wrist and pointed the pistol at the back of his hand.

Click!

Empty chamber. I'd spun the cylinder back while Ellum was taking the guy down. Now he knew I was serious — as if he didn't know before!

I fired again anyway, blowing a hole through his hand. Blood spattered into my hair and across Ellum's vest. He screamed — a rather uninspired howl, really, but this wasn't exactly exquisite torture.

"We have a winner!" Ellum shouted at him, pulling him up to his knees. "Now get up — what the fuck is your name anyway?" I threw the gun on the ground before him and went to gather up his friend.

"K-Kevin," the chump managed to stammer.

"'K-K-K-K-Kevin'!" Ellum sneered. "That's such a fucking white-boy name!" She still crouched behind him, and she snaked her hand around to grab his crotch. "I think we'll call you Judas instead. Pick up the gun, Judas."

He fumbled for it with his good hand; got it.

"Now shoot Stray Cats, here," I said as I heaped the unconscious kid in front of our new friend. Judas pointed the shaking gun at the center of Stray Cats' back.

"No, dumbfuck, shoot him in the back of the head. So it comes out his face."

Bang! Judas had some guts. Of course, he threw up immediately, so no style points for him.

"Good work, Judas. Ellum, my dear, would you do the honors?"

Out came the straight razor, which fluttered across Judas' throat in the blink of an eye. I shoved No Face into the Bel Air and jerked the whole thing up and over. Once it was on its roof, I pushed it around a bit so it would look like the driver

had lost control and flipped it himself. By the time I finished, Ellum (looking like a pristine mother nursing in the moonlight) had her wrist at Judas' mouth.

"And that is *that*, darling!" I took a lick at Ellum's wrist as she stood, and we bound Judas' wrists and ankles with the duct tape I kept in the toolbox. We tossed him in the trunk and finished with a slapdash strip of tape over his mouth, just to be sure.

Ellum hopped atop the capsized Chevy, kicking at the fuel tank after pulling the line free. Gas spilled everywhere, collecting in sludgy pools in the sand. I flicked my lighter and tossed it toward the car, which went up like a Fourth of July display. Ellum writhed and swayed as the fire blazed around her. Damn, she's beautiful.

We leaped into the Merc and sped off toward Vegas as headlights appeared on the horizon behind us.

▼   ▼

Just inside Las Vegas, Ellum and I got married at a drive-through chapel. I didn't have a ring, so I used a loose wingnut I found in the toolbox.

Ellum said the marriage would never work. She cut off her ring finger with the straight razor and handed it to me, singing, "Divorce!" I yelled at her for bleeding all over the car, but it was done as soon as it started.

I still keep that desiccated little thing in my pocket....

▼   ▼

We pulled in to Treasure Island at the Mirage. As we drove up, two giant pirate ships were shooting at each other in the artificial lagoon they have set up while bursts of pyrotechnics exploded all around them. Even the doorman was dressed as a buccaneer — all glitz, no class.

It was getting early, and we needed to hole up for the day. Ellum and I sauntered up to the counter and harassed the clerk, who took it all graciously like the contemptible piece of juicebag shit he was. No doubt he dealt with lots of loudmouths who pretended to be high-rollers.

"No reservation? Then may I have your name, sir?"

"Tom Cruise."

"I see. And this would be Nicole Kidman?"

"No, we broke up years ago. This is my sister, Leisure."

"Mm-hmm. Now, I'll need your real name to get you in the system."

"The name I've given you will do."

"It certainly will, sir. Enjoy your stay!" We passed Robert Goulet on the way to the elevator.

Two minutes after entering our room, we were asleep in the bathtub, wrapped in blankets, having stuffed towels into the crack under the door. I dangled the "Do Not Disturb" sign from the outer door's handle.

▼   ▼

I awoke to a gentle knocking at the bathroom door, and nudged Ellum to rouse her.

"It says 'do not disturb.'" I couldn't find one of my shoes in the dark, and I cut myself on Ellum's straight razor while groping about. She climbed out of the tub and onto the counter as I gathered the darkness around the doorjamb. My shoe hung on one of the shower knobs.

"I'm afraid the matter is of considerable urgency, Mister, er, *Cruise*." It was a man's voice; probably hotel security. Ellum seemed to have a bad feeling about it, because she shook her head as she crouched on the counter. Time to play it crafty.

"Hey, I'll be right out. Damn, my head hurts. Is that girl still out there?" There wasn't anything in the bathroom that lent itself to use as a weapon, but I suppose I didn't really need one.

"No, Mr. Cruise, there's no girl out here."

I mouthed to Ellum, "Meet me at the car in ten minutes," and kissed her. She should have no difficulty getting out of the room, even if our guest was standing right in front of her — he'd never even see her.

Opening the bathroom door, I stumbled out, acting like a hungover juicebag. The visitor was indeed hotel security, but I could tell from the way he looked at me that something was up. He had one of those tragic suits — less than 200 bucks off the rack at Penney's — and a demeanor that suggested he was good at getting his way. I wish I could have looked at his soul like Ellum could, but what the hell. I figured he was a ghoul just from the way he smelled. I straightened up and dropped the drunk act.

"We have rules in this town, Mr. Cruise—"

"Stiers."

"I beg your pardon?"

"Stiers. Adam Stiers. I'm not Tom Cruise. I'm flattered by the compliment, but it's only a superficial resemblance."

"Yes, well, Mr. Stiers, it appears that you care little for the rules in our town. The prospect of your continued presence here is not one we particularly relish." Definitely a ghoul. Probably to a Ventrue, but that suit....

"Why? Because I bullied your check-in clerk?"

"Among other things. I believe that you have left a member of your party in your car. The trunk, to be precise."

"He was tired."

"I see. Truth told, Mr. Stiers, I'm not the one to whom you need to explain yourself. I'm sure you're familiar with our *traditions*, and that you have no intention of flouting them." God damn this guy's thesaurus mouth. "My employer wishes to speak to you, and I am to escort you to his offices." Now we were getting somewhere. With any luck, I could keep this anarch shtick going (the California plates on the car helped) and get some good dirt on how this town ran. A bit of research and a quick report to the archbishop, and Las Vegas would belong to the Sabbat.

"Take me to see Moe Green, Fredo." I looked like hell. This would be good.

I expected to go up, but the elevator went down instead. Curious — those Ventrue bastards usually do everything with as much extravagance as possible. We descended past the lower lobby, the basement and even the garage. The ghoul had a special key that took us down this far; he hadn't pushed a button yet.

The ghoul led me down a long, narrow hallway with bad fluorescent lighting and a smell like mouthwash. We exchanged a few meaningless pleasantries, him trying to cow me and me trying acting all awed that I was about to meet the baddest Dracula in Vegas. I was supposed to meet Ellum back at the car in about three minutes, and it looked like I'd be late. I smiled thinking about it — whoever had the misfortune to be in that parking garage when she started flipping out was going to be in a bad way.

We passed through a pair of swinging doors, like the kind they have in restaurant kitchens, into what I guess was a storage room. Metal shelves lined the room, stocked with large, institutional-sized cans of food or carpet cleaner or whatever. A few 55-gallon drums of some other unknown substance stood in the center of the room, one of which lay on its side, leaking brown goop.

"Duke, this isn't Tom Cruise." From what I saw, only the ghoul and I were in the room; no one had followed us, and there wasn't anywhere to hide. Bad. And what the fuck was this tape on the floor?

"We've already been through this," I said aloud to no one. The lights were weird in here, too yellow to be fluorescent, but too harsh to be normal light bulbs. "Your clerk spelled my name wrong."

All of a sudden, a pair of men stood in front of me. One of them looked like someone had grabbed his neck and the top of his head and given it a good twist. His arms curled up on his distended belly like crippled chicken wings, and his hands had sharp black claws at the ends. The other guy wore glasses and a gray suit with black pinstripes, and he had a short, almost military haircut.

"Welcome to Treasure Island," the distorted guy said in a phlegmy voice. "I am Montrose, and this is my associate, Alexander Cantor." Pinstripes nodded at me. "Perhaps you'd care to inform us as to your business here?"

"Not business. Pleasure. I'm in from California to do a bit of gambling."

"And the Kindred in the trunk?" This guy was damn presumptuous, and I didn't like where the conversation was headed.

"We were driving in shifts. He had the night before."

"Quite an odd set of circumstances, don't you think, Adam Stiers from the Anarch Free State?" That was weird. Either he didn't know anything was up, or he saw through me and was trying to yank my chain. "Perhaps an object lesson in how Prince Benedic keeps the rabble in line would do you some good." The ghoul's hand clamped down on my shoulder.

Of course, I was stronger. Grabbing the toady's wrist, I spun and wrenched his pathetic arm from its socket, leaving it dangling from his shoulder. When I turned back around, the two others — I can only assume they were Licks, too — were gone. Too bad for Duke, I suppose.

The weird light in the room slid away from me as I coalesced the shadows into one thick tentacle. Duke winced when I shoved the tentacle up his ass, but his eyes bulged right back open, when I forced it out his mouth. I dug the elevator key out of his pocket after tearing his wrists open with my teeth. The blood — so much of it — washed over the floor, and I left crimson footprints as I bolted down the hallway to the lift.

▼ ▼

Ellum was upset. Surprize, surprize.

"Ten minutes! Ten fucking minutes, Adam! You said ten minutes!" I saw an arm jutting from underneath the car opposite us, but we could address that later.

The car roared to life, and I gunned the engine, whipping the vehicle out of its parking place. I could see the night sky past the mechanical arm of the parking garage exit. I imagined the sky lit with orange, reflecting the flames licking up from the burning Treasure Island Casino as the screams and chokes of those trapped inside the building issued forth. That, too, could be addressed later.

My eyes were wide as I shoved a twenty at the attendant. She handed me my change and lifted the arm as I grabbed her hand and punched the gas. It's hard to fit a human body through those little sliding glass half-windows, but it can be done, given enough strength. Her head hung limply as I dropped her at the curb. I roared across the street, and Ellum already had herself worked up. She leaned out the window and winged a pedestrian (I think he was wearing some godawful Hawaiian shirt) with the tire iron.

Explain that shit to the cops, Montrose. We'll be back later.

▼ ▼

The sun was almost up when we got back to California. (We ditched my beloved Mercury at a gas station seven minutes out of Vegas and jacked a Jeep Grand Cherokee while the guy who owned it went to pay for his gas. You should have seen his wife's face when Ellum opened up the door and jerked her out by the hair. "Bye, bitch!" she called as we sped away. We had to write off Judas, and I don't envy the stupid fucker who lets him out of that trunk.) We took back roads to avoid the police, then burned the Jeep about 20 miles out of San Fran.

A few nights later, we talked to Bishop Mark about the trip. We had the prince's name, two or three of the individual Kindred's names and a rough idea of who was really pulling the strings (it turns out that some group called the Rothsteins have some significant influence in Vegas, and Montrose has seen a couple of our scouts before, so we had to take his dialogue with a grain of salt). The bishop thinks we'll move against Las Vegas in a few weeks. Give them some time to get over "the Anarch Incident," and as they settle back into their precious Masquerade, we'll be right behind them with torches in hand.

With all that went on in Vegas, I didn't even get a chance to pick up a legal hooker. Maybe next time....

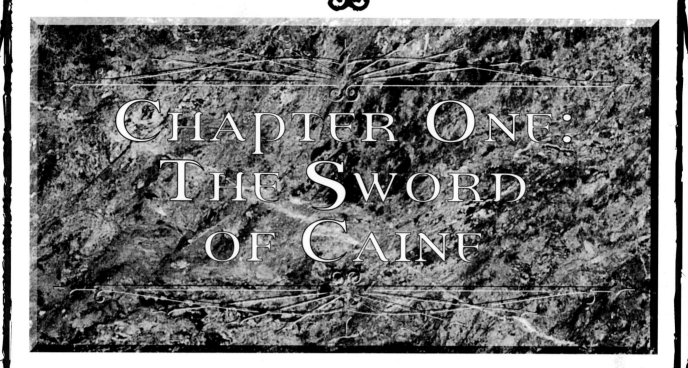

CHAPTER ONE: THE SWORD OF CAINE

The name Sabbat may be held to cover every kind of gathering, although it must continually be borne in mind that a Sabbat ranges from comparative simplicity, the secret rendezvous of some half a dozen wretches devoted to the fiend, to a large and crowded congregation presided over by incarnate evil intelligences, a mob outvying the very demons in malice, blasphemy, and revolt, the true face of pandemonium on earth.

— Montague Summers, The History of Witchcraft

This means war.

War on the Antediluvians. War against Gehenna. War against the Camarilla, the Inconnu and the cagey independents. War against the witch-hunters, the werewolves, the cowardly anarchs and the herds of humanity. For some vampires, this means war on the very sect to which they belong.

Welcome to the Sabbat. Please keep your arms inside the vehicle, otherwise someone might rip them off and hand them back to you.

For the Sabbat, being a vampire means being a soldier in a holy war on the ancient, cannibalistic monsters who passed on the Curse of Caine in the nights of old. The Antediluvians — and their mindless puppets, the vampires of the Camarilla — seek to bring the fiery bloodstorm of Gehenna on the world and devour their wayward childer. The Sabbat really doesn't want to see that happen. As part of those selfsame wayward childer, they have better things to do than die at the fangs of their malignant progenitors. After all, they have a world to conquer.

To the Sabbat, the eternal struggle is a matter of "us versus them," in which "them" means everyone who is not of the sect. Although they aren't above a bit of Borgia-esque intrigue or an alliance of convenience, ultimately, the sect comes first. Fanatics to the last, Sabbat vampires gladly throw themselves into the fire for their sect, falling on their foes in legions, tearing their enemies apart just as a pack of wolves brings down its prey.

At least, this is how the vampires of the Sabbat seem to others. In truth, the matter is much more complex — isn't it always? Neither the mindless barbarians nor the infernal zealots others who know of them portray them to be, vampires of the Sabbat run dangerously close to becoming so. Having turned their backs on humanity, Sabbat vampires understand that they are Damned, creatures of the Beast. Rather than bemoan the loss of what they once were, Sabbat vampires revel in their monstrosity — they are *more* than human, cursed in nature for moving beyond the limitations of humankind. And, as is always the case with the Damned, Sabbat are vampires first and sect-members second.

Of course, this means the sect is as rife with treachery, rivalry and outright hostility as any other group of "Kindred" — a term of weakness among the Sons and Daughters of Caine. The sect is sick, rotting from within, yet rebelling against its own collapse with a ferocity unmatched by other vampires anywhere.

It's not a great time to be alive, and it's a hellish time to be undead. But what choice do you have?

The View from Within

It is inevitable that, as widespread as the Sabbat makes itself, the sect is bound to come into conflict with other denizens of the modern nights. Vampires are secretive creatures, however, as are many of the other things that prowl the darkness, and it is difficult to obtain an accurate picture of who the Sabbat shares the night with. That doesn't stop them from forming their own conclusions, however.

Additionally, the Sabbat suffers its own internal schisms. Elder members of the sect, hundreds of years old and perhaps even present at the formation of the sect over half a millennium ago, see very little in the same light as do the younger Sons and Daughters of Caine. Indeed, most young members have fewer than 25 years under the night, which colors their opinions accordingly.

Young Cainites' Opinions

The Antediluvians

Grade-A, wicked evil on a biblical level. Anything that can boil you away into a fucking puddle of blood by looking at you has no place in this world. Especially when all they want to do is eat you.

The Camarilla

It's a combination of everything that's bad about government, religion and modern culture. Those bastards are greedy, self-centered and they don't even want to know who they're really working for with all their little games of Jyhad. Goddamn, they make me want to tear down everything that gives them comfort. They're so close to fucking humans, they act just like 'em.

The Inconnu

You know, I bet there are about six of these old sons of bitches, and they're so good at playing the game, they've got everybody all terrified of the shit they *must be* doing because we can't see any of it. The ultimate "less is more" shtick.

The Lupines

Sometimes, if you're a real badass, you and your whole pack can take down *one* of these. If you're lucky. Either don't fuck with them or, better, become a real badass.

The Mages

I'm not sure I've ever met one, but they're probably bastards like everyone else. I think they're mortal though, so fuck 'em.

The Wraiths

You know, maybe it's stupid of me to believe in vampires but not in ghosts. I guess you can call me stupid.

The Changelings

Yeah, I know plenty of fairies. They're all in the West End. Out and proud.

The Mortals

I'll have a six-pack, please. Fucking cattle. They're food, nothing more.

Elder Sabbat

Half care only about themselves, while the other half care only about themselves but tell you otherwise.

ELDER CAINITES' OPINIONS

The Antediluvians

Their evil is so pervasive, I cannot help but see it everywhere. Our purpose is to drive these sanguinary cannibals to their Final Deaths, but that is a long, hard road not undertaken lightly.

The Camarilla

The greatest crime is not that they serve the Ancients who would rise and consume us. No, their greatest crime is that they do it out of ignorance, and that even when you show them the folly of their ways, they refuse to see the truth. Cursed, complacent ticks.

The Inconnu

It is just as well that they have withdrawn from the Jyhad, for their power is considerable and their minds are incomprehensible. They would be just as likely to destroy us as they would the Camarilla, and not out of any allegiance or greater purpose that we can divine. They are best left alone.

The Lupines

Loathsome, offensive brutes, who kill first, kill second and ask questions last. They are mindless beasts, of use only if you can direct one toward an enemy. If you can't, step back, because a weapon uncontrolled is a weapon that turns against its user.

The Mages

A diverse, potent and ultimately forgettable lot. They keep to themselves and have their own concerns, and I can't say that I begrudge them.

The Wraiths

Much knowledge may be gleaned from the spirits of the dead, but one must speak carefully. They are as capricious as any of the Daughters and Sons of Caine, but far more fleeting, and their recourse proves difficult for us to prevent. They vanish as they will, and cannot be so easily controlled as other, more tangible contacts.

The Changelings

The Wild Ones cross paths with us more often than we recognize. It is a testament to their peculiar brand of magic that they either leave us alone entirely, as is most often the case, or destroy our kind in the greatest of conflagrations. Even if one knows he deals with a changeling, he is best served by moving on to other avenues. The fae are as random as the winds.

The Mortals

Why, my meal was fine, thank you very much.

Younger Sabbat

Spoiled childer, but not without their merits. They are still impressionable enough, still new enough to Caine's unrelenting curse, that they may be brought to one's own way of thinking. Of course, that's provided he can get past their vulgarity and bullheadedness.

SECT HISTORY

The sect's history prior to the momentous Cainite event known as the Convention of Thorns is less than certain. Some Sabbat claim they recall nights of marauding terror and divine predation, wandering the cities of the Old World as a death cult. Others claim the sect never truly existed as a sect prior to the Anarch Revolt, and instead took the form of roving packs, not unlike the packs of the modern nights. Still others claim that the very name *Sabbat* defines the sect's origin — a loose confederation of witches and self-avowed monsters claiming servitude to Hell.

In light of the various theories as to the sect's origin, one fact remains somewhat reliable: The sect rose to prominence after the Anarch Revolt. When the young vampires of Clans Lasombra and Tzimisce rose against their Antediluvians, the indisputable reign of elders drew to a close, and vampire society changed forever thereafter.

THE ANARCH REVOLT AND DIABLERIE

THE LASOMBRA EARN FREEDOM

Sometime in the 13th or 14th century, Clan Lasombra united against and slew its progenitor. Led by a charismatic Cainite named Gratiano, turbulent Lasombra anarchs decided that the stale rule of elders kept them oppressed. As Keepers, true masters of the night, young Lasombra rebelled against the feudal ties of sire and childe that relegated them to roles of eternal subservience. Flocking to Gratiano's banner, Assamites and anarchs of all clans gathered in Sicily, where it was rumored that the mighty Lasombra Antediluvian made his haven. Overwhelmed and unprepared, the haven fell, and Gratiano consumed the Ancient's blood, setting the clan free from tyranny.

Naturally, the story varies from teller to teller, as time and duplicity have eroded the truth of the affair. Of the vampires present — whether they still exist or have fallen to the thirsty fangs of younger Cainites — none has stepped forward to corroborate any of the story's details.

By varying accounts the leader of an anarch band himself, the treacherous childe of the Lasombra Ancient or the puppet of other masters of the Great Jyhad, Gratiano struck the first blow in what would become the most tumultuous period of vampire history ever recorded, with the possible exception of these Final Nights. It is rumored that Gratiano accepted an archbishop's position after the Sabbat rose to power (some centuries after the diablerie of the Antediluvian), but this rumor conflicts with others. Why would Gratiano, who struck the first blow of the Anarch Revolt, settle for a mere archbishopric? If his cause was true, why would he *accept* an archbishopric? How could this rogue anarch and his motley soldiers fell an entire clan of masters of deception? Numerous questions arose, but for the time between the Ancient's fall and the eruption of the Sabbat, Gratiano and his brood disappeared.

THE FIENDS FOLLOW

Spurred on by the success of the Lasombra (as dreadful news travels quickly among vampires), the Tzimisce took heart and planned to follow suit.

The Fiends were — and still are — a notoriously fractious family of vampires. Characterized by an unfathomable dignity on one side and a twisted deviance on the other, the clan literally fell to war with itself. As the masters of Eastern Europe, the elder Tzimisce held their lands in fearsome iron grips. Entire lines of Tzimisce vampires held lands since time out of mind. A sickness rotted the clan from within, however. The very lands of the Tzimisce's demesnes pulsed with magic — indeed, this magical tie to the land haunts the clan into the modern nights. This magic festered within the Fiends, however, turning them against their sires or causing them to put aside past cruelties and rally to the elders' cause. Transylvanian history reflects this chaos, as does the chaotic history of other Carpathian lands. Vampires literally warred every night, ravaging the "land beyond the forest" in their bloodthirsty crusades.

In the end, the passion of the young anarchs won out against the stagnant, crumbling legacies of the elders. Fiends who had governed their holdings for centuries were turned out into the streets or hunted to extinction, put to death at the fiery brands of the Tzimisce anarchs.

(It is a footnote in the history of the Sabbat that very few Tzimisce claim that many of their elders were diablerized. Cainite scholars and historians regard this claim as ominous — why did the Fiends not claim their elders' power? Why do they diablerize only vampires of other clans? Of course, the Tzimisce remain silent on the matter, pointing out a few infamous cases in which childer *have* committed amaranth on their sires. Other Cainites note the rarity and choose not to press the issue.)

Finally, one night in the late 14th century (according to dubious sources), the Fiends managed to unearth the location of their clan's founder. Converging on the site, a blasted church on a forgotten *tirsa*, Tzimisce anarchs disinterred their Ancient

A SOLITARY CLAIM

What transpired did not.

Lugoj, fool that he was, led us into damnation. And we followed, ever the loyal rebels, dragged into a Hell beyond our comprehension.

Lugoj died that night, impaled on a wooden pike and hidden behind us, as we struggled against the Eldest's servants.

It looked at me, wearing Lugoj's face. Ever since, I have been a good lad.

— From the journal of Lambach Ruthven, present at the fall of the Tzimisce Antediluvian

and committed diablerie on... *it*. After a long and brutal battle with the twisted minions of the Eldest Fiend, the anarchs had won. Lugoj Blood-breaker, the leader who had partaken of the amaranth, then sank into a torpor, weighed down by the potent blood taken from veins cursed by God long before the birth of Christ. None have seen Lugoj since, and tales circulate among younger Sabbat: Even in claiming victory over the elders, still they manage to draw their childer down.

AND THE REVOLT BEGINS

With the success of the Tzimisce and Lasombra anarchs (many of whom proclaimed themselves *antitribu* or "anti-clans" to signify that they had turned their backs on their fathers), widespread patricide erupted all over Europe. Unlike any time before, childer disillusioned with their treatment at the hands of their elders embraced open revolt. Elders fell in droves, often taking numerous treacherous childer with them. Indeed, the Cainite population of Europe dwindled as the war continued. Aided by the potent vampires of the mercenary Assamite clan, the anarchs left no stone unturned in their war on the hated elders.

Although no other clans managed to achieve the same success over their Ancients that the Tzimisce and Lasombra did, it wasn't for lack of trying. Even one of the most powerful elders of those dark nights, Hardestadt of Clan Ventrue, suffered a bold attack, and, though he survived, it became obvious that something must be done about the rampant chaos that the anarchs brought with them.

Soon after the Anarch Revolt entered its most active phase, vampires realized that they had gone too far. Mortals, observing the chaos and terror happening around them, discovered that monsters loomed in their midst. After a desperate appeal to Rome, humankind entreated the pope to turn the Inquisition toward the end of rooting out these devils and heretics.

This mission devastated the Cainite community even more than its internecine war had, as now the Cainites had to fear the torches of the Inquisitors as well as each other. Of course, the excesses of the elders continued unabated, as these old, cowardly vampires left their childer to the Inquisition in order to make good their own escapes.

Finally, everything came to a head. Certain powerful elder vampires, among them the presumed-dead Hardestadt, made a call to all "Kindred," claiming that they had found an end to the need for such warfare. This written accord, known as the Convention of Thorns, promised to restore order and sanctity to the race of Cainites.

Of course, in the hands of the elders who created it, the proposal simply offered a return to how things were before.

The anarchs and Assamites had no choice, however, trapped between the Inquisition and the elders (who had centuries under their belts and were infinitely cagier) as they were. As an informal body, the anarchs agreed to the Convention, hoping that they could at least secure for themselves

some measure of apologetic return to the fold. Admitting failure, the anarchs and Assamites succumbed to the will of the assembled elder Cainites, drawing the Anarch Movement to a decisive close.

Not every anarch gave up so easily, however. The "decisive" return achieved by the vampires of the fledgling Camarilla, the repentant anarchs and the vast majority of Clan Assamite offered little in the way of remedying the situation that had caused the situation to begin with. Enraged, these anarchs and rogue Assamites rampaged through Thorns, leaving nothing but a burning, bloodied carcass of the town behind them. Although they had yet to organize themselves, the sect that would become the Sabbat had committed itself to its immortal course of action that night.

In the half-century to follow, packs ("sabbats") of *antitribu* plagued the night, dragging villagers into the darkness and striking ever more precisely at the foundation of power the Camarilla was building for itself. These rebels organized themselves into a cohesive, ideological sect over those 50 years, agreeing on a rough doctrine of cause against the elders and the Antediluvians who pulled their strings. Freedom from the Ancients' Jyhad became the root of their purpose — even though the Lasombra and Tzimisce managed to destroy their Antediluvians, that only allowed the existing Ancients to fill the vacuum. By the mid-16th century, the entity known as the Sabbat had united in righteous opposition to the Camarilla and blind subservience to greater evil.

THE NEW WORLD

During the late 16th century, the Sabbat found itself in a precarious position. Composed as it was of a few headstrong elder Cainites (who would have been the targets of violence had they claimed allegiance to the Camarilla) and a vast majority of young vampires with little power or influence, it had failed to gain a significant advantage over (or even foothold against) the nascent Camarilla.

Bitter war raged between the vampires of the newly formed Sabbat and the not-much-older Camarilla. The Inquisition continued to claim victims while all of Europe's Cainites drew lines in the sand to mark their allegiance. These were not political boundaries, however, as vampires lacked the ability to control heads of state or claim governmental commissions for themselves (to any great degree, that is; some vampires operate at lower levels of governments to this very night). Rather, the lines of influence fell at the farthest extent to which the Kindred and Cainites could extend their grips. Some major cities in (predominantly Sabbat) Spain held powerful communities of Camarilla Kindred while more than one city in France — where the Toreador and Ventrue exercised their influence — claimed large Sabbat populations. In the end, the war was more a nightly litany of guerrilla attacks than open movements on battlefields. Puppet rulers fell or switched allegiance; knightly orders crumbled, science created terrible new weapons with which to strike

The Convention of Thorns

Many years have passed since the start of our current conflict, now called the Anarch Movement. Be it known that on this night of 23 October, 1493, the Jyhad has ended. The time for self-destruction is over.

This concordat, bound in the Covenant of Caine by sacred vow, represents an unyielding, vigilant truce between the Kindred known unto themselves as the Anarchs, the Clan Assamite, and the freestanding Kindred bound under the title of Camarilla. Henceforth, the parties shall be recognized by faction as the Anarchs, the Assamites, and the Camarilla.

Each of the parties agrees to the responsibility of maintaining peace. Each shall lay its censures on any who breech or oppose this sacred Agreement. Accounting will be made of all parties for violations by them to either the letter or spirit of this Agreement. This document is binding under the social code of all Children of Caine by the accepted Lextalionis of all Cainites as it has passed through the ages. All Kindred are entreated to accept and gain solace from this peaceful accord.

Be it known that the Anarchs will enjoin with the Camarilla as an accepted part, making it whole. Anarchs are expected to work peacefully to achieve their own ends. They must become defenders of all, and they shall receive full entitlement to all rights and privileges belonging to all Camarilla Kindred. All Anarchs shall be accepted back unto their elders and their formerly denounced clans without any fear of reprisal. Only the most vicious of atrocities shall not be forgiven. These shall stand written for the justicars to hear within one year, after which all allegations are no longer valid. All Anarchs shall reclaim all remaining and rightful property confiscated from them. In return they must turn over any war gains taken during the conflict by giving them to their sires or any recognized clan elder.

Know also that if the Anarchs are further warred on, this open Jyhad invalidates their responsibility to maintain peace with their attacker. They may act freely without fear of reprisal from inactive members of the Camarilla. Anarchs are guaranteed the freedom to act as they please, short of breaching the *Masquerade* imposed for the protection of all Kindred from the kine.

It is also noted that any member of any other self-proclaimed sect must openly declare this before his elders and renounce this relation. Failure to do so will result in the destruction of any deemed guilty. No Kindred may be sent knowingly to his death by an elder or sire, unless the security of clan or Camarilla outweighs the possible loss of unlife.

From this night forward, the Assamites shall henceforth no longer commit diablerie on members of other clans. The Assamites must commit themselves to this acceptance by a mark of assurance placed on them in the form of a Thaumaturgical limitation. All members of the Assamites shall become unable to drink freely of the vitae of other Kindred from now unto forever. In addition, the Assamites shall pay the Brujah elders of Spain two thousand pounds of gold, in ransom of the five Assamite elders captured committing diablerie. Also, the Assamites may no longer participate in blood hunts.

Be it also know that the Assamites are guaranteed complete independence from Camarilla demands. The Assamite fortress, Alamut, shall be free from further assaults. Assamites are also granted, out of respect for their beliefs, the freedom to commit diablerie within their own clan without restraint and the right to commit diablerie on all Kindred not recognized as holding membership within the Camarilla.

It is rendered that all parties involved and all showing allegiance to any of these parties shall be held responsible for all aspects of this Convention brought forth here, in the neutral Kingdom of England, outside the hamlet of Thorns, near the town of Silchester. May Caine hold truth and peace for us all.

---

enemies down and havens burned like winter hearth-fires. In the end, however, the tide turned in the Camarilla's favor.

The Age of Exploration, however, had opened new vistas to humankind and Cainite alike. The Sabbat, composed of younger vampires who were less set in their ways, saw the opportunities the Americas presented and took advantage. Leaving behind all but a few Old World territories (notably Madrid, home to Archbishop Ambrose Luis Monçada, and some of the older, Eastern domains of the Tzimisce), the Sabbat established a resounding presence in what would become the United States.

For a while, the sect flourished in the evolving colonies. Amid a revolutionary and radical mortal backdrop, the Sabbat's presence was easy to hide among the insurrectionists of the region. Two factors conspired to keep the New World Sabbat relatively weak, however. Many of the mortals who fled to the New World did so out of religious persecution, leaving a strong contingent of those with True Faith among the colonists. Additionally, being separated from their elders' lairs, the Sabbat found it difficult to wage its nightly war on the elders. Only the presence of the terrible Lupines prevented them from descending into internecine squabbling, as did the occasional rumor of a powerful native elder Cainite or transplanted Methuselah from the Old World.

The relative prominence of the Sabbat faced opposition, though, as disenfranchised Camarilla vampires also journeyed across the oceans, hoping to carve out legacies for themselves away from the ironbound holdings of European elders. Before long, the Camarilla-Sabbat war that started after the Anarch Revolt drew to a close arrived by ship on the shores of the Americas.

Before long, few mortal conflicts in the New World existed that did not hide the more sinister implications of vampiric conflict. The Sabbat rode the trends of these tumultuous times, using the American Revolution, French-Indian War and the incessant violence of the American frontier as screens for their own campaigns of conquest and parasitism. Like the population-choked cities of the Old World, almost every city had a strong population of vampires, which the exodus to the New World had intended to avoid. Sieges — the "starving out" of Camarilla vampires in cities as Sabbat vampires rampaged through and broke the Masquerade, making discrete feeding nigh impossible — became a popular tactic, but it rarely succeeded in the long term.

Arguably the single most crippling characteristic of the Sabbat is its lack of organization. Rather than establish rigid codes of behavior and Byzantine hierarchies of responsibility, the Sabbat instead embraces freedom. This freedom turned against the sect, however, in what became known as the Sabbat Civil War.

The Lasombra and Tzimisce, the most populous clans in the Sabbat in the late 18th century, fell to warring amongst themselves for the rapidly depleting resources of the New World. The continent was huge and underdeveloped, its cities few and far between, and rare was the Cainite who wished to try to survive in the wilds. Cities became commodities to the Sabbat, who struggled against each other for the dwindling communities of kine that sustained their existence. In fact, many Sabbat adopted the guise of marauding Native Americans, turning entire towns and cities into paranoid powderkegs, reasoning that if they couldn't have the city, no one would.

(It bears mention that a good deal of Sabbat culture draws heavily from Native American practices. Several of the sect's *ritae* stem from shamanic practices, and a good deal of the sect's greetings and lesser rituals [sharing blood in handshakes, smoke signals, sweat lodges and vision quests] recall certain tribal customs of the New World's indigenous people — or at least the Europeans' interpretations of said customs.)

Amid the struggle between the various Sabbat clans and factions, the Camarilla crept into the New World undetected. By the time the Sabbat realized that they had been surrounded and, in fact, overtaken, it was too late. In a brief 30 years, the Sabbat's work had been undone by the very enemies they had fled in the Old World.

THE PURCHASE PACT

Unwilling to admit defeat, the Sabbat turned inward, pledging to fix its rifts and turn its attentions once again to the targets on whom they belonged: the Camarilla and the Ancients.

In 1803, the year American president Thomas Jefferson obtained all American territory west of the Mississippi River from the French, the Sabbat made an internal accord, known

as the Purchase Pact (after the Louisiana Purchase). This pact forbade conflict among sect members expressly, and it is a hallmark decision in sect history. Until the Purchase Pact, all Sabbat had complete freedom — if they so wished, they could make open war on other Sabbat or overtly claim another Cainite's sphere of influence. The Purchase Pact ended the possibility for such conflict (at least openly, as many Sabbat find out to their chagrin). Unwilling to risk destruction at the hands of the Camarilla over petty internal struggles, the Sabbat focused its attention on its true enemies.

TERMS OF THE PURCHASE PACT

Let it be know that forthwith, the Sabbat exists as a free entity, though the price of that freedom comes in the form of the sacrifice of certain rights.

On this, the 19th of September, 1803, all Sabbat of good faith and conscience do hereby suspend all grievances with other Sabbat.

Any Sabbat found in open violation of this agreement — e.g., any Sabbat making open war on another for the purposes of his own betterment at the expense of the sect — is hereby declared forsaken, and may be hunted for the blood in his veins. Such abandonment must be pronounced by a duly recognized bishop, archbishop or other elder member of the sect.

In this we are united. In this we are Sabbat.

Signed,

Regent Gorchist

Witnessed,

Cardinal Radu Bistri

Priscus Livia Boleslav Czernzy

Archbishop Enrique Albertos Marquez

Bishop Federic Montaigne

Unfortunately for the Sabbat, the Purchase Pact came too late. The insidious influence of the Camarilla had taken root in what had become the United States, and it had also become part of the impetus for the American drive westward.

Sabbat vampires are survivors, however, and despite the obstacles placed in their path by the Camarilla's encroachment, the sect persevered. Establishing strongholds in Canada (for which certain Sabbat vampires' ties to the Native Americans proved immensely helpful) and Mexico (where impoverished conditions and corrupt governments allowed the society of the undead to flourish), the Sabbat had effectively blocked in the Camarilla. Crusades — brutal blitzes that sent numerous waves of vampires to take over cities overtly or covertly — rose in frequency. The rival sect could move only westward, fenced in as it was by Sabbat presence to its immediate north and south. All the Sabbat had to do was hold its borders....

Remaining cohesive proved difficult, however, as old tempers flared and the Tzimisce and Lasombra blamed each other for allowing the United States to slip through the sect's fingers. Cooler heads in the sect noted that, while the Sabbat may have given up the United States, it had laid relatively undisputed claim to Mexico and Canada, which offered much more geographical territory. Cool heads never prevail in times of war however, and another wave of infighting broke out, which culminated in the Second Sabbat Civil War.

This time, divided by geography as well as lineage, the Sabbat almost destroyed itself in the New World. The Lasombra and Tzimisce allowed no Cainites to remain neutral in the conflict, sweeping up clans, factions, cults — anyone who could lend a fighting arm to either side. Mexico was torn apart in the struggle, which resulted in much of its decrepit state even to the modern nights. Conflict in Canada was more subdued — until the Tzimisce discovered the Lasombra were secretly sending reinforcements to Mexico to aid their cause.

Mortal history conspired to keep the Cainites safe, however, as the conflict reached its greatest peak during the Great War. Americans had focused their attention so greatly on events in the European Theater, they had little time to notice secret vampiric conflicts happening to the north and south. Canadians likewise felt little impact, as the majority of the fighting occurred thousands of miles away in Mexico.

The Camarilla assumed influence in numerous Canadian cities, as the Sabbat presence there had become too weak to repel them.

Finally, after becoming painfully aware that their action had cost them more territory, the Sabbat vampires put their differences to rest... for a short time. Convening in New York, which the sect had managed to hold against all the best efforts of the Camarilla, high-ranking Sabbat reconsidered their commitment to the sect's causes. Not content to merely sign a goodwill agreement as they had before, Sabbat vampires took a long, hard look at what was important to the Sword of Caine. An unheard-of congregation of Sabbat committed to document the Code of Milan, a collection of tenets that composed Sabbat ideology supposedly since the establishment of the sect. Additionally, the assembled vampires submitted a few addenda, to bring the code up to date in light of recent affairs.

The revised code proved to be too little, too late, again. After a few scant years of relative peace (which many Sabbat attribute to fear of the Seraphim, who were present at the code's reaffirmation), trouble arose again.

The Third Sabbat Civil War, the briefest of the three, lasted only 100 nights, in the latter half of 1957. Incited by a failed coup of New York on behalf of the Brujah *antitribu*, violence once again ensued. Ironically, the end of the trouble came as a result of the rarest of Cainite diplomacy — compromise. After the Brujah *antitribu* coup fell, the clan rose against the united Lasombra and Tzimisce, which was bound for disaster. Out of the ashes of the fighting, however, emerged

THE CODE OF MILAN

By the solemn word of Regent Gorchist, this is the one true Code of Milan, revised from the original manuscript this night, December 21, 1933. Out of the ashes of our great war may this peace reign everlasting.

An oath of allegiance has been sworn by the regent and the consistory in the presence of all faction leaders and 50 other witnesses to faithfully follow all regulations imposed by this code in leading the Sabbat. This revised Code of Milan is agreed on by all Sabbat factions, including those of Cardinals Huroff, Bruce de Guy, Agnes and Charles VI; and Archbishops Beatrice, Una, Tecumseh, Giangaleazzo, Toth, Aeron, Marsilio, Rebecca, Julian and Salluccio. All other factions must pledge themselves in support of this revised Code of Milan or claim separation from the Sabbat.

These are the statutes comprising the Code of Milan:

I. THE SABBAT SHALL REMAIN UNITED IN ITS SUPPORT OF THE SECT'S REGENT. IF NECESSARY, A NEW REGENT SHALL BE ELECTED. THE REGENT SHALL SUPPORT RELIEF FROM TYRANNY, GRANTING ALL SABBAT FREEDOM.

II. ALL SABBAT SHALL DO THEIR BEST TO SERVE THEIR LEADERS AS LONG AS SAID LEADERS SERVE THE WILL OF THE REGENT.

III. ALL SABBAT SHALL FAITHFULLY OBSERVE ALL THE *AUCTORITAS RITAE*.

IV. ALL SABBAT SHALL KEEP THEIR WORD OF HONOR TO ONE ANOTHER.

V. ALL SABBAT SHALL TREAT THEIR PEERS FAIRLY AND EQUALLY, UPHOLDING THE STRENGTH AND UNITY OF THE SABBAT. IF NECESSARY, THEY SHALL PROVIDE FOR THE NEEDS OF THEIR BRETHREN.

VI. ALL SABBAT MUST PUT THE GOOD OF THE SECT AND THE RACE OF CAINITES BEFORE THEIR OWN PERSONAL NEEDS, DESPITE ALL COSTS.

VII. THOSE WHO ARE NOT HONORABLE UNDER THIS CODE WILL BE CONSIDERED LESS THAN EQUAL AND THEREFORE UNWORTHY OF ASSISTANCE.

VIII. AS IT HAS ALWAYS BEEN, SO SHALL IT ALWAYS BE. THE LEXTALIONIS SHALL BE THE MODEL FOR UNDYING JUSTICE BY WHICH ALL SABBAT SHALL ABIDE.

IX. ALL SABBAT SHALL PROTECT ONE ANOTHER FROM THE ENEMIES OF THE SECT. PERSONAL ENEMIES SHALL REMAIN A PERSONAL RESPONSIBILITY, UNLESS THEY UNDERMINE SECT SECURITY.

X. ALL SECT MEMBERS SHALL PROTECT SABBAT TERRITORY FROM ALL OTHER POWERS.

XI. THE SPIRIT OF FREEDOM SHALL BE THE FUNDAMENTAL PRINCIPLE OF THE SECT. ALL SABBAT SHALL EXPECT AND DEMAND FREEDOM FROM THEIR LEADERS.

XII. THE *RITUS* OF MONOMACY SHALL BE USED TO SETTLE DISPUTES AMONG ALL SABBAT.

XIII. ALL SABBAT SHALL SUPPORT THE BLACK HAND.

ADDENDA TO THE CODE OF MILAN

OBSERVED BY ALL WITNESSING PARTIES PRESENT ON THIS NIGHT, DECEMBER 21, 1933, AND HEREAFTER UPHELD.

XIV. ALL SABBAT HAVE THE RIGHT TO MONITOR THE BEHAVIOR AND ACTIVITIES OF THEIR FELLOW SECT MEMBERS IN ORDER TO MAINTAIN FREEDOM AND SECURITY.

XV. ALL SABBAT POSSESS THE RIGHT TO CALL A COUNCIL OF THEIR PEERS AND IMMEDIATE LEADERS.

XVI. ALL SABBAT SHALL ACT AGAINST SECT MEMBERS WHO USE THE POWERS AND AUTHORITY THE SABBAT HAS GIVEN THEM FOR PERSONAL GAIN AT THE EXPENSE OF THE SABBAT. ACTION SHALL BE TAKEN ONLY THROUGH ACCEPTED MEANS, APPROVED BY A QUORUM OF PRISCI.

a unified group of Caitiff calling themselves the Panders, after their leader, Joseph Pander. The Panders had the Brujah *antitribu's* support, as they were rabble and outcasts, much like the Brujah had become after the migration to the New World. Seeing the opportunity to avoid another protracted (and dreadfully embarrassing) war, the Lasombra and Tzimisce recognized the Panders as a distinct entity, conferring on the group clan or bloodline status. With the mob appeased and little of import given up on behalf of the Fiends and Keepers, the sect narrowly avoided another crippling setback.

MODERN GEOGRAPHICAL INFLUENCE

Some say the Sabbat has matured remarkably in the intervening years. Indeed, it has become a force to be reckoned with in the modern nights, claiming or reclaiming cities long held by the Camarilla and using sieges and crusades with deadly efficiency. This singularity of vision seems to have overcome at least a modicum of the sect's disorganization. Additionally, the sect is younger and more nimble than the Camarilla, and it is able to adopt the ways of the modern world more quickly. Whatever the cause, in the 40-some years since the aversion of the most recent Sabbat Civil War, the sect has made some astounding coups and become a legitimate contender for the Camarilla's crumbling power.

Not surprisingly, the Sabbat exercises a great deal of influence over Third-World nations and the most squalid cities of the world. There, in hives of homeless and faceless juicebags, the Sabbat's vampires feed with impunity and build their own private empires. Without the threats of organized law enforcement and mass media, the Sabbat can indulge in the widespread violence and feeding demanded by many of the younger and more chaotic vampires.

In modernized parts of the world, the Sabbat is careful to cover its tracks. While scorning the Masquerade of the Camarilla (at least in theory, if not in practice), the Sabbat's leadership realizes that the threat of organized and technologically advanced human resistance is too dangerous to provoke. Thus, in cities of Europe and North America, the Sabbat takes some pains to cover its tracks, though its methods — intimidation and murder — are far cruder than the (usually) subtle machinations of the Camarilla. With its limited influence in mortal circles, the Sabbat suffers in modern cities; the Camarilla influence in many human institutions prevents the Sabbat from spreading with ease.

NORTH AMERICA

Canada and the United States pose perhaps the most successful staging ground for the Sabbat. The sect has recently redoubled its war effort along the East Coast of the United States, solidifying its dominance in Miami, Washington, DC, Baltimore, Philadelphia and Atlantic City. Concerned Sabbat see these victories as paper tigers, however, as the sect's formerly taken-for-granted supremacy in

New York City has become contested. Supporters of the war movement hasten to note that the cities of Atlanta, Richmond, Boston and Raleigh-Durham have recently fallen into contention from former Camarilla strangleholds. Obviously, the Sabbat recognizes that North America represents an extremely powerful financial and international control base, and it continually makes strides to advance its control of the region. Nightly, the sect tightens its grip on the United States' Midwest, hoping to crack the Camarilla like a nut between the combined might of Mexico and the East Coast territories.

The Sabbat steps carefully in North America, all too aware that the heavily technology-oriented populace can easily cause serious problems if people notice the sect's activities. The frenzied media of the United States provides too much of an opportunity for the sect to be revealed to the public at large, and that this forces the Sabbat to avoid too much open warfare against its foes. Unfortunately for the Sabbat, this means that much of the battle takes place through influence, which is one of the primary strengths of the Camarilla. Similarly, the difficulty of obtaining weapons in Canada hinders the Sabbat's crusades, which often rely on discreet direct assaults. North America forces the Sabbat to adopt new tactics and to find creative uses for the resources available to the sect but lacking in its enemies.

Detroit

Once the hub of the United States' automotive manufacturing, Detroit, Michigan has become a shell of its former industrial self. Detroit is valuable territory for the Sabbat despite its economic woes, and the sect seeks to revitalize the city with a shift in industrial focus. With one of the highest murder rates in the United States, Detroit (which has been known as "the murder capital of the US") provides ample feeding grounds for its dwellers. Unlike some of their brethren to the south, the Sabbat of Detroit do not concentrate on capturing neighboring Camarilla cities. Rather, the city's vampires focus on bolstering the flagging fortunes of their home. After all, the Sabbat must have the proper resources if it is to launch a successful attack….

Montreal

As part of the hammer that keeps southeast Ottawa in line (with Detroit as the anvil), Montreal boasts a population of *exceptionally* powerful Sabbat. Highly religious and organized, the packs of the city revel in freakishness. The trade and tourism of the area mean that Sabbat have easy pickings when hunting, and those who dabble in mortal works can lead wealthy and comfortable unlives. However, the same strengths that make the city lucrative and abundant for Sabbat also feed its own rot from within — many members of the sect in Montreal are suspected of being infernalists, and without the constant tests and trials that characterize the sect elsewhere, the Sabbat of the city turn to spiritual decay. The Sabbat Inquisition has taken a keen interest in the affairs of Montreal's Cainites, and several of the latter have fallen to claims of heresy and traffic with demons.

CENTRAL AMERICA

The greatest stronghold of the Sabbat is Mexico, and the sect places its spiritual and political heart in Mexico City. There is not a place in Central America (excepting a few pitiful and pathetic territories in the Yucatan peninsula) that does not see the guiding fist of the sect. Monterey and Guadalajara, Acapulco and Oaxaca — the hub of the Americas teems with Sabbat. Pushing north into the United States, the Sabbat exerts constant pressure; trickling into South America, the sect establishes a small presence among the variegated states of that area. Among the slums of economically depressed Mexico, the Sabbat finds easy hunting grounds and plenty of fodder for footsoldiers in the Jyhad.

Combining the *ritae* of the sect with the ancient practices of indigenous peoples, the Sabbat of Central America are among the most ritualistic and fervent supporters of the sect's policies. This fanaticism, combined with easy access to weapons, mercenaries and criminal gangs, means that the Sabbat of Central America are brutal and warlike. Indeed, in many places, the Sabbat members revel openly in their vampiric status, and the wandering packs of the area battle one another for turf and entertainment. A high rate of violent crime means that situations that get out of hand are easily covered up or dismissed, while the overflowing ghettoes provide a surfeit of blood. It is no wonder, then, that the Sabbat of this territory style themselves as brutal gang leaders or reclusive aristocrats.

Mexico City

The center of Mexico claims a population in excess of 20 million people, with the vast majority living in hardscrabble poverty. Dense smog and befouled water make the city among the most polluted places on Earth. Entire towns built on landfills house generations of people who likely never learn of electricity, writing or numbers. Among these masses of uneducated and dying kine, the Sabbat revels.

The current Regent of the Sabbat, a fifth-generation Toreador *antitribu*, makes her haven in Mexico City, considering the goals of the sect and holding sway over the Black Hand. Vampires who seek true political power within the Sabbat must travel here at some point, to be recognized — or scorned — amidst the hundreds of vampires who fight for prestige and position. Indeed, the vampires here are so numerous that even the city's wardens cannot recognize them all; any vampire who gives the proper countersigns is considered welcome. Entire packs may enter, vanish into the slums, and leave without anyone becoming aware of their existence.

Mexico City epitomizes the Sabbat in many ways: Here, vampires flaunt their powers openly to the kine (even if only frightened street gangs). Blood is always available for the taking (from the faceless denizens of the slums, who will never be missed). Vampires test against one another in bouts of strength and cunning, while industry and trade may be influenced by any Cainite bold enough to exert her will. Some vampires speculate that as many as 1,000 vampires keep their havens in Mexico City, making for a hellish preponderance of urban predators who act in whatever manner takes their whim. So is the mighty, diseased heart of the Sabbat's empire constructed.

Tijuana

Located just across the border from San Diego, California, Tijuana is a coastal city focused on tourism — mainly of the high-school-crowd-looking-to-become-intoxicated kind. As with many of the squalid cities in the throes of economic crisis, Tijuana faces problems with pollution and poverty. Much of the city has a cracked and decaying carnival atmosphere, with winding streets passing huddled clusters of low-life bars and clubs. As the Sabbat's staging ground against the rabble vampires of southern California, Tijuana holds a disproportionate number of Cainites. The high incidence of tourists and poverty-stricken neighborhoods allows the city to support more than its usual share of vampires. Bishop Cicatriz of Tijuana fights a two-front war, organizing War Parties to feel out the anarchs' wartime defenses while simultaneously attempting to exert influence across the border into San Diego — often through the use of immigrants and political conflicts over the border.

SOUTH AMERICA

In a continent overrun with feudal, balkanized vampiric domains, the Sabbat holds only limited sway. Most of the Cainites of South America support private domains backed up by small coteries of influential allies. As these vampires-cum-potentates have little desire to risk their positions by participating in the Sabbat's Jyhad, the sect has little success with converts in the area. Additionally, though major cities are always prime targets for the Sabbat, the economics of South American countries do not hold the appeal of North America and Europe, so they are often considered secondary targets due to their combined lack of financial power and — incorrectly — importance to the Jyhad. In fact, the neutral attitudes of South America make many of the cities perfect middle ground for meetings with members of other sects or organizations, and when a Camarilla or independent vampire needs to make arrangements with the Sabbat, it's as likely as not to happen here, often rubbing elbows with the war criminals, expatriates and other exiles of the mortal world.

Sabbat vampires in South America are disorganized and fractious. The cities of the area are largely independent, and the given presence of Sabbat in any city is usually limited to a single pack. Additionally, given the antagonistic relationship with the seemingly ubiquitous shapeshifters of South America (who appear to be involved in some war of their own), the Sabbat finds the South American continent very troublesome for any sort of travel.

EUROPE

As the home of the elders of the Camarilla and the birthplace of the Sabbat, the countries of Europe are prime grounds of subtle warfare for the sect. Here, the Sabbat still fights to overthrow the decrepit "Kindred" of latter nights. Unfortunately for the sect, the presence of many powerful and paranoid elders makes it difficult at best to besiege cities, and the Camarilla is quick with retribution against any

perceived attack. As a result, the Sabbat has only limited influence in Europe, primarily in Spain and Italy where the Lasombra clan exercises its traditional sway.

As a whole, Europe is staunchly traditional and orderly. Many of Europe's vampires — including a few of the Sabbat — date back to the Middle Ages and beyond, and they still uphold their old ways. To make gains against creatures of such age, power and guile, the Sabbat must move slowly and cautiously. Additionally, with its feet firmly in the modern world (thanks to the induction of many younger Cainites), the Sabbat makes use of modern technology and institutions that are beyond the understanding of some of Europe's anachronistic elders. The end result is a slow cold war as the Sabbat sacrifices its weak pawns in an attempt to undermine the centuries-old pillars of strength supporting the Camarilla of Europe. Since even the eldest among the Sabbat would be hard-pressed to fight the Camarilla's luminaries here, they must content themselves with waiting for that inevitable change or fatal mistake that will allow them to move into a city and take it in one fell stroke.

As mentioned previously, many of the Sabbat in Europe are quite old. Indeed, some vampires claiming to have been involved in the fabled Anarch Revolt still give counsel in the European nations. As a result, upward mobility in the sect is limited here. Despite the Sabbat's cries of freedom and equality, young Cainites of the area chafe at finding themselves unable to rise in position because older and more cunning vampires already hold the reins of power. Only by dint of the most wildly risky and successful schemes can a young Cainite hope to rise in standing. As a result, the Sabbat packs of the area are mostly old, founded packs, also known as *covens*; younger Cainites tend to leave for riper pickings elsewhere after a brief "mentorship" with their sires.

Eastern Europe, with the Russian territories and the former Ottoman provinces, is almost a separate continent as far as vampires are concerned. Here, the hoary Tzimisce ply the ancient ways of their clan, some even existing still as feudal overlords in crumbling castles. Vampires who visit here are best served by upholding the ancient ways, lest they find themselves decorating the walls of some abattoir. In the more rural places in the mountains, small villages are lorded over by howling packs of Sabbat vampires, small-scale imitations of the Sabbat dream.

Sabbat vampires of the Old World generally look on their compatriots in the Americas with disdain, often considering them crude and unworthy. As one European *ductus*, or pack leader, says, "What gravity can freedom have to a Cainite whose greatest moral quandary is deciding whether to take prey from a Burger King or a McDonalds?"

Madrid

Ruled by an ancient and twisted Lasombra, the Archbishop Monçada, Madrid remains a bastion of Sabbat power and prestige. Here, the Lasombra come for confession and to participate in their clan's oldest *ritae*. No Camarilla would dare attack the city — who would be fool enough to challenge the viper in his own lair? — so the sect's control of the surrounding territory is absolute. From Madrid, Sabbat vampires of all clans spread out through the Iberian peninsula, conducting neutral business in Barcelona or traveling to the rest of continental Europe to engage the Camarilla elders in overt or covert schemes.

Although Madrid is not as large a city as Barcelona, it is the capital of Spain, and is therefore a seat of political power. The Lasombra enjoy their chess games of intrigue here, though Monçada brooks no challenge to his power. With the city's beautiful architecture, Toreador and *antitribu* alike flock to the location to study the old stonework and paintings. Cainites with a taste for sport watch bullfights in the evenings; some vampires even cultivate their own ghouled bulls, and watch hungrily as the matadors become the victims. In Madrid, aristocratic Sabbat vampires indulge their every depraved whim. Who would stop them?

Milan

Once a Sabbat stronghold in the middle of Italy, Milan recently changed hands. Giangaleazzo, the former archbishop of the city, masterfully orchestrated a purge of the loyal Sabbat elements and pledged his fealty to the Camarilla in a sudden coup. Enraged, the Sabbat has sworn to destroy Giangaleazzo utterly, and to retake the city. However, since Milan is surrounded by Giovanni and Camarilla elements, direct assaults are difficult at best. It appears that the erstwhile archbishop of the city may have his way.

AFRICA

Considering the fierce rivalry between the Followers of Set and the Serpents of the Light, Africa occupies some of the Sabbat's attention. However, in general, the Followers are too deeply entrenched in their homeland for the Sabbat to confront them effectively. Furthermore, despite their misguided devotion to an Antediluvian, the Setites are less of a threat than the Camarilla. The remainder of the African continent is apparently devoid of vampiric controllers, though rumors of strange native vampires — "Laibon" and other, older names — circulate wildly. Of course, if the loss of Sabbat (and Camarilla) agents in South Africa is any indication, the native vampires, if these "Laibon" are vampires at all, may not see things in exactly the same light.

The Middle East, encompassing northern parts of Africa and some Far Eastern sections of Europe, is an exception to the Sabbat's otherwise minimal presence

in the Dark Continent. As the traditional home of the Assamites, the Middle East countries like Turkey and Saudi Arabia are fortifications of strength for the Black Hand. The shifting allegiances of religious factions in the Middle East also make a fertile ground for recruitment; once the Blood has become involved, it is often a simple matter to turn fervent loyalty from a holy mortal cause to an unholy immortal one.

Australia

As a marginally independent territory, the Sabbat finds Australia frustrating. The princes of the area either pay lip service to the Camarilla or hold completely independent cities. Consequently, the Sabbat has pushed its attacks on Australia, as evidenced by rising crime and political unrest. Without reinforcements from outside, the cities of Australia may soon fall to the Sabbat presence, but many major outposts — Sydney and Melbourne in particular — remain remarkably free of Sabbat influence.

With huge expanses of uncivilized territory, Australia is a perfect place for solitary or nomadic Cainites. At least a half dozen nomadic packs roam the bush, though at least two are known to have disappeared while crossing the wastes. The necromancers of the Sabbat claim that unquiet spirits step out from dreams to assault trespassers here, but no magic has yet been able to summon or bind these spirits. Some Cainite scholars whisper that central Australia may be home to an ancient Nosferatu enemy, and that it may have awakened, hungry.

Asia

The Far East remains shrouded in mystery to the Sabbat. The native vampires have little or no interest in contact or cooperation, and none seem to fear the Antediluvians. Those few captured seem able to withstand privation for a preternaturally long time, and they rarely give up any secrets, even when the most wicked Tzimisce apply their tortures. Worst of all, the Vaulderie apparently has no effect on the Cathayans, as evidenced when a "convert" brought back some associates and slaughtered his entire pack. Even when using the underground smugglers who deign to transport Cainites (albeit at a ridiculously high price), the Sabbat finds itself balked by the enigmatic locals and their disdain for the sect's ruthless nature.

Because of Asia's huge mortal population (primarily in China and India) and financial markets (trade with Japan and Korea), the Sabbat is quite interested in establishing power in this region. Unfortunately, aside from a single agent in Hong Kong and a pack in Tokyo, there are no active Sabbat in Asia. Attempts to influence the region have all failed miserably, with Sabbat agents disappearing or dying before achieving any goals. Direct assaults with large packs of fodder meet horrible demises as Cathayans seem to melt out of the shadows wielding terrible powers. Asia is a deathtrap for the Sabbat, and the sect seethes with frustration at these failures.

The only hint to penetrating Asia may lie with Adonai, nominal leader of the Salubri *antitribu*, who alludes to ancient legends of his former clan's founder's travels to the East. The discovery of a set of ancient and unidentifiable symbols at a ruined temple in Cambodia led to some trepidation when Adonai recognized the signs as a primitive form of the secret writing used by his clan in nights of yore. However, even when confronted directly, Cathayan diplomats refuse to speak of the "family of Zao-lat the traitor."

The Clans of the Sabbat

The Sabbat may have fewer members than the Camarilla, but it is far more cosmopolitan — at least with regard to the lineage of those who make up its ranks. The Camarilla probably has more diversity within the clans that compose it, but the Sabbat prides itself on the universal vision of its vampires. Of course, the vampires of the sect are just as unique as any other Damned in the World of Darkness, though their common ideology tends to unite them more cohesively.

Until recently, the Lasombra and Tzimisce were the most numerous vampires of the sect. In the nights of conquest and siege, however, more vampires of other clans and bloodlines came to populate the Sabbat. Although Lasombra and Tzimisce still outnumber the other vampires, the ratio is no longer as stacked as it used to be. Critics of these two clans wonder if perhaps the leadership of the sect is undergoing a change, as reflected by the increase in "lesser" clans and bloodlines.

The clans of the Sabbat often refer to themselves as *antitribu* or "anti-clans", having turned their backs on the Camarilla or independent clans that originally spawned the. Little love is commonly lost between the *antitribu* and the mainstream clans — their respective members parted ways long ago on matters of philosophy, and it appears that reconciliation is hardly possible, especially as Gehenna approaches in the modern nights. Surely, the details of these old rivalries have been lost in the mists of history, but few vampires meet with hostility like that possessed by the *antitribu* and their estranged parent clans.

What follows is a general description of the clans and bloodlines of the Sabbat. More information on all of them appear in Chapter Two (except the Tzimisce and Lasombra, who are covered in **Vampire: The Masquerade**).

Lasombra

Clan Lasombra is, without a doubt, the dominant clan in the Sabbat. It claims a history of nobility and prestige, though in the modern nights, it would seem that the Sabbat has twisted this nobility into the blackest of mockeries. Lasombra are jaded, depraved leaders, tempered by their own inner darkness and centuries of ruthless plotting and counter-plotting. The Sabbat would likely crumble without the leadership of Clan Lasombra, which claims to have destroyed its progenitor and would lead others to that selfsame victory.

Tzimisce

Eldritch and alien, the Tzimisce are a senescent clan of rotting prominence. Much of the Sabbat's monstrous outlook stems from Tzimisce philosophy and subsequent influence. The Fiends claim a proud history of rulership, governing their vassals in the Old World with iron talons and hoary magic. In the modern nights, many of the sect's priests and councilors hail from Clan Tzimisce, the moral and spiritual backbone of the Sabbat. They possess a twisted honor and a malignant love of knowledge. It is whispered that the legendary Dracula claims this clan as his own, though his allegiance to sect or clan is unknown if it — or he — exists at all.

Assamite Antitribu

The Sabbat Assamites are much like their independent brethren, though their allegiance is to the sect and its purpose rather than the slumbering, antiquated Ancient venerated by the mainstream clan. Assamite *antitribu* inhabit a comfortable niche among the bloody Sabbat, given as they are to murder and diablerie. Most members of this clan join the subsect known as the Black Hand or become templars, paladins and other enforcers of Sabbat policy. Surprisingly, the clan seems to maintain fairly civil relations with its parent clan despite its "heretical" beliefs in the Sabbat's Noddist philosophy. Sabbat Assamites also maintain a vague hauteur over their forebears, as they never succumbed to the curse only recently broken by the non-Sabbat Assassins.

Blood Brothers

A strange bloodline of vampires developed by Thaumaturgical and other mystical means, the Blood Brothers are created rather than Embraced. Although they count few members, the Blood Brothers display a vicious streak a mile wide, and often find themselves serving as muscle or labor for other vampires in the sect. Blood Brothers move in "circles" that consist only of other Blood Brothers, and their bizarre biothaumaturgical Embrace strips them of personal will. As such, while they cannot be said to happily serve the Sabbat, they do so unquestioningly. Additionally, Blood Brothers undergo a fleshcrafting process during the Embrace that reforms their facial (and sometimes bodily) structures to resemble one another exactly. They are most frequently found — which is a bit misleading, as there is nothing "frequent" about them — in the employ of freakish Tzimisce and scheming Lasombra, who use them when they need graceless work done with which they would rather not associate themselves.

Brujah Antitribu

Superficially similar to their parent clan, the Sabbat Brujah are ironically much more conservative than the mainstream clan. Brujah *antitribu* are pillars of stability for the Sabbat, as they care less for causes and more for wanton violence. Many of the Sabbat's shock troops and fodder come from this clan, as their prowess is matched only by their relentless (if simplistic) support of the sect. The Sabbat Brujah are great proselytizers, as well, converting everyone they can with promises of freedom and the destruction of elder tyranny. Unlike the apparent attitude affected by Camarilla Brujah, they do not seem to despise the sect to which they belong.

Gangrel Antitribu

Very little can be said regarding the Sabbat Gangrel as a clan, as their ranks include loners and individualists who would seem to have little use for sects. The clan has two subdivisions, known as the City Gangrel and the Country Gangrel. Country Gangrel are the most like their parent clan, feral and often rustic, preferring their own company to packs and blood-guzzling ritual convocations. The City Gangrel, however, seem to exhibit a more pack mentality, and resemble the creatures of urban nightmare more than their cousins — rather than wolves and bats, their frenzies leave them with the features of spiders, hyenas and… other… beasts. City Gangrel are consummate urban predators, honing their instincts to suit the alleys they prowl. Recently, a great many Gangrel have "defected" to the Sabbat, looking over their shoulders for whatever has spooked them into such a mass exodus and speaking fearfully of "sleeping horrors" awakening.

Harbingers of Skulls

These rare and curious vampires have joined the Sabbat only recently. In fact, until a few years ago, no one had heard of them. The Harbingers present themselves as quiet and conservative, preferring to traffic with the souls of the dead rather than rampage about, leaving wakes of fire and destruction. Nonetheless, they are cold and alien, conducting murder and torture in their laboratories. All of the Harbingers physically resemble corpses themselves; their skin stretches over their bones and gives them a skeletal, emaciated appearance. They affect masks and other manners of hiding their faces, for their skin has stretched so tightly over their heads that they appear as naked, grinning skulls. Some vampires attribute a dark origin to the Harbingers, as their knowledge and power is far superior to any bloodline that has "popped up" recently.

Kiasyd

The enigmatic Kiasyd seem to have little affiliation with the Sabbat, and they are arguably not part of it at all. However, it appears that, for whatever reason, they sympathize with the sect. Those who have heard of the Kiasyd (a rarity in and of itself) believe them to have some mystical connection with the Lasombra, since tangible darkness trails the Kiasyd as it does the Keepers. For the most part, they seem to be content to remain quietly distant from the nightly affairs of the sect, losing themselves in ancient writings and forgotten lore. Few Kiasyd venture outside their havens — which would certainly be memorable, given these vampires' strange, bluish skin, oddly pointed ears, tall frames and pure black eyes. Perhaps it is best that they keep to themselves, for they are obviously unwholesome.

MALKAVIAN ANTITRIBU

The Malkavians of the Sabbat support the sect only nominally, if at all, though they form one of the more populous clans. It would seem that their crippling derangements hinder any attempts at lucidity — they are true monsters, rarely driven by anything other than ravenous hunger or their own rampaging Beasts. In their rare, brief moments of civility, they exhibit the cursed insight of the rest of their clan, often speaking cryptically of events to come or unrevealed secrets forgotten. Sabbat packs are often forced to restrain or incapacitate their Malkavian members, whose explosive and murderous rages are equally as likely to maim friend or foe. Some Sabbat Malkavians have mentioned "infecting" their Camarilla counterparts, but no one outside the clan claims to know what they mean.

NOSFERATU ANTITRIBU

Nosferatu in the Sabbat are studies in extremes — among their ranks are some of the sect's most depraved villains and most humanitarian penitents. Although these latter are derided as "soft" by many others of the sect, the clan as a whole is too useful to the sect to write off. Sabbat Nosferatu are some of the most ardent followers of the Sabbat's Paths of Enlightenment, turning their backs on the values of those they no longer resemble. Nosferatu *antitribu* often form packs with other Nosferatu exclusively and gather secrets much like their Camarilla forebears. In fact, the Nosferatu *antitribu* maintain probably the best relationship with their mainstream clan of all Sabbat vampires, and it is all but assured that they know more about the Camarilla than any other Sabbat clan, as well.

PANDERS

Although they are not a true clan in the strictest sense of the word, the Panders have nonetheless accumulated some small degree of status in the Sabbat. The Panders comprise the cast-offs and detritus of the Sabbat — they are the sect's "Caitiff," clanless and wretched, but still committed to the sect's aims. Unlike the Caitiff, however, the Panders are acknowledged as equals… at least in theory if not in practice.

RAVNOS ANTITRIBU

The Ravnos *antitribu* have turned their backs on their Gypsy heritage, and they no longer maintain any relations (outside of hostility) with their mainstream clan. Sabbat Ravnos are some of the wildest vampires in the sect, as wanderlust still runs in their undead veins and their wicked ways have made them even more malicious than independent Ravnos. Almost all Ravnos *antitribu* are *gorgio* — non-Gypsies; in turning away from their parent clan, the Sabbat Ravnos have also turned away from their archaic ways. Many Ravnos *antitribu* serve as scouts and spies for the Sabbat, taking advantage of their nomadic natures and prowess with Chimerstry.

SALUBRI ANTITRIBU

A recent development in Sabbat history has seen the conversion of a member of the reviled Salubri bloodline to the Black Hand. Bringing and Embracing a small, elite army of followers, this Salubri has declared a personal vendetta against the Camarilla, which he claims has sheltered murderers and kinslayers since its inception. While the Sabbat seems like a strange place for those who take offense at the destruction of elders (at least to other Sabbat) the Salubri *antitribu* seem to regard the sect's larger philosophy with only lip service. In their minds, their allegiance with the sect begins and ends with the war on the Camarilla. In the tradition of the *antitribu*, the Sabbat Salubri have turned utterly away from the "clan" that spawned them, regarding their progenitors with antipathy for what they consider weakness and fatalism.

SERPENTS OF THE LIGHT

It is believed that the Serpents of the Light began as a heretical offshoot bloodline of the Followers of Set. Following more closely to the tenets of *voudun* than the arcane Egyptian faith of the parent clan, the faction left the fold at the urging of the Sabbat in the late 1960s (once the sect had established itself in Haiti and turned back Setite presence). Serpents of the Light consider the Setites' attempts to resurrect their undead vampire-god blasphemous and foolish, as doing so would open the door to Gehenna and rouse the other Antediluvians. The Serpents of the Light still have much to prove to the sect, but not for a lack of conviction — they oppose their forebears' support of their Antediluvian with a ferocity not found elsewhere.

TOREADOR ANTITRIBU

These vampires embody all that is despicable and inhumane in the Sabbat and Toreador alike. Whereas the Camarilla-advocates of Clan Toreador becomes engrossed in beauty, the Toreador *antitribu* — through their long association with the Sabbat — find human suffering, pain and cruelty beautiful. They are truly depraved, taking pleasure in the torment of others and reveling in the gore with which they surround themselves. Sabbat Toreador are simultaneously in touch with and alienated from their human sides — they know mortal urges intimately, though they twist them horrifically. Some Sabbat speak furtively of the Toreador *antitribu*, believing them to be more insane than the Malkavians, claiming that the Perverts are interested only in suffering for its own sake rather than any specific end. Like their counterparts in the Camarilla, the Sabbat Toreador make up the "high society" of the sect, though their society is malefic and bloody, indeed.

VENTRUE ANTITRIBU

The Ventrue of the Sabbat resemble their parent clan of nights past, and they truly loathe what the mainstream clan has become in the modern nights. While Camarilla Ventrue are powerful financiers and corporate merchant princes, the Sabbat Ventrue are paladins and knights, sworn to uphold the Sabbat's way of unlife and atone for the greed of their predecessors. They possess a grim nobility, and many find places within the Black Hand or as templars. The Sabbat Inquisition, devoted to rooting out and destroying infernalism, is composed predominantly of Ventrue *antitribu*. Indeed, the Sabbat Ventrue are — some would say ironically — some of the sect's most ardent supporters.

ON THE TREMERE ANTITRIBU

Brother Saiz had not made the esbat in a month.

I must admit, though we may come or go as we please, this disconcerted me. Perhaps all was not well — he may have fallen to the Lupines or run afoul of the secret magics of the witch men. Perhaps the Devil had come to claim his soul. Or perhaps Brother Saiz' rituals had gone wrong. As I am responsible for the pack, I had to know.

It took me six months to find the place, the Universidad del Tercer Circulo del Serpiente Dorado. It was buried a quarter-mile below the ground.

I had thought there would be untold wards and curses on the doors, or other ways of preventing people from finding it, yet that was not so. You can imagine my surprise as I walked unmolested through the gilded doors of this most secret chamber.

("Unmolested" may not be the best word, for I had to circumnavigate a fetid vestibule that a large, white alligator had claimed as her own at one of the upper tiers of the labyrinth leading to the chantry below the streets of Mexico City.)

All around me appeared the signs of a great, but seemingly brief, conflagration. Ancient books and shelves were charred and blackened, ritual markings on the floor were blasted away in sections and a miasma of choking haze filled the still air of the room. Most curious, I found roughly one hundred pillars of ash, a strange architectural feature of the room. On closer inspection, however, I learned that these pillars were not part of the room's support structure — I discerned that each pillar had a distinctly human face. When I touched one — ever so lightly! — it crumbled to the floor, a partially melted ring of silver resting among the charred remains.

I fear Brother Saiz shall not be rejoining us, nor will any of his Tremere compatriots.

— Matilda Soliz, pack priest, in a letter to Bishop Cicatriz of Tijuana

ORGANIZATION IN THE SWORD OF CAINE

Although it would be difficult to discern from the outside, the Sabbat actually has a codified hierarchy. The sect has leaders and followers, commanders and footsoldiers, like any other war effort.

Of course, the "war effort" is purely subjective to the sect. Sabbat do not spend every night in constant struggle with Camarilla vampires or the insidious Antediluvians. In fact, to the untrained eye, very little exists to distinguish Sabbat-controlled cities from those of the Camarilla, apart from higher crime rates, more missing-persons cases, greater urban human suffering and less hope for salvation. Then again, in the World of Darkness, these things exist on sliding scales, and what may be passable to one city's bishops may earn the Final Death in another.

The Sabbat is not ruled so much as it is led — even the regent and cardinals do what they do out of devotion to the sect's cause. Leadership among Sabbat, however, is a precarious thing. Among the higher echelons, Sabbat vampires tend to lose touch with the younger vampires who fight the battles nightly. At lower tiers of the hierarchy, a *ductus'* or priest's decisions sometimes carry more weight than those of a city's archbishop or bishop. In the end, the Sabbat's fervent support of its cause proves its undoing, as the disorganization endemic to a sect sworn to uphold freedom prevents it from achieving consistent success.

Despite their seemingly slavish devotion to the sect, members of the Sabbat are vampires first and foremost. Eternal, parasitic creatures, Sabbat vampires must deal with the same fears as the other Damned — witch-hunters, fellow Cainites, the mysterious other supernaturals who sometimes pass through cities and even members of "the masses" who catch on to a vampire's depredations all conspire to end a Sabbat's unlife as quickly as they would any other threat. Although they would never call it thus, the vampires of the Sabbat support an unspoken Masquerade; the sect isn't stupid, and it's leaders know that there is no way to succeed if the sect collapses before establishing a way to fulfill its goals.

As such, the Sabbat has created a few "offices" to serve its best interests. These titles are artificial at best, though any vampire who has managed to acquire one certainly has the personal power or influence to back it up. Sabbat vampires, being the passionate creatures they are, also harbor grudges as deeply as any Camarilla harpy or anarch dissident — intra-sect politics are as murky as the Camarilla's, though the Sabbat pretends to be above such things (at least in front of others). Vampires at various levels of the power structure invariably owe some fellow Sabbat favors, harbor vendettas toward others and manipulate all the resources at their disposal toward making things difficult for their foes while gaining (or erasing) debts sworn by (or to) others. It is even said that the recent upheaval wrought by the Inquisition (see

TITLES

The Sabbat places a great deal of emphasis on propriety and ritual, albeit in their own special way. In a practice similar to that of "other" religious orders, the sect has adopted a body of titles to indicate each soldier's place in the "army." Such titles are often honorifics, though some vain vampires of the sect claim titles far in excess of their actual accomplishments.

Here are a few of the titles used by the sect, as well as their forms of address. While the titles themselves are universally male, the forms of address reflect the bearer's gender; female forms of address are given in parentheses if they differ from the masculine. Players and Storytellers are encouraged to create their own titles as well — it is more memorable to meet the Vicar of the Incarnadine Covenant than it is to meet the priest of yet another unnamed pack.

TITLE	SIMILAR TITLES	FORM OF ADDRESS
REGENT	NONE	OUR MOST DISTINGUISHED EXCELLENCY
CARDINAL (ALWAYS ASSOCIATED WITH A SPECIFIC REGION)	HIGH LORD (LADY)	HIS (HER) EMINENCE
PRISCUS	GRAND MASTER (MISTRESS), MONSIGNOR	VERY REVEREND SIR (MADAM)
ARCHBISHOP (ALWAYS ASSOCIATED WITH A SPECIFIC REGION)	ARCHDEACON, FATHER (MOTHER) SUPERIOR	HIS (HER) EXCELLENCY
BISHOP (ALWAYS ASSOCIATED WITH A SPECIFIC CITY)	DEACON, HIGH FATHER (MOTHER)	HIS (HER) EXCELLENCY
TEMPLAR/PALADIN	LORD (LADY)	SIR (LADY)
DUCTUS	LORD (LADY), SERGEANT, CHIEF	BY TITLE
PRIEST	FATHER (MOTHER), MASTER (MISTRESS), MINISTER	REVEREND SIR (MADAM)
PACK MEMBER	NONE	NONE, THOUGH SOMETIMES BROTHER (SISTER)

Many young Sabbat disdain the use of titles and honorifics, believing them to be outdated relics of the former nights of aristocracy. Indeed, some of the more radical elder members of the sect agree — if the Sabbat opposes elder oppression, how can it, in good conscience, cling to sobriquets that imply distinction? Regardless, almost all Sabbat know the titles and their proper forms of address; to remain ignorant is to risk embarrassment… or worse.

below) in Montreal is the direct result of one vampire trying to play too many factions off each other — a consequence any Cainite familiar with the workings of the Camarilla has seen innumerable times.

That said, the Sabbat has pulled itself up by its bootstraps, leading a campaign of conquest unheard of since the colonization of the New World. Recent crusades in Miami, Atlanta and Atlantic City have turned the tide of the Sabbat's war effort on the East Coast of the United States, while relatively bloodless seizures of power in Washington, DC and parts of Europe prove the Sabbat is as capable with intrigue as guerrilla tactics. Conservative members of the sect warn against resting on their laurels, however, arguing that "complacency has lost more than one war." More often than not, Sabbat crusades fail, even as early as the scouting stages, because lines of communication and duty break down, leaving the sect unable to improve its lot.

To delineate responsibilities, the Sabbat has created for itself a rough organization. In theory, this organization provides a strong base for sect leadership, as skilled vampires claw and plot their way to prominence. In practice, however, the model breaks down, as elder vampires demand anachronistic subservience from the Cainites below them, and younger vampires rebel openly against the leaders who should be establishing coups rather than plotting against each other like the depraved Licks of the Camarilla. The Sabbat is perhaps its own greatest enemy, with many of the battles fought in the hearts and minds of the sect's members.

THE REGENT

The *regent* of the Sabbat supposedly coordinates the grand-scale master plan of the sect, much like a mortal dictator or corporate president. Supported by a *consistory* of other powerful vampires, the regent holds little sway over the sect as a whole, however. Young Sabbat often make a big show of rejecting this hypocritical figure of authority as elder Sabbat flout her rule for their own personal gain. In the end, the regent may demand service, fealty and respect, but she had best be able to back it up, as the Sabbat has no lack of wide-eyed megalomaniacs who would not hesitate to usurp the position for themselves.

The regent's nightly affairs — if such can be said of a vampire who spends as long as a month at a time in the cold arms of sleep — consist primarily of entertaining sect luminaries, hearing progress reports, plotting against other vampires (both in the sect and out) and deciding which tactical or strategic maneuvers to make. Add to this list the incessant cultivation of influences, moving and counter-moving to keep one's enemies at bay, presiding over *ritae* and weathering the countless intrigues inherent to centuries among the undead.

The current regent of the Sabbat, Melinda Galbraith, makes her haven in Mexico City. A member of the Toreador *antitribu*, Galbraith draws much fire from her many detractors as being more involved with the petty affairs of the sect than with the Sabbat's larger purpose. Apparently content to offer

"bread and circuses" to those below her, the regent stages elaborate *ritae*, replacing actual accomplishment with much pomp and observance of ritual. Galbraith has been instrumental, however, in providing support to some of the key sieges in North America. For this reason, she finds little approval among the Sabbat of the Old World, who tend to believe she concentrates on her immediate surroundings too greatly to see the big picture.

The Cardinals

Cardinals oversee Sabbat affairs in grand geographical regions. As the superiors of the archbishops, cardinals coordinate the Sabbat in their cities and direct them in the Great Jyhad.

Cardinals wield immense amounts of power as their influences cross great distances. Yet, even if they have no direct influence in a particular arena, their underlings generally do. The office of cardinal is far more than simply regional management, however. The cardinals bear the responsibility of the crusades — it is their direct duty to bring cities within their *diocese* under the Sabbat's sway. Of course, doing so is quite difficult: The fall of a city takes years to plan and execute. Additionally, sweeping in and taking over requires finesse. Simply firebombing an entire town leaves nothing within the town to be desired.

Obviously, the responsibilities of the cardinals are vast. On one end of the spectrum, cardinals must appease their political peers and betters, proving their worth as cardinals and maintaining the Great Jyhad. On the other end, they must exercise caution and restraint, as turning their cities into hellholes diminishes their worth.

Most Sabbat see their cardinals no more than once per year, if at all, as the duties of the office keep them in constant communication with bishops, archbishops, prisci and of course, the regent herself. When the lower echelons of the sect do see their cardinals, it is often during various sect rituals or honorific festivals.

Cardinals vary widely in style — some are bellicose warlords, leading their crusades at the front of the columns and destroying those who stand against them with frightening powers. Others are clever tacticians, carefully orchestrating every move the vampires they lead make. Still others are charismatic firebrands, whipping their charges into frenzies and turning them loose on the unsuspecting, soft Camarilla "Kindred." Almost all cardinals are feared by those beneath them, as their tremendous physical and political power makes them terrible foes, in whose good graces one must remain, lest one meet Final Death.

The Prisci

Preeminent among the Sabbat, the prisci are vampires of great age or power, selected by the consistory to join its ranks as advisors. Prisci require little or no temporal power; they are not responsible for maintaining Sabbat influence in a city, nor must they coordinate sieges or other war efforts. Rather, the prisci offer their unique insight to other members of the sect, particularly the regent, cardinals and archbishops.

Often, however, prisci do achieve some degree of political influence, usually at the expense of those who have failed them. Most prisci belong to Clans Lasombra, Tzimisce and Toreador *antitribu*, though no formal rules exist as to whether or not a member of a given clan may belong. Of course, becoming a priscus requires that one prove oneself to be of inestimable value to the sect — no vampire younger than 200 years has ever attained a priscus' position.

To young vampires, prisci epitomize the hypocrisy of the Sabbat. Sure, they've proven themselves, but they don't do it consistently. Maybe in some long-forgotten night over a century ago, Priscus So-and-so did something memorable, but what has he done lately?

Naturally, young vampires rarely have a chance to see the prisci in action. Devoted as they are to the regent and her support, much of the prisci's affairs take place in the Sabbat's hallowed catacombs of power. Young vampires have not entirely missed the mark, however. The consistory (which also includes a few cardinals) greatly resembles the upper layers of the Camarilla, as elder vampires stab each other in the back and usurp each other's influence in endless Cainite games of supremacy. The priscus' role is to ensure the Sabbat's long-term success through good advice and careful planning. This role serves the interest of all Sabbat, since it lets the younger vampires see actual results for their efforts as it lets the sect's elders enjoy the luxuries acquired from unlives of treachery and double-dealing along with the occasional important effort.

Most prisci, having reached advanced age, spend a good deal of time in torpor, rising only when needed or when a masterstroke demands their attention. Prisci are responsible for much of the upper-level advancement in the Sabbat — a priscus' patronage is required to become an archbishop, for example, and the consistory selects its own members from lesser ranks of the sect.

Being a priscus not all Blood Feasts and Epicureanism, as should be duly noted. Many prisci were lords or military strategists before becoming vampires, and their vast experience (tempered with the caginess required to attain the position in the first place) serves the sect well. Often, a siege's success or failure rests on a bit of information, such as what defenses a given prince can muster, or which sympathetic vampires may be convinced to look the other way as the Sabbat roars into town. Such is the role of the priscus: to maximize the flaws of the others through proven strategies. Some cities even have prisci on hand to advise the archbishop or bishop's council on matters of Cainite relevance. As kingmakers, they are often the true power behind the obvious figurehead.

THE ARCHBISHOPS

Archbishops officiate the nightly affairs of individual cities, often as the most powerful vampire in the locale. Appointed by the cardinal of a given region, archbishops bear the responsibility for all vampires underneath them, and they must see to the maintenance of the city in the Sabbat's best interests. Of course, the Sabbat's best interests are not always (and in fact, are rarely...) the best interests of the mortals of a given city. As mentioned before, Sabbat-held cities are urban wastelands or teeming dens of violence — which suits the Sabbat reasonably.

Most archbishops support "nondisclosure" policies similar to the Masquerade. Less strict than the Masquerade, however, the Sabbat attitude toward mortals bears more disdain than secrecy. Such is the reason crime rates in Sabbat cities skyrocket; it's often easier to kill a mortal who has observed a vampire in action than it is to clean up afterward. Given the general feeling toward mortals that most Sabbat vampires espouse, most archbishops are fine with this arrangement.

The archbishop, as his title suggests, is the foremost spiritual authority of a given city. Most archbishops were pack priests before attaining their positions. (This fact reveals much about the title, as few archbishops are over 200 years in age. Those who are, however, are often vastly more than 200 years old, and have become *de facto* archbishops as they are the oldest and most influential vampires in their cities, as is the case with Archbishop Monçada in Madrid and the former Archbishop of Milan, Giangaleazzo. Truly old Sabbat Cainites tend toward the ranks of the prisci and cardinals, or bear no titles at all, allowing their potency to speak for itself.) Archbishops take active roles in many of the *auctoritas ritae* of their city's Cainites, and they may have a hand in determining local or regional *ignoblis ritae* as well. In the end, the archbishop balances temporal power with skilled administration: Cities in which the packs run wild become barren, and cities that become barren cannot support the race of vampires.

THE BISHOPS

If a city has no archbishop, it generally hosts a council of three to five bishops depending on the city's size. Similar to the archbishops, bishops bear the responsibility of maintaining Sabbat influence in their cities, as well as the spiritual growth of the vampires therein.

Sabbat bishops often hail from the ranks of the pack priests, but many originate among the ducti as well. Because bishops are generally younger and/or less capable than archbishops, the Sabbat installs the councils. In this manner, no bishop needs to function in a capacity to which he is ill-suited. For example, a charismatic and iron-fisted administrator may not know the first thing about presiding over the mystical *ritae*, so the sect makes sure it covers all its bases with the bishops. Most bishops, promoted directly from the packs in which they serve, are 200 years old or younger.

This division of power among multiple figureheads often creates conflict. Sabbat priests are rarely known for their even tempers, and a council of headstrong leaders often hamstrings itself. For this reason, bishops answer directly to cardinals, who have no qualms about beating or twisting problematic bishops into their proper places. In some ways, the position of bishop demands more from its title-bearer than that of the archbishop, as diplomacy is key to a bishop while an archbishop can push through his own agendas with less resistance.

THE DUCTI

Leaders of individual packs, ducti attend to the operation matters of their charges. As most packs number between three to seven individual members, ducti resemble gang leaders or chiefs of small tribes.

The title of ductus is largely honorific, according recognition to the most accomplished member of a pack. Some authority accompanies the title, however, but the ductus who throws his weight around is likely to find his ass kicked and dumped unceremoniously in a trash bin, if not staked out to welcome the next sunrise. Ducti rely more on presence and force of personality to motivate those in their packs. They work closely with pack priests to coordinate attacks, grow sect and pack influence, and act as liaisons to the bishops and archbishops.

Ducti may call *esbats*, which are pack meetings, and most usually do so weekly. At esbats, the priest generally conducts the most important *ritae*, after which the ductus assesses the pack's progress. Ducti also assign duties to pack members that fit the group's needs; someone has to maintain the haven, someone has to get rid of the bodies, et cetera.

The position of ductus is, with a notable few exceptions, the highest position to which a nomadic Sabbat may rise. Nomadic Sabbat travel from place to place, obviously, and most are unfit to hold the titles of archbishop or bishop. Nomadic Sabbat have no explicit prohibition from holding the titles of priscus or cardinal (or regent...), but few, if any, ever have.

In matters of rank, the ductus supersedes all others in the pack — though not always the oldest member, he is certainly the most *something else*, which most ducti can bring to bear should their authority come into question. The wise ductus, of course, listens to his pack, resorting to rank only when others refuse to see the strength of his arguments.

THE PACK PRIESTS

Priests bear the responsibility for the spiritual well-being of their packs. Most priests are Tzimisce, but anyone of any clan may become a priest with the proper instruction.

Second in command to the ductus, the pack priest officiates all *ritae* observed by the pack, and often creates a few for the sole use of the pack. This creates great bonds of loyalty and also bestows a sense of self on the pack — they become valuable, unique individuals with the tradition to prove it.

All packs have at least one priest, though some rare and large packs have two. In the event that the ductus is eliminated, the priest becomes the pack leader *pro tem*, until a new leader can be appointed by the bishop or archbishop (or in nomadic or autonomous packs, the pack itself).

Priests shoulder a tremendous responsibility: They must keep their packmates from succumbing to infernalism and from letting their Beasts rise to uncontrollability. Priests, most often, have abandoned their Humanity (adopting instead a Path of Enlightenment), and they are encouraged to support their packmates' journeys down their own paths. Obviously, the priest is as much counselor as he is a witch.

THE TEMPLARS

Also known as paladins, the templars are an elite force of bodyguards appointed by a bishop or greater leader. Although they have no formal organization, being named as a templar is a great honor for the Cainite so titled. Being recognized as such is a symbol of strength in the Sabbat and a public acknowledgment of one's fighting skills.

Templars serve a variety of duties, always in a martial capacity. Most archbishops keep a cadre of paladins in their retinues to handle delicate matters best solved by a judicious application of violence, while the Inquisitors tend to being templars with them as backup muscle for their travels and trials.

Templars are forbidden from becoming members of the Black Hand, which is seen as a conflict of interests as the paladins generally have no secondary factional agendas. Sometimes referred to as bloodhounds or buttonmen by other Cainites, templars are almost always found in the employ of sect leaders, though some may belong to packs for periods of inactivity or have been honorably discharged from their duties in times when said leaders have no need for standing paramilitary attendants.

FACTIONS OF THE SABBAT

The Sabbat is hardly a unified entity, as its history, cosmopolitan makeup and penchant for personal freedom illustrates. The sect is home to numerous splinter groups, factions of vampires who have united under the Sabbat's banner to achieve their own ends (which often correspond with those of the sect), or to direct the greater body of the sect. In the chaos of the Sabbat, it is not unlikely to find members of these factions among the packs, though by no means does every member of the Sabbat support a faction — most simply support the Sword of Caine itself. Nonetheless, these factions claim a great number of members, and some have become integral to the existence of the Sabbat itself.

THE BLACK HAND

The Black Hand is best described as a sect within a sect; a unique group of vampires distinct from all other Sabbat. The Black Hand (also known simply as the Hand or, less frequently, the *manus nigrum*) is not a wholly independent sect, however, as all Hand members are loyal members of the Sabbat.

The Black Hand consists of vampires of many different clans, but it draws most of its members from the Assamite and Gangrel *antitribu*. It also includes many militant vampires, for whom clan is often a tertiary concern at best, as they pursue the Sabbat's ideal of freedom. Members of the Black Hand rarely exist in all-Hand packs; the group instead disperses its number among the other vampires of the sect. A notable few packs made exclusively of Black Hand members exist, but these are rarely seen outside momentous Sabbat events like sieges and crusades.

Conceived as a special militia, the Black Hand is , at its simplest, a military force at the disposal of Sabbat leaders. Like a true army, the Hand specializes in numerous aspects of warfare, from intrigue and intelligence to assassination to outright physical combat. The Black Hand seldom remains active for any long period of time, instead sending small, focused units or packs to attend to the issue at hand. Indeed, very few vampires can even remember a time when the whole of the Hand acted simultaneously at all. Sabbat elders seem to prefer this arrangement, and some secretly fear that the sect-within-a-sect would attempt a coup if kept active for too long a time. Throughout its history, however, the Black Hand has always served the Sabbat with unwavering loyalty.

Sabbat leaders most commonly activate cells of the Black Hand for leading assaults on Camarilla-held cities or sieges already underway. The Black Hand includes many of the deadliest Cainites on earth, and they specialize in terror tactics and breaking the Masquerade. Calling for Black Hand assistance when it is unnecessary, however, casts an individual in unfavorable light — the sect's presence is grave and not necessarily subtle, and calling on it is literally "bringing out the big guns." Any Cainite with a title of bishop or greater may call for the Hand's assistance, and most Hand members are able to contact and request aid from other members of the faction.

High-ranking members of the Hand select other Sabbat Cainites for membership in their group on an individual basis. Membership is a matter of much prestige among the Sabbat, akin to belonging to an elite military force (which, in fact, it is). Knowledge of this practice has disseminated among the sect somewhat, and Cainites who want to draw the Black Hand's attention often make grand displays of their martial skills, sometimes participating alone in Wild Hunts, taking great responsibilities in city sieges and even challenging Black Hand members to personal duels.

The Hand tests its would-be inductees with rigorous trials and ordeals designed to test a vampire's endurance, strength, willpower, cunning and martial ability. Such tests include walks over flaming coals, confounding packs of established Hand members sent to hunt the individual and full-scale "capacity for violence" tests that often leave crowds of mutilated mortals wondering what the hell just happened to them. If the prospective member is accepted, the Hand usually assigns the Cainite a mentor, who instructs the new recruit in the ways of the faction and teaches him to be a better soldier.

Members of the Black Hand bear a distinguishing mark — the faction brands its members with a permanent, mystical sigil on the palms of their right hands. Once the vampire receives this mark, she has become a true member of the Black Hand, and must heed the group's call whenever she receives it.

Although this brand may be concealed or made over (which spies for the group often do to keep from revealing themselves), it may never be removed. Membership in the Black Hand lasts until the vampire meets her Final Death.

A group of vampires known as the Seraphim acts as the high military council of the faction, the generals and leaders, as it were. These four Seraphim answer directly to the regent, and they have been known to join the consistory at times when war is imminent or a consideration. Below the Seraphim are the dominions, lower-level sect leaders who organize individual regiments of Black Hand warriors. Beneath the dominions, sergeants, lieutenants and the rank-and-file (if such may be said of such an elite group) conduct most of the actual operations of the faction.

Many Sabbat credit the Black Hand with the cohesion of the sect through difficult times. Indeed, the Black Hand remained solvent during the first and second Sabbat Civil wars, enabling the sect to maintain influence in cities that would have otherwise fallen to the Camarilla once word of the struggle broke out.

One of the Seraphim, Djuhah, has created permanent packs of Black Hand members, much to the consternation of other Sabbat Cainites. To what end Djuhah has assigned these *columns* is unknown, though some vampires have observed what they call a "quiet" in the Black Hand's activities in the past several years. In fact, much of the Sabbat's successful war effort seems to have come without much visible assistance from the Black Hand, which has many of the faction's detractors questioning its utility.

THE SABBAT INQUISITION

Taking its cue from the mortal Spanish Inquisition, the Sabbat Inquisition is a political faction charged with rooting out heretics and infernalists. Originally established to combat followers of the Path of Evil Revelations who had hidden themselves inside the Sabbat, the Inquisition has met with tremendous success in the past few years, with notable performances in Detroit and Montreal (as well as several notorious nomad packs). Of course, the faction resembles the mortal Inquisition in other ways as well: If it labels someone as an infernalist, the accusation is unlikely to be denied, and the faction makes a practice of using similarly torturous tactics to their mortal counterpart.

The Sabbat Inquisition has recently doubled in size, from 15 to 30 members, largely owing to its success. All members of the Inquisition are respected and trusted (and powerful...) members of the Sabbat. Cells of Inquisitors travel to all Sabbat-held territo-

ries, presiding over and delivering punishments against accused Sabbat. Despite its success in exposing infernalists, however, the Inquisition has acquired quite a reputation for cruelty, which stems from its interrogation methods and punishments. A Sabbat accused of infernalism can expect to be branded, burnt, dismembered and physically beaten, while a vampire who admits to (or is proven guilty of) infernalism receives a long, slow Final Death, complicated by painful torments that, while not intended themselves to kill the subject, certainly make his death a painful ordeal. Many Inquisitors take twisted pleasure in delivering death sentences (known as *auto da fé*), cutting their victims, delivering insects underneath their skin or flaying their flesh. Most other Sabbat indulge the Inquisitors this eccentricity, at risk of their own accusation.

The Sabbat Inquisition is a political entity as well, in that it possesses the power to depose bishops, archbishops, pack priests and ducti. It stands on the cusp of becoming a political *tool*, but has yet to do so, largely because its members are devout in their duties and respond poorly to attempts at manipulation.

The Inquisition has unprecedented power, able to move and accuse as it will. Nomadic Inquisitors usually travel in groups of five, accompanied by a pair of templars. Although their success leaves the Sabbat better for its interference, the Inquisition has made few friends among the Sabbat. Many bishops and archbishops actually resent the Inquisition's presence, as the Inquisitors tend to disrupt the usual affairs of the sect and dig up dirt on all Cainites in a given city.

Inquisitors prefer to conduct their business unannounced, as knowledge of their arrival allows those who should hide from them to avoid their ire. On visiting a city, Inquisitors question *everyone*, from probationary pack members to archbishops and cardinals. The faction considers evidence against all Cainites and will accept any accusation, from any member of the sect. Of course, groundless accusations rarely turn up any evidence, and the Inquisition prefers to leave wrongful accusers, embarrassed, to the whims of the unjustly accused.

Inquisitors have brusque, harsh demeanors, and they don't hesitate to use intimidation in their proceedings. Inquisitors, for all the good they do the sect, are almost always regarded with respectful fear, as all Cainites know their unlife rests in the hands of these stalwart individuals.

A rumored antagonism exists between the Black Hand and the Inquisition. Members of one faction are expressly forbidden membership in the other, and some suspect this rivalry has resulted from the Inquisition's recent successes and the growing complaints of the Hand's impotence.

THE LOYALIST FACTION

The Loyalist faction claims that it is the legacy of the "true" Sabbat, those vampires who shook off the yoke of their elders and desperately grabbed their freedom for themselves. Other Sabbat tend to dismiss Loyalists as anarchists, sociopaths and spoiled childer who want the benefits of the Curse of Caine without the responsibilities.

The Loyalists' philosophy is simple: Each vampire is his own master. The freedom to do whatever one will belongs to all vampires, whether he wants to destroy the Antediluvians or go on a rampage through a suburban mall. In practice, few Loyalists stoop to such recklessness, as they know local law enforcement would hunt them down and destroy them, often at the behest of other vampires who actually value their secrecy.

Obviously, the Loyalists have no organization, and they are considered a faction only in the sense that numerous individuals support the ideology. Most Sabbat have little respect for Loyalists, as they tend to act against their leaders' order just for the hell of it — or because they *should*, to hear a Loyalist tell it. Naturally, this contrariness for its own sake results in trouble, complicated missions and needless conflict more often than not, but nonetheless, the Loyalists persist.

On the inside, however, Loyalists truly believe in their cause. They point at decadent, staid elders and complain that the sect has left its ideals by the wayside. The night no longer belongs to the Sabbat, Loyalists contest. Sect is irrelevant given the modern state of affairs; Sabbat packs are as powerless as Camarilla neonates or rabid anarchs, because of the apathy and antagonism of their elders. Loyalists do what they do because they *must*, as did the original anarchs and *antitribu* in the nights of the Anarch Revolt.

Loyalists accept anyone into their ranks, and they have no codes or secret rituals to identify themselves to one another. The Loyalist sect has no hierarchy of responsibilities, and it is largely composed of young Sabbat (though many older Sabbat once supported the cause, they have since moved past it). Status among the faction comes from tales of elders snubbed and derring-do and other escapades of being "as fucking punk-rock" as a Loyalist can be.

The Loyalists are obviously fairly powerless in the larger picture of Sabbat politics, but their numbers continue to grow. Many elders make the mistake of dismissing the Loyalists, but cautious Cainites see the potential (or menace) they possess, pointing to the Panders as a recent example of what young Sabbat are capable of.

Lesser Factions

Smaller in power and number than the Black Hand, Inquisition and chaotic Loyalists, lesser factions exist among the Sabbat to help the sect and themselves. These lesser factions come and go, springing up almost overnight and then falling out of favor or being wiped out entirely in some grandiose but doomed war effort, like the now-extinct Sabbat Fabians. Some of the longer-standing intra-Sabbat factions include the following.

The Status Quo

As their name suggests, things are good enough for the Status Quo as they are. Made up of a great many Lasombra, Tzimisce and key members of the Black Hand, the Status Quo accepts the nature of vampires and knows that change is relatively impossible. The Great Jyhad continues, for better or worse, and shaking the foundations of the Sabbat serves only to distract it from its greater goal.

The Status Quo supports Lasombra leadership and the internal stability that allows them to present a stern façade to the Camarilla. The Status Quo points to the recent success of the Sabbat war effort as proof that things are happening the way they should, and talk of radical change in any form is unnecessary.

The Status Quo does not want to increase the authoritarianism of the sect — its members aren't after hoarding all the power for themselves (read: any more) because it promotes rebellion in the lower ranks. At the same time, increasingly unreasonable demands from overly vociferous Loyalists and concerned Moderates serve only to agitate other members of the sect, and a compromise must be struck.

Many Sabbat leaders belong to the Status Quo (it stands to reason), but these leaders are not the mad tyrants or megalomaniacs of the sect. Rather, these are the proven leaders who have attained their stations through merit, who phrase their orders as requests and respect the rights of those under them — or at least they pretend to, knowing it gets results.

Moderates

The Moderates oppose what they see as increasing rigidity intruding into the sect. Edicts such as the Purchase Pact and the revised Code of Milan limit the rights of individual Sabbat for the good of a few.

While not as vehement as the Loyalists, Moderates nonetheless oppose the encroachment of "rules and guidelines that have no place among such creatures as" vampires. The faction rests between Loyalist dogma and Status Quo conservatism, acknowledging the need for order and structure, but not adherence to arbitrary codes that offer no benefit to offset their inconvenience. Moderates generally oppose sieges and crusades (though they usually follow orders), but they do not hesitate to question those in charge if an order seems foolish or reckless.

Most of the sect, if it cared to declare such things, would apathetically fall into the ranks of the Moderates — things

are good enough, but could get better. This faction includes the most diverse membership of the sect, claiming members from a great many clans and bloodlines. It possesses a bit of political clout, but the shifting allegiances of its members (which often taper off once they find something more interesting than political diatribe) keeps the faction as one of relatively minor power.

Ultra-Conservatives

Predictably composed of the eldest members of the Sabbat, most of whom belong to Clans Lasombra and Tzimisce, the Ultra-Conservatives favor centralization and authoritarianism, hoping to turn the Sabbat into a military force against the Antediluvians and the Camarilla.

The time for freedom is over, claim the Ultra-Conservatives. Gehenna looms around the corner, and it's time to stabilize the Sabbat, lest it fail utterly. The Ultra-Conservatives ironically support the acceptance of the Panders, hoping to rely on them in the coming apocalypse.

Ultra-Conservatives favor strong leaders and *Monomacy*, ritually removing weak leaders through duels. The Black Hand seems to be slowly leaning toward support of the Ultra-Conservatives, but it remains characteristically quiet when confronted with the issue.

Young Cainites see the Ultra-Conservatives as fat old bastards, more likely to use the sect to settle personal vendettas than to forestall the impending Gehenna. Others view them as millennialist crackpots, fighting a war against invisible enemies out of vampiric senility. When confronted with differing arguments, however, the Ultra-Conservatives are quick to quote the *Book of Nod*, identifying the portents and omens all around them that foretell the awakening of the Antediluvians.

Old World Tzimisce

Not every Tzimisce supports the Sabbat with her whole heart. Indeed, when it comes to the arcane Tzimisce of the Old World, few support it at all. Of course, aligning oneself *against* the Sabbat is a good way to end up facing down a pack of self-important rabble who want to strike at the elders for the good of the Sabbat and all such rubbish, so it's often easier to join the society yet abstain from its meetings.

The Tzimisce of the active sect harbor little love for their apathetic old cousins, who seem content to slumber away in rotten castles and disembowel a peasant for sport every now and then. However, the Sabbat Tzimisce reason, at least these vampires keep to themselves instead of plotting away and obliviously working the will of the Antediluvians. There are worse crimes than being an elder, and for all the trouble it would take to annihilate these eldritch Fiends, it's easier to focus on those worse crimes.

Lasombra Antitribu

In the nights following the Anarch Revolt and the Convention of Thorns, the Lasombra were quick to obliterate their elders and assume their fortunes and power. Those Lasombra who opposed the Lasombra anarchs met swift and terrible deaths. To the Lasombra mind, the purge is complete.

In actuality, however, a rogue Keeper arises every now and then, often as a staunch supporter of the Camarilla. The Lasombra loathe the elders and *antitribu* of their clan, as they remind the Lasombra of precisely why they joined the Sabbat in the first place. While some would argue that there is little difference between a modern Keeper and those who the clan destroyed during the Anarch Movement, Clan Lasombra is quick to point out that it was the anarch Lasombra who set the entire revolution in motion. The Keepers are what all Sabbat should become, to their line of reasoning, and not the least of that transformation is the elimination of rogue elements.

Lasombra *antitribu* rarely appear more than one at a time — it would seem the clan has done an excellent job of reinventing itself at the expense of what it used to be. They are often Moorish or Spanish in heritage, and many (if such a word has meaning in this context) have taken to the seas, adopting unlives of piracy, for whatever reason. The rest of the clan is quick to rout out the traitor, however, and other Sabbat clans often take cruel glee in the sight of the normally territorial Lasombra uniting in rabid abandon against one of their erstwhile brethren.

The Order of St. Blaise

In Europe during the 14th century, the Church established an auxiliary of 14 saints to protect the plagued masses. One of the 14, St. Blaise, was known for his healing abilities of throat maladies. It became wide practice at this time that on February third, devotees would have their throats blessed by a pair of crossed candles. Cainites active in the Church found it particularly ironic that those same blessed throats would provide a sacred meal for vampires.

It also struck some Sabbat that St. Blaise's feast day is February third, the day after the pagan holiday Candlemas, an ancient fire festival. Several Sabbat members thought that this coincidence contained some synchronistic irony, and they formed the secret society and it's defunct monastic counterpart. (At the time of the order's inception, the monastery proved remarkably useful for shielding vampires of the order from the Inquisition.)

Vampires of the Order of St. Blaise lead dangerous unlives, integrating themselves into the hierarchy of the Roman Catholic Church. Through careful manipulation of Church resources and "good works" done at the community level, members of the order influence aspects of their cities in ways most Sabbat traditionally neglect. By establishing herds in soup kitchens and exempting certain buildings from tax status, the Order of St. Blaise expands the Sabbat's power on local levels. Indeed, most Sabbat cities, rife with murder, rape and skyrocketing crime rates, see an increase in Church attendance, brought about by desperate mortals' attempts to find any salvation they can in the World of Darkness.

Lately, the order has established small cloistered monasteries throughout the world. Vampires within the sect maintain minimal contact with the higher levels of the Church, preferring instead to hide among the lower echelons. On the Feast Day of St. Blaise, the order or its ghouls still provide services, usually at a large church.

CHILDREN OF THE DRACON

A bizarre knightly order of Tzimisce vampires, the Children of the Dracon seem to bear more Hellenic features than the Slavic heritage of Clan Tzimisce suggests. The Children seem to be a cultural division, almost like a bloodline, but the distinction is more artificial than that which would be caused by a deviation in the vitae.

The exact agenda of the Children of the Dracon is unknown, but they seem to be at intellectual odds with the rest of the Tzimisce. Perhaps this is due to some past transgression, or perhaps it lies in the difference of mortal stock from which the vampires were originally drawn. Whatever the case, the Children of the Dracon do not antagonize the other Tzimisce, so much as they take a consistent role of the Devil's Advocate. If the Tzimisce favor a siege, the Children posit the values of holding back; if the Fiends support the Inquisition, the Children argue against giving any faction too much power.

Although this seems arbitrary, the Children seem to see themselves as the warders of their brothers. Apparently, sometime in the mists of history, a Tzimisce made a decision that affected the entirety of his clan (perhaps resulting in the clan's odd weakness). The Children of the Dracon have sworn to make the Tzimisce consider the full gravity of their actions... or perhaps atone for them.

The Tzimisce report that no Child of the Dracon has ever held the title of *voivode* in the clan, and that the Children are either incapable of learning their *koldunic* magic or they steadfastly refuse to. The distinction means little outside the clan and faction, and others regard it as a curious family affair.

INFERNALISTS

Infernalists — devil-worshippers, Satanists, followers of the Path of Evil Revelations — are not truly a faction within the Sabbat. Rather, they are a sickness that plagues it. The Sabbat infernalist serves himself first and foremost, or so he thinks. The reality is much less glamorous.

Infernalists have no formal structure, as they rarely associate with one another. The business of trafficking with demons is downright medieval — the infernalist is a lone conjurer, dealing only with devils for his forbidden knowledge.

The practice of infernalism runs contrary to everything the Sabbat believes in. While most infernalists see themselves as taking a quick route to great power, the truth is that they are selling themselves into demonic servitude. Sooner or later, the Devil will literally come to collect his due, the infernalist's soul. To the Sabbat, such servitude annihilates the freedom to which the sect is sworn. The sect has had immense problems with infernalism in the past, however, and it has created its own Inquisition to combat it. Their great success, while laudable for its own sake, indicates a darker

THE DEVIL'S DUE

We present infernalism with much less emphasis in this book than has been the standard in prior Sabbat supplements. This is intentional. Much less space has been devoted to the infernal, as it is no longer as important to the sect, or to the game.

If you like infernalism in your games, by all means, use it. Dealing with the Devil predestines a character, however; Old Scratch claims her in the end, which strips a lot of the free will and the significance of the vampire's actions, which, in turn, lessens the impact of **Vampire**'s theme of standing against the Beast and fighting the monster one has become.

Infernalism has been included to this lesser degree for Storytellers. Sometimes, it's fun to put the characters in conflict with a guy who sold his soul for power, especially if they're Sabbat. Do they want quick power? Or is their freedom more important to them? Such moral questions are the reason for infernalism's inclusion here, not an easy route to min-max characters or for cheap shock value.

problem for the sect — so many infernalists found and punished come only as a result of a large number of infernalists to begin with.

UNLIFE IN THE SABBAT

Fraught with violence and unrest, the unlife of the Sabbat vampire tends to be short, and it often ends in a burst of flame or at the fangs of another Cainite. Between the Embrace and Final Death, however, much takes place. Crusades, intrigues, run-ins with the Camarilla, political treachery — all these unique events occur during the unlife of a Cainite. The nightly affairs of the Sabbat, however, are no less fascinating.

The following aspects of unlife apply predominantly to young vampires of the sect, who still travel in packs and observe *ritae* with other Sabbat. The unlives of Sabbat elders, by comparison, differ a great deal. Sabbat elders generally keep solitary havens and carry out scheming, sequestered unlives, punctuated by gatherings with other sect luminaries and nightly plots to confound their rivals. Elders of the sect ironically (though some say hypocritically) resemble the elders of the Camarilla, having acquired great wealth and some degree of undead comfort. They tend to distance themselves from the packs, spending most of their nights in torpor or plotting against rivals. In fact, "sect" seems to have little real meaning to the older members of the Sabbat — it appears that they adopt its trappings only when it would serve to incite a pack of young vampires against a potential enemy. The Curse of Caine, timelessness and stagnation, affects these vampires profoundly, as they find themselves drawn all too often into the hated Jyhad. In the end, all that matters is that one has become undead, as the flames of passion for any cause die and the centuries progress.

CREATION RITES

Vampires of the Sabbat perform the Embrace like any other vampires, selecting their candidates with all the care or haplessness that befits them. However, these new vampires must prove themselves to the sect before being accepted as *True Sabbat*.

Proving oneself generally requires participation in a crusade, siege or other combative trial by fire. (This statement is not universally true, however, as some Sabbat prove themselves with daring bits of espionage or outstanding service to another vampire, such as assisting with a complex *ritus* or giving aid to a Sabbat in dire need of it.) Ultimately, the decision to give a childe the Creation Rites belongs to the sire. Even so, such rites are not given without just cause — a childe who proves an embarrassment to her sire may never receive her Creation Rites, provided she is not simply destroyed soon after the embarrassment.

Vampires who never receive the Creation Rites are not considered vampires by Sabbat Cainites. As such, they may be ordered around, fed on, even sent into battle with no chance of surviving (as is often the case with mass-Embraces in Camarilla cities). Sabbat vampires feel no hypocrisy over this; they have not made childer and forced them into demeaning unlives. Instead, they have simply created monsters, who may prove one night to be worthy of Sabbat membership, and thus, full recognition as a vampire.

The rites themselves vary, but they are always officiated by the pack priest (or a bishop or archbishop in the case of an elder's childe). The sire determines what sort of special, symbolic form the act should take. Tzimisce, for example, sometimes fleshcraft their childer into hideous monsters, considering the rite to be the childe's restoration (or alteration) of his features. Lasombra Creation Rites often involve meeting one's sire's sire or reciting a litany of one's lineage. Among more violent Cainites, Creation Rites may involve gang-style initiation killings, robberies or other entry-level crimes. A Toreador *antitribu*'s Creation Rite may entail torturing a victim to death — ever so exquisitely! — while a Malkavian *antitribu* might be bound by the wrists to a speeding truck, and must chew off his own hands to work himself free.

Obviously, Creation Rites are a very personal matter to the Sabbat. No two need be exactly alike, but sometimes certain styles come into vogue or all members of a pack use the same symbolic act. In the end, it's all up to the sire.

PACKS

Vampires, at their core, are solitary creatures. In non-Sabbat cities, some vampires may never come in contact with others of their kind, or they may see other Cainites only once in a decade. Solitary, urban predators, vampires stalk the nights alone, as Caine did so many nights ago.

Vampires of the Sabbat do not practice such solitude.

Sabbat vampires move in packs, rude, unnatural families of vampires who share a common purpose. Much like coteries of

CAINITES EX TERRAM

The recruits climbed out of the dank earth, brushing the soil from their clothing. As their captors snatched away their shovels, the prisoners shifted uneasily. The silence was unnerving; the open graves seemed to call out to them. The recruits cowered in the presence of their grinning captors. From studded leather to priestly robes and vestments, this group had a macabre sense of fashion.

What could only have been the "head" priest walked a circle around the group as a drummer beat out the rhythm of a heartbeat. As the priest emptied a vial of red fluid on the ground, he chanted, "As I walk, we come to the place and the time between worlds; a place without place, a time without time; for I am the resurrection and the light, he who drinks of me shall live a new life, with Raphael before me, Gabriel behind me, Michael to my right, Auriel to my left here in this circle of fire." The flame moved swiftly in its circular path as the perimeter erupted in flames.

The drum halted as each vampire stood before his captive. The priest bellowed, "If you wish to follow me, you must leave all behind. Only then can you drink the elixir of life. Now close your eyes, for only in darkness can you see the true light."

As each candidate closed her eyes, a vampire drained her body of blood. The priest circulated among the motionless bodies. Ceremoniously he proclaimed, "The Body of Christ, the Blood of the Sabbat?"

"Amen," replied each soon-to-be sire as he grasped the chalice and smeared an inverted ankh onto the head of the dead recruit saying, "Glory be to Thee, Father of the Undying, Mother of the Unborn. For thy glory flows out rejoicing, to the ends of the earth."

After all the recruits received the mark of Caine, the vampires Embraced them, the cloying aroma of vampiric vitae filling the air. Before the candidates had a chance to regain a new, undead consciousness, the priest proclaimed, "Ashes to ashes, dust to dust!" The vampires struck their childer savagely with shovels and threw the victims into the open graves. Howling, they filled the graves with dirt and covered them with wood.

Vestments fluttering in the wind, the priest walked a circle around the graves, covering the entire area with the volatile liquid. "The fire purifies all," he decreed as the area burst into flames. "We rejoice in the power of the flame; we dance in the light of wisdom and strength; we rise to the mercy of the fire; the fire holds resurrection in its flames."

The drum grew louder and faster as the priest leapt the flames. The vampires danced about the fire as the priest approached them with the Vaulderie. Each member drank and then leapt the flame.

As the spectacle continued, the priest exclaimed, "Like the phoenix, we all shall rise; like the risen Christ, gods we all shall become. Go now, to love and serve the Sabbat."

As the flames dispersed, the vampires vanished. Only the drummer remained, reducing his rhythm to a heartbeat, the beat of the Sabbat. And God help the city when the drummer's audience arose from their makeshift graves.

other vampires, packs often have an overriding reason to have been put together by their elders. Whether as simple as combat or as esoteric as a performance pack that interprets the *Book of Nod* when the local archbishop oversees the Sermons of Caine, a pack performs some fundamental function.

Naturally, most packs have some martial bent — the Sabbat is a sect of holy warriors, after all. Infinite variations on this theme exist, however. Some packs might specialize in guerrilla warfare while others scout ahead for the packs that follow them. Other packs may focus on breaking the Masquerade in Camarilla cities, while still others may have military or police skills that allow them to fly aircraft or operate SWAT-grade weaponry. A pack may practice duels, fighting its enemies in dramatic hand-to-hand combat while yet another pack may be a biker gang, unloading shotguns through Main Street windows at 60 miles per hour and then circling in the city park as a challenge for anyone to come take them on. The variations are as endless and unique as the vampires who make up the pack in question

Not every pack serves an exclusively martial purpose, however. The Sabbat creates a pack to handle anything it needs. Spy packs are common among the Sword of Caine, as are teams of computer hackers, relic-hunter packs that dig up forgotten artifacts or search after fragments of the *Book of Nod*. Some bold (or insane) packs even hunt Lupines, demonstrating their bravery (or lunacy) by bringing down some of the world's most dangerous prey.

To the Sabbat vampire, the pack is everything. It is a surrogate family, in that members share ties of mutual blood (as embodied by the Vaulderie). This unity does not imply that the family isn't *dysfunctional* — packs are some of the most hellish conglomerations of savage personalities in the world — but some level of sympathy always exists, otherwise the pack simply disbands and the members join another.

The pack also functions as a spiritual guide. The priest leads the individual members of her pack on a journey into what it means to be a vampire. The family that prays together, stays together, after all, and the Sabbat practices an enormous amount of *ritae*. By confronting their Beasts — or embracing them — members of Sabbat packs have seen each other at their worst, and they depend on the others to help them deal with the curse of being a vampire.

Packs serve as protection as well. Given the intense nature of the sect, their acceptance of the fact that they are vampires, their loathing for humankind and their competitive urges, Sabbat vampires often run afoul of one another. Whether vying for control of the drug trade or hunting an elder during a War Party, packs are going to conflict with other packs, and woe be to the weaker group. Pack members watch each other's backs at almost all times (unless the rivalry within the pack has grown so fierce that some members want others dead, and stranger things have happened...). Yet, packs need not fear only other packs; the World of Darkness veritably boils with danger. Marauding Lupines, vicious elders, Camarilla spies and even mortal threats like gangs, police and rowdy rednecks may make short work of an individual whereas the pack offers its members safety in numbers (it's less likely with the mortals, but hey, still *stranger* things have happened).

Sabbat leaders use the packs for their war efforts, for attacks on elders and also, perhaps most importantly, to maintain Sabbat influence in their cities. With Sabbat vampires, who adopt a rough semblance of the Masquerade in their own cities, the packs need to prevent Camarilla vampires from using the Sabbat's own tactics against it. Granted, many Camarilla vampires are loath to expose themselves to mortals (as does the Sabbat when it begins a crusade), but packs are the Sabbat's equivalent of social circles, and the entities with which visiting vampires are likely to come in contact. When Cainite moles show up, they've got to fool an entire (likely hostile) pack into believing their story, not just one vampire. Additionally, should the Camarilla ever stoop to overt violence, packs are going to have the numbers to deal effectively with the situation.

All this talk doesn't go to say that Sabbat vampires do everything in packs — just most things. Sabbat vampires still pursue their own agendas, make their own contacts, deal with people they prefer and otherwise lead private unlives. That's part of the freedom of belonging to the Sabbat. The role of the individual, though, is equally as important as the role of the group, as far as the sect is concerned.

Havens: Parishes and Oases

Unlike most vampires, who seclude themselves in private and secretive havens where they can be safe from prying eyes, the members of the Sabbat often share communal havens that support entire packs. Although a full pack may not always be present in a particular haven at any given time, it is not unusual to find half a dozen Sabbat residing in one domicile. In general, each haven has its own single pack, and thus, as the unliving quarters for the followers of the pack priest, that haven becomes the pack's "parish."

Sabbat are not picky about their choice of parishes: Utility serves over appearance for the vast majority of Sabbat packs. As long as the Toreador *antitribu* has room for "art" without disturbing the cache of methamphetamines cooked up and prepared for "distribution" by the Pander, the haven can take any form at all — abandoned house, hotel, condominium, church, sepulcher, warehouse or business structure. Some Sabbat vampires do enforce their selections of personal tastes on the pack, but even a Tzimisce or distinguished Lasombra may stay in a run-down apartment building if it serves as the best territory for the pack.

Of course, because the Sabbat fanatically fears the influence of the Ancients and the Camarilla, many permanent havens boast spectacular traps and escape routes. It's a poor haven that doesn't have a locker for weapons and a room for *ritae*. Most buildings are modified to include some sort of emergency exit (since enemies and rival Sabbat alike are fond of burning down pack havens) and may boast additional security if the pack can afford or scrounge up the necessary material. Multiple locks and alarms are ubiquitous, and many havens sport small crossbow-type or explosive traps around important areas, to prevent incursion by the enemy.

Pilgrims, nomadic packs that travel from city to city without a permanent home, often make use of "oases," or semi-settled caches of equipment and material. Typically, a pack of pilgrims leaves behind tools and money when times are abundant, often in a small abandoned hovel, a cavern or even a burned-out car hulk in the back roads and woods. Special signs mark the cache, so that other Sabbat can recognize it and find directions to it through the founded packs of nearby cities. The information about oases thus spreads as nomadic packs place and use them, relaying the appropriate updates to settled packs so that other pilgrims in the area will know where to go for supplies while "on the road." Rumors have spread recently, however, of Lupines learning the signs that identify oases; more than one nomadic pack has met a bloody end in a werewolf ambush near what they thought was a secure site.

RITAE

The Sabbat practices numerous rituals and ceremonies, all intended to foster loyalty inside the sect as well as unite the disparate Vampires that make it up in the face of their foes. These rituals, known as *ritae*, build bonds that no other society of free Cainites can hope to emulate.

The sect maintains a body of 13 "high rituals" known as the *auctoritas ritae* and any number of lesser rituals known as the *ignoblis ritae*, which vary from pack to pack and city to city.

The sect observes these *ritae* often, generally at esbats and other key times (such as certain weeks or nights of the year, whenever certain packs gather, etc.). The *ritae* are vital parts of any Sabbat pack's existence, and they are covered in depth in Chapter Five.

Hiding from the Herds

Fun and Games

Sabbat vampires lead tense unlives, sworn to eternal righteous duty against the Camarilla and Antediluvians in the Great Jyhad. Not every night sees the hunt of an elder or the siege of a city, however, and the Sabbat has adopted numerous bloody "sports" with which to pass the time on nights when they have no active sect responsibilities to address.

As a whole, the elder body of the Sabbat looks down on these "games," seeing them as vulgar and senseless. The elders admit, however, that fun and games keep the footsoldiers of the sect in fine fighting order. Indeed, when an elder thinks the sect at large isn't looking, she may be known to engage in a few herself.

• **The Races** — A game in which sect members steal any car they can find (police cruisers, delivery vehicles, private cars) and take them out on the streets or highways. Invariably, the races involve accidents, crashes, police pursuit and other opportunities for the Cainites to kill mortals and sometimes feed after the fact.

• **Drive-By** — The vampires literally perform drive-by shootings against other vampires (preferably Camarilla, but rival packs of Sabbat will do). These drive-bys rarely kill the other vampires, but mortals often get in the way and it's great fun to see the people supposedly killed get up and crawl to recuperate. This is one of the key Masquerade-breaking tactics employed by the Sabbat during sieges of other cities.

• **Football** — Just like it sounds, football with the Sabbat tends to be a bit rough. Normally, packs simply go to a park or other recreation site and challenge a group of mortals to a game of football. Of course, blood-frenzied vampires with Celerity and Potence aren't always the best opponents, and the Sabbat rarely play fair, so the games usually result in broken necks and legs for the mortals, who are just as likely to meet their deaths when the vampires "juice up" after the game.

• **Trick or Treat?** — It need not be Halloween for the Sabbat to play this game. Trick or Treat usually takes a violent turn as the homes the Sabbat visits are rarely prepared to offer "treats" during the middle of the summer. Instead, the vampires may take their own treats, (killing the residents and drinking their blood), or they may practice a trick, such as boarding up the house and setting it on fire with the residents still inside.

• **Human Gladiators** — A true bloodsport, this game involves capturing two or more mortals, hyping them up on speed or PCP and turning them loose on each other. The survivor, it is explained, may keep his life (which may or may not be true), and to make things interesting for the Sabbat, they often give the competitors makeshift weapons such as chains, broken bottles, broken-off broom handles and other implements that take a long time to kill their victims but still hurt like hell. Some Sabbat eschew this game, since it is more of a spectator sport than an actual vampiric endeavor.

These are just a few of the pastimes in which the Sabbat engages. Some packs prefer games of their own invention, and it is considered the height of Sabbat pack chic to create a game that others adopt.

Sect Justice

The Sabbat tolerates no treachery. As any army would, the Sabbat protects its secrets with a ruthless code of justice. Final justice rests in the hands of those wronged — most packs enforce their own punishments — but truly grievous crimes against the sect are punished by the local bishop or archbishop

Crime	Punishment
Treason against the sect	Torture and dismemberment, in whatever poetic fashion the "judge" decides (includes being thrown off buildings, being drawn and quartered, having limbs removed, etc.)
Murdering a fellow Sabbat	Diablerie at the hands of the murdered vampire's pack (or a pack of an elder's choice, should the victim have been an elder)
Deceiving Sabbat leaders	Burning or flaying
Revealing a Sabbat secret to one outside the sect	Death by fire, or a Wild Hunt (see Chapter Five)
Failure to respond to a leader's call	Branding or mutilation (often, the vampire loses a hand)
Striking a vampire of greater station	Blinding, mutilation (often, the vampire suffers several broken bones)
Associating with Camarilla vampires	First offense: censure; second offense: flogging; third offense: staking or death

| Failure to accomplish an important mission assigned by leaders | "Spite" punishment, generally of a humiliating nature (such as cutting off the vampire's nose, branding his forehead with an "F," dashing out his teeth, etc.) |
| Displays of cowardice | Blood Feast (see Lexicon and Chapter Five) for fellow pack members, though the vampire is usually left undead to atone for himself later. |

A Sabbat Lexicon

The vampires of the Sabbat have evolved their own specialized patois, much of which takes into account their holy war on the Antediluvians and the attendant rituals and practices that follow it. Particularly old Sabbat vampires even recall terms and phrases that have long since passed into the nights of forgotten history. Although many of these terms are in common use among Sabbat vampires, some of them take on different meanings colloquially, given the lack of formal communication among sect members. Vampires who would "talk the talk" are advised to be aware of everything they say and what it means.

Abbot A vampire or ghoul charged with the maintenance of a Sabbat pack's communal haven.

Antitribu Literally, "anti-tribe" or "anti-clan." The *antitribu* are vampires who have turned their backs on their "parent" clans and now espouse the policies of the Sabbat instead. One notable exception to this rule are the Lasombra *antitribu*, who have abandoned the Sabbat in favor of independent or Camarilla unlives. *Antitribu* are generally held in extremely low regard by their parent clans, which is especially true in the case of the Lasombra.

Archbishop: A vampire who serves as the leader of a city under the Sabbat's influence. Not every Sabbat-held city claims an archbishop; some have councils of bishops.

Auctoritas Ritae: A collection of 13 rituals practiced by all vampires of the Sabbat, upheld in a manner similar to the Biblical Ten Commandments.

Bishop: A vampire who serves or advises an archbishop, or a vampire who maintains Sabbat influence in a city with the aid of others of equal status. (Those who are in the know liken bishops to the primogen of the Camarilla.)

Black Hand: The secret militia of the Sabbat. Some references allude to *another* organization with the same name. The "true" meaning of this term, if there is one, is a matter of much uncertainty, even among those who claim to be members.

Blood Feast: A victim or group of victims, bound and suspended upside down. Said victims serve as refreshment at Sabbat functions.

Brave: A vampire participating in a war party.

Cainite: A vampire. Sabbat vampires use this term in places where other vampires would use the term *Kindred*. Sabbat vampires accept and claim descent from Caine, while the Camarilla largely claims him to be a myth.

Cardinal: A Sabbat vampire who oversees the influential affairs of a large territory. Each cardinal is attended by a group of archbishops, who govern affairs on local city levels.

Chief: The leader of a war party.

Code of Milan: An oft-referenced but rarely seen document developed as a code of conduct for Sabbat vampires. Some Sabbat scoff at it, claiming that codifying the sect's behavior runs counter to everything the Sabbat stands for.

Column: A permanent pack of Black Hand members, usually nomadic.

Communal Haven: A single haven shared by an entire pack.

Consistory: The body of advisors to the regent, composed of key prisci and cardinals.

Convention of Thorns: The treaty that supposedly ended the Anarch Revolt and resulted in the formation of the Sabbat.

Coven: A pack of Sabbat that makes a permanent haven in a city; used to differentiate between "founded" packs and nomadic packs. Most Sabbat cities host numerous covens, in addition to providing "hospitality" to a seemingly endless stream of nomadic packs.

Creation Rites: The special ritual marking a Sabbat vampire as becoming a true member of the sect. The Creation Rites differ from the Embrace in that anyone can be Embraced, but until he receives the Creation Rites, the recruit is not a member of the Sabbat (and thus, not considered a vampire…).

Daughters and Sons (of Caine): All vampires. A similar term with the same meaning is "brothers and sisters."

Ductus: The leader of a Sabbat pack. This title is a highly subjective one, sometimes held by the meanest thug in a pack while acquired through genuine merit or ritual combat at other times. The ductus decides the logistical affairs of her pack, though the wise ductus gives careful ear to her packmates' voices.

Esbat: A weekly meeting held by a pack, whether nomadic or founded. Central to the esbats are discussions of events that affect the pack as well as the *auctoritas* and *ignoblis ritae*.

Festivo dello Estinto: The "Festival of the Dead," a grand celebration held during the second week of April in Sabbat cities. All covens attend the festival, as do any nomadic packs that can make it.

Fire Dance: A ritual and rough celebration in which Sabbat vampires prove their loyalty and bravery by jumping through raging fires. Many Sabbat war efforts and other events begin with fire dances.

Founded Pack: A coven; a pack of Sabbat vampires that maintains a permanent haven in a city.

Great Jyhad: The war for supremacy in the New World, begun in the 17th century and arguably raging during the modern nights.

Hand: The Black Hand.

Headhunter: A Sabbat vampire who collects the skulls of his fallen foes as trophies. Some headhunters collect only vampire skulls, while others collect Lupine skulls, mortals' skulls or the skulls of witch-hunters. These trophies are considered great honors in the Sabbat, according to the degree of difficulty associated with claiming them.

Horseman: A nomadic Sabbat vampire, thought to have been inspired by the Four Horsemen of the Apocalypse.

Hulul: The figurehead of the Assamite *antitribu*, who is rumored to be ritually destroyed every 100 years.

Ignoblis Ritae: The rituals practiced by individual Sabbat packs to reinforce unity, loyalty and the causes of the Sabbat. These rituals vary from pack to pack, and they are considered less important individually than the *auctoritas ritae* because they are not as universally useful. Some Sabbat members observe no *ignoblis ritae* at all.

Jyhad: The eternal conflict with other vampires. Sabbat vampires use this term more loosely than other vampires, because almost all struggle is a holy war from the Sabbat point of view. In his mind, a Sabbat takes part in the Jyhad any time he fights.

Kindred: Non-Sabbat vampires. Most Sabbat use this term derisively, considering Camarilla vampires to be their inferior and laughing at their "big, happy family" of vampires who cower from humankind. Many Sabbat also apply the term "Kindred" sarcastically to vampires of independent clans, whom they perceive as too selfish or foolish to take up the cause against the Antediluvians.

Loyalist: A Sabbat vampire who refuses to acknowledge leaders among the sect out of loyalty to its original goals. Loyalists believe that to be truly loyal to the Sabbat, they must have total freedom. Loyalists are commonly viewed as agitators and dissidents, and they are watched warily by their packmates and elders. Much of the Sabbat's terrifying reputation among other vampires may stem from the actions of particularly fervent loyalists.

Monomacy: A ritual duel between vampires of the Sabbat, held under formal rules. This duel is a traditional Sabbat means of settling disputes, and it often results in the Final Death of one of the participants.

Nomadic Pack: A pack that travels constantly in its duties to the Sabbat. Nomadic packs maintain no permanent havens, but they sometimes keep hidey-holes and emergency havens throughout their regions of travel. Nomadic packs may also stop in cities for indeterminate periods of time, but they eventually return to the roads.

Nomads: Members of nomadic packs.

Pack: A group of Sabbat who have sworn the Vaulderie to one another. A Sabbat may belong to only one pack at a time — usually the one that enacted her Creation Rites — though she may have ties of blood to other packs from her past.

Paladin: A Sabbat vampire who serves another important vampire as an assassin or bodyguard. Also known as templars, paladins are greatly feared for their disciplined martial prowess. Paladins are forbidden from membership in the Black Hand.

Palla Grande: A grand and terrible festival held on All Hallows Eve, when all Sabbat vampires in a city gather to celebrate and revere the sect. It often takes the appearance of a masquerade ball, and humans are sometimes invited as guests — or refreshments.

Path of Enlightenment: A belief system followed by the more alien members of the Sabbat in place of Humanity. Paths of Enlightenment are moral codes that serve to anchor the Sabbat vampire against her ravening Beast, though some paths encourage "riding" the Beast rather than controlling it. The most common paths practiced by the Sabbat include the Path of Caine, the Path of Cathari, the Path of Death and the Soul, the Path of the feral Heart, the Path of Honorable Accord, the Path of Lilith and the Path of Power and the Inner Voice. Some Sabbat follow the Path of Evil Revelations, though these vampires are hunted by the Sabbat Inquisition as heretics and traitors to the sect.

Priest: The leader of Sabbat *ritae* in a given pack. The spiritual leader of a pack, the priest is (theoretically) below the ductus in "rank," though this is not true of every pack.

Prior: An abbot (*vide*).

Priscus: A Sabbat vampire, often quite advanced in age and/or generation, who advises the regent and cardinals. Plural *prisci*.

Recruit: An vampire Embraced against her will, usually in the interests of providing cannon fodder for the sect's conquests.

Regent: The "leader" of the Sabbat, insofar as the sect recognizes one. Only one regent exists at a time.

Sabbat: 1. The vampiric sect that opposes the Camarilla and the machinations of the Antediluvians

2. A vampire belonging to the sect. Usage: *Jasmine is Sabbat, through and through, baby.*

3. A group of vampires belonging to the sect. Usage: *Yeah, those Sabbat over there have been giving us the once over, and I think the shit's about to go down.*

True Sabbat: A Sabbat who has proven himself to the sect and has received the Creation Rites.

Vaulderie: A mingling of the blood of all vampires in a pack, which is then consecrated by the pack priest and consumed by all members of the pack.

Vinculum: A "blood tie" that creates an artificial loyalty to another member of one's pack, like a minor blood bond. Vinculi result from partaking in the Vaulderie

VULGAR ARGOT

The Sabbat is a violent, hostile, youthful sect, and the young ones' language reflects as much. Hereafter are some of

the (more printable) terms Sabbat vampires casually drop. Many of these terms take their roots from modern slang, with added meaning to vampires, and some even transcend the boundaries of sect, and may be used anywhere.

Bat: An elder vampire of the Sabbat, who often has little in common with younger members of the sect.

Bitch: A probationary pack member, or a Sabbat of lesser status than the speaker.

Chica: A female Sabbat vampire.

Costello: Dismissive term for the Camarilla. (This is suspected to have arisen after some mispronunciation of "Sabbat.")

Counting Coup: Taking the head of a fallen foe as a trophy (see *Headhunter*). This practice is sometimes called "scalping."

Crowley: A derogatory or dismissive term for followers of the Path of Evil Revelations, or vampires who make ostentatious shows of evil for their own sake. These individuals are also known as Ozzys or Mansons by some packs.

Did: Killed. Usage: *Yeah, we did the cop, but only after we caught him snooping around the bishop's haven.*

Dog: A Lupine. In certain circles, dog also means an infectious carrier of blood-borne diseases (short for plague dog).

Go Down: A vampire who, usually out of habit, perversity or derangement, commits sexual acts regardless of his or her own vampiric impotence. Also known by a host of other charming epithets including dick, handjob, hummer, etc., usually custom-tailored to the specifics of the vampire in question's behavior.

Headache: Accidentally killing while feeding. Usage: *Danny gave that skinny girl a headache.*

Injun or Indian: A member of a nomadic pack.

Juice: Blood.

Keg: A "member" of a Blood Feast. In some packs, these individuals are referred to as pints or longnecks.

Pimp: A vampire charged with gathering vices for packmates. The pimp may procure drugs, alcohol, prostitutes, children or any other indulgences for fellow vampires (or mortals…).

Pipes: An exceptional failure, or an object of derision. Usage: *That scouting run you guys did was the pipes.*

Poet: A member of the goth subculture, especially one who "dresses like a vampire." Also known as Shelleys or Byrons.

Shovelhead: A Sabbat vampire created during a siege or other event that necessitated the "quick and dirty" mass Embrace. Also known as a Thwack or a Clang (after the

sound a shovel to the head makes, presumably), which is sometimes used as a verb.

Tongue: Sabbat propaganda, or a Sabbat proselytizer, often spread among the anarchs of Camarilla cities.

V: A vampire.

Vato: A male Sabbat vampire.

Witch: Irreverent term for a pack priest, best used out of earshot of the individual in question.

OLD FORM

Despite its war on the elders, the Sabbat claims some members who are quite advanced in age themselves. These vampires recall the nights when the Sabbat was born, and have carried over or adopted phrases as old as they are. Beware the vampire who speaks in the tongue of the Sabbat elders, for she is surely formidable and wicked beyond belief.

Angellis Ater: The "black angels" of Clan Lasombra, often young vampires who embrace the stereotypical and shallow evils of the modern night in blatant attempts to become monsters.

Kamut: A nomadic pack of Sabbat formed for a specific purpose, such as hunting Lupines, scouting Camarilla cities or exposing heretics.

Lacheur: A young Sabbat, particularly an insolent one. May be used to refer to any young vampire in some cases.

Manus Nigrum: A mysterious subsect of the Sabbat, or one entirely independent about which very little is known. Younger vampires refer to this group, apparently erroneously, as the Black Hand.

Revenants: Individuals who are born as ghouls. Revenants are families of ghouls that have existed for so long with the blood of their undead masters in their veins that it now passes on to each of their descendants as well. The vampires of Clan Tzimisce seem to use revenants most often, and they are often held in suspicion by others who know of their natures.

Shakari: The eldest vampires among the Assamite *antitribu*.

Sword of Caine: The Sabbat.

Voivode: The leader of Clan Tzimisce. Some vampires postulate that there is no single *voivode*, and the title is one of inscrutable significance to only the Fiends themselves.

CHAPTER TWO: AROUND THE FIRES

He who makes a beast of himself
gets rid of the pain of being a man.
— Dr. Johnson

The Sabbat claims a very cosmopolitan membership. Composed of 14 clans and bloodlines, the sect possesses a diversity of lineage not found in any other society of vampires. However, because the sect is smaller than the Camarilla, a greater number of clans and bloodlines means that each consanguinity has fewer members. For example, while the number of "mainstream" Brujah may number in the thousands, only several hundred Brujah *antitribu* populate the ranks of the Sabbat.

The Sabbat has little problem with this, though, as it prides itself on the diversity, individuality and freedom of its members. Who wants to be just another cog in the Ventrue machine when one can be a member of the few, the proud, the Ventrue *antitribu*?

This chapter explores the new clans and bloodlines that belong to the Sword of Caine. The majority of the sect consists of members of the Lasombra and Tzimisce clans, which are detailed in Chapter Two of **Vampire: The Masquerade**.

ASSAMITE ANTITRIBU

In the nights following the Anarch Revolt and the Convention of Thorns, Clan Assamite found itself in a deadly predicament. In light of the overwhelming opposition posed by the young Camarilla, the Assamites became targets for the ire of all vampires. To temper the threat the Saracen Assassins posed, the Camarilla subjected Clan Assamite to a powerful Tremere curse, rendering the Assamites unable to partake of Cainite vitae, which was core to many Assamite's ethical codes.

Not every Assamite succumbed to the blood curse, however. A few bold Assamites, led by the first *hulul*, al-Numair, went into hiding. In the nights that followed, al-Numair and his band of rebel assassins joined the young Sabbat, more out of defiance to the Camarilla than support for the sect's still-nascent philosophy. Since that time, however, the Assamite *antitribu* have assumed an important role in the Sabbat and become some of the most feared members of the notorious Black Hand.

Assamite *antitribu* serve their clan first and the Sabbat second, though many of their beliefs coincide with those of the sect. Unlike members of their original clan, Assamite *antitribu* do not revere Haqim. Rather, they see him as they see all of the loathed Antediluvians, as a corrupt, malignant force that will one night rise and devour his children. Instead, Assamite *antitribu* seek to grow ever closer to Caine, whom the mainstream Assamites regard as an abomination. Regardless, the two clans seem to be on fairly civil terms, though no outsider has come up with a credible reason why. Indeed, the Assamite *antitribu* seem to bear a hauteur over their mainstream brethren, whom they chide mercilessly for accepting the Camarilla's curse even after they have broken it.

Like the members of their original clan, Assamites are masters of assassination and silent killing. The Angels of Caine are a valuable martial addition to the Sabbat, which would lack a good deal of prowess and tactical brilliance without them. Many Assamite *antitribu* attain significant military rank in the sect, and many more go on to become some of the sect's

greatest killer-heroes, leaving the corpses and ashes of fallen infidels to mark their silent passing.

Assamite *antitribu* do not typically assume the roles of pack priests, though many become ducti, especially if combat or assassination is their pack's purpose. Most Angels of Caine belong to exclusively Assamite *antitribu* packs, though more and more of them have broken this mold, becoming valuable additions to more diverse packs. They do not proselytize as strongly as the non-Sabbat clan does, believing that converting others to their faith is vanity. In the end, Caine shall recognize his own, and others will have been given the choice to follow him or take their own path.

Nickname: Angels of Caine

Appearance: Assamite *antitribu* bear similar appearances to their non-Sabbat counterparts, though many more *antitribu* bear the features of European or mixed cultures. Elders wear traditional Middle Eastern or Mesopotamian garb, while young Assamite *antitribu* favor a more modern wardrobe, even adopting gang or cultic garb to better hide among these violent subcultures. As with the Assamites, an Assamite *antitribu*'s skin grows darker as the Cainite ages.

Haven: Assamite *antitribu* favor communal havens, which may take the form of pack havens, assassins' cells of other Assamite *antitribu* or other "nests" of vampires. Favored locations include refrigerated warehouses, abandoned slums and slaughterhouses, where bodies may be disposed of with minimal difficulty.

Background: Most members of the Assamite *antitribu* hail from Middle Eastern, North African or Asiatic cultures, though these may be several generations removed from their places of origin. More and more, however — especially among the higher generations — lineage has grown less important, taking a back seat to ability. Newly Embraced Assamite *antitribu* do not typically become active in the sect immediately, serving seven-year "apprenticeships" at Black Hand strongholds or under the guidance of skilled masters instead. These *mustajib* — deserving ones — must prove themselves to the clan before being offered the opportunity to prove themselves to the sect.

Character Creation: Assamite *antitribu* can come from any racial or ethnic stock, though Middle Eastern and North African lineage is still the most common. Like non-Sabbat Assamites, many Assamite *antitribu* are ex-soldiers, criminals, holy men and explorers. Their Natures are usually brusque and direct (and likely violent), but their Demeanors can be anything at all. Physical Attributes tend to be primary among the Assamite *antitribu*, as do Skills. Common Backgrounds for the Angels of Caine include Black Hand Membership, Mentor, Generation and sometimes Sabbat Status. Many Assamite *antitribu* follow the Path of Caine, and as such, the Assamite *antitribu* are often regarded as heretical by their parent clan.

Clan Disciplines: Celerity, Obfuscate, Quietus

Weaknesses: The Assamite *antitribu* never suffered the curse that the Camarilla placed on the mainstream clan. While the Assamites are only now returning to the bloodlust endemic to those of Haqim's line, the *antitribu* have possessed this weakness all along.

Assamite *antitribu* become addicted to Cainite vitae easily. Whenever an Assamite *antitribu* drinks the blood of another vampire, he may become addicted. The player must make a Self-Control roll (difficulty 3 + the number of blood points taken). If the player fails the roll, the Assamite has become addicted. Once addicted, every time an Assamite *antitribu* partakes of vampire blood, the player must make another Self-Control roll (difficulty 6) or succumb to frenzy, in which he will take as much blood from his vessel as possible. Storytellers should encourage players to roleplay this craving for undead vitae — Assamite *antitribu* do not subjugate their bloodlust, they indulge it.

Organization: The Assamite *antitribu* maintain a structure similar to that of the original Clan Assamite. Members follow a hierarchy, unusual among the clans of the Sabbat (because most other clans devote their duty to the sect first). Instead of the Old Man of the Mountain, however, the Assamite *antitribu* follow the guidance of the *hulul*, the eldest member of the clan. Every 100 years, the Assamite *antitribu* ritually destroy their *hulul* as an offering to Caine, and one member of the clan is selected to partake of the slain vampire's blood and become the new *hulul*. The *hulul* is attended and advised by the *shakari*, the wisest and most accomplished members of the clan. Vampires below these stations operate much like normal Assamites do, taking assassination contracts and indulging in wanton diablerie.

Quote: *You are so frail, I am almost ashamed to take your blood. Almost.*

STEREOTYPES

Camarilla: Scavengers playing at being lions.

Sabbat: I against my brother; my brother and I against our cousin; my cousin and I against the stranger.

THE VIEW FROM WITHOUT

The Camarilla

Antitribu? What's the difference? A killer's a killer. Maybe these guys are even more untrustworthy than their independent kin, but how can you tell when Assamites are concerned?

— Stevie "The Butcher" Reno, Sheriff of Houston

The Sabbat

Beneath their facade of sincerity lies a dead heart of treachery. For the time being, however, they are useful enough.

— Laika, Tzimisce *koldun*

The Independents

It is true they are heretics. But when matters of faith arise, who can say which Child of Caine is correct? Perhaps our righteousness shall seal our damnation, should the heretics emerge, proven correct, when Gehenna arrives.

— Khuf Ramalza, Assamite *rafiq*

BLOOD BROTHERS

Conceived and created in crumbling Old World castles and chantries by the newly vanished Tremere *antitribu* and a few twisted Tzimisce sorcerers, the Blood Brothers are an artificially engineered bloodline of shock troops and servitors. The Blood Brothers are the dubiously successful result of extensive experiments in blood bonding, intended to create a cell of servants that thought and acted as one.

To some degree, the Blood Brothers are a hive mind, sharing the same conscious thoughts and experiencing their surroundings vicariously through other members of their individual "chapters," known as circles. This link allows them to work effectively apart from each other — the bloodline excels at coordinated combat missions and espionage, provided no one realizes what they are (which, due to their rarity and the difficulty of their creation, is unlikely). They practice an unusual, disturbing Discipline that allows them to "loan" their limbs to one another, heal their compatriots and even capitalize on their shared minds.

Blood Brothers commonly form exclusive packs, in which they undergo Tzimisce fleshcrafting to make themselves look exactly alike — the better to unsettle their foes. The bloodline is notorious for its lack of personal drive, which makes its members ideal servants; no master needs to fear the Blood Brothers' fangs at his throat. Unfortunately, the bloodline has very little creativity, and it usually lacks the ability to outmaneuver opponents or outthink them, which is a flaw common to any enforced conformity. This is not to say the Brothers are dull-witted or slow; rather, they do not possess much self-awareness.

Few outside the Sabbat have come in contact with the Blood Brothers, and fewer still have escaped to tell about it. Indeed, not many Sabbat have dealt with the Frankensteins, or even know about them. Blood Brothers have become increasingly uncommon in the modern nights, mostly due to the fact that the Tremere *antitribu* no longer exist to create new ones

while the existing Blood Brothers have typical Sabbat rates of Final Death. Blood Brothers cannot Embrace (a fail-safe put in place by clever experimenters who had no desire to repeat the Gargoyle fiasco), yet they are vampires in every other respect, including the ability to create ghouls.

Nickname: Frankensteins

Appearance: Barring a few scars here and there, Blood Brothers look exactly like other members of their circle. Most shave their bodies completely before the Embrace, ensuring an eternity of hairlessness, though this is not always the case. Additionally, many Blood Brothers tattoo numbers or other symbols on their bodies before their Embrace (often on the base of the neck, but sometimes on their stomachs or ankles), which identify which circle they belong to and in what capacity. Blood Brothers most often dress in styles similar to that of the skinhead culture, wearing T-shirts, jeans, military-surplus boots and braces or suspenders. They cultivate their image for an air of obvious, but not ostentatious, menace.

A Word on Blood Brothers

Blood Brothers are intended more as a Storyteller device than as a bloodline for players to portray. There aren't a huge amount of roleplaying opportunities open to a family of servants with little personal drive. The decision to allow players to play members of this bloodline is, as always, the Storyteller's to make, but we don't recommend it.

Players, unless your character knows a good deal about the Sabbat, it's unlikely she's ever even heard of the Blood Brothers, let alone known one. Remember to keep your knowledge and your character's knowledge distinct, to better enjoy the mystery and horror of **Vampire: The Masquerade**.

Haven: Blood Brothers most frequently stay in whatever haven their master or patron keeps for them, which may even be part of the master's own. Blood Brothers always stay with each other in communal havens. Some critics speculate that the undead mind of the Blood Brother in incapable of coping with situations of prolonged absence from other members of his circle, but the few notable individual vampires of the bloodline have proven able to adapt to this eventuality.

Background: The Blood Brother's background ceases to have relevance after his Embrace. Vampires of this bloodline become devoted entirely to their circle and sect, and all other concerns vanish. Tzimisce (and Tremere *antitribu*, in the past) usually select mortal families, gangs or other extant groups from which to create Blood Brothers, capitalizing on the conformity and camaraderie therein. Female members are exceeding rare, but at least one has been reputably reported.

Character Creation: Blood Brothers have uncomplicated, martial concepts, but these often matter little to the vampire in question. Most are simple vampires, with similar Natures and Demeanors. Physical Attributes are almost always primary, as are Skills. All Blood Brothers in a circle must begin the game with the same Generation; the bloodline pursues few other Backgrounds other than Mentor and Resources. Few Blood Brothers have the initiative or contacts to learn Disciplines outside those the bloodline develops normally. Blood Brothers tend to uphold Humanity, often because they don't know any differently, though these scores often drop quite low before too long.

Clan Disciplines: Fortitude, Potence, Sanguinus

Stereotypes
Camarilla: They are the enemy, I am told.
Sabbat: Yes.

The View From Without
The Camarilla

Oh, right, like there's any such thing as Blood Brothers. And we drink infant's eyeball fluid and bite the heads off bats and take out our ribs so we can blow ourselves, too. For Caine's sake, isn't there *anything* you fools think the Tremere haven't done?

— Everett Thig, Tremere apprentice

The Sabbat

With such practices, we place ourselves among the same ranks as the Camarilla and the manipulative Antediluvians. I cannot approve.

— Lutz Persson, Lasombra Bishop of Oslo (Contested)

The Independents

I have other matters to worry about than bedtime stories.

— Pisanob Hecstapolapiquatl, Giovanni thanatologist

Weaknesses: Blood Brothers may not Embrace — they must be created via Thaumaturgy or sorcerous rituals. Should a Blood Brother attempt to Embrace a mortal, that mortal simply dies, robbed of all her blood.

The Frankensteins also feel each other's pain. If one takes damage, every Blood Brother of the circle suffers the same wound penalty for the next turn. Only the greatest wound penalty applies — if two are wounded, all members of the circle (including the less wounded one) suffer the largest penalty. This effect is not cumulative, though all members may feel wound penalties for multiple rounds (assuming one of their number suffers damage every turn).

Organization: For most Blood Brothers, unlife begins and ends with the circle, which consists of three to seven members. They may attend other Sabbat functions, but their master or patron dictates most of their purpose. Blood Brothers feel no inherent allegiance to other circles, above and beyond that of duty to the Sabbat. The bloodline treats others with cold deference, and its members seem somewhat reluctant to let outsiders know much about it. Perhaps their ends are best served in secrecy.

Quote: *You are not supposed to be here. We will show you the way out; one piece at a time, if needs be.*

BRUJAH ANTITRIBU

During the Anarch Revolt, the young majority of Clan Brujah was the first and most vocal to rally to the cause. The elders of the clan, after a passing interest in the challenge to other elders' status quo, judged the anarchs to be in error. After much debate and posturing, the elders and loyal childer of Clan Brujah turned their backs of the "daft and dangerous" vampires who called themselves anarchs. As a result, the Brujah anarchs, who almost unanimously refused to bow to the Convention of Thorns, bear a tremendous grievance against the parent clan and support the Sabbat with fervor. Unlike Camarilla Brujah, Sabbat Brujah often feel very strongly for their sect — while Camarilla Brujah bemoan their apathetic elders and spend their nights fighting in the parking lots of punk rock nightclubs, the Brujah *antitribu* have taken the Great Jyhad to the elders and Antediluvians themselves.

Of all the clans of the Sabbat, the Brujah *antitribu* are probably the most like their parent clan, with a few striking differences. The clan not only supports its sect with enthusiasm, it takes an active part in the nightly conquest and Jyhad that has made the recent Sabbat war effort so successful. Although still waters may run deep, the sanguinary turbulence among the Brujah *antitribu* does not indicate a lack of intellect or profundity on their part.

Brujah *antitribu* make brutal shock troops and effective footsoldiers for the Sabbat, and they find their greatest comfort in this role. Ruthless and vicious to the last, the Brujah *antitribu* enjoy their martial roles. As the Damned, they reason, why not indulge in a little violence and sadism to pass the innumerable nights? Fewer dissidents find their place among the Sabbat Brujah than in the ranks of the Camarilla, but that seems to be because the Brujah *antitribu* have better luck — or skill — choosing childer who are not so arbitrarily contrary.

The Sabbat Brujah are likely the most numerous non-Lasombra or Tzimisce members of the Sabbat, due to the fact that the clan is the least disposed to seeing the big picture. They take what they want when they want it, whether it is new childer, desirable vessels, shares of their cities' vice trade or the money in your pocket, and woe be to whomever would stand in their way. Other Sabbat frequently consider the Brujah *antitribu* base and classless, while the clan sees itself as the closest in ideology to the Sabbat's original intent — freedom.

Of late, many Brujah *antitribu* have grown frustrated with the antiquated leadership of the Lasombra and Tzimisce, and they have plotted their own spectacular plans and won their own victories. Most members of this clan find places among the Loyalist faction, and some few manage to transcend their atavistic urges to become productive members of the Black Hand or Inquisition. Indeed, the Brujah *antitribu* seem to be on the cusp of something momentous, and only time will tell what their nights hold in store.

Nickname: Brutes

Appearance: Brujah *antitribu* want to scare the hell out of those who look on them. Shocking hairstyles, painful piercings, tattoos and severe clothing all earmark the members of the Brujah *antitribu*. Some packs composed exclusively of Brujah *antitribu* adopt similar styles of dress, like urban gangs, while individual Brutes tend to affect whatever makes everyone around them uncomfortable (which takes some doing among the Sabbat). Members of this clan may resemble punks, gangsters, Mafiosi, soldiers of fortune or anything else they feel like, pal.

Haven: When the Brujah *antitribu* bother with establishing a private haven, it tends to occupy the back corners of their minds. As such, abandoned gas stations, disreputable nightclubs, churches and other "why would you go there?" places enjoy favor among the clan. For the most part, however, Brujah *antitribu* don't give a toss about where they stay. After all, haven maintenance is someone else's responsibility — the Brujah *antitribu* have asses to kick.

Background: The Brujah *antitribu* select childer from a wide range of backgrounds; members have very little in common other than nasty, rebellious natures and a penchant for violence. Most Brujah *antitribu* hail from blue-collar upbringings, and few have completed much in the way of formal education, but aside from those broad caveats, Brutes Embrace whomever they think would be useful or mean.

Character Creation: Brutes may have any concept, and they display a wide variety of Natures and Demeanors (which tend toward the martial or sadistic). Physical Attributes tend to be primary, as are Talents and Skills. Brujah *antitribu* tend to forego Backgrounds, considering them weak ties to the mortal world, but a growing minority have some form of Resources (generally from illegal or clandestine operations). Sabbat Brujah tend to uphold Humanity throughout their entire unlives, less out of moral preference than a simple lack of interest the philosophies of more rigorous ethical codes. Of course, these Humanity Traits tend to hover around the 4-6 level, and those rare Brujah *antitribu* who achieve more than a century of unlife have low scores indeed. Most are barely able to keep their Beasts at bay.

Clan Disciplines: Celerity, Potence, Presence

STEREOTYPES

Camarilla: Roll over and kiss your masters' feet, cowards.

Sabbat: As long as it doesn't get in my way, I'm all for it. When it starts telling me what I can and can't do, I'm going to have to take a look at what it does for me to make up for it.

THE VIEW FROM WITHOUT

The Camarilla

Mindless doesn't *necessarily* mean stupid, but they're not mutually exclusive. The *antitribu* embody all that is weak and flawed in Clan Brujah.

— Horatio Ballard, Ventrue industrialist

The Sabbat

Too brutal to trust; too simple not to.

— Van Bailey, ductus of the Riverside Cutthroats

The Independents

Their lack of sophistication makes them easy to win over to your way of thinking, but they're not good for much more than hurting others. Still, that can be useful.

— Verdigris, Setite mistress

Weaknesses: Like Camarilla Brujah, Sabbat Brujah have the same undead passion and inclination toward excitement burning in their blood. All frenzy difficulties increase by two for Brujah *antitribu* characters, to a maximum of 10. Brujah *antitribu* tend to be less offended about their radical moods than Camarilla Brujah, and many take perverse pleasure in their boiling tempers.

Organization: Organization is an uncomfortable concept to many Brujah *antitribu*, who prefer to take things one night at a time and do what they will whenever they get the urge. Brutes sometimes support the ideals of the Loyalists, and enjoy the lack of formality associated with allegiance to that cause. The Brujah *antitribu* sometimes hold Raves (and, less frequently, Rants) like the Brujah of the Camarilla, though these bashes are more likely to revolve around carnage and wanton destruction than discussion and debate.

Quote: *Fuck! Did you see how easy that guy's arm popped off? I barely pulled on it! These fucking juicebags make me sick.*

GANGREL ANTITRIBU

Feral and untamed, the Gangrel *antitribu* show an animalistic face to the Sabbat. Having grown apart from the Gypsy heritage of the mainstream Gangrel, the Sabbat Gangrel have returned to their bestial sides, becoming deadly hunters whose skill in the pursuit of prey is unmatched. The clan includes subtle slayers and savage berserkers alike, and the skill with which the Gangrel take on their foes lends a powerful strength to the sect. Gangrel *antitribu* are not sadistic bullies like the Brujah or mindless automatons like the Blood Brothers, however. Rather, they are instinctive, predatory creatures, enjoying the thrill of the hunt almost as much as the heady rush of feeding.

The Sabbat Gangrel have seen a recent influx of defectors from the Camarilla in recent nights, though few of these vampires seem to want to share the reasoning behind the exodus. Many whisper of "sleeping horrors" awakened, and the fact that the Sabbat has been "right all along." The sect as a whole seems frustrated by this turn of events and the apparent reluctance of the defectors to speak about their motives, but whatever it is that scares these urban predators, it must be of epic scale.

Gangrel *antitribu* divide themselves into two sub-clans, based on a deviation of clan blood thought to have occurred in the late 18th century. The "original" Gangrel, known in the Sabbat as Country Gangrel, are similar to their erstwhile Camarilla counterparts, shunning society and eking out unlives as lone hunters. They resemble the monstrous vampires of mortal legend, possessing the abilities to assume animal forms and call on nature's lesser creatures. The Country Gangrel support the Sabbat as scouts and warriors, using their animal contacts to retrieve information and their martial prowess to rend foes to bits.

City Gangrel are rumored to have become a distinct bloodline during the time of the Industrial Revolution, when cities became larger and less dependent on the resources of the countryside. Rather than forage for themselves in the hinterlands, a certain few Gangrel made havens for themselves in the cities, becoming monsters of urban legend and spreading terror in the wake of their feeding binges. No less animalistic than their Country Gangrel siblings, City Gangrel hide among the refuse and alleys of the city rather than the Lupine-infested copses other Gangrel prefer.

More so than other Gangrel, however, Gangrel of the Sabbat realize the importance of watching each other's backs during these tumultuous nights before Gehenna. The cities and outlands alike harbor many dangers, and a pack stands a better chance of dealing with them than an individual does. In this way, Sabbat Gangrel consider themselves more in touch with their animalistic sides than Camarilla or independent Gangrel by emulating the wolves and lions of the wilds.

Nickname: Hunters

Appearance: Most Gangrel don't give a damn about their appearances, considering vanity secondary to functionality. They typically appear sloppy or disheveled. Despite their abandonment of their Gypsy heritage, many Gangrel still bear swarthy features and dark hair. Some City Gangrel have adopted the slick, fashionable styles of the mortal world, but only as a form of "urban camouflage" that allows them to stalk their prey with greater ease. Often Gangrel are Embraced without a great deal of forethought, and many still bear unshaven beards or unkempt hair (though they may remedy these rugged features as they rise each night, if they wish).

Haven: Gangrel of both ilk are equally at home in the ground, under rocks or hidden behind garbage cans. Most Gangrel eschew permanent havens, communal or otherwise, and have adopted the nomadic unlifestyle. Any place a Gangrel may rise at sunset and stalk her prey is fine. Gangrel also keep few possessions other than what they can easily carry, so they have no real need for a place to cache large collections of belongings.

Background: Gangrel *antitribu* draw their childer from the ranks of those who possess a tenacity or survival instinct. Uncomplicated folk, Sabbat Gangrel often Embrace individuals like themselves when they bother to Embrace at all, so that they may have packmates of similar outlooks. Strangely enough, Hunters often act as patrons and mentors to their childer, perhaps out of animalistic duty as alpha to their pack members. City Gangrel choose particularly resilient folk for their childer, or those who would bear a grudge against the mortal world; thus, many City Gangrel come from the ranks of the homeless or foreign cultures resigned to ghettoes in the vast urban sprawls. For some inexplicable reason, many of the Country Gangrel in North America seem to have Native American ancestry, and some suspect this has a good deal to do with the Sabbat's prominence during the time of the American Manifest Destiny.

Character Creation: Most Country Gangrel are outsiders, drifters and the like, while City Gangrel favor more social concepts like soldiers or traveling entertainers. Physical Attributes are most often primary, though many Sabbat Gangrel display keen Wits and Perception. Gangrel *antitribu* favor Talents almost universally. As mentioned before, many Sabbat Gangrel have Mentors, and some few become Black Hand members or accomplished Sabbat with some measure of Sabbat Status. When Gangrel forsake Humanity, it is usually in favor of the Path of the Feral Heart or, far less common, the heretical Path of Lilith.

Clan Disciplines: Animalism, Fortitude, Protean (for Country Gangrel); Celerity, Obfuscate, Protean (for City Gangrel)

STEREOTYPES

Camarilla: Fools! If the Antediluvians do not exist, why have so many of you left the ivory tower to join us?

Sabbat: A fine pride of night monsters, with a few gentrified exceptions.

THE VIEW FROM WITHOUT

The Camarilla

If they do for the Sabbat what the Gangrel did for us, the Black Hand's welcome to 'em.

— Cinda Lowell, Toreador novelist

The Sabbat

I miss the nights of Transylvanian legend, when such beasts curled at our feet in our manors or died on our spears in the woods. They have become so shiftless in the past few centuries.

— Count Vladimir Rustovich, Tzimisce *voivode*

The Independents

Well, at least they've given up those ludicrous claims of *romani* blood.

— Aleksandr, Ravnos nomad

Weaknesses: As with other Gangrel, the Beast Within never lurks too far from Sabbat Gangrel, leaving its indelible mark on their bodies. Whenever a Sabbat Gangrel frenzies, she gains an animalistic feature. The Storyteller and the player should work together to determine this feature. Every five of these features acquired reduces one of the Gangrel's Social Attributes by one (Storyteller's choice as to which is most appropriate). These animal traits should be subtle yet unnerving — a tough hide, pronounced fangs, slitted pupils, et cetera. In recent nights, many City Gangrel seem to have acquired the features of urban animals, like rats, pigeons, dogs and even certain insects.

Organization: Country Gangrel and City Gangrel bear a certain animosity toward each other, which is likely a result of the clan's division so many centuries ago. City Gangrel believe their Country brethren to be bumpkins and rustics, while the Country Gangrel feel that the City Gangrel have debased themselves, becoming carrion-eaters and dwellers-in-trash. This dispute appears to be primarily a "family matter," however, and few outside the sect see it, because the Gangrel certainly don't advertise. Gangrel *antitribu* tend to respect accomplishment among their members, and many amass some degree of temporal power in the sect (often to their chagrin). Rather than shirk their sect responsibilities, however, the Gangrel *antitribu* bear their burdens with a certain savage nobility.

Quote: *Watch carefully — if you bite your prey like this, you reduce the spray of blood from their veins, which means more for you and less waste. Just leave the body behind that dumpster and we'll move on.*

HARBINGERS OF SKULLS

A recent addition to the Sabbat, the bloodline calling itself the Harbingers of Skulls claims a history of treachery, for which it seeks to exact a hellish vengeance. Members of the bloodline are quite powerful without exception, and they claim to have returned from their banishment to the realms of the dead. Long ago, they whisper, a rogue society of sorcerers hunted them for their blood, stealing immortality to further their own arcane lusts for power.

Few Sabbat believe this fairy tale of ancient injustice in these modern nights, but the Harbingers are afforded a wide berth nonetheless, given the immense potency of their magics and their discomforting eccentricity. The Harbingers of Skulls are necromancers on par with (and some say exceeding) the dreaded Giovanni, surrounding themselves with miasmas of death, murder and mortification, all toward the end of righting their legendary wrong. It would seem, however, that for all their polemics, something rots below the surface they present. Like the corpses they themselves resemble, something eats away at them from within.

The Harbingers of Skulls have been members of the Sabbat for only a few years, and few of the youngest members of the sect have ever heard of them, let alone seen one. Apparently, one of their number came forth with a proposition to the cardinals, prisci and regent, who conferred and welcomed the Harbingers to the Sword of Caine. Since then, the Harbingers of Skulls have amassed unheard-of power in the sect (given their small number, which is estimated in the low hundreds). The Black Hand, the Inquisition and even the ranks of the prisci now claim members of the Harbingers among them. Scions of the Sabbat appear to reap great benefits from the Harbingers' death magic, maintaining contact with fallen allies or tormenting enemies from beyond the wall of Final Death. Indeed, the Harbingers seem more than willing to offer aid to Sabbat compatriots — in exchange for favors to be determined later.

Cursed by Caine's blood with the countenances of corpses, the Harbingers often flay the tattered, grave-tainted flesh from their heads, leaving them with the grinning rictus of their namesake. Masks and ceremony play an important part in the bloodline's culture, and elders among these Cainites maintain vast collections of ritual masks and implements that they wear and use in their necromantic rites. It has been rumored that the vitae in their veins is ancient and quite potent, and perhaps their claims of grandiose history are not far from the mark. Whatever the case, the Harbingers of Skulls simply ignore inconvenient lines of questioning, preferring instead to spend their hours amid the tombstones of cemeteries or in deep contemplation of the powers of the dead.

Nickname: Lazarenes (after Lazarus, who observed Christ's return from the dead)

Appearance: The Harbingers of Skulls have an emaciated, corpselike appearance, accentuated by flesh that shrinks to fit the vampires' skulls. They are seldom seen outside their havens or the secret halls where powerful Sabbat convene to plot their intrigues. Harbingers prefer loose-fitting, flowing cloaks and burial shrouds, the better to represent their death magic and make dramatic impressions.

Haven: Harbingers of Skulls never belong to packs, and thus, they never make their havens with packs (unless doing so is temporary — the Sabbat rumor-mill is rife with tales of a Harbinger calling himself the Capuchin accepting brief hospitality from certain packs, priests or ducti). Lazarenes prefer their own, private havens, which often have laboratory annexes where they may conduct

A Word on Harbingers of Skulls

Like the Blood Brothers, Harbingers of Skulls are not intended for players to portray. Unless the Storyteller plans on running an elders game, it is impossible to create a Harbinger of Skulls under the new character generation system.

Harbingers of Skulls are all *at least* eighth generation, and hundreds (if not thousands) of years old. Most have more Disciplines than many starting packs, and could easily prove a match for the wiliest Tzimisce or most duplicitous Lasombra elder. In fact, almost every Harbinger predates the Sabbat altogether...

The bottom line is, don't do it, unless you really, *really* want to, and even then, Storytellers are encouraged to put the kibosh on your plans. Storytellers, choose wisely when allowing players to portray these types of characters. Millennia-old vampires aren't likely to pick people off the street and turn them into vampires, and they're better off being used for you to weave your elaborate plotlines than as powerhouse players' characters.

Also, don't let your players' knowledge color their characters' knowledge in this matter. In the World of Darkness, there's no master **Vampire** book for characters to consult on these matters of mystery. Let them unearth the secrets of the malignant world for themselves.

their grisly studies. Such havens tend to be far from prying or mortal eyes, beneath places like cemeteries, mausoleums, morgues and slaughterhouses.

Background: The backgrounds of those who become Harbingers of Skulls is unknown — it is believed that the bloodline has not Embraced since its introduction to the Sabbat. If this is true, murmur the young members of the sect, the Harbingers must be ancient, accomplished and critical, as they seem not to deem children of the modern nights worthy of their brand of Caine's curse.

Character Creation: Harbingers of Skulls have morbid concepts, many of which are archaic or foreign to the modern nights. The bloodline favors Mental Attributes and Knowledges, and its members cultivate numerous Backgrounds. Few Harbingers deign to follow the tenets of Humanity; they are more frequently attuned to the Path of Death and the Soul or some bizarre variant of the Giovanni's Path of the Bones.

Clan Disciplines: Auspex, Fortitude, Necromancy

Stereotypes

Camarilla: It is a shame how these children sing and dance as the very Ancients they stubbornly ignore pull their invisible strings.

Sabbat: As a vehicle of vengeance, the Sword of Caine is an admirable vehicle. As for it's intended purpose, the Sabbat is a laughingstock.

The View From Without
The Camarilla
What the hell are you talking about?
— Dennis Rundgren, Ventrue broker
The Sabbat
I don't like them. I've already fucked up dying once. I don't want to see what lies in store if they find me when I do it again.
— Rooster, Brujah *antitribu* fixer
The Independents
Oh, shi—
— Andreas Niccolo Giovanni, deceased

Weaknesses: Regardless of the quantity of blood a Harbinger of Skulls consumes, her skin maintains a deathly pallor. Additionally, the Harbingers' skin shrinks to make these Cainites appear skeletal, with bony limbs and faces frozen into an immortal death's grin. Because of this decidedly unwholesome and morbid visage, Harbingers of Skulls have Appearance Traits of zero. All Social rolls involving the Appearance Trait automatically fail for Harbingers of Skulls.

Organization: The Harbingers of Skulls have little organization, and most eschew social company, preferring to be left alone to study or hatch their plots. They do gather infrequently, but to what purpose has never been confirmed. Vampires outside the Harbingers' circles suspect everything from schemes to bring down the Sabbat from the inside to symposiums on the most recent research involving the lands of the dead. The Harbingers of Skulls do maintain some form of visible hierarchy, however, as evidenced by their masks and rituals. The more esteemed or accomplished members of the bloodline wear much more elaborate masks, and they are ritually acknowledged by lesser Harbingers, though the precise system has eluded onlookers to date.

Quote: *Nothing — nothing — burns as hot as the wound left by the knife of treachery, especially when it has been left to fester for eons.*

KIASYD

The origins of the strange Kiasyd bloodline have been lost to the passage of centuries, but their affection for pomp and their curious powers lead some Cainites to suspect that their roots lie with the Lasombra. The most pervasive theory attributes their creation to unholy experimentation with the blood of the Wild Ones and forbidden deals made with demons. Whatever the truth, the result is one of the strangest consanguinities of vampires in the World of Darkness.

The Kiasyd are scholars and keepers of secrets. They tend to be observers rather than taking an active part in acts such as War Parties. Kiasyd don't like to take physical actions against an opponent, preferring to spar with wits and words instead. They jealously guard their knowledge and their private collections. While a Kiasyd's home is always open to visiting members of the bloodline, all Kiasyd are viciously territorial, and most cities house one member of the bloodline at most. Weirdlings don't like to compete with each other for knowledge. If one encounters two Kiasyd together, it is likely an elder with her childe, who may study with the elder for upward of 50 years. Eventually, however, the time will come when the childe will seek his own haven, almost always in a different community.

The Kiasyd are well known for being very calm and studious. Their *raison d'être* centers around their collections of scrolls, books, spells and vampiric lore piled high on their library shelves. Their unusual stature and unquenchable thirst for knowledge make for very high-stacked shelves indeed.

As to the Kiasyd's membership in the Sabbat, the theories again involve Lasombra influence. Whether the Keepers have struck a bargain with the Kiasyd, trading secrets for protection, or whether their relationship is a more sinister brand of master and servant, few can say. Their inquisitive natures hide devious, twisted personalities, warped by massive amounts of forbidden lore and probably the fae blood that contributed to their initial creation. In fact, some Kiasyd are rumored to be addicted to the blood of the changelings, drawing sustenance only from its magical nourishment rather than the pale, tepid taste of mortal blood. Other Kiasyd are suspected of even more perverse tastes, feeding only while violating their vessels in impotent parodies of sexual ravishment or stealing children away under the light of the full moon to eat their flesh in their own libraries. In the end, all that is truly known of them is that they are enigmas, suffered only for their knowledge.

Nickname: Weirdlings

Appearance: The Kiasyd have retained the unusual beauty of the fae folk. Their skin is a chalky white, which takes on a faint bluish glow in moonlight. Rumor has it that the tone of a Kiasyd's skin is an indication of the age of the vampire, but the Kiasyd are much too polite to talk about themselves, so no one knows for sure. They are willowy and tall — six to seven-and-a-half feet — and they have angular noses, cheekbones and ears. The eyes of Kiasyd have been similarly distorted, showing only inky blots with no discernible whites or pupils. Some Kiasyd prefer to dress in Victorian or goth clothing to reflect their studious, somber mood, much to the amusement of more modernized vampires. Long hair or a bandana, and sunglasses hide their unique appearance from prying eyes.

Haven: Permanent, nondescript havens are important to the Kiasyd. They often seclude

A WORD ON THE KIASYD

Kiasyd interact with others rarely — they are better implemented in a story as wise, eccentric vampires sought out for knowledge than players' characters amid desperate, violent cities where rape and murder sometimes outnumber annual births.

Storytellers should exercise discretion when permitting players to assume Kiasyd roles. Although they are not as disruptive or limiting as some other clans (for players — in the hands of a Storyteller they work fine as dramatic devices), the Kiasyd are content to spend their unlives in research and contemplation, which hardly makes for an exciting chronicle. ("You wake up again. What do you do?" "I read for 300 years.")

Players, here's the usual caveat: Don't pretend your characters know much, if anything, about the Kiasyd.

STEREOTYPES

Camarilla: Are you sure these are vampires you're talking about?

Sabbat: Excess can result in a sickness of the soul. Beware your Beasts, my brothers and sisters, lest you leave the world worse than when you entered it.

THE VIEW FROM WITHOUT

The Camarilla

Ah, yes; I have long wanted to question one of these fey chroniclers.

— Athosides, Tremere archivist

The Sabbat

I don't know what they have to do with the rest of us. Don't they just read and write? That shit's for pussies.

— Joey Two-Cuts, Malkavian *antitribu* renegade

The Independents

You can tell when they craft lies for your sake — their lips move.

— Hesha, Setite

themselves in their havens, whiling away the innumerable hours in study until forced to leave, either due to the curious prying of unwelcome guests, or to the eventually rundown condition of the haven. They often choose a private library, museum, art gallery, historical ruins or catacombs in which to establish havens. Whatever the style, the haven almost invariably has a very large and well-stocked library, and many of the accouterments of genteel "living." Kiasyd pride themselves in being gracious hosts, and some keep vintage vitae for guests.

Background: Kiasyd choose polite and intelligent mortals as progeny. Potential childer are well disciplined in their studies and share the Kiasyd's love of books and curiosity for unearthing new knowledge. Likely choices include librarians, educators, students or museum curators. These childer usually have more professional contacts that personal friends, and they value education and learning above self-gratification.

Character Creation: Most Kiasyd come from scholarly or socialite Concepts, as attractive and studious people draw their attention. Demeanors tend toward the conservative, but their Natures are often vastly different. Mental and Social Attributes are prized, as are Knowledges and Skills. Few Kiasyd have any Backgrounds other than the odd smattering of Resources, Generation and Mentor, as they rarely traffic with mortals to the degree necessary to grow them. Oddly enough, most Kiasyd still cling to the tenets of Humanity.

Clan Disciplines: Dominate, Mytherceria, Obtenebration

Weaknesses: The Kiasyd's shortcoming can be attributed to their mixed blood. Pure iron causes great discomfiture in the Weirdlings. Being in the presence of iron — within a number of yards equal to the Kiasyd's Stamina — raises the Kiasyd's frenzy difficulties by one. Touching it causes an immediate frenzy roll, and wounds caused by iron weapons inflict aggravated damage.

Organization: Weirdlings have a formal, almost Victorian organization, based on numerous distinctions that have meaning only to other Kiasyd. Every 50 years, all Kiasyd attend a formal affair at the haven of a duly-selected member of the bloodline, where they discuss new lore they've unearthed and new mysteries they've unraveled. Very rarely, the Kiasyd invite an outsider or Sabbat pack, who are expected to converse intelligently in the matters the Weirdlings raise. Boorish or obstinate packs are dealt with in appropriately malevolent fashions, from wicked snubbing to unbreakable curses.

Quote: *Be very careful. That's an original Gutenberg Bible you're holding. If you damage it, I shall have no choice but to exact reparations; I doubt you'd live long without your skin.*

MALKAVIAN ANTITRIBU

Cainites are humankind's base nature made flesh, and the Sabbat are Kindred who accept their nature and revel in the power of the Beast. The Malkavian *antitribu*, then, are the Beast unrestrained. While Camarilla Malkavians may instruct or illustrate an idea using their madness, the *antitribu* seem more concerned with spreading madness, much like a disease. If a Malkavian is crazy like a fox, their *antitribu* are rabid foxes.

The Malkavian *antitribu* wield their dementia like double-edged swords. To the *antitribu*, insanity is a weapon, albeit one that hopelessly distorts them. Mastery of its use may take decades, or even centuries. At once completely independent, yet strangely joined to other Freaks by an inscrutable group consciousness, a member of this clan is not easily forgotten — no matter how badly one may wish it so. Malkavian *antitribu* are skilled at psychological abuse. By combining forceful words with subtlety, and the use of trust violated by moments of sheer terror, the Freaks can pry information from the most stoic victim or mortify even the staunchest of captives. It is for this reason the Sabbat hasn't destroyed the clan outright; it's too useful. From the most distinguished archbishop to the lowest ductus, vampires who have dealt with the Malkavian *antitribu* know that they are holding a weapon that may fully intend to annihilate its wielder.

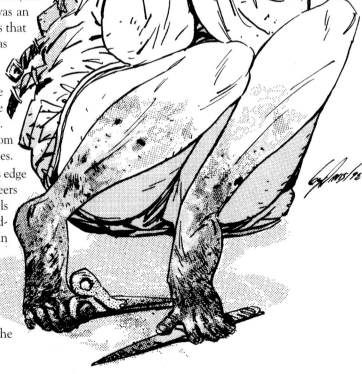

Like other Malkavians, the Malkavian *antitribu* suffer the permanent mark of madness, though few know that they are incurably insane, and many outlets for their "philosophy" exist in the Sabbat. They seem to have the least fear of Final Death of any Cainites, both inside and outside the Sabbat. They make fine soldiers or officers in times of war as well, for they are not afraid to do what is necessary to win. The Malkavian *antitribu* believe that it doesn't really matter who fights the battles, as long as chaos comes out of order, and the cycle of chaos continues.

For a time the Sabbat were unsure of how to deal with the Malkavians in their midst. The Freaks could follow the rules when it served their purposes, but for the most part, they were uncontrollable. Some Sabbat packs kept their Malkavian members locked away, bound in basements and crypts until the sect needed to loose the psychotics on their enemies.

According to popular rumor, it was this lack of respect for their unique insights that promoted the great Malkavian "disease." Starting in the depths of a thought-starved delirium, the seeds of mass psychosis started to form. Maybe it was an attempt by the Malkavian *antitribu* to show the clans that they would not be so easily manipulated. Maybe it was just a neat thing to try at the time. Whatever the case, one thing is certain — the parent clan outside the Sabbat has become "infected." What this means, none outside the Malkavian *antitribu* know, but its possible repercussions set even the stalwart Lasombra on edge. Even this minuscule bit of knowledge comes only from consistent corroboration on the part of worried Cainites.

The Malkavian *antitribu* display a keenly vicious edge to their insanity. Rumors abound of Sabbat packs' seers who divine a War Party's success by reading entrails ripped from a still-living human and of blood-maddened prophets who presage the coming of Gehenna in this, the Time of Thin Blood. The most dangerous of all — the serial killers, suicide cultists and the like — may be "bred" for special missions into fast-held Camarilla territory, sent to spread the madness with which they are burdened, to pave the way for the Great Jyhad.

Nickname: Freaks

Appearance: A Malkavian *antitribu's* mode of dress depends on her dementia, from the very strange to the extremely conservative. A bag lady conspiracy theorist or crack addict holing up in a flop house in stolen thrift-store regalia could be a Malkavian *antitribu*, as could a stressed-out former Wall Street stockbroker in a rumpled Armani suit or a morose housewife in suburbia. Malkavian *antitribu* often have a wild, savage look in their eyes, appearing on the verge of frenzy. Many are poorly groomed, wearing unkempt — or gore-spattered — clothing.

Haven: Better the devil you know when it comes to the Malkavians, reason most Sabbat. Most ducti prefer to keep their crazies where they can keep an eye on them, at communal havens or other acceptable locales. Left to their own devices, the Malkavian *antitribu* establish havens in asylums, the basements of clinics or in transient hostels. A Sabbat Malkavian with multiple personalities may have two or three very different havens to choose from, depending on which personality is dominant when dawn nears.

Background: Inmates of asylums, hospitals for the criminally insane, street bums, lawyers — Malkavian *antitribu* choose almost anyone from any walk of life. While those outside the clan see no rhyme or reason for the selection of childer, the Sabbat Malkavian looks for individuals who are strong enough to bear the liability of their madness, while developing the clan's unique insight.

Character Creation: With the Malkavian *antitribu*, any concept, Nature or Demeanor may be apropos. Mental Attributes are almost always primary. Any Ability category can be primary, depending on the focus of the Cainite's derangement. Common Background Traits include Herd, Contacts and Mentor: A Mentor might be an older Sabbat Malkavian trying to attune the younger one to their own madness, while Contacts include doctors, psychiatrists or police investigators. Few Malkavian *antitribu* can summon the cogency to adopt a Path of Enlightenment, but those who do may most often be found on the Paths of Caine, Power and the Inner Voice or Lilith.

Clan Disciplines: Auspex, Dementation, Obfuscate.

Weaknesses: The Malkavian *antitribu*, like their Camarilla counterparts, are all insane. Many of them are given to bouts of extreme violence with no concern whether the carnage is being directed at packmates or enemies. When a Malkavian character is created, the player must choose a derangement (see **Vampire: The Masquerade** pp. 222-224) for that character at the time of the Embrace. This derangement can be temporarily overcome with Willpower, but can never be permanently "cured" or eliminated.

Additionally, Sabbat Malkavians are often too undisciplined (or too indulgent in their own monstrousness) to resist frenzy. A Sabbat Malkavian's player may never spend a Willpower point to avoid her character's frenzy. As one might think, many Sabbat Malkavians' unlives are short and punctuated by a great deal of violence. Members of this clan often lead very… dynamic… unlives and end up destroying themselves in one form or another before too many nocturnal years pass.

Organization: Sabbat Malkavians claim that no sort of organization exists within their clan. It seems that any "clan" activity that occurs is completely random and coincidental. The Malkavian *antitribu* agree wholeheartedly with this supposition, citing as an example the "infection" of their Camarilla peers. In fact, some Sabbat Malkavians maintain that no such things as Malkavian *antitribu* exist — they profess to be Panders.

Supposedly, the most depraved, dangerous members of the clan are locked well below ground behind strong metal bars, with only a few Sabbat leaders holding the keys for their release. When needed, the rumors say, these prisoners are released to be used as weapons. It is also suspected that the Sabbat Malkavians carry rabies, and create rabid human and animal ghouls.

Quote: *Who would have thought a woman that size would have so much blood in her? Besides God, of course — God knows everything. Can we get someone to clean this up?*

Nosferatu Antitribu

Cainite historians suspect that the Nosferatu *antitribu* joined the Sabbat not out of resentment for their elders, but out of something more malevolent underneath the clan's pustulant façade. Indeed, the Nosferatu *antitribu* seem to be on at least civil terms with their Camarilla counterparts, but this apparent cohesion may simply be due to the fact that they are beyond such things as petty allegiances and concentrate instead on the force that threatens their clan nightly. Of course, the Nosferatu and their *antitribu* are silent when asked about it, which inclines vampires to believe that this matter is theirs alone.

Like Camarilla Nosferatu, the Nosferatu *antitribu* are hideously deformed, damned to an eternal unlife of hiding from or (given their Sabbat tendencies) tormenting mortals. The Creeps make their havens in vast nests of sewers underneath their cities, forming clutches and broods that horrify those who come down to meet with them. Some Nosferatu *antitribu* even revel in their monstrous ugliness, going out of their way to disgust Cainite and kine alike. In this sense, the Sabbat has greatly influenced the Nosferatu *antitribu*; they have given up on all that is human and accepted their damnation with stoic resolve.

Ironically, or perhaps because of their disfigurements, the Nosferatu *antitribu* are perhaps the most humane (if not *human*) of the Sabbat clans. Having transcended the need for ostentatious brutality, the Creeps have come to grips with their monstrousness. They do not caper in blood or senselessly slaughter mobs of kine; rather, a Nosferatu *antitribu's* every move is one of calculated precision, designed to get the exact response she seeks, whether that be respect, fear or understanding. Many young Sabbat consider the Nosferatu *antitribu* soft — until they step into the sewers and see the true malice of the Creeps' black souls.

As the Nosferatu have since time out if mind, the Sabbat Nosferatu traffic in the trade of information. Creeps cultivate vast networks of information and secrets while permitting little of their own dirty laundry to air publicly. Many Sabbat turn to the Nosferatu *antitribu* when seeking information of the common variety (as the clan is not known for too much dabbling in the occult), such as who dueled whom for their position and which of the traveling templars is actually an Inquisitor. "The Creeps know everything," or so goes the sentiment, and the Nosferatu *antitribu* don't dispute this supposition, fading into darkness and conversing with their vermin spies.

More than any other clan, the Nosferatu *antitribu* fear their Antediluvian (whereas other clans may be said to despise their progenitors). To hear a Creep speak, fear is the most sensible emotion when dealing with the Ancients, and only the Nosferatu *antitribu* have enough awareness to realize this. In the grim legends of the clan, the Antediluvian, disgusted by his childer and scorned by Caine, turned loose a great evil on the clan, to absolve them of their heinousness. If this is true, all vampires everywhere should feel a tinge of fear, as whatever it is that hunts these hunters must surely be terrible indeed.

Nickname: Creeps

Appearance: The Nosferatu *antitribu*, like their Camarilla counterparts, are all blighted by the Blood of Caine. They are so unsettling to look on that other considerations such as clothing and grooming habits are secondary — what does it matter whether one wears a designer cocktail dress or a burlap bag if one resembles the twisted, broken bodies left behind in an automobile accident? As such, most Nosferatu *antitribu* dress for comfort, preferring loose shifts, broken-in casual clothes and other leisurely ensembles. Some Nosferatu *antitribu* go to the opposite extreme, however, and affect cutting-edge *couture* or the severe wardrobes of S&M subcultures, to better leave horrid impressions with those who observe them.

Haven: Nosferatu *antitribu* tend to congregate in nests and warrens beneath the cities, where few venture and even fewer return. Despite their great ugliness, Nosferatu *antitribu* do not tend to be morbid, and they eschew the grim surroundings of morgues, graveyards and the like. When Nosferatu *antitribu* reside at a communal pack havens, they tend to take the most isolated and inaccessible portions of it for themselves. Most of their packmates don't mind so much.

Background: The Creeps are hardy survivors, and they are no strangers to derision. They draw their childer from society's castoffs most often, though many still possess some small mean streak and Embrace beautiful or popular individuals out of spite. For some reason, most Nosferatu *antitribu* seem to be male, but what does it matter when one's gender is practically indeterminate?

Character Creation: Nosferatu *antitribu* favor Mental and Physical Attributes, as eking out an existence among the rats and refuse requires sense and prowess. Most also prefer Talents, though tales of wise and scholarly Creeps who have studied Knowledges and can provide the answers to vexing questions are on the rise. Popular Backgrounds include Contacts, Generation, Resources and animal Retainers. Most young Nosferatu *antitribu* still maintain their Humanity, but most older members of the clan adopt Paths of Enlightenment such as the Path of the Feral Heart, the Path of Power and the Inner Voice, the Path of Cathari and the Path of Caine. There have been no reports of any Nosferatu *antitribu* following the Path of Lilith.

STEREOTYPES

Camarilla: Why bother?

Sabbat: I'd say, "Why bother?" here, too, but some smartass would sell me to the Inquisition or the high-and-mighty Black Hand.

THE VIEW FROM WITHOUT

The Camarilla

There's no such thing as Nosferatu *antitribu*. We're all hiding from the same mad gods.

— Peter the Cockroach, Nosferatu tunnel-digger

The Sabbat

They know more than they pretend to, which is about half as much as we give them credit for.

— Alexei Guylaine, Sabbat templar

The Independents

How do they tell each other apart from the regular ones? Secret invisible forehead tattoos?

— Vance Rosselini, Giovanni diplomat

Clan Disciplines: Animalism, Obfuscate, Potence

Weaknesses: Given their startling deformations, all Nosferatu *antitribu* have Appearance Traits of zero. This Trait may never be increased, though it may sometimes be hidden by disguise or magical means. Most Social rolls, with the exception of such things as intimidation or inflicting terror, fail automatically.

Organization: Nosferatu *antitribu* recognize age and accomplishment, often putting the needs of their clan or individual members before the needs of the Sabbat. Still, they are upstanding members of the sect, and they rarely do things half-assed. Since they often share havens, the Nosferatu *antitribu* have little need for formal clan convocations or self-important meetings. Most Creeps simply go about their business and keep others out of it while learning as much about others as they can.

Quote: *Don't ask me why I'm looking over my shoulder, girlie; that's my fucking business. Now do you want dirt on the bishop or not? If you don't, I'm sure the bishop wants dirt on you.*

PANDERS

Although not truly a clan in the strictest sense of the word (as they have no progenitor from the Third Generation), the Panders have made much of the Sabbat's egalitarian society, carving a niche of respectability for themselves in spite of their bastard pedigree. Like the Caitiff — which, for all practical purposes, they are — the Panders have no formal, recognized lineage. Any vampire who joins the Sabbat and doesn't know what clan she is becomes a Pander, as do those childer Embraced by established Panders. The group consists of a wide variety of Cainites, most of whom are young and untested. It should be noted, however, that Panders are True Sabbat, not just a dumping ground for rejected or unproved vampires of other clans.

The Panders arose in the aftermath of the most recent Sabbat civil war, during the late 1950s. A clanless vampire known as Joseph Pander united the clanless Sabbat under his own banner and led them against the Moderate faction at the behest of several key Lasombra and Tzimisce. Impressed with his efforts, the elders of the Sabbat rewarded the sect-loyal Panders with a formal recognition, which immediately touched off a powderkeg of ill response from more "legitimate" clans. In the end, though, the Panders won out, earning recognition time and again, through bloodshed and diplomacy. Joseph Pander still exists in the modern nights, but rumors of assassination attempts spurred by disapproving elders run rampant through the Mutts' circles.

Of course, the Panders are loose cannons and X-factors, the "rebels of a rebellious sect." Lasombra in the modern nights consider them threats to security, worrying that their lack of cohesion or millennia of tradition might make them unpredictable. The Panders understand their own position, though, and they accept their cannon-fodder role with resolve. Indeed, at any Sabbat siege, the front line is most often composed of Panders out to prove themselves. As cunning as any Lasombra and as brutal as any Brujah *antitribu*, the Panders do what needs to be done for the good of the sect.

Panders lack the sophistication and the years of formalization held by the other clans; they truly are a motley bunch of rogues and thugs. Unlike some of the other clans, however, they have the Sabbat at heart, and their terrible escapades are often fronts for conquest "for the good of the Sword of Caine!"

With the sect's good-faith gesture in recognizing the Panders, it has earned an ally for the entirety of its existence, but the Panders are still the low Cainites on the totem pole. The Mutts almost invariably draw the worst duties, the most dangerous missions and the riskiest *ritae*, all because they're still the newest and least established. Those Panders who are aware enough, accept this "honor" as a badge of courage, while the dimmer ones simply do what they're told in hopes of getting to feed first from the pack's kills. It is this reason — this devout and reckless drive to get the job done — that has paid off for the Panders, and they have grown in number and power because of it.

Nickname: Mutts

Appearance: Most Panders are young (at least in terms of Cainite age), and they affect contemporary styles. Because of their rebellious natures and counterculture origins, many Panders wear styles adopted by "rebel" cultures — biker leathers, punk mohawks, goth makeup, skinhead boots or gang colors. In fact, the Panders sometimes seem frozen in the mindset they held at the time of their Embrace, wearing styles years, if not decades, out of mortal fashion. This is less likely a counter-fashion statement than it is a simple lack of awareness that times have changed. Many elders smirk at this, realizing that even the youngest of vampires becomes a static individual, much like themselves, who sometimes continue to wear the styles popular in their own mortal days.

Haven: Panders often make their havens wherever the pack does, and they are frequently charged with the haven's maintenance if no ghoul exists to take care of it. Panders almost never maintain private havens, finding some security in being with the pack at all times. The Mutts also prefer havens with some connection to their lives before becoming vampires—motorcycle mechanic shops, crackhouses, heroin dens, nightclubs and the like.

Background: Panders generally Embrace from the low levels of society, recruiting from the miscreants and excitable rebels who make excellent fodder for the Sabbat's war efforts. A number of true psychotics and sociopaths have made their way into the Panders' ranks, but these individuals often die merciful deaths among the fires of the sieges. Still, the Panders are hardly a stable bloodline, populated by those too angry with society at large (for whatever reason) to become a useful part of it.

Character Creation: Panders have violent or rebellious concepts, and they often possess strongly individualistic Natures (though there are a fair share of Conformists who simply want to belong). Demeanors can be literally anything. Physical Attributes, Talents and Skills are the most popular among the Panders, and few have much in the way of Backgrounds. Most Panders still cling to their Humanity, but a few of the more critical thinkers among the Mutts sometimes adopt the Path of Cathari or the Path of Honorable Accord.

Clan Disciplines: None. Like non-Sabbat Caitiff, Panders may take any Disciplines they want (subject to Storyteller approval). Additionally, Panders increase their Disciplines with adjusted experience costs, just as Caitiff do (see **Vampire: The Masquerade**, page 143).

Weaknesses: Panders have no inherent, Blood-bestowed weakness. Note, however, that the Panders are given only grudging respect, and they generally get stuck with the Sabbat's shit work. Also, no Pander may begin the game at better than Ninth generation (though they may increase this via diablerie or other means during the game).

Organization: The organization of the Panders depends largely on their pack. Some all-Panders packs have ganglike structures, or are organized like skinhead chapters. Others have no formal structure; they simply resemble gatherings of subcultures. When Panders become part of cosmopolitan packs, they often find themselves low in the ranks. Most Panders roughly acknowledge Joseph Pander, though many believe his time has past and that the bloodline should just get on with the business of being vampires.

Quote: *I'm not interested in your holier-than-thou shtick. I have business to do, and if you're not with me, you're against me. And I break those who stand against me.*

RAVNOS ANTITRIBU

There is a saying among the Sabbat that it might be better to deal with the Devil himself than to bargain with a Ravnos *antitribu*. You won't get the better of either of them.

In the forgotten nights of history, likely some time after the Convention of Thorns, a faction of the Ravnos split from their Gypsy heritage after discovering the Sabbat. Although the Sabbat had a grandiose ideology behind it, these separatist Ravnos found themselves more enamored of the "nightlives" these vampires led. They didn't confound themselves with complex Hindu *dharma* riddles, nor did they subvert their bestial natures. The Sabbat was composed of vampires through and through, and it offered many possibilities for the malicious deceit and wanderlust of these young defectors, who became the first Ravnos *antitribu*.

Since then, the Sabbat Ravnos have had little to do with the sect, serving it when it's convenient, and otherwise taking advantage of the lack of communication presented by constant travel. Some wonder why they bother with sect allegiance at all, but when a piece of Rogue-discovered information turns the tide in a siege or an enterprising Ravnos *antitribu* manages to seduce a Camarilla prince's progeny, all these fears evaporate. It would seem the Ravnos *antitribu* have turned their backs on their original clan, if only to be free of their elders' overbearing presence. And such is the nature of the Sabbat.

The nomadic existence of most Sabbat packs suits the Ravnos *antitribu* quite well. The idea of a permanent haven is almost anathema to the Rogues, who like nothing better than to serve their pack by setting up a temporary base to scout enemy territory, knowing that they can pull up stakes and move locations whenever the pack's needs change. Such pilgrimage is their preference in the modern nights, but many suspect that its roots go much deeper, possibly stemming from the prejudices of race and culture that victimized the Ravnos *antitribu*'s human ancestors, and the centuries they spent fleeing persecution. A Sabbat Ravnos is also less likely to feel

bored or stagnant than his independent counterparts, as he rarely supports the complex philosophies they do.

While the average Rogue possesses a rakish charm that may win her a temporary companion or two, the Ravnos *antitribu* has virtually no mortal allies she can rely on with regularity. Ravnos are very much the "love them and leave them" type. They use their smooth talents with either sex both for personal pleasure and information-gathering.

Sect notwithstanding, the Ravnos *antitribu* have a traditional code of conduct for dealing with their clanmates. This code may be difficult for those outside the clan to follow, but nonetheless, a Ravnos' word to his pack is his law. They follow the "spit and shake" rule of all Ravnos on verbal agreements, but the Rogues take this one step further. If a Sabbat member wants an agreement in writing, it will be signed in blood, the pen dipped in an open wound on the Ravnos' own arm. This binding in blood is as strong as the Vaulderie to the Sabbat Ravnos, and it can be broken only by Final Death. Violating the code costs the perpetrator a considerable loss of face with other Ravnos, which has been adopted by the sect at large. Few Sabbat Ravnos feel comfortable giving this guarantee to Sabbat members outside their clan, and most do get quite indignant should the other party suggest it.

Nickname: Rogues

Appearance: Ravnos of the Sabbat generally have swarthy, Romantic good looks. They often have black hair, dark eyes and olive complexions. When on the road, they dress in a functional, nondescript manner — jeans, T-shirts and riding leathers for both men and women — so as not to draw attention to themselves when in enemy territory. When they set up temporary camps or become part of founded covens, however, they tend to dress with a bit more flash. Male and female Ravnos *antitribu* alike wear bright colors, often ornamented with jewelry or other accessories.

Haven: Hanging their hat wherever the pack pleases works just fine for the Ravnos *antitribu*. They hole up wherever and whenever the need arises, in whatever accommodations are available at the time. If one chooses a permanent haven, he may appropriate a crumbling old mansion, plantation manor or similar structure, or he may prefer a simple, easily portable affair for ease in travel. Ravnos *antitribu* tend not to keep too many personal items — though they may steal, trade for and otherwise come into possessions on the road, Rogues rarely keep anything for very long. The challenge is in the acquisition, not the ownership.

Background: Sabbat Ravnos look to the decadent underbelly of humankind for their childer. Any young, charismatic individual with a penchant for deception may make a noteworthy Ravnos *antitribu*. A quick wit and callous disregard for the feelings and property of others are key elements in the choosing of someone to Embrace. Much of their mortal Gypsy blood has been forfeit, and the Ravnos *antitribu* are more a clan in the Cainite sense than a vampiric outgrowth of the mortal Rom families: Most Rogues are *gorgio* (non-Gypsies), especially in the United States and South America.

Character Creation: The Ravnos *antitribu* generally have loner, drifter or entertainer concepts, though a great many are criminals as well. They may have any Nature, usually juxtaposed with a radically different Demeanor (to keep others guessing). Social and Mental Attributes are most common, usually with Physical Attributes as secondary, to weather the hardships of the road. Most Ravnos *antitribu* cultivate Skills over Talents and Knowledges, and few have much use for Backgrounds beyond the odd Contact or Ally. Many Ravnos *antitribu* follow the Path of Cathari, the Path of Caine and the Path of Death and the Soul, though some retain Humanity indefinitely.

Clan Disciplines: Animalism, Chimerstry, Fortitude

STEREOTYPES

Camarilla: Why would one suffer the pain of rebirth only to shackle himself to the passions of another?

Sabbat: We have an arrangement: We each give each other what we get in return — very little.

THE VIEW FROM WITHOUT

The Camarilla

These worthless vagrants are the only thing that comes to mind when I am asked, "What is worse than a Ravnos?"

— Heather Dowd, Brujah revolutionary

The Sabbat

They don't seem to care much for the sect, but their word is their honor.

— Dash, nomadic Sabbat priest

The Independents

I'd sooner invite an Irishman into my haven.

— Giancarlo Giovanni

Weaknesses: Like their independent siblings, the Ravnos *antitribu* have had a long history of catering to their increasingly depraved whims. Each Rogue specializes in an area of vice in which she is particularly interested, and she takes every opportunity for practice sessions. In fact, she must make a Self-Control roll (difficulty 6) to resist her vice when given the chance to indulge it. The player decides what type of "crime" the character will be addicted to during character creation. It could be pickpocketing, con games, carjacking, murder or any other concept the player and Storyteller can agree on.

Organization: The Ravnos *antitribu* have little formal organization, instead making their own ways on the interstates at night. Rogues do respect skill and prowess, however, and when Ravnos *antitribu* gather, they tell tales of their own accomplishments, of Lupines baited or slain, and grand schemes elaborately concocted and flawlessly executed. As is to be expected, of course, many of these tales are lies or exaggerations, but storytelling is often prized as much as the deed itself.

Ravnos *antitribu* deal with Ravnos and Gypsies with great difficulty, showing a particular hatred for those of Romany descent. Many suspect that the clan had long been shunned by the vampires and Gypsy folk of purer blood, treating the Rogues as inferior, and the Ravnos *antitribu* have finally decided to return the antipathy. Ravnos *antitribu* extend a "thieves' honor" to Sabbat Ravnos, and all other members of the sect, believing that harming one's own brothers and sisters can lead only to another schism, which would leave the Rogues utterly alone.

Quote: *This is what the Sabbat is all about — the freedom to roam the highways, feed wherever I will and take what catches my fancy. This is the best unlife could hope to be, and I would proudly die defending it. You gotta die for your own, though. You're not my responsibility.*

SALUBRI ANTITRIBU

The tumultuous approach of Gehenna has wrought many strange events in the modern nights, not the least of which is the introduction of the Salubri to the Sabbat. While the mainstream Salubri suffer reputations as soul-stealers and diablerists, the Salubri *antitribu* have put the nigh-incomprehensible practices of that bloodline behind them. With a rage borne of centuries of persecution, the Salubri *antitribu* have developed a consuming hatred for the Camarilla and joined forces with the Sabbat to bring about its destruction.

The Salubri *antitribu* have existed among the Sabbat for a mere handful of nights, and probably little before that. During this time, however, they have made names for themselves as vicious opponents of the Camarilla, whom they blame for the destruction of some powerful vampire somewhere back in their lineage, whose name has been forgotten in the modern nights. They have little love for the philosophy of the Sabbat, choosing to ally themselves with the sect out of martial necessity rather than subscription to the grand scheme. The Sabbat will take any soldiers they can get, however, and the Salubri *antitribu* know how strongly the Sabbat despises the Camarilla.

The Sabbat Salubri have made bold claims as to their effectiveness, saying that they have destroyed the cabal of sorcerers who brought about their bloodline hero's demise. (The name Salubri *antitribu* is a bit of a misnomer, as the Salubri do not have a Third Generation progenitor, but this matter is one of semantics and — if brought to the Furies' attention — histrionics.) They profess to have taken the war to the Camarilla, which they claim has hunted and persecuted them for close to a millennium. Spurred on by ven-geance, Salubri *antitribu* have little time to pursue the rumors of Golconda put forth by the cowards of the bloodline from which they split. Indeed, non-Sabbat Salubri supposedly give themselves up when they Embrace a new childe, sacrificing themselves so that the childe may have every advantage she can get. This "sacrificial lamb" metaphor offers little to the Salubri *antitribu*, who reason that the flawed shall fall in battle while the strong uphold the clan's private Jyhad.

The Salubri *antitribu* serve the Sabbat as reluctant warriors, easily distracted by their own internal quests. The rest of the Sabbat considers them anomalies, useful allies in times of war, but intolerable proselytizers when not in combat. To the Sabbat Salubri, this is fine — unlife is a hell of endless torment, ameliorated only by glorious death or victory in battle.

Nickname: Furies

Appearance: The Furies wear motley assemblies of piecemeal "armor," to protect them in their personal crusade against the Camarilla. They may look like modern leper mercenaries, bedecked in loosely assembled scraps of sheet metal and heavy padding, or they may be grim knights, resplendent in riot gear, carrying an archaic sword at the ready. Whatever form they take, Salubri *antitribu* look like they mean business, and few want to stand in their way.

All Salubri *antitribu* acquire a mysterious third eye in the center of their foreheads when they develop the second level of their Discipline, Valeren, much like the independent Salubri bloodline. Unlike other Salubri, the Sabbat Salubri often don't bother to hide this oddity, displaying it proudly as a herald of the destruction that awaits their enemies.

Haven: Salubri *antitribu* generally stay in the same havens as their packs. Many Furies keep their own private havens in addition to those of the pack, however, in the cellars of museums, libraries, hospitals and funeral parlors. These places are often ramshackle, secondary affairs, used more as boltholes or weapons caches than chambers in which to spend the innumerable nights of immortality.

Background: The Sabbat Salubri choose their progeny carefully, and they never use the Mass Embrace technique so popular during sieges and crusades. They choose individuals with strong wills, passion and the drive to do whatever needs to be done. Becoming a Salubri *antitribu* is far beyond the scope of most mortals' philosophies, however, as their plight has significance only to other vampires. As such, most new Salubri *antitribu* spend many of their early nights being indoctrinated by their sires, who couch their lessons in the forms of prophecies and parables of holy war. Only when the childe has been completely fired up and instilled with a hatred for all things Camarilla is she turned loose on her unsuspecting foes.

Character Creation: Furies share no Traits universally, though many play up loner or soldier concepts. Headstrong Natures and Demeanors such as Director, Fanatic, Bravo and Monster are common. Salubri *antitribu* prefer Physical Attributes and Skills, and they develop few Backgrounds other than Resources and Allies. Those Salubri *antitribu* who exist long enough to adopt more vampiric codes of ethics (rare, in light of their recent establishment) usually support the Path of Caine, the Path of Honorable Accord and the Path of Power and the Inner Voice.

Clan Disciplines: Auspex, Fortitude, Valeren

Weaknesses: Vitae taken outside the heat of passion offers no sustenance to the Salubri *antitribu*, nor does blood given freely. Unless the Fury takes blood by force, drinks in the throes of undead passion or slakes her thirst on a fallen foe, any blood points she consumes do not replenish her blood pool. Additionally, no Salubri *antitribu* may start the game lower than Tenth Generation or higher than Twelfth Gen-

eration, as the bloodline's vitae has yet to spread across the broader spectrum of Cainite potency.

Organization: The Sabbat Salubri organize themselves in a manner similar to the knightly orders of ages past. The bloodline recognizes foes killed, vampires diablerized and secrets uncovered in its quest to avenge the destruction of Saulot and the bloodline in its place of prominence. The eldest Salubri *antitribu* is Adonai, a vampire of the Seventh Generation, who awards title and honor to accomplished Furies in an annual ceremony during the *Palla Grande*. It is assumed that fewer than 100 of these vampires exist, and they tend to fall in battle frequently, as their fervor is not always a match for the sheer power of elder Cainites.

Quote: *I have the power of gods in my veins. You have tattoos, a velvet vest, a top hat and a cane. Now get the fuck out of my way, little "vampire," or I'll cleave you in twain.*

Serpents of the Light

The Serpents of the Light is an independent and proudly heretical sect of the Followers of Set. Its pride lies within its adopted independence from the Setites; the Serpents have no affiliation with their parent clan. While many Setites trace their history to ancient Egypt, the Serpents claim they originated in the West Indies.

The Serpents of the Light came into being when the Sabbat moved into Haiti in the 1960s. Before then, the group that became the Serpents may have been a rogue cult of Setites, studying *voodoun* and how its mysticism could be used to its undead advantage. Until the 1970s, the Sabbat was too disorganized to pay much attention to the Caribbean, despite some degree of presence there — Sabbat activity simply lay dormant. In fact, the Sword of Caine had no idea that this "lost tribe" of Setites even existed in Haiti. Once the sect became aware of the cult, however, the Sabbat recognized the ruthless strength in the group and gave protection to it in its infancy. It is possible that the first Serpents were younger Setites, who agreed with the political philosophy of the Sabbat. When the news of the Sabbat's discovery reached the Setites' ears, their elders forbade their childer's interaction with the Sword of Caine. Citing the Sabbat's "intent to destroy the god-king," they sent emissaries to Haiti who insisted that the cult disassociate itself from the Sabbat.

The splinter sect, out of habit, vampiric wile or otherwise, chose to ignore their elders, and they sought asylum in the ranks of the Sabbat. The rift grew nightly, until the Serpents of Light proclaimed total independence from the Followers of Set. This schism may have been achieved by experimenting with their ophidian Discipline and the local mysticism of the Caribbean. The modern Serpents recognize that they would have been crushed by the Setites if not for the Sabbat's intervention, and they give their undivided loyalty to the Sabbat cause.

Because the Serpents chose to ally with the Sabbat, they have earned the enmity of the Followers of Set, and vice versa. Hatred between these two now-separate bloodlines runs deep, and the Setites consider the Serpents traitors to their clan. Indeed, the Serpents of the Light consider Followers of Set to be abominations intent on destroying the world via the resurrection of their undead vampire god. The two groups spare no effort in antagonizing each other, playing out a deadly holy war across the distance of continents. Serpents of the Light also oppose the other Antediluvians for similar reasons, citing a Haitian Voodoo prophecy similar to the Gehenna foretold in the *Book of Nod*. As Sabbat, their ideology fits perfectly.

Manipulation by seduction is the tool of choice for the Serpents of Light, who play a dangerous game of attack and counterattack against their Setite rivals with mortal pawns. Members of the bloodline wield the weapons of addiction and decay. They are expert at discovering a target's weakness, and using that tool — be it drugs, sex, power or whatever — to gain control of the target. They relish the opportunity to bring down a prince's city from the inside out, like any dedicated Sabbat. A few Serpents set loose in a major metropolis can magnify the drug-trade substantially, entice many innocent victims into prostitution, and much more. They prefer to operate behind the scenes, extending their control through human and Cainite underlings, without becoming an obvious target themselves. Rooting out a Serpent of the Light from a city is much like peeling an onion — you must slice away many layers before you get to the core. They maintain an attitude of "fight fire with fire" when it comes to foiling the plans of the Setites and, to a lesser degree, the Camarilla.

Elder Cobras instill a great loyalty in their childer from the night of their Embrace. The Serpents of the Light compare their struggle to split from the Followers of Set to the history of their West Indian roots. Much of their speech when conversing with each other occurs in Haitian patois and Voodoo references. While they take a sybaritic pleasure in the Jyhad between Sabbat and Camarilla and make superb espionage agents for the Sabbat, their loyalty remains with their patron cult above all. A Serpent of the Light serves the need of her particular chapter of the cult she belonged to before her Embrace above the needs of the Sabbat.

Nickname: Cobras

Appearance: The Serpents of the Light wear clothing derived from their peculiar brand of Cainite *voodoun*. They select colors based on the symbolism of their faith; colors tie the Cobra to certain spirit *loas*. White follows the *loa* of wisdom, blue the *loa* of harmony, red the *loa* of war, black the *loa* of death and so on. Serpents mix these colors into their everyday clothing, even combining them into patterns in some cases. When they have no need to "blend in" with non-Serpent cultures, they adopt traditional Haitian dress, including soft caftans and linen blouses.

Haven: Members of this clan prefer structures near water to pass the daylight hours, trusting the flow of water to ward off the curse-*loas* of Set. They sleep with their pack when possible, preferring to at least be in a place where they can hear moving water or waves. They decorate their havens in many different ways, but often favor Caribbean motifs with macabre wood carvings, metalwork and batik wall-hangings. Many Serpents of the Light also keep secret havens, where they erect altars to their spirit guides.

Background: The Serpents of the Light often choose Haitian or North African individuals as clan members, if it is practical. Otherwise, anyone can serve the Serpents of Light, as long as they exhibit high intelligence, an aggressive bent and a willingness to learn. All Serpents of the Light must study and practice Voodoo theology, or some form of occultism. The clan has been growing in strength and number, due to its desire to become a power-player in the Sabbat.

Character Creation: Serpents of the Light may have any concept, but they often have priestly, occult or religious inclinations. Natures tend to be self-serving, though Demeanors reflect a feigned altruism. Social Attributes are most

often primary, followed closely by Mental Attributes. Knowledges and Talents are equally prized. The Cobras frequently entwine themselves with the local mortal cultures, developing strong Backgrounds in Allies, Contacts, Influence and Resources. Some Serpents of the Light learn Necromancy or Thaumaturgy, specializing in the Bone Path and Spirit Manipulation. Many Serpents of the Light also find purpose and stability on the Path of Power and the Inner Voice, as well as the Path of Lilith.

Clan Disciplines: Obfuscate, Presence, Serpentis.

Weaknesses: The Serpents of the Light share the same weakness as the Followers of Set. They both hail from primordial darkness, and thus they react identically severely to light. Serpents suffer two additional health levels of damage when wounded by sunlight. Serpents of the Light also subtract one die from all dice pools when subjected to particularly bright light, artificial or otherwise (sunlight, spotlights, chemical flares, etc.).

Organization: Knowledge is strength, and the Cobras recognize this principle. They participate in all Sabbat pack meetings and *ritae*, sometimes organizing pack actions, especially War Parties and scouting sorties. They also maintain a loose communications network among their clan members, to stay informed about Sabbat and personal clan activities.

Quote: *Your trial is hopeless. Only with the aid of my loa can you hope to survive. Here; carry this with you. It will keep the eyes of the hungry dead from seeing you and alert you to the barrows where the still-living are buried.*

TOREADOR ANTITRIBU

The Toreador *antitribu* were instrumental in the formation of the Sabbat, and much of what came out of the Convention of Thorns did so under the direction of Toreador anarchs who would later guide the sect. With the organizational efforts of the Lasombra and Tzimisce, and a few Ventrue *antitribu*, the Toreador created much of the sect's structure, as well as codifying many of the sect's beliefs. Indeed, the early, anarchic nights of the sect may have seen its destruction, "if not for the masterful misdirection of our esteemed *artistes*."

In the modern nights, the Toreador *antitribu* have similar interests as their Camarilla siblings, only their appreciation for the aesthetic has grown to include pain, savagery, cruelty and depravity. How is a rose, sonnet or portrait any more enrapturing than a masterfully executed flaying, reason the Toreador *antitribu*? What is beauty, if not subjective?

The Perverts' talent for torture rivals even the Tzimisce in pain and duration. Young clan members begin on human subjects, while their elders graduate to° other° subjects. Some of the more practiced members have actually gotten their art introduced into Camarilla salons and Elysia, where they have garnered much Cainite support, to the dismay of the vampires whose bastions have been violated. In the 1980s, an anonymous artist showed "Woman's Submission at the Hands of Man" through the medium of a dress made of raw meat. This exhibit toured several Camarilla-held national galleries and made headlines in every city it visited. No one ever questioned the type of meat used, nor the method of creating the sculpture.

Tattoos, scarification and body piercing among Toreador *antitribu* provide another opportunity as well — one to which very few members inside the Sabbat (and none outside) are privy. The artists have created their own language of symbols and codes, which they use to pass information to each other for their own benefit and the benefit of the pack. A certain lattice of keloids or a particular stone in a nose-stud can provide vital information to those pack members who can read the hidden message. Tattoos and piercings heal over and force themselves out of Vampire bodies unless they existed before the Embrace: Toreador *antitribu* can send different messages each night, relishing the exquisite pain of the process every time they do so.

Of all the Sabbat clans, the Toreador *antitribu* interact most frequently with mortals. They move in the most glamorous mortal circles, plying their trade in art and society, feeding as they will from the rich and indolent. Like the Toreador of the Camarilla, the Sabbat Toreador are lethal social butterflies, moving visibly yet mysteriously through mortal circles. Little do their sycophants and admirers know that behind every invitation, innuendo and expression lies the horror of the Sabbat.

Nickname: Perverts, Pervs

Appearance: Most Toreador *antitribu* are attractive — often horribly so — or at least flamboyant. They dress in the latest and most blatant fashions, and most have flashy jewelry in their piercings or intricate tattoos. They sport the latest hairstyles, listen to newest music, and speak the coolest street lingo. They're the people everyone else aspires to be — on the surface.

Haven: Toreador *antitribu* often keep lofts or apartments in the part of town known for its fashions, fine food and scintillating conversation. In cities where the Sabbat is the prominent influence, they mingle with the high-class "beautiful people," attending theater premieres, art exhibits and private balls, and keeping havens in the heart of the hip neighborhoods. If a Toreador must spend time in a communal pack haven, it is usually because he has been asked to organize an upcoming event for the Sabbat. Not that Sabbat Toreador mind their packmates, necessarily; they just don't want to share the attention or be seen someplace gauche.

Background: Toreador *antitribu* seem to select childer from a wider range than their Camarilla counterparts. They Embrace from the expected ranks of artists, writers and creative types, but they also select childer from the medical profession or the military — anyone they feel practices their talent in an exemplary fashion. Often they watch their potential victims for months or even years, to ensure that they have the talent and ability to sustain their fellow clanmates' interest and be useful to the pack at large. Toreador *antitribu* do not choose shallow childer, in spite of the image they present, and more than one arrogant Sabbat has learned painfully that the Pervs are not the "limp-wristed art fags and rotten cheerleaders" he thought they were. Allowing one's rivals to underestimate one is the surest way to maintain the upper hand, as many vampires know too well.

Character Creation: Sabbat Toreador usually have artist, entertainer or dilettante concepts, unless they are not of the traditional creative upbringings. They have flamboyant Demeanors and unique Natures, the latter of which tend to be selfish, vain or otherwise self-interested. Social Attributes are almost always primary, with a secondary focus on Mental Attributes. Talents and Skills take precedence over Knowledges, as the Perverts prefer to *do* rather than *know*. Common Background Traits include Contacts, Fame, Herd, Resources, Retainers and Sabbat Status. Toreador *antitribu* often maintain their Humanity for a few years, but they almost always "transcend" into the beliefs of the Path of Death and the Soul, the Path of Cathari or the Path of Power and the Inner Voice.

Clan Disciplines: Auspex, Celerity, Presence.

Weaknesses: The Toreador *antitribu* once possessed the same flaw as their non-Sabbat counterparts, though their indulgence in blood-games and twisted passions has warped

this failing somewhat. While they once found beauty even in extreme violence or sadism, they have since become needlessly cruel, inflicting their own viciousness on those around them. If presented with an ample opportunity (feeding, a rival embarrassing herself, torturing a captive Cainite), a Toreador *antitribu* will inflict physical or emotional pain on her subject more often than not. When confronted with such a situation, the player must roll the vampire's Self-Control (difficulty 6) or spend a Willpower point. If the roll fails or the player refuses to spend a point (which must be declared before the roll is made, as leaving things to fate has its consequences), the character must indulge her need to "act out" against the subject. Whether this acting out is as simple as a devastating remark or as base as cutting the victim's thumbs off is up to the vampire in question, and is a darkness best explored by the player.

Organization: The Sabbat Toreador have their own division between poseurs and artistes, but no one on the outside can figure out exactly what it is. Most serve themselves first, the Sabbat second and their clan third, though some forego the glory of the sect for the vanity of the clan. Toreador *antitribu* interact with greater ease than most Sabbat do with mortals, and some distorted Perverts prefer kine company to Cainites. Most Toreador *antitribu* have some instrumental role in the *ritae* of the *Palla Grande* and *Festivo dello Estinto*.

Quote: *Really, darling, you must not squirm so. It spoils the overall effect.*

VENTRUE ANTITRIBU

Long ago, before the Sabbat and Camarilla existed, before the Anarch Revolt and before the Lasombra slew their Ancient and drank his precious vitae, the Ventrue were knights and lords, masters of their manors. After the powderkeg of the Anarch Revolt and Tyler's bold attack of Hardestadt the Elder came the Renaissance, and the Ventrue changed with the times. Driven by greed and power-lust, the Ventrue shifted tack. Rather than maintain their noble status, they pursued greater interests in the merchant class. Leaving behind the duty of nobility and the divine right of kings, the Ventrue surrounded themselves with excess and filthy lucre.

So believe the Ventrue *antitribu*. The few Ventrue anarchs who had originally opposed their elders' iron-fisted rule had grown frustrated with the static reins of power held by the aged Blue Bloods. As mortal currents changed, these elder powers still clenched tightly to their empires, forever preventing younger and more able Ventrue from taking their rightful places. By selling themselves, the Ventrue had given up true nobility. For the Ventrue anarchs, their leaders had failed, tempted by material wealth and corrupted by power. In proclaiming themselves *antitribu*, the Ventrue who joined the Sabbat carved for themselves a unique niche that occupies their valorous hearts to this very night.

The Ventrue *antitribu* practice a chivalrous *noblesse oblige*. They are grim knights and paladins, sworn to combat the Antediluvians and bring down the degenerate Camarilla. Although their aims may seem noble in comparison to the hellish violence of the Sabbat, they support the Sword of Caine to the bitter end. The Ventrue know, as their preserved medieval chronicles attest, that Gehenna lurks just around the corner. In these final nights of chaos and Thin Blood, the only way to avert the impending Armageddon is to pull it out by the roots. Cainites and kine alike serve the Antediluvians unknowingly, and only those with the drive to fight their secret masters shall survive past the rain of fire and blood. The Ventrue *antitribu* have pledged to do just this.

Ventrue *antitribu* see their Camarilla counterparts as failures, and they have assumed the roles of the race of Cainites' saviors to atone for this. They believe mortals to be ignorant cattle, sufficient only for food and service to their terrible vampire lords. The world will become a hell, surely, but Cainites, as tools of God's vengeance and the Devil's will, are fit to be rulers of the Children of Seth. To accept anything else is to take the path of the disgraced Ventrue of the Camarilla, and the Sabbat Ventrue are not willing to accept that failure.

Nickname: Crusaders

Appearance: Ventrue *antitribu* wear clothes that befit their anachronistic minor noble status. Many still have significant money, held over from nights and families long past, and they dress the part in tasteful clothes and luxurious accouterments. The Crusaders do not consider this behavior hypocritical; they present themselves as they believe they should. After all, they have the money, so what good does it do them to deny themselves? Who commands greater respect: the knight who cleans his armor and grooms his horse, or the unkempt barbarian with stained clothes and broken talons? Sabbat Ventrue command attention, as do their Camarilla cousins, by looking the part.

Haven: Ventrue *antitribu* keep private havens when they can, though they have no aversion to sharing communal havens with the rest of their packs. Most Crusaders prefer lavish appointments, so that they may spend their time away from the Great Jyhad in relative comfort. They collect few trappings of materialistic cultures however, enjoying a few fine appointments rather than extensive collections of gadgets, cars and personal effects. In this manner, their havens, both personal and communal, may be described as austere. Ventrue *antitribu* also honor the ages-old custom of hospitality: Should another Sabbat Ventrue require a haven for the day, the Crusader will do his best to provide it.

Background: Sabbat Ventrue select childer from the ranks of high society, but not trust-fund brats or dilettantes. A Ventrue *antitribu* must have the means to support his station and the strength of character to do everything it takes to fulfill his duty. Crusaders may come from any cultural or ethnic upbringing — indeed, the mortal stock from which Sabbat Ventrue Embrace their childer is probably the most diverse in the entire sect — but the potential childe must have a strong sense of responsibility, a trait that the Crusaders find of short supply in the hedonistic final nights.

Character Creation: Ventrue *antitribu* adhere to soldier and aristocrat concepts, for the most part. Natures reflect their unfaltering sense of duty, and most have similar Demeanors, though the clan has had its share of Thrill-Seekers, Monsters and Deviants. Sabbat Ventrue prize all Attributes and Abilities equally, considering the "true" knight to be as capable with the computer and pen as he is with the sword and automobile. Ventrue *antitribu* also cultivate extensive Backgrounds, among which Allies, Influence and Sabbat Status are most important. Most Sabbat Ventrue keep some semblance of Humanity for a short time after their Embrace, until they can fully devote themselves to their monstrous chivalric code, which almost universally takes the form of the Path of Honorable Accord (or, less frequently, the Path of Caine or the Path of Cathari).

Clan Disciplines: Dominate, Fortitude, Presence

Weaknesses: Sabbat Ventrue suffer the same rarefaction of tastes as Camarilla Ventrue, and they may feed only from certain vessels (as decided at the time of character creation). For example, the Crusader may be able to derive sustenance from only Christians, or the blind, or perhaps might be able to drink

STEREOTYPES

Camarilla: I spit at them — they are single-handedly responsible for bringing Gehenna down on all our heads.

Sabbat: Undisciplined, but sincere. Usually.

THE VIEW FROM WITHOUT

The Camarilla

Knights? Please. That is *so* 800 years ago.

— Pagi, Nosferatu jet-setter

The Sabbat

Maybe their manner is a bit arrogant, but you know what? I'm glad they're on our side.

— Cherise DuChamp, coven ductus

The Independents

The fruit falls closer to the tree than they would have us think.

— Hesha, Setite

only cold blood from crystal flutes. The character will feed on no other vessels, even if frenzied or starving. Ventrue *antitribu* may feed on vampiric vitae normally.

Organization: The complex neo-feudal hierarchy of the Ventrue *antitribu* is based on accomplishment, acquisition and enemies slain. The clan supports a fair number of warlords and administrator-lords alike, who may choose to battle in the streets or over Gross Annual Profits. Anything is acceptable as long as the Crusader keeps his cause in his cold, unbeating heart. The majority of the Sabbat Inquisition is composed of Ventrue *antitribu*, and some members of the clan find their calling among the ranks of the Black Hand as well. Additionally, many Ventrue *antitribu* become templars and paladins for the Sword of Caine.

Quote: *Heretic, traitor, spy or coward; it's all the same to me. Now stick out your hand and silence that tongue, or I'll cut it out and take off your arm at the shoulder. Accept your punishment as a true Childe of Caine.*

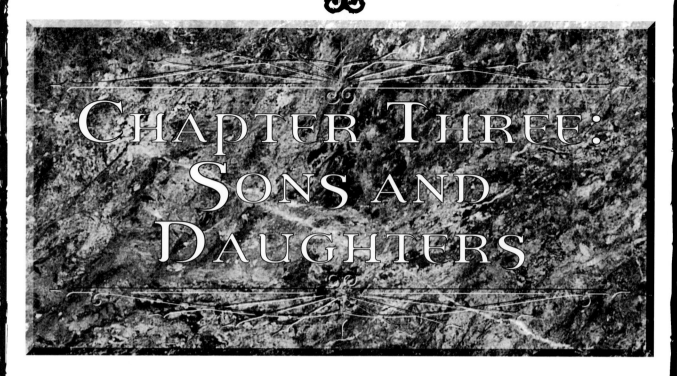

CHAPTER THREE: SONS AND DAUGHTERS

Is evil just something you are?
Or something you do?
— Morrissey, "Sister I'm a Poet"

This chapter points out the minor changes and considerations necessary in creating a Sabbat character for a **Vampire: The Masquerade** chronicle.

Before you begin to play a Sabbat vampire, you should take a few things into account. Remember that you're trying to create an interesting and unique character who reflects the darkness and the struggle of the Sabbat to not only survive but prove itself superior, rather than the one with the "best" Traits. Additionally, the Sabbat is not an inherently evil sect. It strongly believes in what it does — it has morals, even if those morals appear warped and perverse to others.

Another unique aspect of the Sabbat is that its members function in packs. Consider how well your character can interact with a group, for if your character disrupts the story because he doesn't fit in, no one will enjoy the game. The Storyteller may ask you to create a new character, or your character might meet a quick Final Death. Even if you wish to play a character who secretly works against her pack's greater interests, that character must be able to hide among the pack, lest she be found out immediately.

Finally, remember that the Sabbat is not all blood and gore. It is a vicious sect, heedless of mortals and just as likely to slit an old woman's throat as it is to ignore her, but an unliving, *thinking* infrastructure lies beneath that depravity and disregard. If the Sabbat was composed of nothing more than murderous maniacs, it would have fallen before the torches of the Society of Leopold or the Camarilla long ago.

The Sabbat is not only wicked, but fervent, canny and intelligent as well — not every character should be a mindless brute. In fact, mindless brutes should be in the minority, unless the Storyteller has expressly stated that yours will be a combat-heavy game (and even then, violence can be done with panache). Players are encouraged to explore the intellectual evil of the Sabbat as well as the physical violence.

STEP ONE: CHARACTER CONCEPT

In creating a Sabbat character it is vital to remember the goals of the Sabbat and your particular pack. Ideology is the most important difference between the Sabbat and other Cainites, so how does this mindset manifest itself to assist your character in his survival? When creating your character, also remember that there is a high mortality rate among newly sired Sabbat. What is it that allowed your character to survive and become True Sabbat?

CONCEPT

This step is simple. Ask yourself who your character was before he became a vampire, and who he has become since. For more information on character concepts, see **Vampire: The Masquerade**, page 105.

CLAN, *ANTITRIBU* AND BLOODLINE

A Sabbat character has many more options when it comes to lineage due to the *antitribu* and several exclusively

Sabbat bloodlines. *Antitribu* are often radically different from their Camarilla or independent counterparts, if only in ideology. Acquaint yourself with the clans as presented in Chapter Two, then select the one that best fits your vision for the character — or choose one that runs counter to it. If none of the clans or bloodlines excites you, you can also choose the "Panders." Clanless and outcast, the Panders have any number of vampires without pedigree among their ranks.

The Pack

As a member of the Sabbat, your character almost certainly belongs to a pack consisting of vampires of various clans (though in reality, you often find that you're stuck with whoever Embraced you and his pack). More than likely, all characters in the chronicle belong to the same pack, so players should discuss and have input as to its nature. The two kinds of packs that make up the Sabbat are the nomadic and founded ones.

Pilgrims or nomadic Sabbat enjoy their freedom by wandering the country and having ties to no particular place. Throughout their journeys, they frequent many colorful locales and encounter many interesting people. While many Sabbat view this unlifestyle as the ultimate freedom closest to the sect's anarch roots, it takes true inner discipline to survive in this environment. While many Camarilla Kindred view nomadic Sabbat as dangerous and deranged vampires — who would voluntarily choose an unlife of running from Lupines and sleeping in the earth or abandoned buildings? — many pilgrims feel that the greatest victory of all is to acknowledge no master except themselves. Of course, nomadic Sabbat serve the sect, but they do so without being bound to one location.

Coven members or founded Sabbat have established a permanent home in a particular city. A haven in the city lends itself to intriguing politics and colorful recurring characters. Dangers within a city are also fairly predictable based on the pack's prior history within the city. The open road is fraught with unpredictable adventures and hazards.

Nature and Demeanor

The Sabbat have specific Archetypes that reflect and accent their evolutionary nature, their strong survival instinct and their self-avowed vampiric superiority. While a character's Nature is the "truest" component of his personality, it is imperative to remember that the Sabbat constantly adapt so that they may survive. This evolution tends to manifest itself in a character's Demeanor; over the course of your character's unlife, you should note changes in his Demeanor ranging from subtle to extreme, depending upon chronicle experiences. To begin with, however, select a Demeanor Archetype that describes how your character acts *now*. Some new Nature and Demeanor Archetypes particularly suited to the Sabbat appear on pages 86-87.

Paths of Enlightenment

Some vampires outside the sect believe the Sabbat has no morals. Outsiders usually see only fire, death and terror in the wake of many Sabbat vampires' passage. The truth of the matter, however, is that Sabbat vampires adhere to very rigid codes of behavior based on their ideology, philosophy and theology. These codes are known as the Paths of Enlightenment. There are seven known Sabbat paths, and some vampires not affiliated with the sect are believed to uphold similar moral outlooks. While a character's morality and actions may not make sense to outsiders (particularly those who cannot comprehend inhuman values and acts as sacred), his path strongly influences every aspect of his existence. Keep your character's clan, pack and Nature in mind when choosing the path best suited for him.

(**Note:** Paths are not recommended for beginning players. For more about Paths of Enlightenment and advice on using them in a chronicle, see the Appendix of **Vampire: The Masquerade**.)

Despite the dehumanizing aspects of the Sabbat Embrace, however, most vampires of the sect continue to cling to the vestiges of Humanity, though their Humanity Traits tend to erode a little more quickly than other vampires'. Particularly in the cases of young Sabbat, many vampires simply haven't had the time or environment to cast off all that was important to them before their Embrace. Neonate characters typically spend less than 25 years as vampires, which is hardly enough time to adopt a radically different frame of mind. Nevertheless, should a player wish to portray a character who subscribes to a Path of Enlightenment, she may feel free to do so (with the Storyteller's final approval, of course). Usually, a mentor in a character's pack aids her in finding her path before she becomes an inhuman monster. Only the most precocious of neonates will be on a path when the chronicle commences; typically, this individual may have had extended contact with the Sabbat — as a revenant, toady, favored ghoul, etc. — before she was Embraced.

Step Two: Choosing Attributes

Point allocations for the Attributes of Sabbat characters are identical to those of other vampire characters. A player receives seven points to distribute among his character's primary Attributes, five points for his secondary Attributes and three points for his tertiary Attributes. Additionally, like all vampires, Sabbat characters receive one free "starting" dot in all Attributes.

Step Three: Choosing Abilities

For the most part, Sabbat Cainites can use any Ability presented in **Vampire: The Masquerade**, as well as the Secondary Abilities presented in the **Vampire Storytellers Companion**, should the Storyteller choose to allow them. Additionally, the Sabbat practices some Abilities developed especially for its terror tactics and violent existence. These Abilities are discussed in depth later.

STEP FOUR: ADVANTAGES

Sabbat Advantages differ a bit from other vampires'. As the sect sees itself in a constant state of war, it places significant emphasis on learning the inherent powers of vampires. Also, as members of the sect are expected to put as much of their former lives behind them as possible, Sabbat Cainites have far less influence in the mortal world than independent or Camarilla "Kindred."

DISCIPLINES

Sabbat vampires start the game with four dots in Disciplines to reflect not only their strong will for survival but also the rigorous trials they undergo after the Embrace. These four points must come from the vampire's clan Disciplines (see Chapter Two). Pander vampires, on the other hand, may choose four dots from *any* Disciplines. Of course, any player may spend freebie points during character creation to acquire out-of-clan Disciplines for her character (pending Storyteller approval).

BACKGROUNDS

When a Sabbat vampire Embraces a new childe, it is normal for all of the childe's mortal ties to be severed. In addition to obliterating the character's human existence, the Sabbat have a cultic initiation known as the Creation Rites designed to bond the newly sired Lick to his pack. Because of the dehumanizing aspects of Sabbat Embrace, the isolation and rigors of Sabbat training and the extensive abuse a character endures from the pack in order to be accepted, the character begins the chronicle without any Background points, having spent all his post-Embrace time with the pack. Designed to ensure loyalty, the methods of the Sabbat leave the neonate feeling completely dependent upon his sire or his packmates for a sense of belonging. Players may use freebie points to purchase Background points at the Storyteller's discretion, but even if you have the points to purchase the Background, it must make sense why the character would have it. It is improbable, for instance, that a nomadic Malkavian *antitribu* biker has any appreciable Influence beyond a dot or two.

VIRTUES

Here's where it gets a bit sticky.

Most young Sabbat vampires, as mentioned before, still have some degree of Humanity left. If your character is one of these vampires, you receive five dots to allocate among your Virtues. (Remember that you have one free dot in each Virtue, as normal.)

Nasty bastards who follow a Path of Enlightenment, however, follow different rules. Certain Paths of Enlightenment subscribe to Virtues other than Conscience and Self-Control — check the details of the path in question (in Chapter Five) to see which virtues apply to your character's path. Characters on Paths of Enlightenment receive the Sabbat-standard five points of Virtues (vampires outside the Sabbat get seven, but such is the price of freedom), and freebie points may be spent to increase these Virtues later. Finally a few other guidelines apply:

• **Alternate Virtues begin at zero:** Every human (and thus every recently Embraced Kindred) has some degree of his "natural" Virtues left, but unnatural vampiric Virtues must be cultivated outside the cultural human norm. Although a character with Conscience, Self-Control and Courage receives one free dot in each Virtue, a character with Conscience, Instinct and Courage begins with only two free dots (in Conscience and Courage). A character with Conviction, Instinct and Courage begins with only one free dot (in Courage). Sabbat characters *must* buy their inhuman Virtues to at least 1, if not higher. This restriction may seem unfair, but the effort required to adopt a morality so antithetical to humanity is not a light one.

• **A vampire following a Path of Enlightenment must begin the game with a Willpower Trait of 5, minimum:** Spending points on Courage or raising Willpower with freebie points will provide this minimum. Without sufficient will to stave it off, a character would fall to her Beast within a few nights of adopting such a heinous code of ethics.

• **Beginning characters may not start the game with path scores above 5:** If a character's Virtues would indicate a path score of higher than 5, disregard the extra. Freebie points may not be spent to increase a beginning character's path rating above 5, either. Newly created vampires have not had sufficient time to gain a greater understanding of their wicked nature. It takes decades — perhaps even centuries — to create a true monster.

• **In all other ways, unless otherwise specified, inhuman paths and Virtues function like their human counterparts.** So, if a roll calls for the player to use Charisma + Conscience, and the character has Conviction, roll Charisma + Conviction.

STEP FIVE: LAST TOUCHES

At this point, the character is almost done. You receive 15 freebie points to round out any of the Traits on your character sheet. Before you spend these points, however, you must record the base scores for your character's Willpower, path rating, and blood pool.

WILLPOWER

Your character's Willpower is equal to his Courage rating. When playing a Sabbat character, you should probably consider raising it even higher by using freebie points (especially if you are playing a path-follower, whose Willpower must start at 5 or greater). Willpower is vital to the Sabbat, and the sect brooks no cowards in its ranks.

HUMANITY/PATH OF ENLIGHTENMENT

A character's starting Humanity or path score depends on his Virtues. Add the two Virtues other than Courage (Conscience or Conviction and Self-Control or Instinct) to determine this Trait. Remember that new characters on Paths of Enlightenment may not have path scores greater than 5 at the beginning of the game.

BLOOD POOL

Simply roll a die to determine the character's starting blood pool.

VINCULI (BLOOD TIES)

Members of Sabbat packs have bonds of loyalty to one another formed by practicing the blood-drinking ritual known as the Vaulderie. Each Vinculum has a rating that determines how strong or weak it is (see page 155 for specific details on Vinculum scores). At this point of character creation, write down the names of every other character in your character's pack. For every other character in the pack, roll a die, add one to the results, then record those results next to that character's name.

(**Note:** Vinculum scores may not exceed 10.)

FREEBIE POINTS

The player may now spend 15 freebie points to purchase additional dots for a character's Traits. Each dot has a freebie-point cost based on the Trait's type — consult the chart on p. 104 of **Vampire: The Masquerade** for these costs. Remember that Disciplines purchased with freebie points need not come from the character's clan Disciplines (though buying certain Disciplines may require some explanation or the Storyteller's approval).

SPARK OF LIFE

The following details will help you make your character a complete and unique vampire. You do not necessarily need to write these things down, but you should certainly think about them — not only now but throughout the entire existence of your character.

PRESENTATION

The nature of the Sabbat is most readily visible in its appearance. With minimal formal concern for a "Masquerade," Sabbat individuality comes out in the way characters physically express themselves. How does your character's clothing, hairstyle and choice of accessories reflect her superior self-image? How do your character's Traits come across to show that he is a survivor? What does your character's Appearance of 3 mean? Does his Strength of 4 make him a hulking brute or is he surprisingly strong for his small frame? Bring the character to vivid unlife with a bit of consideration for the *character* rather than just the Traits.

SPECIALTIES

Given the guerrilla training Sabbat members often undertake and the self-discipline necessary just to *be* a Sabbat member, Sabbat characters sometimes have specialties or areas of refined expertise. A character may take a specialty in an Attribute or Ability when one of those given Traits has a rating of four or higher. Although most players select specialties for their Traits during play, you can pick them immediately, provided that it makes sense. Specialties allow you to reroll every 10 scored in your area of specialization, adding successes on the reroll to the successes you have already accumulated.

Example: Brian's character, Vaughan, has a Computer specialty in "the Internet." During play, Brian has Vaughan searching for the location of a vital bit of information on the World Wide Web. The Storyteller has Brian roll Vaughan's Intelligence + Computer (a pool of six dice) against a difficulty of 7 and decides that he needs four successes to find what he is looking for. Brian rolls a 10, 8, 7, 6, 3 and 2 — three successes. However, Vaughan's specialty entitles Brian to reroll the die that came up a 10, counting it as a success and providing him an opportunity for an additional one. Brian rolls a 9, which is indeed an additional success, and the last one he needed, in fact. Vaughan's extra study and work on the Internet has paid off.

EQUIPMENT

Due to the severity of the Sabbat Creation Rites, it is highly unlikely that a character would have any remaining possessions or pieces of equipment from his human existence at the start of a chronicle. If you feel your character needs equipment now, you should work out these details with the Storyteller before the game begins. The search for appropriate gear takes time, and it is not automatically successful. Almost any piece of mundane equipment that fits your character's concept *can* be obtained, provided either your character has sufficient dots in the Resources Background, or it just makes sense. A street thug probably knows where to get a hold of a gun, while a derelict has little business with a bandoleer of military-surplus grenades.

QUIRKS

By giving your character unique details, personal anecdotes and personality quirks, you can add a great deal of depth and interest to your roleplaying experience. For the Sabbat, many quirks are residual effects from the trauma they experienced during the Embrace and Creation Rites. For other Sabbat members, peculiarity in mannerisms may arise out of the character's struggle to feel superior while still having a low self-esteem. Contemplate the strange and interesting aspects that define your character. The possibilities here are infinite — consider every little thing your character may do and add color by making it unique. Does your character bother to lick her victims' wounds after she feeds? Does she wear a special kind of earrings? Does she drive a signature car or speak in certain slang? How does she carry herself? Does the sight of children upset her? Anything that adds depth to the character helps set her apart from the myriad other members of the sect, and other vampires.

MOTIVATIONS

What makes your character a superior being, above the masses of humankind and the cowering Camarilla? How does she view her existence and purpose within the Sabbat and her pack? Does she believe Gehenna is a real and impending threat? Where does she see herself and her pack in five years? A decade? A century? Considering these aspects of your character will give you a better understanding of how she might react in any given situation in the game.

MORTAL IDENTITY

A final point for consideration is your character's mortal identity. Most Sabbat view humans as little more than fast food. Because of their views on these creatures, they have little use for a formal Masquerade or mortal society. Yet, a few vampires may still have connections. Whether you're a priest with the Mother Church or a drug lord with human runners, you need to evaluate your identity and your attitudes in the human world. In spite of its disdain for humankind, the Sabbat nonetheless finds itself having to deal with "pathetic mortals" more often than they might like. Does who your character once was have any effect on these interactions?

PRELUDES

For the most part, Sabbat vampires become Damned like any other vampires: Another vampire selects a prospective childe, drains him of blood and replaces that blood with a bit of her own. Details on how the character became a vampire typically resolve themselves in the prelude before play begins. More information on preludes appears in **Vampire: The Masquerade**, pages 108-9.

The Sabbat, however, offers an interesting variant on the prelude: the mass Embrace. In the nights of the sect's ongoing holy war, it is entirely possible that the players' characters' pack has been Embraced as fodder during a siege, or otherwise "on the fly" as the sect has a need for bodies to help win the war. If the Storyteller wishes, she may run a prelude for *all* the characters at once (with perhaps a bit of individual detail, to explain how she managed to be in the wrong place at the wrong time with the rest of the characters), turning them loose on the Jyhad knowing as little ("It's your first night, and your sires turn baleful glances upon you before charging into the fray.") or as much ("You have proven yourself as valuable spies and soldiers in the siege of Miami; you are now True Sabbat.") as she prefers.

NEW TRAITS

During the course of its evolution from disparate packs of indolent anarchs to the terrible and righteous holy sect of the modern nights, the Sabbat has developed several new outlooks, capabilities and resources with which to wage its ceaseless war. The following new Traits are most suited to Sabbat characters and chronicles, though Storytellers may feel free to adapt or include them in other chronicles, should they so wish.

NATURE AND DEMEANOR ARCHETYPES

These new Archetypes reflect the extremism and violence of the Sabbat. To be sure, many of the vampires of the sect are not slavering, psychotic mass murderers — but then, many are. Storytellers are reminded to be judicious in rewarding Willpower for acting in concert with one's Nature. Even killers grow jaded and need to challenge themselves with new atrocity, so mindlessly gutting one's umpteenth victim should net the killer little return.

Capitalist

Why give it away for free when you can sell it? You are the ultimate mercenary, realizing that there is always a market to be developed — anything can be a commodity. You have a keen understanding of how to manipulate both kine and Cainites into thinking that they need specific goods or services. Appearance and influence are everything when it comes to the big sale, though you'll use anything to your advantage. Salesmen, soldiers of fortune and bootlickers all adhere to the Capitalist Archetype.

— Regain a point of Willpower whenever you make a successful "sale" or barter of any commodity. Commodities need not be physical items; they may be bits of information, favors or other such intangibles.

Chameleon

Independent and self-reliant, you manage to blend into any situation. You carefully study the behavior and mannerisms of everyone you come in contact with so you can pass yourself off as someone else later. You spend so much time altering your mannerisms and appearance that your own sire may not even recognize you. Spies, con artists, drag queens and impostors best represent the Chameleon.

— Regain a point of Willpower whenever you fool someone into thinking you're someone else for your own (or your pack's) benefit.

Creep Show

You strive to shock and disgust those around you with gratuitous acts and ostentatiously "evil" mannerisms. You realize, of course, that it's all show and merely a way to intimidate and control others. Outsiders, on the other hand, think you are the Devil incarnate, and you revel in this image. Shock-rockers, rebellious teenagers and the attention-starved exemplify the Creep Show Archetype.

— Regain a point of Willpower whenever someone recoils from you in horror or otherwise reacts in fear.

Enigma

Your actions are bizarre, puzzling and inexplicable to everyone except yourself. Your strangeness may be residual effects from the Creation Rites, or the most effective way for you to carry out the work of the Sabbat — to see the movements of the Antediluvians and counter them. To the rest of the world, however, your erratic actions suggest that you're eccentric if not completely crazy. Conspiracy theorists, deep-cover agents and Jyhad fanatics all live up to the Enigma Archetype.

— Regain a point of Willpower whenever someone is completely perplexed or baffled by one of your actions that later turns out to be a fruitful endeavor.

Eye of the Storm

Despite your calm subtle appearance, chaos and havoc seems to follow you. From burning cities to emotional upheaval, death and destruction circle you like albatrosses. For you, unlife is a never-ending trial with uncertainty around every corner. Gang leaders, political figures and other influential individuals exemplify the Eye of the Storm Archetype.

— Regain a point of Willpower whenever a ruckus, riot or less violent phenomenon occurs around you.

Guru

Your enlightenment draws others to you. You may be a mentor of a particular Path of Enlightenment, a priest with the Church or merely an idealist in your pack. Whatever the case, your presence motivates and moves others to engage in spiritual or ideological pursuits. Your peers view you as calm, centered and "with it," even when you are preaching about violence as a means to an end. Cult leaders, Zen masters and pack priests are examples of Gurus.

— Regain a point of Willpower whenever someone seeks out your help in spiritual matters and your guidance moves that individual to an enlightened action that he normally would not have taken. Also, regain a point of Willpower whenever you achieve an epiphany that relates to your personal philosophy.

Sadist

Your exist to inflict pain and suffering upon others. Killing is too easy — torture is the best way to *truly* harm a person, and you seek the slowest, most painful means to push others to the ultimate limits. Pain — *others'* pain — gives you immense pleasure. Drill sergeants, jilted ex-lovers and some of the terminally deranged may all display Sadist Archetypes at one time or another; sadism is rare enough to appear only in aberrant cases, rather than reliably in one type of person or another.

— Regain a point of Willpower whenever you inflict pain upon someone for no reason other than your own pleasure.

Sociopath

All inferior beings both living and undead should be exterminated in order to bring about a harmonious existence. You likely feel no remorse when you kill (depending upon your Humanity or path). On the contrary, you are doing a glorious deed for society. Some Sabbat are critical of your violent nature, but you sometimes manage to sway them with arguments like, "Darwin would agree that I'm only helping nature along!" and, "Only the Sabbat shall survive!"

— Regain Willpower whenever you are the greatest contributor to a body count after everything has settled down. This count includes times when you are the only killer, and it need not result from a massive combat — like killing every member of a movie audience or gunning down defenseless patrons in a bank robbery.

New Abilities

In addition to the Abilities listed in **Vampire: The Masquerade**, you may find the following Secondary Abilities of interest. They are designed to reflect the Sabbat member, her unlifestyle and her nightly activities. If your Storyteller does not permit Secondary Abilities, simply ignore them. (The Secondary Abilities, not the Storyteller.)

Talents

Fortune-Telling

"You are in flight — a tall, gaunt man haunts you even in your dreams."

"That's right! Oh, my god!" Tara gaped. "He's been chasing me for weeks, and even when he's not there, I think I see him!"

"That's right, dear. But relax. You and he are fated to be," cackled the old Gypsy, his one good eye gleaming in the candlelight.

"Really? That's odd. Then why does he seem so scary?"

"Why, because he is, my dear. Yes, you will be his. You will be his forever!"

A shadow fell over Tara, blotting out the candle's dim light.

Whether you scry with a crystal ball, consult the yarrow sticks like your Chinese ancestors, read Tarot cards or tea leaves, divine with a pendulum or cast runes like your Celtic forebears, you have learned the ability to forecast the future. You may or may not have the gift to really tell fortunes, but you can make people believe you do.

(**Note:** It is up to the Storyteller whether or not Fortune-Telling truly works in her chronicle. She should share this information with players whose characters have this Talent — charlatans know when they're faking it — though they may certainly choose to lead others along, if they so wish.)

- • Novice: You are able to use one method of divination adequately, and you treat it as a pastime.
- •• Practiced: You are proficient in one method, with the ability to provide general information.
- ••• Competent: You are familiar with many divinatory systems and proficient in several. You can provide specific and detailed information from your readings.
- •••• Expert: You are adept in multiple methods of fortune-telling. Not only can you provide detailed information, but you can tell people specifically what they want to hear.
- ••••• Master: An oracle; the Gypsies take lessons from you.

Possessed by: Gypsies, Psychics, Quacks, New Agers
Specialties: Tarot Cards, Tea Leaves, Runes, Yarrow Sticks, Mirrors, Crystal Balls, Palms

Panhandling

Dezra shook his cup and forced a cough into the still night air, mumbling to passersby and pulling his blanket more tightly around his shoulders.

"Any help for a vet'ran down on his luck? Anything? Every little bit helps, even just a dollar. Hey, lady?"

Jackpot. Dezra caught a sweet young woman in a business suit looking at him. With only a glimpse of his brown eyes and a waver in his voice, he had her for 20 dollars, and even a ride to the shelter if he wanted it.

"No, thank you, ma'am. This is more'n enough. God bless you, ma'am." Under his breath, he added, "And I didn't even have to kill you for it. Damn, I'm good."

You are a skilled beggar. You are able to get people to give you money just by asking for it. You know whom to ask, how to approach them, what to say and how to avoid the police. This Talent is useful for picking up quick cash or creating a cover.

- • Novice: You get most of your money shaking cans and washing windshields. You're still working on a hard-luck story.
- •• Practiced: You're working on the story and using the classic lines, but you still manage to get little more than spare change.
- ••• Competent: You're really smooth — you can even hit the hard-hearted for a few bucks.
- •••• Expert: Who needs a sob story when you can hustle and scam your way into big bucks from tourists and little old ladies?
- ••••• Master: Dinners, rides home, cash for a bus ticket — easy as pie.

Skills

Vamp

Lucita sidled up to the doorman of the Digital Lounge, all hips and lips. A few fleeting, vacuous promises and a carefully placed hand on his chest and groin made him bend to her will. He knew damn well she wasn't supposed to be here tonight — Andrei specifically stated that she was to be denied entrance — but the doorman didn't care anymore as her mouth met his and his sex stirred beneath her touch. That was precisely how Lucita wanted it.

You can use your seductive means to get any information from anyone. Whether you're acting out the role of the empathetic girlfriend, the barroom floozy, the loving wife or the adventurous mistress, you know how to please. You can be subtle or overt, coy or wanton, depending on what promises the best results, and you can interpret your subject's turn-ons to better accomplish your seduction. If the vampire practicing this Skill actually goes through with the acts he suggests, he may need to spend blood points to function properly; see **Vampire: The Masquerade**, pages 138-9 for details.

(**Note:** This Skill relates only to using sex to achieve an end. Being charming, alluring or desirable is an application of Empathy, Expression, Performance or Subterfuge, likely coupled with Appearance or Charisma. Only the dullest of victims may fail to realize the carnal pleasures proposed by a user of this Skill, and many vampires consider its use distasteful or vulgar, as they no longer concern themselves with such base mortal acts, especially among the Sabbat.)

- Novice: You know how to gain a partner's interest and extract information without being blatantly obvious.
- •• Practiced: You perceive the subtle innuendoes in determining what a partner likes, and you use this insight to extract information.
- ••• Competent: From talking to someone for a few minutes, you can determine his fantasies. You enact them with skill often withdrawing vital information easily and within the context of your role-playing games.
- •••• Expert: You can discern your mark's ultimate fantasies, enacting dialogue and mannerisms perfectly. Your partner usually becomes obsessed with you, and the sap may tell you *anything*.
- ••••• Master: Some wonder if you are too good to be true; a veritable succubus or incubus.

Possessed by: Hookers, Spies, Lasombra, Bored Housewives
Specialties: Lingerie Modeling, Bondage, Role-playing, S&M, D&S

FIRE DANCING

Flames roared and cinders fluttered underneath the Flatiron Building — tonight, the Sabbat would strike at the feeble Camarilla Licks of Atlanta. In preparation, the archbishop had called a gathering beneath this, their temporary headquarters in order to incite her soldiers. After a rousing speech, she had built the bonfire, leading the Sabbat in chants and catcalls. Now was the time — time to cast herself into the fire and show her charges the meaning of fearlessness.

The archbishop threw herself through the flames without a second thought, her eyes glazed over and a fine sheen of blood-sweat on her forehead. Flames licked at her hair and engulfed her clothes, yet she emerged from the other side unscathed. To the vampires who watched her, she appeared to be the Devil herself, passing through the flames as if she were rising from the mouth of Hell. They rallied behind her, ready to follow this devil back into Hell, if need be.

You can enter a trance-like state that allows you to leap through flames. This Skill is vital in the Fire Dance and other *ritae*. Demonstrating this Skill often equates to being a powerful and dominant member of the pack. This Skill does not grant any immunity from the fire, but it does allow the vampire to avoid being burned or succumbing to a frenzy. This Skill cannot be part of a split dice pool: The user must concentrate on Fire Dancing and nothing else. When the vampire tries to Fire

Dance, damage should be rolled normally, but for every success with this Skill, reduce the amount of damage done by one health level. Few vampires outside the Sabbat have this Skill.

(**Note:** Unless the fire is actually a bonfire meant for the ritual dance, you do not suffer Rötschreck any less frequently than any other vampire.)

- • Novice: You make the necessary leaps to prove that you're not a coward. You usually wait until the fire has died down quite a bit before you leap though.
- •• Practiced: You no longer feel that "Oh, shit," panic when you jump.
- ••• Competent: You are usually the first to jump, for you do not fear the flames. You live by the motto, "Build it higher, jump the fire!"
- •••• Expert: An acrobat in the flames, you command a prowess and fearlessness that serves as inspiration to all who observe you.
- ••••• Master: A legend among the Sabbat, your moves are simultaneously unholy and magnificent.

Possessed by: Sabbat, Mystics, Primitive Tribesmen, Performers
Specialties: Leaping, Acrobatics, Distance, Looking Tough

KNOWLEDGES

BLACK HAND LORE

"So you are a member of the mighty Hand, correct, Ismail?"

"You are correct, Your Excellency," answered the Assamite. He certainly looked the part, down to a flawless tattoo of an open palm that adorned the back of his shaven head.

"I see. And to what circle of mastery have you ascended?"

"The fifth, Excellency. I am a Keeper of Caine's Word and paladin to Bishop Cicatriz himself."

The bishop reached out almost carelessly with his claws, and the Assamite's head fell to the ground. "'Circle of mastery,' indeed. What foolishness. And members of the Hand are forbidden to be paladins. When you wish to lie to me, at least learn the nature of the falsehoods you would craft. But I suppose it is a bit late for you to learn these lessons, eh jackal?"

Soundless and wide-eyed, the Assamite's head stared at the bishop, who walked into the shadows from whence he had come.

You have learned information about the Black Hand — which may or may not be true since this information is known to few outside the organization. You have heard rumors and legends about the history, strategies, intrigue and rituals of the Hand. Additionally, you may be able to recognize numerous agents of the Hand within your own city and the surrounding area.

- • Novice: You know mostly rumor and hearsay.
- •• Practiced: You have decent second-hand information.
- ••• Competent: You have a steady — and *reliable* — source for second-hand information.
- •••• Expert: You have numerous steady and reliable sources that provide you a great deal of information.

- ••••• Master: You have a powerful contact within the Hand, along with other sources within the group who provide you intricate and detailed information that only an experienced member could know.

Possessed by: Black Hand Members, The Order of St. Blaise, Sabbat Leaders, Assamite *Antitribu*, Assamites, Nosferatu *Antitribu*
Specialties: History, Famous Leaders, Tactics, Strategies, Secrets, Rituals, Local Members

UNDERWORLD LORE

Vincent shrugged as the man in the pinstriped suit asked him who he'd come to see.

"Names ain't important. I came to see an old friend and bring him a gift," Vincent replied. He handed the other man a bottle of imported liqueur and three coffee beans. Nodding his head and smiling, the man led Vincent past a huge, heavy set of mahogany doors and into the offices of the most powerful mortal in the city.

You know the politics and figures of organized crime within your city. You understand how the system works, whom to pay off, whose arm to twist and who gets the cement shoes. Whether it's street drugs or vampiric blood for a secret cult of ghouls, you know the source and who's playing the game. This Knowledge encompasses members of all criminal organizations, ethnic and otherwise, including the Mafia, Yakuza, and street gangs.

- • Novice: You saw *The Godfather* a couple times.
- •• Practiced: You know a few button men or soldiers and can name most of your city's prominent gangsters.
- ••• Competent: You know as much as most connected men.
- •••• Expert: If it's happening in your city, you know about it.
- ••••• Master: If it's happening, *period*, you know about it.

Possessed by: Mafia Dons, Yakuza, Government Leaders, Police, Connected Thugs
Specialties: Loan-Sharking, Drug-Running, Smuggling, Slavery, Politics, Ethnic Organizations

SABBAT BACKGROUNDS

For the most part, the Sabbat looks with disfavor upon Backgrounds, considering them co-dependent ties to the mortal world. Nonetheless, Backgrounds often come in handy, and rare is the Sabbat who would rather die than avail himself of their resources. This section looks at Sabbat views concerning the core **Vampire** Backgrounds as well as introducing a few new ones specific to the sect.

EXISTING BACKGROUNDS

ALLIES

The Sabbat views allies as an occasional dirty necessity. Trusting no one outside the sect, much less wanting to be indebted to anyone, a member of the Sabbat chooses allies with great reservation. Because allies are mortal, the Sabbat consid-

ers them expendable, and practically no Sabbat would entrust his unlife to something as fragile and inferior as a human being. Few Sabbat keep allies for any length of time, preferring to either pay off or bully prospective help into cooperation.

CONTACTS

Sabbat may still have mortal contacts whom they can manipulate, bribe and hit up for information. These people hail from all walks of life, though if a player wishes to cultivate contacts, those contacts must have some reason to be involved with a Sabbat character (considering the sect's overall dislike of mortals). As a whole, the sect regards mortal contacts with little more respect than mortal allies, but it recognizes the occasional necessity of them. After all, when Sabbat vampires need guns, sometimes mortal gun-runners have the best wares. In truth, most Sabbat vampires can and do benefit from contacts at many points during their unlives, though they tend to keep quiet about such things. It wouldn't do to have other Cainites know that one is dependent on the mortals around him.

For the Sabbat, it is more commonplace to have many minor contacts spread throughout the city than any single, particularly powerful contact. Of course, bishops, archbishops, prisci, cardinals and the like typically have influence they can exert over key powerful individuals, but this relationship, obviously, falls more into the category of Influence than Contacts.

FAME

Most Sabbat avoid turning movie stars into vampires, but it has happened. For a sect that prides itself on exclusivity and supremacy, fame can bring unwanted attention to the sect. Besides, once Embraced, even the famous tend to lose interest in their mortal fans (largely due to their deteriorated Humanity). Those with Fame who do not gracefully fade from the limelight must use it with the greatest of care. If for any reason, a Sabbat member with Fame is deemed a threat to Sabbat security, the Sword of Caine suffers no reservations in eliminating her. One almost apocryphal tale tells of a budding Hollywood actor who, after being Embraced into the sect, refused to devote his attention to the Great Jyhad and instead used his vampiric powers to make a name for himself. Incensed, the Sabbat destroyed him, leaving an overdosed, fleshcrafted body-double in his place, dead in front of a popular nightclub. Such ignominy awaits those who fail to draw the distinction between mortal renown and Cainite duty.

HERD

Vampires of the Sabbat have differing views on the matter of herds. Some Sabbat argue that herds promote laziness; nightly hunting hones survival skills, and herds are impossible to maintain for nomadic packs. Other Sabbat members, however, fear disease and use a herd to minimize chances of infection. Some keep herds to prevent mortals populaces from ever becoming aware of their presence. Ultimately, it's a matter of convenience and pack preference as to whether or not

members support herds. It should be noted, though, that most Sabbat keep only small herds so as to minimize threats to security. Many a herdless Sabbat boasts that the Sabbat should drink from whomever they damn well please!

INFLUENCE

Influence is a character's ability to sway the mortal world. The Sabbat has some influence on mortal society, but does little to further or exploit these human ties. Actually, the Sabbat finds it difficult to view humans and their affairs as anything more than a potential liability. Besides, the Sabbat sees little reason to be involved with humans. Many packs have extensive rules governing such interactions. This is due in part to the Sabbat's disdain for humanity. After all, a Cainite with only shreds of Humanity — let alone the palpable evil that exudes from her when she follows a Path of Enlightenment — will have a difficult time subtly manipulating any human if those around her are uncomfortable.

Some Sabbat view the human world as a giant chessboard to manipulate at will, but this tactic is dangerous indeed. Most Sabbat, with the exception of leaders and elders, simply stay out of mortal matters.

MENTOR

Since Sabbat unlife demands so much from its ranks, many members look to their packmates, sires and superiors for guidance. In Sabbat society, the mentor may teach and guide the Sabbat member on his chosen Path of Enlightenment, give advice, provide protection from elders by acting as a buffer, offer caution when intruding on the affairs of other elders and provide information regarding opportunities for power and advancement.

- •   Mentor is a ductus or pack priest.
- ••   Mentor is a prominent elder or priest.
- •••   Mentor is a bishop.
- ••••   Mentor is an archbishop.
- •••••   Mentor is a priscus or cardinal.

RETAINERS

Because the Sabbat is known for its secrecy — secrecy that has enabled its survival over the centuries, its members are apprehensive at thought of letting a bunch of humans know their secrets. Even when a Sabbat vampire takes a retainer, he is much more likely to choose a ghoul or an animal. There is also an ideological basis for the Sabbat's restricted use of retainers; why would a superior being choose such an inferior being for a servant, assistant or companion?

Retainers must always be controlled in some way, either through a salary, the donation of Cainite blood or direct mind-control. They may not always be loyal, though typically they are, considering the consequences. Depending on how well they have been treated, some retainers feel the temptation to betray their masters if given the chance. Sabbat members keep tight reins on their retainers. Usually, a retainer is killed at the slightest sign of mistrust or disobedience.

NEW BACKGROUNDS

ALTERNATE IDENTITY

Danya bowed to the prince, averting her gaze toward the ground. "I humbly present myself before you, my prince, as you request of all your subjects on each full moon."

"Thank you, Danya," the prince boomed in his deep baritone. "Your loyalty and honesty are greatly appreciated. You may go."

Back in the parking garage, Danya dropped her act and once again became Sabrina. Quickly, she moved a pair of desiccated corpses from the trunk of her car into the prince's and strewed a handful of spent pistol cartridges around the area. At the base of the garage, Sabrina stopped at a pay phone, dialed 911, dropped the handset and fired a few rounds into the air before leaving. Perhaps Danya was loyal and honest, but Sabrina was a real bitch.

You maintain an alternate identity outside your own, complete with papers, birth certificates or any other documentation you desire. Only a few may know your real name or identity. Your alternate persona may be highly involved in organized crime, a member of the Camarilla, a con artist who uses alternate identities for her game or you may simply gather information for the Sabbat about the enemy. Indeed, some Sabbat may know you as one individual while other Sabbat believe you to be someone else entirely.

- • You are new at this identity game. Sometimes you slip and forget your other persona.
- •• You are well grounded in your alternate identity. You are convincing enough to play the part of a doctor, lawyer, funeral salesman, drug-smuggler or a capable spy.
- ••• You have a fair reputation as your alternate persona and get name-recognition in the area where you have infiltrated.
- •••• Your alternate identity has respect and trust within your area of infiltration.
- ••••• You command respect in your area of infiltration, and you may even have accumulated a bit of status. You have the trust (or at least the recognition) of many powerful individuals within your area.

BLACK HAND MEMBERSHIP

As midnight tolled, Armin crept silently from the tall cabinet in which he had hidden himself all day. Slinking down a moonlit hallway, he sniffed the air for the telltale scent his target always wore. He detected a subtle hint of the fragrance — she was close by — mere seconds before hearing her approaching footsteps. Armin ducked behind a writing desk and watched his mark move absently past him.

As soon as her back was to him, Armin struck, burying his poisoned blade between her shoulders. She turned, a look of rage on her face, forcing blood to her limbs to make herself stronger, but Armin had already vanished into the nothingness from which he seemed to come. Calling upon the blood had been her mistake — Armin's poison coursed through her veins, doing its deadly duty.

Moments later, Armin withdrew across the front lawn as his target lay in a frothing heap on her rich carpet, calling breathlessly to her attendants.

You are a member of the feared Black Hand, the body of assassins and soldiers that serves the Sabbat fervently. Having this Background indicates that you are a full-fledged member of the organization, and you have all the responsibilities and benefits that accompany membership.

You may call upon members of the Black Hand to aid you, should you ever need it. Of course, this ability is a two-way street, and other Hand members may call upon you to aid them. Thus, you may find yourself assigned to perform assassinations, lend martial aid or even further the political ends of the Hand as a diplomat or spy. You may also be required to attend crusades that take you away from your pack. All members of the Black Hand *must* heed the call of another Hand member, especially the superiors of the faction.

Being a member of the Black Hand is a prestigious matter, and other members of the Sabbat respect the organization. When dealing with other Sabbat, should you choose to reveal your affiliation with the Hand, you may add your rating in this Background to any Social dice pools, even after other Status or Abilities have been taken into account. Most Hand members, however, choose not to reveal their allegiance. Also, the Black Hand is remarkably adept at hunting down Sabbat who claim membership in the sect but do not truly belong — liars, beware.

- • You are a grunt; you may call upon one Black Hand member once per story.
- •• You are known and respected in the Black Hand; you may call upon two Black Hand members once per story.
- ••• You are held in the Black Hand's regard; you may call upon five Black Hand members once per story.
- •••• You are a hero among members of the Black Hand; you may call upon seven Black Hand members twice per story (but you'd better have just cause — if it seems you're becoming soft, you may lose points in this Background). You may also lead large numbers of Hand members into action should it ever become necessary.
- ••••• You are part of Black Hand legend; you may call upon 12 Black Hand members twice per story (but see the preceding caution). You may also lead large numbers of Hand members into action should it ever become necessary. The Seraphim may even seek your counsel on matters of import.

RITUALS

Sayle raised the chalice over his head, intoning the ancient koldunic incantations and consecrating the Vaulderie. He closed the ritus with a blessing of his own.

"Let he who partakes of this sacrament feel the righteousness of the Sabbat. Let him never fall in battle, and let his packmates ever guard him vigilantly. Let him earn the valor for which his unbeating heart cries, and let all his enemies fall beneath his fangs. In the name of Caine, Lilith and the dark Angel Uriel, I bless this blood."

With that, Sayle dipped his finger into the vessel and drew a bloody cross on each of his packmates' foreheads, ending with himself. After that was done, Sayle took a deep draught from the chalice and passed it to Brother Teague, on his left.

You know the *ritae* and rituals of the Sabbat, and you can enact many, of them. This Background is vital to being a pack priest — without this Background, *ritae* will not function. This Background is actually a supernatural investment, drawing on the magic of the eldest Tzimisce sorcerers. Sabbat vampires who are not their pack's priests should have an outstanding reason for acquiring this Background, as pack priests are loath to share their secrets with more secular members of the sect.

- • You know three of the *auctoritas ritae* (your choice).
- •• You know nine of the *auctoritas ritae* (your choice) and three *ignoblis ritae* (your choice).
- ••• You know all 13 of the *auctoritas ritae* and nine *ignoblis ritae* (your choice). Also, you may create your own *ignoblis ritae*, given enough time (consult your Storyteller for development time and game effects).
- •••• You know all the *auctoritas ritae* and 20 *ignoblis ritae* (your choice). You may create your own *ignoblis ritae*, given enough time (consult your Storyteller for development time and game effects). You are also familiar with the functions of numerous re gional and pack-specific *ignoblis ritae*, even if you cannot perform them.
- ••••• You know all the *auctoritas ritae* and 40 *ignoblis ritae* (your choice). You may create your own *ignoblis ritae*, given enough time (consult your Storyteller for development time and game effects). You are also familiar with the functions of almost all re gional and pack-specific *ignoblis ritae*, even if you cannot perform them; if it's been written down or passed around in lore, you've heard of it.

SABBAT STATUS

Vykos stood in the dim hallway of the New York mansion, its body cutting a strange yet commanding presence just out of sight of the assembled Sons and Daughters of Caine. It walked forward as the ghoul herald called out its name, and the myriad voices fell immediately silent, deferring to the great priscus who was about to appear before them.

Respect had its perks, not the least of which was the ability to quiet the rabble when one must speak directly to them.

While the Sabbat values individuality, the strength of the packs lies within the strength of its leadership. Only leaders who are respected and revered within the pack and the sect can achieve this level of recognition. Status plays an important role in getting and keeping a leadership position. Members of the Sabbat do not recognize Clan Prestige (see the **Guide to the Camarilla**) for the most part (though a few Tzimisce do, as do a fair share of Lasombra). Rather, sect comes before clan to most Sabbat, and thus, it is better to be recognized by the sect as a whole. At the Storyteller's discretion, Sabbat Status may add to a character's Social Trait when she makes a point of it. Obviously, Sabbat Status confers no particular benefit — and is more likely a detriment — when dealing with members of the Camarilla or even some independent Cainites.

- • Ductus or pack priest/Well-known
- •• Templar or paladin/Respected
- ••• Bishop/Renowned
- •••• Archbishop/Pillar of the Sabbat
- ••••• Priscus or cardinal/Luminary

MERITS AND FLAWS

In addition to the Merits and Flaws listed in **Vampire: The Masquerade**, the following may be used to effectively enhance your character. As always, Merits and Flaws may be used only with Storyteller approval.

PHYSICAL

EARLY RISER (1 PT. MERIT)

No one can explain it, but you seem to have the ability to exist on less rest than your fellow packmates, tending to rise at least one hour before everyone else. You always seem to be the first to rise and the last to go to bed even if you're been out until dawn. While your packmates may still be groggy, you tend to be awake and aware.

VULNERABILITY TO SILVER (2 PT. FLAW)

To you, silver is as painful and as deadly as the rays of the sun. You suffer aggravated wounds from any silver weapons (bullets, knives, etc.) and the mere touch of silver objects discomfits you.

LAZY (3 PT. FLAW)

You are simply lazy, avoiding anything that requires effort on your part. Preferring to let others do the hard work, you lounge around. For any action that requires preparation, there's a good chance you didn't properly prepare. Difficulty rolls for spontaneous Physical actions (including combat, unless it's part of a planned offensive) increase by one.

INFERTILE VITAE (5 PT. FLAW)

During your Embrace, something went horribly wrong causing your blood to mutate under the stress of dying and rising again. All those you try to Embrace die. No matter what you do, you may not create any childer. However, your blood can still be used in the Vaulderie or for any other vampiric need, including making ghouls.

SOCIAL

SANCTITY (2 PT. MERIT)

This Merit is sometimes called the halo effect; everyone considers you pure and innocent, though not necessarily not naïve. You have a saint-like quality that is hard to pinpoint but cannot be denied. You are trusted, even if you are not trustworthy. At the Storyteller's discretion, you tend to receive lesser punishments for wrongdoing, and you are liked by most.

SPECIAL RESPONSIBILITY (1 PT. FLAW)

Shortly after your Embrace, you volunteered for some task in order to gain respect and approval from your pack members. Now, you wish you had never opened your damn mouth! While you are not given any special credit for performing this duty, you would lose much respect from the pack if you were to stop. The nature and the details of your duty should be worked out with the Storyteller in advance. Ideas can range from lending money to pack members to acting as pack messenger or possibly gathering victims for Blood Feasts.

MENTAL

INTROSPECTION (1 PT. MERIT)

You have keen insight into the ulterior motives of all your actions. Through this nightly exercise, you also have incredible insight into the underlying motives of others' actions. Add two dice to your Perception dice pool when you must take an action against someone with the same Nature or Demeanor as you.

FLASHBACKS (6 PT. FLAW)

You managed to make it through the Creation Rites, but not wholly intact. The most insignificant thing can throw you into a different mood or state of mind. Your behavior is extremely unpredictable. Because of your precarious emotional state, your Willpower fluctuates. At the beginning of each story, make a Willpower roll (you may not spend Willpower for an automatic success, obviously). If you succeed, you may participate in the story as normal. If you fail, however, your Willpower is considered to be 1 for the duration of that session. You may roll again at the beginning of the next session to see if you regain your wits.

A WORD TO STORYTELLERS

Merits and Flaws are included here to build character depth, not to enable players to generate super-characters. Feel free to disallow any and all Merits and Flaws to which you take exception. Additionally, Storytellers who wish to run Sabbat chronicles are encouraged to deny players from taking the Merits: Iron Will and Unbondable.

CHAPTER FOUR: THE GIFTS OF CAINE

...scarlet and black wounds
burst upon the splendid flesh.
— Arthur Rimbaud

The Sabbat practices several of the standard vampiric Disciplines, and a few that are unique to the sect. Of these, some are derivatives of other Disciplines (like Sanguinus, which borrows heavily from the Vicissitude used in the Blood Brothers' creation) while others seem to have been resurrected after long periods of disuse (like Valeren, which is thought to have been practiced by ancient Salubri warriors long before the birth of Christ). Still others have a more nefarious cast — only demons and other malevolent spirits teach the paths and rituals that belong exclusively to Dark Thaumaturgy.

In practice, the Sabbat encourages the teaching of Disciplines among its ranks. As the inherent powers of the Blood bestowed by the Curse of Caine, Disciplines represent the pinnacle of vampiric evolution, according to Sabbat doctrine. As such, many Sabbat focus more on Disciplines than they do on other aspects of their learning; Sabbat are frequently proven to have broader or more accomplished ranges of these undead gifts than their Camarilla or independent rivals. Elder Sabbat warn their childer, however, that skill in Disciplines is no match for the ability to use them effectively. All the Potence in the world won't help you if a cagey coterie of Camarilla neonates influences the police to raid your haven at high noon.

Storytellers are encouraged to exercise a bit more leniency when their Sabbat players express interest in out-of-clan Disciplines. It's not unreasonable for a Serpent of the Light to teach a packmate Serpentis in exchange for a bit of instruction with Obtenebration. Of course, some bit of restraint should exist — despite all their preparation for the Great Jyhad, Sabbat are still very fractious, and they have their own agendas. Most Cainites teach Disciplines to others only on a *quid pro quo* basis.

"Incomplete" entries in this chapter signify that the vampires who practice a given Discipline do not have clan members of sufficient generation to wield the higher-level powers. For example, the Salubri *antitribu* are known to have no members lower than the Seventh Generation. As such, their Discipline of Valeren is known only to the sixth level of mastery.

HOME BREW

The powers covered in this chapter are the most well-known (or notorious) high-level variations of the vampiric Disciplines, but are by no means the only ones. Once a vampire has sufficient skill and power (and generation) to master Discipline Levels Six plus, she also gains a sufficient understanding of her Discipline's essential nature to allow her to create her own powers. That does not mean that a sixth-generation priscus can do whatever the hell he wants with shadows by using Obtenebration, but rather that he may conceive and develop a new Level Six power and purchase it with experience instead of the power presented herein.

New powers that a character creates *must* be cleared with the Storyteller before it may be used during the game. Power

Discipline Level	Cost (Clan Discipline)	Cost (Non-Clan Discipline)
6	30	42
7	35	49
8	40	56
9	45	63

Storytellers, think long and hard about allowing players' characters to master high-level Disciplines, even if they somehow acquire sufficient generation to do so — the goal is not to find new ways of wreaking more havoc on the environment but to gain an increased understanding over the curse of undeath.

Level 10 Disciplines are available only to vampires of the Third Generation, and have been left undisclosed deliberately; who knows what powers the godlike Antediluvians wield?

level, game balance and suitability to the chronicle should dictate which powers fly and which powers deserve a roll of the eyes. A Storyteller has the right to gun down a proposed power at any time in the best interests of the game. Just because a character has the potential to create a new power doesn't mean that she can — or should — do it.

DARK THAUMATURGY

Despite the inexplicable disappearance of the Tremere *antitribu*, Dark Thaumaturgy has entrenched itself into the malignant underground of the Sabbat. A basic tenet of Sabbat unity is the sharing of Disciplines among pack members. This sharing strengthens the pack as a whole, and it better prepares the pack for a stand against the Camarilla. Although this tenet is true, however, students of Dark Thaumaturgy are still rare, due to the innate dangers in dealing with the infernal.

Dark Thaumaturgy is simply Thaumaturgical knowledge gleaned from demons, rather than a separate Discipline. The distinction is made merely for the purposes of illustrating the danger of dealing with infernal forces — learning a path or ritual from a text or another vampire does not leave the taint of the infernal on a vampire. Trucking with demons, however, stains the soul in a serious way.

In the absence of traditional Tremere training and research, some Sabbat who want to learn the secrets of Thaumaturgy turn to demons. These demons pride themselves on taking over the beings to whom they teach their dark magics and bending them to their infernal will. Practitioners of Dark Thaumaturgy think they work to control the "Devil on their shoulder", lest it take over entirely. In reality, Dark Thaumaturgy is practiced predominantly by fools who think they're going to outsmart the Devil, those who want a quick route to power and people too weak to resist infernal temptation.

Dark Thaumaturgy has levels and paths, just like Thaumaturgy. The mechanical difference between Thaumaturgy and Dark Thaumaturgy is relatively moot — paths and rituals still create the same effects. However, Dark Thaumaturgy comes with a price. Traffic with the Devil's minions permanently scars the soul, and the taint of infernalism manifests in the Dark Thaumaturge's aura. Before long, the unmistakable marks of the Devil's favor may even appear physically, as a wart on the nose, a "witch's claw" behind the ear or even (among the most Damned of the Damned) withered limbs, freakish scars, horns or cloven hoofs! Needless to say, once these visible traits appear, the Inquisition is sure to follow close behind, hastening the infernalist to deliver his soul to whatever dark power has claimed it.

YOU'RE GOING TO HELL

In case you didn't get the clue, Dark Thaumaturgy is a *Bad Thing*. Storytellers, you don't owe it to the players to let them take it. Thaumaturgy and Dark Thaumaturgy alike are dying among the Sabbat because the best practitioners of arcane magic, the Tremere *antitribu*, have vanished from the sect.

This Discipline is included for those Storytellers who would like to introduce this element into their stories. You're not going to find any Traits for demons in this book (or very many other places in **Vampire**); they're left up the Storyteller to do with exactly what she will, which may be nothing at all. The methods for characters (*not* players — this is a game, not a Demon Summoning 101 primer) to contact the infernal host is likewise left to Storyteller discretion. If you don't want to use it, you don't have to.

If you, as a Storyteller, decide to implement Dark Thaumaturgy, you may wish to restrict it to Storyteller characters. Should you allow players' characters access to its powers, you should temper its appreciable benefits with significant disadvantages. Quite simply, learning Thaumaturgy from a demon requires service to that demon. Sure, a player gets to learn the Path of Phobos at little experience point cost, but he must do what the demon says, *whenever it wants him to*. Should some character actually *want* to enter into pacts of this nature (it does make for a good "damnation" chronicle or tragic character flaw), don't feel guilty about dragging him off to Hell at the demon's slightest inkling. That's what you get when you deal with the Devil.

Again, Dark Thaumaturgy is simply Thaumaturgy learned from demons — there is no separate Dark Thaumaturgy Trait. Demons may teach any of the "normal" paths and rituals of Thaumaturgy, but a few powers may *only* be learned with demonic tutelage. Increasing path and Thaumaturgy Traits is less difficult when dealing with the minions of Hell, but that ease is more than compensated for by the ruthless pursuit and persecution the infernalist faces when (not *if*) her unholy leanings come to the fore. (Buying Thaumaturgy as a "New Discipline" with demonic instruction costs only 8 experience points. New paths cost only 5 points. Increasing a Thaumaturgy Trait with infernal assistance costs the current rating x 5 experience points, while increasing a path rating costs the current rating x 3 points.)

DARK THAUMATURGICAL PATHS

Like normal Thaumaturgy paths, Dark Thaumaturgical paths require a Willpower roll (difficulty equal to the power's level +3) and the expenditure of a blood point. Only one success is necessary to invoke these powers, unless otherwise noted. Failure on this roll signifies that the effect fails, while a botch costs the thaumaturge a permanent point of Willpower.

THE FIRES OF THE INFERNO

This path of Dark Thaumaturgy allows the thaumaturge to manipulate the supernatural flames conjured from the depths of Hades. It appears in a malignant, green, and it is impossible for the infernalist to hide. This "balefire" is supernatural fire, and it affects those with protection from mundane flames normally.

Balefire is not subtle. The sickly, green flame springs from the conjurer's hand in jets or globes, its sole purpose to damage opponents. Unlike the Lure of Flames, Fires of the Inferno are not intended for fine or discrete purposes.

System: The higher the level of mastery the practitioner possesses, the hotter the flames are. Hellfire can be extinguished in the same way as normal flames, though the green color implies that something less than normal is happening. A botched roll results in the caster losing control of the flames, which may turn on him or engulf him. Remember that vampires wishing to soak this damage must possess the Discipline of Fortitude. For details on how fire damages vampires, see **Vampire: The Masquerade**, page 227.

- • Lighter (difficulty 3 to soak, one health level of damage/turn)
- •• Stovetop (difficulty 4 to soak, two health levels of damage/turn)
- ••• Blowtorch (difficulty 5 to soak, three health levels of damage/turn)
- •••• Flame-thrower (difficulty 7 to soak, four health levels of damage/turn)
- ••••• Conflagration (difficulty 9 to soak, five health levels of damage/turn)

P O L Y

THE PATH OF PHOBOS

This path allows infernalists to wield the fears of their victims as a weapon. Practitioners of this path mystically tap into the depths of their victims' psyches, prying the terrors from their minds and making them seem very real. Many more sophisticated Sabbat infernalists prefer this path over physical ones, as they enjoy the sublime effects of using the subjects' own fears against them rather than vulgar, brutal displays of fire and demonic servants.

Infernalists using this path often experience nightmares and night terrors, which result from the many horrible memories they have leached from their victims. Storytellers should make Manipulation + Empathy rolls (difficulty 7) for characters who use the Path of Phobos more than once in a given story. The number of successes indicates how long the character must cope with the sea of stolen terrors roiling in her own mind. Botching results in the nightmares not only recurring for a week, but draining an additional nightly blood point from the vampire, due to the lack of sound sleep. Such is the price of hellish insight.

1 Success	One Week
2 Successes	Five Days
3 Successes	Four Days
4 Successes	Two Days
5 Successes	One Day

• INDUCE FEAR

This power causes the victim to feel extremely paranoid. Subtle shapes and shadows move in and out of the victim's vision, tormenting her by lurking just beyond her range of sight.

System: The infernalist can use this power on any target within his view. For the duration of the effect, the subject becomes noticeably upset and preoccupied, which should be roleplayed. The victim must make a Courage roll (difficulty 5 + the number of successes the thaumaturge garnered) to take any action other than looking for the imagined stalker. If the character enters combat while under the effects of Induce Fear, she loses one die from all dice pools (provided she even makes the Courage roll), as her invisible stalkers distract and disconcert her.

1 Success	One Turn
2 Successes	Five Minutes
3 Successes	One Hour
4 Successes	One Night
5 Successes	Two Nights

•• SPOOK

This power turns suspicion to dread, as the flitting shadows become visible threats. The victim feels that something terrible is about to happen to her unless she leaves the area quickly. She might imagine she sees the flash of a gun barrel or hears the clicking of hard-soled shoes on the pavement just behind her. She might even believe she smells her pursuer's sweat or feels his damp breath on the back of her neck.

System: The nagging sense of discomfort in the back of the character's mind becomes more tangible. Mortals must make a successful Courage roll (difficulty 7) to keep from fleeing the area in terror. Vampires must make the same roll, but if they fail they enter Rötschreck. The thaumaturge must see her victim for this power to work.

••• Terrorize

The infernalist can draw out his victim's fear and present him with it. The victim sees that which terrifies him the most. If he fears spiders, he may imagine spider webs brushing his face and hands as thousands of illusory arachnids scuttle across his flesh. He may hear them skittering across the floor or clicking their horrid chelicerae. To the victim, the effects seem very real, though they are simply illusions.

System: The Willpower roll to activate this power also determines how long its effects last. Should the terrorized character wish to take any action, a Courage roll (difficulty 7) is required to allow her to shake off her fear, otherwise she simply cowers, feebly hiding from her imagined object of terror. Botching this Courage roll results in a derangement, preferably suited to the fear visiting the victim. The vampire must see his victim in order to use this power.

1 Success	One Turn
2 Successes	Five Minutes
3 Successes	30 Minutes
4 Successes	One Hour
5 Successes	One Night

•••• Fear-Plague

The victim's most deep-rooted fear reveals itself to the infernalist with this power, who then forces the victim to deal with it head-on. The fear plagues the victim in every waking moment, and often in his sleep as well. A person afraid of drowning would feel the air thicken and coagulate in his throat and lungs, until he cannot take a breath, for example, while a person afraid of vampires may see fanged nemeses in his coworkers or lurking behind every corner. Eventually, the victim becomes so exhausted that he is unable rise and face a new night of swarming horrors.

System: This power lasts for a week, during which the victim suffers his fear at every turn. Weakened by his constant state of fear, the character cannot spend Willpower, and the player makes all Willpower rolls as if his permanent rating is three lower (to a minimum of 1). The thaumaturge must see his victim to activate this power, but once it takes effect, it works regardless of whether or not he maintains a line of sight.

••••• Leech of Fear

This power enables the infernalist to temporarily feed on fear as though it was blood. This experience gives a euphoric high stronger than conventional feeding, but it is a dangerous practice if used too frequently. The thaumaturge converts the pure emotional charge drawn from the victim's terror into a mystical substitute for vitae. This power may

have something to do with old legends of vampires being able to "smell fear."

System: As long as a thaumaturge with this power has a victim in sight, he may attempt to gain sustenance from that victim's fear. The victim must have cause to be afraid of something or someone while the infernalist practices this power, but those fears may not be caused by other applications of this path. The number of successes equals the "fear pool" the Cainite takes from the victim. This pool may be spent like blood pool, but must be used before sunrise. Any unused points disappear at that time. In addition to the lost Willpower point, a botch means that the infernalist gets no "fear pool" from the victim, and cannot use the power on that victim again for 24 hours.

The Taking of the Spirit

This path allows the infernalist to strip away the Willpower of his victim, leaving an almost soulless automaton ready to serve the Cainite without question. Some fiendish vampires have built entire legions of servants for themselves with this power, and it works on vampires and kine alike.

System: The victim loses a number of temporary Willpower equal to the vampire's mastery of this path (see table). Should the victim know what is taking place (having heard of it, or having had it happen before), the player may resist with her own Willpower roll (difficulty 7). If the victim's player accumulates more successes on this extended, resisted roll than the thaumaturge before being reduced to zero Willpower, this path may not be used against her character by the same thaumaturge for a full year. If the victim is reduced to zero Willpower, she must do the vampire's bidding, not speaking, staring blankly forward, in a state much like a zombie. The victim regains a Willpower point per night, which the thaumaturge may continue to try to steal away. If she sees her "master" killed, she regains full Willpower pool immediately. The Cainite must touch the victim to perform the Taking of the Spirit.

A botch on the part of the thaumaturge has unique results: He loses the corresponding number of temporary Willpower points (which also return at a rate of one per night). If all points are lost, he may come under the control of otherworldly forces.

•	Loss of one Willpower point
••	Loss of two Willpower points
•••	Loss of four Willpower points
••••	Loss of six Willpower points
•••••	Loss of eight Willpower points

Dark Thaumaturgical Rituals

Like the rituals of regular Thaumaturgy, these rituals have ratings. The ritual's rating is the lowest level of Thaumaturgy a vampire may have before attempting to use it. For example, a character must have mastered the third level of Thaumaturgy before attempting to use the *Felis Negrum* ritual. Also, like the rituals of Thaumaturgy, these rituals must be learned before they can be used. Generally, the higher the level of the ritual, the longer it takes to learn, though the aid of demons does speed up the process.º

Dark Thaumaturgical rituals require a successful Intelligence + Occult roll, for which the difficulty equals the level of the ritual + 3 (to a maximum of 9). Only one success is required for a ritual to work, but some spells may require more successes or have variable effects based on how well the player rolled. Should this roll fail, the spell may simply have no effect, or the Storyteller may come up with an interesting side effect. Should the player botch the roll, he's managed to anger some denizen of the Abyss, which can't be good for the character's long-term well-being. Unless mentioned otherwise, rituals require five minutes per level to cast.

BIND THE INTERLOPER (VARIABLE-LEVEL RITUAL)

This ritual allows a character to force a demon summoned by another thaumaturge into servitude, allowing him to command the demon as if he summoned it himself. Some methods may include promising a bounty of souls to the infernal in payment, knowledge of the demon's True Name (which probably differs from its summoning name) or a sacrifice of a valuable object or commodity like the caster's blood.

System: The ritual's level varies depending on the potency of the entity being bound (see the table for Call Forth the Host), and the ritual requires 10 minutes per level to perform. The thaumaturge must know the demon's name and achieve more successes on the roll than the original summoner accumulated when calling the demon forth. Should the binding succeed, the demon serves the thaumaturge for the remainder of its servitude period, without beginning a new one.

CALL FORTH THE HOST (VARIABLE-LEVEL RITUAL)

This ritual draws forth a demon or tortured spirit from the Inferno. The creature appears through the power of the ritual and follows the thaumaturge's instructions to the letter (but *not* the spirit — demons are known for warping their orders to serve their own ends). Note that most demons resent being summoned and ordered around in this way; they may return later of their own volition to torment the would-be sorcerer. The character must know the name of the demon she wishes to summon for this ritual to take effect. Demons take many forms, though they may generally disguise themselves to walk unnoticed among humankind.

System: This ritual requires one hour per level to perform (for example, summoning an imp takes only one hour, while summoning a shade takes three). The summoned demon serves the character for a number of hours equal to 10 minus the level of the ritual (again, by way of example, an imp would serve for nine hours while a shade would serve for only

seven). During this period of servitude, the demon may not harm the caster, and it must follow her instructions exactly. When the duration of servitude expires, the demon vanished in a puff of sulfur and returns to Hell (though it may return of its own accord later to even the score).

Level	Demon
One	Imp (a mindless, slave demon — Physical Attributes of 1, Intelligence 1)
Three	Shade (a tormented soul — Physical Attributes of 2, Mental Attributes of 2)
Five	Pit Lord (a demonic sergeant-at-arms — Physical Attributes of 3, Social and Mental Attributes of 2)
Seven	Lesser Demon Noble (a ruler of some territory in Hell — all Attributes of 3 or greater, likely with 10-12 points in Disciplines)
Nine	Greater Demon (what are you thinking? — all Attributes of 5 or greater [though these may rise to godlike levels], with a daunting array of Disciplines)

CURSE OF OEDIPUS (LEVEL ONE RITUAL)

This ritual completely blinds the target. It requires the thaumaturge to light a stick of heavy incense, the smoke from which is believed to mystically cloud the target's vision.

System: This ritual blinds the target — who need not be seen, though the caster must know her name or what she looks like — for a number of hours equal to five minus her Stamina.

VIDEO NEFAS (LEVEL TWO RITUAL)

The caster entreats demons to answer his questions, revealing secret knowledge or unearthing mysteries. Most demons are not omniscient, however, and this ritual's effectiveness is limited by the demon's knowledge. This ritual has no visible effect, but individuals with Auspex sometimes claim to have seen imps or homunculi whispering into a thaumaturge's ear. The caster must break a dried bone in two for this ritual to take effect.

System: The number of successes accumulated on the roll determines the extent of the information the demon must reveal. The caster may ask only one question of the demon, but he may cast this ritual as many times as he wants.

1 success	Yes or No
2 successes	A short sentence
3 successes	A descriptive synopsis (3-4 sentences)
4 successes	A complete answer
5 successes	An encyclopedic answer, which may include the topic's history, interesting personages involved or even apocryphal lore never before known to mortals or Cainites.

FELIS NEGRUM (LEVEL THREE RITUAL)

This ritual turns the thaumaturge or another individual into a black cat. The thaumaturge must burn the whisker of a black cat or the skin of a white cat and inscribe the subject's name on a piece of glass in her own blood.

System: If the infernalist uses the ritual on herself, she can change back at will. If used on a ghoul, the spell lasts only 24 hours. If used on another vampire, the spell lasts for 12 nights minus one per Willpower point (permanent, not pool) the victim possessed at the time of the transformation. The target may resist whether she knows precisely what is happening or not, by winning a resisted roll against the thaumaturge's Willpower. This ritual requires the caster to spend one blood point. The subject acquires all Traits — including Mental Attributes — of a cat for the duration of the transformation.

PLAGUE'S SECRET DOMAIN (LEVEL FOUR RITUAL)

This ritual causes the victim to become "sick at heart." The subject loses interest in his regular activities or his personal appearance, and he eventually sees no reason to continue his life or unlife, falling into torpor or chronic depression. The infernalist must perform the ritual in front of a smoking censer, which she extinguishes with freshly spilled blood from a source other than herself at the ritual's completion.

System: Each success (above two) adds a day to the victim's depression. If it continues for 10 days (this ritual may be cast more than once), the victim enters torpor if he is a vampire. If used on a mortal it works the same, except at the end of the 10 days, he dies, taking his own life to end the misery and drudgery of it all. This ritual requires two blood points that must be taken from a "donor" other than the thaumaturge.

CLOSE THE WAYS (LEVEL FIVE RITUAL)

The infernalist who calls on this ritual does not do so lightly, for it is much more difficult to undo the curse than to call it down on an enemy. While this curse does not necessarily kill, it does deluge the subject with a tide of terrible fortune. It is generally only invoked in the weeks leading up to a War Party or crusade, and it is conducted during one of the Sabbat's *auctoritas ritae* such as the *Festivo dello Estinto* or *Palla Grande*. The caster extinguishes 14 flames with his bare hands, naming his intended victim with every flame doused.

System: A successfully cast ritual brings untold bad luck to the victim. Success causes an automatic botch to the victim's rolls for a specified period of time. Treat this botch as a "ghost" 1 on die rolls, as if the victim always had an additional 1 turn up. Thus, if the subject rolled no successes but no 1s, he would still botch, as the "ghost" 1 turned his failure into a botch. Likewise, if the victim's rolls garner any successes, subtract one for the "ghost" 1. The caster must sacrifice two points of *permanent* Willpower when enacting this ritual, to stave of the Rötschreck of the flames and to bring the curse down on her victim's head. This curse may be broken only by the thaumaturge invoking it, and to do so she must cut off her own left hand and spend two more points of permanent Willpower.

1 success	One night
2 successes	One week
3 successes	One month
4 successes	One year
5 successes	10 years

INTO THE ABYSS (LEVEL FIVE RITUAL)

This ritual allows the caster to step into Hell itself. Why anyone would want to do this is unknown, but some Sabbat claim to have had packmates dragged into the Inferno, or that ancient Cainite artifacts lie among the Devil's hoards. To enact this ritual, the caster must wash an entire wall with the blood of children; the wall then becomes the portal into Hell.

System: This ritual requires 24 hours to cast, during which the thaumaturge must remain awake. At the end of the ritual, the portal opens, and it will remain so for a number of hours equal to the caster's Willpower. Denizens of Hell may not escape through this portal, though they may attempt to deny exit to any vampires who have invaded their realm of eternal torture.

DEMENTATION

Dementation, the madness-inducing Discipline of the Malkavians, originally belonged solely to the Malkavian *antitribu*, as the Camarilla Lunatics instead adopted Dominate. As such, the Discipline is covered in this volume rather than in the companion **Guide to the Camarilla**, as the undisputed masters of the higher-level uses of Dementation are among the Sabbat. Such truth is never immutable, however, and the Malkavians of the Camarilla are adapting to their recent "infection" with the Discipline with alarming speed. It's almost as if they were naturals....

●●●●● LINGERING MALAISE

While lesser Dementation powers allow a Malkavian to inflict temporary (though often long-lasting) madness upon a victim, elders of the clan have developed the ability to infect the minds of their victims with permanent dementia. Lingering Malaise causes permanent psychological shifts within the victim, making him, as one Gangrel elder remarked, "an honorary Lunatic."

System: The character speaks to his victim for at least a minute, describing the derangement that Lingering Malaise will inflict. The player rolls Manipulation + Empathy (difficulty of the victim's Willpower); the victim resists with a Willpower roll (difficulty 8). If the user of Lingering Malaise scores more net successes, the victim gains a permanent derangement chosen by the individual who inflicts it. Lingering Malaise may only be used to inflict one derangement per night on any given victim, though multiple attempts may be made until the derangement takes hold.

●●●●●● SHATTERED MIRROR

Although Dementation's low-level effects are primarily to initiate or promote insanity rather than to create it spontaneously, some of its more potent manifestations are not as subtle. The wielder of this fearsome power can transfer her own deranged mindset into the psyche of a hapless victim, spreading her own brand of insanity like a virus.

System: The vampire must establish eye contact with her intended victim to apply this power. The player then rolls

Charisma + Subterfuge (difficulty of the target's Willpower) resisted by the target's Wits + Self-Control/Instinct (difficulty of the Malkavian's Willpower). If the aggressor wins, the target gains *all* of her derangements and Mental Flaws for a period of time determined by the number of net successes the aggressor scored:

1 success	one hour
2 successes	one night
3 successes	one week
4 successes	one month
5 successes	six months
6+ successes	one year per success over 5

RESTRUCTURE

The elder with this fearsome power has the ability to twist his victims' psyches at their most basic levels, warping their very beings. The subject of Restructure retains her memories *in toto*, but her outlook on life changes completely, as if she has undergone a sudden epiphany or religious conversion. This effect goes much deeper than the implantation of a derangement; it actually performs a complete rewriting of the victim's very personality.

System: As the description says, this power allows the Malkavian to change his target's Nature to one more suitable to his ends. To accomplish this, the character must make eye contact with his intended victim. The player rolls Manipulation + Subterfuge (difficulty of the victim's Wits + Subterfuge). If he rolls a number of successes equal to or greater than the target's Self-Control/Instinct, the target's Nature changes to whatever the player desires. This effect is permanent and can be undone only by another application of Restructure (though subtle differences from the character's original Nature may still remain, as it is impossible for such a grave change to occur flawlessly). A botch on this roll changes the character's own Nature to that of his intended victim.

DEMENTATION AND IRON WILL

The Merit: Iron Will (**Vampire: The Masquerade**, p. 299) grants immunity to Dementation in the same manner as it does versus Dominate: By spending a Willpower point, the player negates the effect of a successful application of Dementation to her character. However, as is the case with Dominate, high levels of Dementation may overwhelm even this resistance. Rather than completely negating the effect of an elder Dementation power, the use of Iron Will raises its effective difficulty, which may reduce the number of successes rolled. Against Dementation Level Six, the expenditure of a Willpower point through Iron Will raises the difficulty of the Dementation roll by two. Against Dementation Level Seven, the same expenditure raises the Dementation difficulty by one. Dementation Level Eight and higher cannot be resisted with Iron Will.

PERSONAL SCOURGE

Similar to the Auspex power of Psychic Assault (see **Guide to the Camarilla**), this fearsome ability allows the elder to turn the very strength of her victim's mind against him, inflicting physical harm with the power of his own will. Victims of this self-powered attack spontaneously erupt in lacerations and bruises, spraying blood in every direction and howling in agony. Those who have observed such an attack with Auspex note that the victim's aura swirls with violent psychosis and erupts outward in writhing appendages — a sight that can make even the most hardened Tzimisce quail. Some callous vampires call the victims of this power Blairs, apparently some sort of pop-culture reference.

System: The vampire must touch or establish eye contact with her target. The player rolls Manipulation + Empathy (difficulty of the target's Stamina + Self-Control/Instinct) and spends two Willpower points. For a number of turns equal to the number of successes rolled, the victim rolls his own permanent Willpower as lethal damage against himself (soaked with his own Humanity or Path of Enlightenment [difficulty 6] — Fortitude does *not* add to this soak dice pool, nor does body armor). He may take no other actions during this time other than thrashing and gibbering; this includes spending blood to heal.

LUNATIC ERUPTION

This fearsome ability is only known to have been applied a few times in recorded Kindred history, most spectacularly during the final nights of the last battle of Carthage. It is effectively a psychic nuclear bomb, used to incite every intelligent being within several miles into an orgy of bloodlust and rage. It is suspected that the Malkavians have used the threat of this power as a bargaining chip in several key negotiations with Camarilla elders.

System: The player spends four Willpower points and rolls Stamina + Intimidation (difficulty 8). The radius of effect is determined by the number of successes scored:

1 success	one city block or 500 feet
2 successes	an entire neighborhood or one mile
3 successes	a large downtown area or three miles
4 successes	several neighborhoods or 10 miles
5 successes	an entire metropolitan area or 30 miles
6+ successes	an additional 10 miles for every success past 5

Within this area, all sentient creatures fall prey to their baser instincts. Mortals spontaneously riot, looting and burning between bouts of mass violence. Kindred enter hunger-induced frenzies, draining dry as many vessels as they can sink their fangs into. Other supernatural beings run amok according to their base natures: Lupines under the effect of this power enter their warforms and frenzy indiscriminately at anything that resembles an enemy, mages temporarily fall into states of magic-induced delusion, and the fae bask in the sudden influx of energy and revel in their temporary power. An entire city can quite literally be driven temporarily insane by this power. Lunatic Eruption's effects persist until the next sunrise, and anyone entering its radius of effect (centered on the site at which it was used, not on the character who applied it) falls under its spell. However, inertia may carry the violence spawned by this power much farther — and keep it going much longer — than the power itself can force.

Victims of Lunatic Eruption may resist with Self-Control/Instinct rolls (difficulty of the character's Willpower); each success provides one hour of lucidity, which most wise individuals use to leave the power's area of effect (leaving the "blast radius" does remove the power's influence). The source of Lunatic Eruption may be pinpointed if a character is using Heightened Senses or an equivalent power at the time it is used; this is automatic and requires no roll. However, this grants no knowledge of what actually happened — the observer simply "feels" a massive psychic shockwave explode from the character using the power.

MYTHERCERIA

The curious blood coursing through the undead veins of the Kiasyd has done some remarkable things, not the least of which has been the creation of the odd Discipline known as Mytherceria. A collection of powers attributed to the faeries and inclined toward the exposure of new knowledge, Mytherceria has driven many of its victims to babbling madness, or at least frustration. The Kiasyd are loath to teach its ways to others outside their bloodline — they know that were it turned against them, they may be forced to reveal secrets the world is better off not knowing.

• FOLDEROL

It becomes increasingly difficult to deceive the Kiasyd as they absorb more and more knowledge. This power reveals lies told to the Kiasyd in several different ways, which varies from vampire to vampire. Some Kiasyd perceive lies via their teller's tongue glowing in an unnatural color, while others' eyes well up with blood tears when lied to. The manner varies from Kiasyd to Kiasyd, but the effect is always the same — he knows you have lied to him.

System: The player rolls Perception + Expression (difficulty equal to the suspected liar's Manipulation + Subterfuge). If the roll succeeds, the Kiasyd gets an inkling as to whether or not the subject is lying. One roll must be made for each statement, should the Kiasyd be so suspicious as to check out everything the speaker says.

•• FAE SIGHT

Attuned to the blood of the Wild Ones, Kiasyd have some propensity for seeing the true nature of the changelings. Kiasyd can identify changelings on sight, and they can even see through to the Wild blood underneath. Additionally, they are able to recognize areas of faerie influence.

System: Kiasyd see changelings for what they truly are. Also, in any area of recent magical faerie activity (cantrips,

summoned chimera, etc.), the Kiasyd knows that the fae have been present on a Perception + Occult roll (difficulty 6).

••• AURA ABSORPTION

This power works much like the Auspex power of The Spirit's Touch. The Kiasyd must touch or pick up the object being read. Instead of just receiving and interpreting the psychic impressions left on the object by the last person who came in contact with it, the Kiasyd absorbs the impressions into her mind. This leaves her with a very clear interpretation of the aura, and wipes the object "psychically clean" so no one coming afterwards can get an impression from the item by using this ability or Auspex. Kiasyd also use this power to mask their own possession of an object.

System: The player must make a Perception + Empathy roll, for which the difficulty is determined by the Storyteller's assessment of the age of the impressions and the mental and spiritual strength of the person who left them.

The number of successes determines the amount of information gained, both in terms of images of the scene when the object was being held or touched, and the nature of the person who was holding the object. One scene-type image and one aspect of the person's identity (Nature, Demeanor, aura, name, sex or age) becomes clear for each success the player garners on the roll.

Anyone attempting to use this power or The Spirit's Touch on the same object subsequently must accumulate more successes than the Kiasyd did to get any impression at all. The first Kiasyd's successes subtract from the number of successes scored by anyone subsequently trying to read the object thereafter.

•••• CHANJELIN WARD

The vampire can create mystical wards, symbols of occult power that disorient onlookers. Many Kiasyd use these glyphs to protect their libraries, though some spiteful vampires use them as curses by placing them on individuals who have earned their disfavor.

System: The vampire creating the ward inscribes the symbol in a visible location — on a library door, bookshelf or an individual's clothing — and the player rolls Intelligence + Security (difficulty 7 for inanimate objects or the subject's Willpower +2). Anyone entering the warded area or touching the warded object loses two dice from her Intelligence dice pools as long as she maintains contact or proximity to the ward. Additionally, anyone seeing the ward becomes addled and lost unless she makes a Wits + Investigation roll (difficulty 8). The glyphs last for a duration indicated by the number of successes on the Intelligence + Security roll, and the Kiasyd is immune to his own wards.

1 success	One hour
2 successes	One night
3 successes	One week
4 successes	One month
5 successes	One year

••••• RIDDLE PHANTASTIQUE

The Kiasyd has knowledge of many hidden and intriguing truths. He can phrase these enigmas as a vexing riddle, causing whoever hears the Riddle Phantastique to do nothing but try to solve it. The Riddle is so impenetrable that it can actually damage the fragile brains of those who think about it. Malkavians and other deranged individuals sometimes have easier times solving the Riddle, but at other times it plagues them by driving them even more insane.

System: The player rolls Manipulation + Occult (difficulty of the victim's Willpower). After a successful roll, the victim can do nothing but sit and ponder the Riddle until she accumulates three times the riddler's successes. The subject rolls Wits + Occult (difficulty 8, plus or minus the number of derangements the victim has, at the Storyteller's discretion). She makes this roll as soon as she is told the Riddle, and then once per hour until she has gathered enough successes. Should the victim botch on a roll to solve the Riddle, she takes one level of lethal damage as the mystical enigma racks her body, and she loses one success from the accumulated total. This damage cannot be healed until the Riddle has been solved. The riddler can end this trance just by telling the victim the answer, but no one else can do so.

•••••• STEAL THE MIND

This power is a further extension of the Kiasyd's mystical lore-gathering abilities. In their ever-increasing quest for knowledge, the Kiasyd have found a way to rip memories and knowledge from sentient beings. The Kiasyd's victim becomes a mindless fool for the duration of this power's effect, able to function only on a basic autonomic level (mortals continue to breathe, while vampires simply stand in stupor). Normally in this state, the victim is so confused that she wanders aimlessly, or sits and does nothing. As soon as the Kiasyd purloins the memories, she often records them in a more permanent form such as a scroll or book, before they escape her own memory. This power accounts for some reports of individuals being left, foolish and duped, by "the Good Folk."

System: The player rolls Perception + Subterfuge (difficulty equal to the target's Willpower). While the Kiasyd has "stolen" her subject's mind, she retains her own consciousness, but has complete access to all of the subject's thoughts and memories. Subjects have no knowledge that they have been affected in this manner, though any attempts to harm them — by the Kiasyd or anyone else — return their wits to them immediately. Those who are victims of this power for long periods of time may starve, but they will eat food presented before them. The number of successes determines the duration of the effect, though the Cainite may return the subject's mind at any time before this period ends.

1 Success	10 minutes
2 Successes	One hour
3 Successes	One night
4 Successes	One week
5 Successes	One month

•••••• •• ABSORB THE MIND

The Kiasyd absorbs the Abilities from her victim's mind, and she is able to call on them immediately, even though she might have never had knowledge of them before. This power is invasive, actually stealing the Abilities permanently, leaving their original owners ignorant and inept.

System: The player rolls Perception + Empathy (difficulty of the target's Willpower). The target may resist with a Willpower roll (difficulty of the Kiasyd's Willpower). The difference between the two determines the effect. If the target gets more successes, he resists completely. The Kiasyd, if successful, may select a combination of Abilities to her satisfaction. Taking some of a victim's Ability dots may leave a remaining bit — the Kiasyd need not take *all* of a subject's dots in a given Ability. (For example, a character with three dots in Occult, from whom a Kiasyd steals one, retains an Occult of 2.) Also, if a Kiasyd takes less dots than she already has in a given Ability, these points do not serve to raise her own score. (In the previous example, the Kiasyd would not increase his Occult score if he already had a score of one or more, as he took only one dot.) No subsequent attempt can be made by the Kiasyd on a target against whom he fails the Perception + Empathy roll for at least a year. In all cases, the maximum to which the Kiasyd can raise an Ability is the level the target has in that Ability. (Again by example, if a victim has a dot in Law and the Kiasyd gets 2 successes, she can't gain 2 dots in Law.) Also, generation restrictions apply; a Sixth Generation Kiasyd can have a maximum of seven dots in an Ability. All losses of Abilities on the part of the victim are permanent, though they may be returned to their original levels via experience-point expenditure.

1 Success	Steal 1 dot
2 Successes	Steal 2 dots in One Ability
3 Successes	Steal 3 dots in up to Two Abilities
4 Successes	Steal 4 dots in up to Three Abilities
5 Successes	Steal 5 dots in up to Four Abilities

••••• ••• THE GRANDEST TRICK

For an exceedingly brief time, the Kiasyd may call his fae blood to prominence to subdue the Curse of Caine. The Kiasyd may become mortal again, discarding all of the benefits and drawbacks of being a vampire. While (temporarily) mortal, the Kiasyd has no knowledge or memory of being a vampire, though he retains all other knowledge and memories. Kiasyd sometimes use this power to pursue lore accessible only by day (for whatever reason), though they sometimes use it to throw witch-hunters off their trail or simply for the bittersweet pleasure of seeing sunrise without fear.

System: The player spends eight blood points and makes a Willpower roll (difficulty 9). If this roll is successful, the character becomes mortal at the next sunrise for a duration determined by the number of successes on the roll. The Kiasyd knows, however subliminally, the duration of the power, and he automatically seeks to return to safety, should daylight be a problem at the duration's end (though "safety" is impossible to reach in some situations). After this power ends, the Kiasyd retains all memories of his brief return to the world of mortals. During his time as a mortal, the character's Traits are limited to scores of 5 (which return to their original levels when the character becomes a vampire again), and the character has no access to her Disciplines. Likewise, the character may not use blood points for any vampiric benefits while mortal.

1 success	10 minutes
2 successes	One hour
3 successes	Four hours
4 successes	12 hours
5 successes	24 hours

NECROMANCY

Widely believed to be practiced by only the loathsome Giovanni, Necromancy has actually been adopted by the Harbingers of Skulls, who claim to have learned the magic of death while trapped in the Underworld. Harbingers seem to know little of the Bone or Sepulchre Paths, instead learning their own Mortuus Path and the Ash Path. Harbingers of Skulls have not been known to interact with the Giovanni, but they may have acquired some knowledge of other paths from the Samedi, with whom they share some inexplicable tie. Harbingers of Skulls learn the Mortuus Path as their primary Necromancy Path; they can only learn their first level of the Ash Path after achieving the third level of mastery in the Mortuus Path. That aside, they learn Necromancy like other vampires.

THE MORTUUS PATH

• REAPER'S SHROUD

This power allows the Cainite or the subject of her choice to take on the semblance of death. Skin stretches tight over bones, flesh grows pale and sallow and joints seize as the body grows rigid. This power may be used to "play dead" and look the part, or to curse another with the appearance of the walking dead.

System: The vampire must touch her target for this power to take effect. If the Necromancer assumes this form, she merely spends a blood point. If attempting to use this power on another, the character's player spends a blood point and makes a Stamina + Occult roll (difficulty equal to the victim's Stamina +3). The effects of this power last until the next dawn or dusk, when the shriveled individual slowly regains her normal state over the course of an hour. While under the effects of the Reaper's Shroud, characters lose two points from their Dexterity and Appearance Traits (to a minimum of 1). Vampires may spend two blood points to reverse the effects of Reaper's Shroud.

•• BLIGHT

This power allows the vampire to accelerate the aging and decrepitude processes in his intended victim. The subject suffers the effects of old age: brittle bones, dry and thin skin and various rheumatic pains among others. Some victims

have even acquired certain ailments normally experienced by the elderly, including bone diseases and arthritis..

System: The vampire must touch his intended victim. The player then rolls Manipulation + Medicine (difficulty equal to the victim's Willpower) and spends one point of Willpower. If this roll is successful, the target suffers the debilitating effects of advanced age. For the duration of this power (until the next dusk or dawn), the target, Cainite or otherwise, must subtract three points from all Physical Attributes (to a minimum of 1). Vampires and ghouls affected in this manner may still spend blood points to increase their Physical Attributes.

Mortals who undertake stressful activity while affected by Blight run the risk of heart failure. For each round the mortal continues strenuous activity, the player must make a Stamina roll (difficulty 6). If the roll fails, the mortal suffers a heart attack.

●●● RESUME THE COIL

This power allows vampires to wrench themselves free from death's long slumber. A character who possesses this level of mastery may throw off the darkness of torpor or aid another in doing so.

System: The player spends two Willpower points. She then makes a Willpower roll, for which the difficulty is ten minus the target's Humanity or path rating. Obviously, the vampire uses her own rating if attempting to rouse herself from torpor. For example, if a vampire seeks to rise from torpor and has a Path of Death and the Soul score of 5, his difficulty for the Willpower roll is 5. If the vampire wishes to awaken another Cainite in torpor, she must touch that vampire. If the vampire so raised entered torpor because of a lack of blood, she awakens with one blood point in her veins.

●●●● TRUE DEATH

The Necromancer may temporarily cheat the Curse of Caine, albeit briefly, by becoming truly dead. While invoking this power, the character suffers none of the traditional banes against vampires. He is not burned by sunlight, holy water does not harm him, and he does not rise from the dead each night. He has literally become a corpse.

System: There is no cost to assume the corpse-body, but awakening from the slumber requires two blood points. While the character is in corpse form, he may obviously take no actions, nor may he use any Disciplines, even "automatic" ones like Fortitude. The corpse-vampire does not consume blood nightly — he retains the same amount of blood as he did when he entered the state of True Death (remember that it costs two blood points to leave the corpse state), which may prove damning should anyone cut him open in the interim. A character who has been staked through the heart is still paralyzed when he returns to vampiric consciousness. This power has no maximum duration, other than the time the vampire chooses to remain dead.

● ● ● ● ● MERCY FOR SETH

Named after mortals — the Children of Seth — this power causes a victim to contract a virulent plague, similar to the epidemics of the 11th through 15th centuries (the Black Plague, the Red Death, etc.). This illness causes death within 24 hours for mortals and sends vampires to torpor within the same period of time. Mortal victims of plague exhibit terrible plague symptoms — sunken eyes, blackened limbs, bloody sweat and excretions, swollen nodes and weeping lesions.

System: The vampire touches her victim, and the player must spend one blood point (which must come in contact with the victim to communicate the plague) and one Willpower point. The player also rolls Stamina + Occult (difficulty equal to the target's Willpower). Success indicates that the vampire has afflicted his victim with plague, who dies or succumbs to torpor within 24 hours.

NECROMANTIC RITUALS

These rituals use the same system presented in **Vampire: The Masquerade** (p. 165). The following rituals were developed by the few Sabbat practitioners of Necromancy, but are not exclusive to the Sabbat. However, they may prove difficult to learn (or even locate), and Storytellers may wish to grant non-Sabbat characters versions of these rituals that operate at higher difficulties and/or lessened effectiveness, or to deny them altogether to such characters.

ELDRITCH BEACON (LEVEL ONE RITUAL)

Eldritch Beacon takes 15 minutes to cast. The material component is a green candle, the melted wax from which must be collected and molded into a half-inch sphere. Whoever carries this sphere, whether in his hand or in a pocket, is highlighted in the Shadowlands with a sickly-glowing green-white aura. All wraithly powers affect this individual with greater ease and severity (Storytellers using **Wraith: The Oblivion** should apply a -1 difficulty to all Arcanoi affecting the bearer of the beacon). The sphere retains its power for one hour per success on the casting roll.

PUPPET (LEVEL TWO RITUAL)

Used primarily to facilitate conversations with the recently departed, though also applied as a method of psychological torture, Puppet prepares a subject (willing or unwilling) as a suitable receptacle for ghostly possession. Over the course of one hour, the necromancer smears grave soil across the subject's eyes, lips, and forehead. For the remainder of the night, any wraith attempting to take control of the subject gains two automatic successes. The ritual's effects remain even if the soil is washed off.

DIN OF THE DAMNED (LEVEL THREE RITUAL)

This ritual is similar to the Level One Ritual Call of the Hungry Dead (see **Vampire: The Masquerade**, p. 165) in that it makes the sounds of the underworld audible in the physical realm. However, Din of the Damned is an area-effect ritual used to ward a room against eavesdropping. Over the course of half an hour, the necromancer draws an unbroken line of ash from a crematorium along the room's walls (this line may pass over doorframes to allow entrance and egress). For the rest of the night, any attempt to listen in on events inside the room, be it simple (a glass to the wall), electronic (a laser microphone), or mystic (Heightened Senses), requires the eavesdropper to score more successes in a Perception + Occult roll (difficulty 7) than the caster of the ritual scored. Failure to beat this mark gives the listener an earful of ghostly wailing and moaning and the sound of howling winds; a botch deafens him for the rest of the night.

PEEK PAST THE SHROUD (LEVEL FOUR RITUAL)

This hour-long ritual enchants a handful of ergot (a mold that grows on grains prior to harvest in cold, damp weather) to act as a catalyst for second sight. By eating a pinch of the magical mold, a subject gains the benefits of Shroudsight (Ash Path Necromancy Level One, p. 164 of **Vampire: The Masquerade**) for a number of hours equal to the necromancer's Stamina score. Three doses of the enchanted ergot are created for every success on the roll. Ergot is normally poisonous to some degree; this ritual removes its toxic properties. However, a botch renders the ergot highly and instantaneously toxic, inflicting eight dice of lethal damage on any subject who ingests it — including vampires.

CHILL OF OBLIVION (LEVEL FIVE RITUAL)

Performed over the course of 12 hours (reduced by one hour per success on the casting roll), this ritual infuses the Necromancer or a willing subject with the very cold of the grave. The ritual's material component is a one-foot cube of ice, which is slowly melted on the subject's chest (inflicting three health levels of bashing damage on mortal subjects). The subject must lie naked on bare earth for the entire duration of the ritual. Once the ritual is completed, its effects remain for a number of nights equal to the caster's Occult rating.

An individual affected by the Chill of Oblivion treats aggravated damage from fire and high temperatures as if it were lethal damage. Furthermore, he may attempt to extinguish any fire by rolling Willpower (difficulty 9); each success reduces the fire's soak difficulty (see **Vampire: The Masquerade**, p. 227) by 1, and a fire with a soak difficulty of 2 dwindles to glowing embers. However, this ritual has several drawbacks. First and foremost, the subject's aura is laced with writhing black veins that resemble those left by diablerie and may well be mistaken for such by any observer who is not familiar with this ritual. The subject also radiates a palpable aura of cold that extends to about arm's length from him; this can be extremely disconcerting to mortals, though it causes no damage, and its game effects mirror those of the Flaws: Touch of Frost and Eerie Presence. Finally, the mystical nimbus of the ritual draws hostile ghosts to the subject (for Storytellers using **Wraith: The Oblivion**, the difficulties of all Dark Arcanoi used against the character are reduced by 3 while the ritual is in effect), who may plague him with unwholesome acts.

OBTENEBRATION

•••••• THE DARKNESS WITHIN

This power allows the Lasombra to call forth the darkness contained in her black soul. This enormous, turbulent shadow vomits from the Lasombra's mouth, though some Keepers are said to cut themselves and let the blackness seep from their veins. The shadow-cloud engulfs a chosen target, burning it with a soul-scarring chill and siphoning its blood away in torrents.

System: The player makes a Willpower roll and spends a blood point. The resulting shadow envelops the target and, though it does not physically harm the victim, it may strike terror into him. Individuals observing the Darkness Within, whether as targets or onlookers, may suffer the shadow Rötschreck as described in **Vampire: The Masquerade**, page 169, unless they are familiar with the Lasombra's power over darkness.

Individuals touched by The Darkness Within lose one point of blood per turn, though players may resist this effect by succeeding on a Stamina roll (difficulty 6) each turn the vampire remains in contact with the cloud.

The Cainite invoking The Darkness Within must devote all her attention toward maintaining the cloud. If the vampire is attacked, the darkness immediately returns to her, through whatever orifice it originated. The Cainite can summon the darkness back at any time, gaining a number of blood points equal to one-half the number the shadow siphoned from its victims (round up). Taking blood from another in this fashion is similar to drinking from that vampire — blood bonds may result if it happens enough. Additionally, the Darkness Within may take blood from only one individual per turn, though it may be in contact with many.

•••••• SHADOWSTEP

The vampire has such fine control over the darkness that he may become it briefly and reform himself from other darkness close by. The vampire may Shadowstep through walls, floors and even mystical barriers. The Cainite simply steps "into" a shadow and re-emerges from another shadow a short distance away.

System: The player rolls Dexterity + Occult, and on a successful roll, the character may emerge from another shadow no more than 50 feet away. Failing the roll means simply that the character cannot step through the shadow-realm, while a botch signifies the character has become trapped between shadows (which fiendish Storytellers should have a heyday with). Pulling another individual through the shadow requires a Strength + Occult roll, with consequences for failure similar to failing by oneself.

••••• •• Shadow Twin

The vampire's control over darkness has progressed to such a degree that he may bestow it with a limited degree of sentience. By animating his own shadow or that of another, the Lasombra can actually "set free" the shadow cast by light. While this power is active, the subject casts no shadow, as it has left to pursue the Lasombra's commands.

Needless to say, this power unnerves mortals and even a few inexperienced vampires. The Lasombra commands the individual's shadow, and some vampires report having seen mortals literally scared to death, as their shadows leapt away to taunt or menace them.

System: The player spends a blood point and makes a Willpower roll (difficulty 8). If the roll succeeds, the shadow springs to unholy freedom for one hour per success on the roll (though it disappears at sunrise regardless of how many successes the Lasombra had). The Shadow Twin has Attribute and Ability ratings equal to half those of its parent body; they won't do much talking or thinking, so Mental and Social Traits don't matter much, though Wits may come into play. Additionally, the Shadow Twin has an Obtenebration score equal to one-half of that of the Lasombra who animated it (rounded down).

The twin may separate itself from the parent and travel up to 50 feet away, crawling through crevices or sliding up walls. It may attack and be attacked, though it takes and does only half-damage (again, round down); flame and supernatural attacks (werewolf claws, vampire fangs, magical spells, etc.) do full damage, however. If the Shadow Twin is killed, its parent loses half her Willpower pool and must roll to avoid Rötschreck (difficulty 9).

••••• ••• Oubliette

By creating a "chamber" of pure darkness, the Lasombra may entrap or smother her enemies. No air exists in this shadow-trap, and mortals suffocate within its chilling void. Even vampires have little recourse once trapped — they may leave only at their captor's whim. The Oubliette appears as a dense patch of shadow, unaffected by ambient light around it.

System: The vampire spends a blood point, but no roll is necessary to create the Oubliette. To actually create the Oubliette around someone requires a contested Wits + Security roll against the target's Dexterity + Occult (difficulty 7 for both rolls). Mortals suffocate within a number minutes equal to their Stamina (though the Lasombra may choose to leave their head exposed or trap a quantity of air inside as well), while vampires are simply suspended impotently in darkness and may not use Disciplines or take other actions. The Oubliette vanishes instantly when touched by sunlight — which has left more than one vampire under the sun's unforgiving rays — or when the Lasombra chooses to relax it. A vampire may maintain only one Oubliette at a time, which leads some Cainite philosophers to argue that it is a prison created from the vampire's very soul, and thus limited to a single incarnation.

••••• •••• Ahriman's Demesne

This power allows the vampire to summon a darkness so obliviating that it extinguishes the light of life — or unlife — of any victim trapped within it. Ahriman's Demesne creates a 50-foot radius of void that issues from the Cainite's hand and takes away the bodies of those it claims when it vanishes. The overwhelming darkness destroys friend and foe alike, claiming anyone unfortunate enough to be within its circumference.

System: The player spends two points of Willpower and concentrates for three turns. During this time, the blackness billows out of the character's hand, growing to fill the area. At the end of the third turn, the player rolls Manipulation + Occult (difficulty 6). Everyone in the darkness' area suffers that many health levels of damage (aggravated, if the victims are vampires) outright — six successes yield six levels of damage, not six dice of damage. After Ahriman's Demesne does its damage, it collapses, taking with it the bodies of any who died when they came in contact with the dreadful shadow.

Sanguinus

Sanguinus is the unwholesome Discipline granted to the Blood Brothers by the Tzimisce who created them. A curious relative of Vicissitude, Sanguinus allows vampires who practice it to combine parts of their bodies, loan them out to others and coordinate their minds and appendages. Even low levels of it are unsettling (at best) to watch. Use of the higher levels is disgusting, indeed, as flesh parts and exposed organs, atrophied by the Blood Brothers' state of undeath, merge and pulse. Mortals observing the spectacle of this Discipline's more obvious powers must make Courage rolls (difficulty 4), spend a point of Willpower or flee the area in nausea.

• Brother's Blood

The Blood Brothers share a mystical bond established at their creation. The blood of one courses through the undead veins of all members of a certain circle. By using his own blood, a Brother may heal the wounds of another in his circle. In this manner, Blood Brothers can heal great amounts of damage without exceeding their generational blood-expenditure limits, and they may even have one of their number withdrawn from combat so that he may heal others without concentration.

System: The player spends a blood point, which may be used to heal any member of the circle, regardless of distance from the character. The Blood Brother may also "bank" blood, spending five points to heal another's aggravated wound over the course of several turns. This power takes place automatically; no roll is necessary.

•• Octopod

This grotesque power allows the Blood Brothers to share limbs and appendages. The organs so "borrowed" travel mystically over a distance, and some vampires have told stories of fighting single members of Blood Brother circles who grew extra arms to carry weapons or extra legs to brace

themselves from falling. The most unsettling aspect of this power is not the additional limbs acquired by the recipient, however; rather, the quadriplegic, eyeless or mouthless Blood Brothers littering the battlefield when this power is invoked is a far more grisly sight.

System: The "donor" player spends a blood point for each limb or organ he wishes to loan to the other circle member. (This may only be done among circle members, but only the donor needs to have this level of mastery of Sanguinus.) The loaned organs appear at the end of that turn, in whatever location the recipient wishes — eyes on the back of heads or on the ends of hands have been seen, as have entire heads located between a Blood Brother's legs. Use of this power does not impart any extra attacks inherently, but it may allow for additional sensory input, more blood to be consumed in a single turn or extra hands to hold weapons or pin down foes. Only external organs may be loaned in this manner — hearts, stomachs and brains cannot.

••• GESTALT

The Blood Brothers may activate the unique ties of blood that bind them, establishing a "hive mind" of sorts. This expanded consciousness allows them to perform efficient and powerful attacks, avoid surprise attacks and even communicate with each other telepathically.

System: This power confers several benefits on the Blood Brothers. For this power to work, however, every Blood Brother in the circle must spend a blood point. If even one member cannot or refuses to spend a blood point, this power fails. Once a Blood Brother has met the Final Death, he is no longer a part of the circle, so the power continues to function among the still-undead members of the group. Gestalt lasts for once scene. While this power is active:

— Dominate, Presence, etc. take effect against the highest Willpower score in the circle. For example, if a vampire attempts to Dominate a Blood Brother under the influence of Gestalt, she must roll against the highest Willpower score any of the vampires in the circle possesses, even if her subject has the lowest Willpower score in the circle. Additionally, a Blood Brother affected in this manner drops out of the Gestalt, though the power remains active for others. The Tremere supposedly created this mental "fuse" to prevent the entire circle from being Dominated by a vampire looking into the eyes of one Blood Brother.

— Perception difficulties for all Blood Brothers in the circle decrease by three, as they share the sensory input of other vampires in the circle.

— By taking no action other than concentrating, a Blood Brother may "loan" an Ability to another brother. For example, a wounded vampire with Melee 4 may step out of combat and loan a circle-mate with Melee 2 his mastery of that Skill. The "borrowing" vampire makes Ability checks against the loaned Trait as if it were his own.

— Blood Brothers in the Gestalt share open, two-way telepathic communication with other members of the circle. This is not a chance to read the minds of other Blood Brothers, but simple, silent communication.

Note that not all Blood Brothers need possess Sanguinus at this level to gain the benefits of the Gestalt. Players of vampires of the circle who have not mastered Sanguinus to this level, however, must make a Wits + Occult roll (difficulty 7) to gain the benefits of the link. This roll is made before the Gestalt becomes active — no "loaning" Occult for this roll! If they fail this roll, they may not gain the benefits of the Gestalt for the scene, though their applicable Traits may be used (high Willpower) or loaned (but not borrowed).

•••• WALK OF CAINE

By using this power, a Blood Brother may concentrate his own blood by drawing on the inherent Cainite curse in other members of the circle. In effect, he may lower his generation temporarily at the expense of raising the generation of other members of the circle. Some Blood Brothers have used this power to terrifying effect, lowering their generation to such a degree that they can perform truly monstrous feats, such as greatly increasing their strength or healing grievous wounds in the blink of an eye.

System: A Blood Brother may temporarily borrow one generation from other members of his circle. No vampire may loan more than one level of generation in this manner. For each level of generation he borrows from a member of the circle, the vampire using this power lowers his own generation by one level, while the Blood Brother from whom he borrowed it increases his generation by one. The Brothers loaning generations need not have Sanguinus at this level, but if they don't, they must make Stamina + Occult rolls (difficulty 7) to loan their generation. If this power takes a Blood Brother to 14th generation, see **Vampire: The Masquerade**, page 297 for the flaw "14th Generation" and apply all penalties thereof to the Cainite in question. This power lasts for one scene.

••••• Coagulated Entity

This frightening power allows the Blood Brothers of a given circle to unite physically as well as mentally. The vampires combine into one monstrous heap of undead flesh, exposing entrails, spraying foul fluids and flailing deadly limbs. These horrid mounds have proven effective in more than one Sabbat siege, sweeping over enemy vampires or smashing their way into fortified havens.

System: Every vampire in the circle who wishes to become part of the Coagulated Entity spends three blood points. Three turns after the process begins, the monster becomes complete and able to act. The vampire of the lowest generation who is part of the construct guides the creature's actions. The actual generation of the creature itself, however, is the *highest* generation of any vampire present in the construct, less one for each additional vampire present in the construct. The creature's Strength, Stamina and Perception are equal to the lowest-generation vampire's in the construct +1 for every additional vampire contained within (though generational limits do not apply to this creature — through sheer size, a Coagulated Entity may have a Strength of 7 or even more). All physical actions undertaken by the monstrosity gain one extra die to the pool for each vampire beyond the first present in the construct (before splitting dice pools). Only one vampire in the circle needs to possess Sanguinus at Level Five for this power to work. Body parts tend to shift during the creation of a Coagulated Entity — fanged maws at the ends of hands and eyes atop fleshy stalks have been reported by terrified survivors. Storytellers should feel free to give any bonuses (or penalties, as some legs may be too weak to support the creature, or arms may be too short to strike effectively) to the construct they see fit. Sanguinus is an imperfect practice, obviously.

A Coagulated Entity may not be staked, as it has too many hearts in unconventional places for any but the blindest of luck to impale. It has a vampire's normal seven health levels, plus two for each additional vampire who becomes part of the entity (treat these extra health levels as Bruised). The entity remains congealed for one scene.

Thaumaturgy

Thaumaturgy in Sabbat society has suffered much upheaval, and none of it is for the better. The Discipline is going to pot — stagnating, due to the sect's loss of Tremere *antitribu* support and the resulting lack of insightful research and training.

Thaumaturgy has, however, acquired numerous practitioners among the sect. Most pack priests seek out Thaumaturgical knowledge, even if they have yet to come into any true ability with it. Likewise, many elders of the sect favor the Discipline, as they believe it emulates Caine's legendary ability to create new and potent powers at his whim.

What follows is a collection of Sabbat Thaumaturgical knowledge. Whether paths and rituals created by the Tremere *antitribu* before their mysterious destruction or older formulae, practiced in the early nights of the sect by sorcerers who refused to share their knowledge with the Camarilla, these powers belong exclusively to the Sabbat. While it is conceivable that some Camarilla Tremere somewhere practices a path or ritual herein, it's none too common.

Thaumaturgical Paths

Sabbat Thaumaturgy works exactly like normal Thaumaturgy — it is distinct only in the sense that these paths are proprietary to the sect. These paths use the systems described in **Vampire: The Masquerade**, page 178.

Learning Thaumaturgy in the Sabbat

Now that the Tremere *antitribu* have disappeared, how does one garner knowledge of blood magic? With difficulty.

Naturally, many Cainites had learned some degree of Thaumaturgical knowledge from the Sabbat Tremere. These vampires may choose to impart this wisdom as a favor, or they may be coaxed into sharing some of their secrets.

Storytellers should use this opportunity to enthrall the characters to another vampire, or to advance the story. Players' characters have no "right" to Thaumaturgy — it exists in such a sorry state among the Sabbat and among so few vampires of the sect that they likely don't even know anyone who practices it. Additionally, it should be very hard to increase one's Thaumaturgical knowledge in the Sabbat: The only blood magic that exists at all is that brought by the Tremere *antitribu*. Other vampires lack the greater comprehension necessary to truly innovate, and they should have difficulty learning or creating new paths and rituals. Although the Tremere *antitribu* shared their secrets a bit more readily than the Tremere of the Camarilla, the relative rarity of the Discipline in the modern nights should prove an equally daunting obstacle to those who would wield its power.

The Path of Mars

The few Sabbat who have retained Thaumaturgical talents have turned their focus to the assistance of the sect in times of war. This path has proven useful to Sabbat War Parties, and it has turned the tides of several confrontations with elder vampires. It is quite unusual among Thaumaturgical paths, in that it adopts a very martial stance, whereas other blood magics tend to have subtler, less violent effects.

• War Cry

A vampire on the attack can focus his will, making him less susceptible to battle fear or the powers of the undead. The vampire shouts a primal scream to start the effect, though some thaumaturges have been known to paint their faces or cut themselves open instead.

System: For the duration of one scene, the vampire adds one to his Courage Trait. Additionally, for the purposes of hostile effects, his Willpower is considered to be one higher (though this bonus applies only to the Trait itself, not the Willpower pool). A character may only gain the benefits of War Cry once per scene.

•• Strike True

The vampire makes a single attack, guided by the unholy power of her Blood. This attack strikes its foe infallibly.

System: By invoking this power, the player need not roll to see if the vampire's attack hits — it does, automatically. Only Melee or Brawling (or Martial Arts) attacks may be made in this manner. These attacks are considered to be one-success attacks; they offer no additional damage dice. Also, they may be dodged, blocked or parried normally, and the defender needs only one success (as the attacks' number of success is assumed to be one). Strike True has no effect if attempted on multiple attacks (dice pool splits) in a single round from one character.

••• Wind Dance

The thaumaturge invokes the power of the winds, moving in a blur. She gains a preternatural edge in avoiding her enemies' blows, moving out of their way before the enemy has a chance to throw them.

System: The player needs not split her dice pool if she wishes to make multiple dodges in a single round. This advantage applies only to dodges — if the character wishes to attack *and* dodge, the player must still split her dice pool. This power lasts for one scene.

•••• Fearless Heart

The vampire temporarily augments his abilities as a warrior. Through the mystical powers of blood magic, the character becomes a potent fighting force.

System: Fearless Heart grants the vampire an extra point in each of the Physical Attributes (Strength, Dexterity and Stamina). These Traits may not exceed their generational maximums, though the player may use blood

points to push the character's Traits even higher. The effects last for one scene, and a character may gain its benefits only once per scene.

The vampire must calm down for two hours following the use of Fearless Heart, or he loses a blood point every 15 minutes until he rests.

●●●●● Comrades at Arms

This ability extends the power of the previous abilities in the path. It allows any of the earlier effects to be applied to a group such as a pack or War Party.

System: The player chooses one of the lower-level powers in the path, invoking it as normal. Afterward, he touches another character and (if the roll for Comrades at Arms is successful) bestows the benefit on her as well. The same power may be delivered to any number of packmates, as long as the rolls for Comrades at Arms are successful and the thaumaturge pays the appropriate blood point costs.

The Path of the Father's Vengeance

This path, based loosely on powerful thaumaturge's interpretations of the *Book of Nod*, devotes itself to delivering justice to the race of Cainites. Each power supposedly has some precedent in the parables of the ancient book, and focuses on teaching the lessons of Caine via the power of blood magic. Use of this path is hotly debated in the Sabbat, as some consider it tantamount to claiming to hold Caine's right over all vampires oneself.

The power of this path comes not only from the magic of blood, but also incantation of verses from the *Book of Nod*. For any of these powers to take effect, the thaumaturge must speak the actual condemnation. For example, to invoke the third-level power, the caster must state plainly to his target that she may eat only ashes. Obviously, the subject must be able to hear the thaumaturge for these powers to take effect, though writing them and showing them to the subject will do.

These powers apply to Cainites only. They do not affect Lupines, mortals or ghouls.

● Zillah's Litany

Zillah, the wife of Caine, unknowingly drank from her husband and sire three times, thus becoming bonded to him. This power reveals existing blood bonds and Vinculi to the thaumaturge.

System: If the subject has any blood bonds or Vinculi to other vampires, this power reveals them to the caster. Although the caster may not know the vampires in question, this power does reveal the names and gives rough psychic impressions of the individuals in question.

●● The Crone's Pride

This power inflicts the curse of the crone, who bound Caine to her as he fled his wife's spurning. Hideously ugly, the crone had to resort to trickery to get others to help or serve her.

System: This power reduces the target's Appearance to zero. All Social rolls during this time generally fail, unless the character attempts to intimidate or browbeat the subject. This power lasts for one night.

●●● Feast of Ashes

Primarily used against wanton or excessive vampires, this power temporarily removes a vampire's dependency on blood. While some would say this negates the Curse of Caine, it reduces the vampire to little more than a wretched scavenger, as he must consume literal ashes, though he gains little sustenance from them.

System: The victim of this power can no longer consume blood, vomiting it as he would mortal food or drink. Instead, the victim can eat only ashes, and the "blood points" he gains from this may be used only to rise each night. Ashen "blood points" may not be used to power Disciplines, raise Attributes or feed ghouls. (though actual blood points in the character's body at the time this power is invoked may still be used for such). One blood point's worth of ash is roughly one pint, and any ash will do — cigarette ash, campfire leftovers or vampire corpses destroyed by fire or sunlight. This power lasts for one week.

●●●● Uriel's Disfavor

This power invokes the darkness of the Angel of Death. All but the dimmest of light causes the subject excruciating pain, and some artificial forms of bright light may even damage the vampire. Uriel delivered God's curse on Caine, shielding him in the blackness of his wings.

System: The presence of any light makes the subject uncomfortable, and bright light of any kind — flashlights, neon beer lamps, headlights, etc. — inflict one health level of aggravated damage on the character for every turn he remains under its direct focus. Most vampires who suffer this curse elect to sleep for the duration, hiding away in the darkness of their havens until they can walk again among the living without pain. This power lasts for one week.

●●●●● Valediction

Many Sabbat rightfully fear this power, though none has ever seen it used. It levies a punishment for breaking one of Caine's greatest commandments — the ban against diablerie. As most Sabbat attain their power and station through some measure of diablerie, they must reconcile their beliefs with the admonitions of Caine, and this power engenders a great sense of humility.

System: When this power takes effect, the subject immediately reverts to her original generation. This change may entail losing points in certain Traits due to generational maximums. This power lasts for one week, after which any Traits reduced to higher-generation maximums return to normal. It takes three turns to speak the full verse that implements this power's effects.

THAUMATURGICAL RITUALS

As well as becoming more rare by the night, Sabbat Thaumaturgy often requires some sort of ceremonial catalyst to perform its rituals. At the Storyteller's discretion, a Sabbat ritual might need some additional requirement such as formulaic circles, phylacteries and/or a good deal of prior preparation. This is not to say that their rituals are less powerful than the equivalent rituals practiced by Camarilla Tremere, but it indicates a less refined understanding of the tenets of the Discipline in some cases. Sabbat Thaumaturges might also use grisly components for activating spells, given the grim nature of most Sabbat thaumaturges. Common implements include rocks with a Thaumaturgical symbol, bone rattles, particular animal or human body parts or certain kinds of vitae or ichor.

Most Sabbat know about rituals, due to the group's predilection for *ritae* and sharing information at esbats. However, the actual practice of Thaumaturgical rituals is quite rare. Rituals are hard to learn, and they take time to study, in addition to demanding a certain level of basic Thaumaturgical understanding. Usually, only members of founded Sabbat packs have the time to study Thaumaturgy. Even then, the nature of Sabbat unlife does not lean itself to quiet, intense study of bookish subjects.

Sabbat Thaumaturgical rituals work like any other Thaumaturgical rituals, as described on pages 182-183 of **Vampire: The Masquerade**.

LEVEL ONE RITUALS

BLOOD RUSH

This ritual allows the vampire to create the sensation of drinking blood in himself without actually feeding. The ritual can be used for pleasure, but it is more often used to prevent frenzy when confronted with fresh blood. The vampire must carry the fang of a predatory animal on his person for this ritual to work.

System: Performance of the ritual results in the Beast being kept in check automatically. Blood Rush allays the Beast for one hour, at which point the Cainite feels hungry again (assuming he did before). This ritual takes only one turn to enact.

DOMINOE OF LIFE

A vampire wanting or needing to simulate a human characteristic can do so once Dominoe of Life is cast. For one entire night, the vampire can eat, breathe, maintain a 98.6-degree body temperature, assume a human flesh tone *or* display some other single trait of humankind she desires. Note that only one trait can be replicated in this fashion. The vampire must have a vial of fresh human blood on his person to maintain this ritual.

System: Using this ritual adds one die to the thaumaturge's Masquerade dice pool (see the **Vampire Storytellers Companion**). Unless onlookers are especially wary, the Dominoe of Life should fool them into thinking the caster is mortal — not that they should have any reason to suspect otherwise.

ILLUMINATE TRAIL OF PREY

This ritual causes the path of the subject's passing to glow in a manner that only the thaumaturge can see. The footprints or tire tracks (or whatever) shine distinctly, but only to the eyes of the caster. Even airplane trajectories and animal tracks shine with unhealthy light. The ritual is nullified if the target wades through or immerses himself in water, or if he reaches the destination of his journey. The thaumaturge must burn a length of white satin ribbon that has been in her possession for at least 24 hours for this ritual to take effect.

System: The thaumaturge must have a mental picture of or know the name of her prey. The individual's wake glows with a brightness dependent on how long it has been since he passed that way — old tracks burn less brightly, while fresh tracks blaze.

WIDOW'S SPITE

This ritual causes a pain, itch or other significant (but not deadly) sensation in the subject. Similar in effect to the old "voodoo doll" effects, this ritual is used more out of scorn or malice than actual enmity. In fact, it requires a wax or cloth doll that resembles the target, which bleeds when the power takes effect.

System: The ceremonial doll must resemble, however rudely, the victim of the ritual. It produces no mechanical effect, other than a simple physical stimulus. The caster may determine where on the subject's body the pain or itch appears.

LEVEL TWO RITUALS

EYES OF THE NIGHT HAWK

This ritual allows the vampire to see through the eyes of a bird, and to hear through its ears. The bird chosen must be touched by the vampire when the ritual is initiated, and it must be a predatory bird. At the end of this ritual, the caster must put out the bird's eyes, lest she suffer blindness herself.

System: The vampire is able to mentally control where the bird travels for the duration of the ritual. The bird will not necessarily perform any other action than flight — the thaumaturge cannot command it to fight, pick up and return an object or scratch a target. The bird returns to the vampire after finishing its flight. If the vampire does not put out the bird's eyes, she suffers a three-night period of blindness. This ritual ceases effect at sunrise; if the bird has not reached its destination or is too far from the vampire for the final step to be taken, too bad, Dracula.

MACHINE BLITZ

Machines go haywire when this ritual is cast. It takes effect instantly and lasts as long as the vampire concentrates on it. This ritual may be used to kill car engines, erase computer media, crash ticker-tape machines, stop life-support machines, et cetera. Essentially, Machine Blitz ceases any machine more complex than a rope-and-pulley. The thaumaturge must have a scrap of rusted metal in her possession for this ritual to work, though some vampires use a variant that requires a knot steeped in human saliva to be untied.

System: This ritual only stops machines; it does not grant any control over them. The effects of this ritual are invisible and not necessarily obvious — these things just seem to happen by coincidence.

RECURE OF THE HOMELAND

The vampire calls on the power of the earth to heal grave wounds she may have received. The thaumaturge must use at least a handful of dirt from the city or town of her mortal birth and recite a litany of her family tree as she casts this ritual.

System: The Cainite must mix the earth with two points of her own blood to make a healing paste. One handful will heal one aggravated wound, and only one handful can be used per night.

LEVEL THREE RITUALS

CLINGING OF THE INSECT

This ritual allows the thaumaturge to cling to walls or ceilings, as would a spider. She may even crawl along these surfaces (as long as they can support her). Use of this power seriously discomfits mortal onlookers. The character must place a live spider under her tongue for the duration of the ritual (though the spider may die while in the thaumaturge's mouth).

System: The character may move at half her normal rate while climbing walls or ceilings. This power lasts for one scene., or until the vampire spits out the spider.

MIRROR OF SECOND SIGHT

This object is an oval mirror no less than four inches wide; no more than 18 inches in length. It looks like a normal mirror, but is much more useful in the hands of a Sabbat thaumaturge. Once created, the mirror is used by the vampire to see the supernatural; it reflects the true form of Lupines and faeries and enables the owner to see ghosts as they move though the Underworld. The thaumaturge creates the mirror by bathing an ordinary mirror in a quantity of her own blood while reciting a ritual incantation.

System: The ritual requires one point of the vampire's blood. Thereafter, the mirror reflects images of other supernatural creatures' true forms — werewolves appear in their hulking man-wolf shapes, mages glow in a scintillating nimbus, wraiths become visible (in the mirror) and changelings appear in their natural aspect. Sometimes, the mirror also reveals those possessed of True Faith in clouds of golden light.

LEVEL FOUR RITUAL

FIREWALKER

This ritual imbues the vampire with an unnatural resistance to the bane of all vampires, fire. Only a foolish vampire would actually attempt to walk on or through fire, but this ritual does grant an advanced tolerance to flame. Some Sabbat use this ritual to show off or perform dramatically at Fire Dances, while others use it only for martial concerns. To enact the ritual, the thaumaturge must cut off the end of one of his fingers and burn it in a Thaumaturgical circle.

System: Cutting off one's finger does not do any health levels of damage, but it hurts like hell and requires a Willpower roll to perform. This ritual may be cast on other vampires (at the expense of the caster's fingertips...). If the subject has no Fortitude, he may soak fire with his Stamina for the duration of this ritual. If the vampire has Fortitude, he may soak fire with his Stamina + Fortitude for the duration of the ritual. This ritual lasts one hour.

LEVEL FIVE RITUAL

PAPER FLESH

This dreadful ritual enfeebles the subject, making her skin brittle and weak. Humors rise to the surface and flesh tightens around bones and scales away at the slightest touch. Used against physically tough opponents, this ritual strips away the inherent resilience of the vampiric body, leaving it a fragile, dry husk. The thaumaturge must inscribe his subject's true name (which is much harder to discern for elders than it is for young vampires) on a piece of paper, which he uses to cut himself and then burns to cinders.

System: This ritual causes the subject's Stamina and Fortitude (if any) to drop to 1. For every generation below eighth, the subject retains one extra point of Stamina and Fortitude (though she may not exceed her original scores). For example, a vampire of the Fourth Generation targeted by Paper Flesh would drop to a Stamina + Fortitude score of 5 (assuming the score was more than 5 to begin with). This ritual lasts one night, and it is popular among packs that regularly undertake War Parties and Wild Hunts.

KOLDUNIC SORCERY

The practice of Koldunic Sorcery is a well-kept secret among the Tzimisce of the Sabbat. Once exceedingly rare, even among the Tzimisce, the lower levels of this dark art are becoming more readily available among the covens. Now that the Tremere influence has suddenly vanished from the sect, the ancient sorcerous arts of the Fiends seem to be on the rise in popularity.

Although Koldunic Sorcery roughly resembles Thaumaturgy, it has no connection to the Hermetic practices of Clan Tremere. Rather, the ancient magic of the Tzimisce has its origins in the sick, magically rich soil of the Old World demesnes of the Fiends. Its paths and rituals are not compatible with Tremere magic, but paths similar to Thaumaturgical paths have existed since time out of mind. Koldunic Sorcery is most often practiced — if such can be said — in covens with Tzimisce of 400 years or more under the shadow of undeath. Rarely, some secret ritual or blasphemous path makes it into the rank-and-file of the sect, and astute Cainites cannot help but wonder how these guarded secrets escape the clutches of the Tzimisce.

VALEREN

According to the Salubri *antitribu*, Valeren is a forgotten Discipline unearthed in their research into their progenitor's history. While the mainstream Salubri practice a healing Discipline, the *antitribu* instead follow the warrior's path, dedicating themselves to one of the many faces of their inscrutable father.

Valeren is a Discipline of righteous wrath, originally developed by the demon-slayers and questing knights of the Salubri from nights long past. It shares a bit in common with the Obeah Discipline upheld by the Salubri, but it quickly diverges into its own focus and ideology. Salubri *antitribu* walk the road of the crusader, and they refuse to become soul-stealers or sacrificial lambs.

Like Obeah, Valeren imparts its practitioners with the fabled third eye of Saulot. The third eye appears at the time the vampire masters the second level of Valeren. The precise nature of the eye, as well as its purpose, are all but unknown to vampires outside the Salubri *antitribu*. Some suspect the eye grants them sight beyond sight, while others venture that the eye allows them to see the infernal taint in the non-Sabbat Salubri themselves.

• SENSE VITALITY

The vampire can feel the flow of a subject's life force after touching him. Sense Vitality may be used to determine how much damage a person can withstand before death, which can be useful in sizing up a potential opponent. It can also aid in medical diagnosis or feeding, as it can reveal infections and diseases.

System: The Salubri *antitribu* must touch the target to see how close to death she is. This action also requires a Perception + Empathy roll (difficulty 7). One success on this roll identifies a subject as a mortal, vampire, ghoul or other creature (or none of the above). Two successes reveal how much damage the subject has suffered. Three successes tell how full the subject's blood pool is (if a vampire) or how many blood points she has left in her system (if a mortal or other blood-bearing form of life). Four successes reveal any diseases in the subject's bloodstream, such as hemophilia or HIV. A player may opt to learn the information yielded by a lesser degree of success — for example, a player who accumulates three successes may learn whether or not a subject is a vampire as well as the contents of his blood pool.

Alternately, this power may be used as a sort of limited "aftersight," revealing to the Cainite how the subject came to be in her current state. Each success on this roll allows the player to ask the Storyteller one question about the subject's health or health levels. "Was he drugged?" or, "Are his wounds aggravated?" are valid questions, but, "Did vampires do this?" or, "What did the Lupine who killed him look like?" are not. The Salubri *antitribu* may use this power on herself if she has injuries but has somehow lost the memory of how she received the wounds.

•• Anesthetic Touch

This power may be used to block a voluntary subject's pain from wounds or disease, or to put a mortal to sleep. As with Sense Vitality, physical contact is required to anaesthetize someone. This power may not be used to block the Cainite's own pain.

System: If the subject is willing to undergo this process, the player needs to spend a blood point to block the subject's pain and make a Willpower roll (difficulty 6). This power allows the subject to ignore all wound penalties for one turn per success. A second application of this power may be made once the first one has expired, at the cost of another blood point and another Willpower roll. If the subject is unwilling for some reason, the player must make a contested Willpower roll against the subject (difficulty 8).

To put a mortal to sleep, the same system applies. The mortal sleeps for five to 10 hours — whatever his normal sleep cycle is — and regains one temporary Willpower point on awakening. He sleeps peacefully and does not suffer nightmares or the effects of any derangements while asleep. He may be awakened normally (or violently).

Cainites are unaffected by this power — their corpselike bodies are too tied to death.

••• Burning Touch

The vampire touches his subject, shocking her with a searing pain. This power causes no actual damage to the subject, though prolonged exposure to this unnatural pain sometimes leaves victims traumatized. The Salubri *antitribu* use this power to extract information from their enemies, and also sometimes to cause additional pain to those who have hunted and persecuted them before delivering true Final Death.

System: The vampire must touch his subject for this power to take effect, and the effects diminish rapidly after he removes his hand. Also, the player spends at least one blood point to activate this power. Each blood point so spent reduces the victim's dice pools by two. This power is often used in conjunction with Interrogation and Torture, wearing down the subject's resistance and rendering him much more tractable.

•••• Ending the Watch

The watch referred to in this power's name is the death watch. An ancient tale unearthed by the Salubri *antitribu* refers to two Salubri who prowled the streets of Caine's Second City, granting merciful release to those who suffered and rotted in the streets. If a person truly wished to die because of great grief or unbearable illness, these Salubri would bestow the gift of death. Particularly revered by the street urchins, the "Death Angels" were seen as truly divine entities by those who sought their solace. In modern nights, the Salubri *antitribu* use this power frequently, as many nihilistic and desperate individuals seek any escape they can from the bleakness of the Final Nights.

System: To End the Watch, the vampire places his hand over the subject's heart, and the player spends a Willpower point. The subject must be willing to end his life; if she struggles or harbors a spark of hope, this power fails. Otherwise, the subject's heart slowly ceases to beat, and death comes like an eternal sleep, restful and painless. Subjects of Ending the Watch may not be subsequently Embraced, and none has ever been reported to have become a wraith.

••••• VENGEANCE OF SAMIEL

By invoking the names of mighty Salubri warriors of nights past, the Salubri *antitribu* strikes his foe with inhuman force and accuracy. This power causes the third eye to open and glow with a baleful redness. Some Salubri *antitribu* who use this power close their normal eyes, signifying their disdain for their foes and horrifying them at the same time.

System: This power costs three blood points. Any single attack made by the vampire automatically hits the target as mystic forces guide the blow. Attacks made in this manner may not be dodged, though they may be blocked, parried and soaked as normal. The blow strikes as if the Salubri *antitribu* had succeeded with all of his Dexterity + Melee or Brawling dice pool (which makes for significant damage). This power may be used only once per turn, and only when the Salubri *antitribu*'s sole action is the attack. Additionally, this power does not work for ranged weapons, only bare hands or melee weapons.

•••••• BLISSFUL AGONY

The vampire may cause pain with a mere touch, as per Burning Touch, but this pain lingers and swells even after the Fury has removed her hand. It is believed that this power was originally used to acclimated warrior Salubri to the pain they would experience in battle, but among the Sabbat Salubri, Blissful Agony has been turned to more brutal uses. If applied with enough intensity, Blissful Agony can drive vampires to the point of frenzy, incapacitate Lupines and even kill mortals outright.

System: The player makes a Willpower roll (difficulty 8) and spends a blood point. The power lasts for one scene, though this duration may be prolonged if the Salubri *antitribu* wishes with a subsequent Willpower roll (though no additional blood points need be spent). The character must touch her subject for the power to take effect initially.

At the vampire's option, she may cause actual physical damage to the victim at the rate of one health level per blood point spent, though touch must be maintained for this to happen. Damage to vampires and other supernatural creatures in this fashion vanishes at the next sunset, but mortals must heal the damage normally. This damage is considered lethal damage, and it may not be soaked by mortals (though vampires and other supernatural entities may).

To induce a frenzy in a victim, the Salubri must cause damage in excess of the subject's Willpower. At that point, the subject must make a Willpower roll (difficulty 6) or succumb to frenzy.

VICISSITUDE

•••••• CHIROPTERAN MARAUDER

Similar to the lesser Vicissitude power of Horrid Form, the Chiropteran Marauder is a terrifying, bipedal bat, bearing a wickedly fanged maw and veined, leathery wings. This power confers all of the benefits of the Horrid Form, in addition to a few others. The mere sight of the marauder is enough to make mortals or weak-willed vampires flee in horror.

System: The vampire gains all the effects of the Horrid Form (see **Vampire: The Masquerade**, page 187). Further, the fluted wings allow flight at 25 mph, during which the vampire may carry, but not manipulate, objects of reasonable size. If the vampire wishes, the player may make a Strength + Body Crafts roll (difficulty 6) to extend bony claws at the ends of the wings, where the hands would be. These claws inflict Strength +2 aggravated damage. Also, the vampire subtracts two from all hearing-based Perception rolls (though he adds one to vision-based Wits and Perception rolls). Assuming the mantle of the Chiropteran Marauder costs three blood points.

•••••• BLOOD OF ACID

At this level of mastery, the vampire has converted his blood to a viscous acid. Any blood he consumes likewise becomes acid, which is corrosive enough to burn human (and vampiric flesh) as well as wood. This effect is particularly potent when the vampire assumes the Bloodform. One of the side effects of this power is the complete inability to create new vampires and ghouls, or give blood to another vampire — the acid would corrode them as they drank it. The obvious benefit, however, is that would-be diablerists are likewise unable to devour the Cainite's blood.

System: Each blood point that comes in contact with something other than the vampire himself does five dice worth of aggravated damage. If the vampire is injured in combat, his blood may spatter on an opponent — foes must

---

BODY ARMORY
Protean •••, Vicissitude •••

This power enables the vampire to form wicked weapons from her own body. The vampire may create sword blades, axes and even spiked mauls, and these weapons do terrible damage to their targets. Many Tzimisce make sword-arms and knife-bladed knuckles and the like, but more° dramatic° implementations are possible.

System: This power costs two blood points per weapon crafted (though larger weapons like two-handed swords and great axes cost four), and the player must roll Dexterity + Body Crafts (difficulty 7). Weapons created in this manner cause aggravated damage (from the Protean Discipline); lesser weapons that do only lethal damage may be created using Flesh- and Bonecraft, as per **Vampire: The Masquerade**, pages 186-187. Learning this power costs 20 experience points.

TAINTED BLOOD

Since time out of mind the Fiends of Clan Tzimisce have worked their magic, fleshcrafting their minions, shaping deadly weapons and painful modifications from their very bones. The magic of the Tzimisce homeland, Eastern Europe's "land beyond the forest," resonated with the arcane power in the Fiends' blood.

Over time, however, the land grew sick, and corrupted with it the Tzimisce ties to that selfsame earth. Their blood became cursed, possessed of a bizarre unlife of its own. The mystical vitae that once sustained them now twisted the Tzimisce, making them alien and freakish.

Indeed, the Fiends' prized Discipline, Vicissitude, has become a disease, and it may infect anyone with whom it comes in contact. Indeed, rare cases have been reported of mortals learning the Discipline, and some apocryphal tales even speak of Lupines learning the fleshcrafting art. Anyone who partakes of Tzimisce blood — even the smallest of quantities — may be at risk of contracting the disease.

THE FATE OF FIENDS

Note: These rules are optional, to be used at the Storyteller's discretion.

Rather than functioning as a normal Discipline, Vicissitude may be used in a special manner. Whereas other Disciplines have set costs to learn and improve, Vicissitude varies by the individual, as it mutates her body to its own malignant end. Some individuals find the Discipline difficult to learn, while others seem to have an unnatural affinity for it.

When a player creates a Tzimisce character, or whenever a non-Tzimisce character tastes the blood of a Fiend, the Storyteller should make a few quick, secret die rolls and record the results. This represents the character's relationship with the disease.

The first roll determines whether or not the character "catches" the sickness. Roll the character's Stamina (difficulty 6); failure indicates the character has become infected, and a botch not only infects the character, but also yields an immediate derangement. Succeeding on this roll means the character has not caught the disease and needs not roll on the table below. (All Tzimisce have inherently contracted Vicissitude at their Embrace, and need not make this first roll.)

The second roll determines how strongly the disease "takes root." If the character in question ever actively attempts to learn Vicissitude, this is the experience-point price she pays for learning it as a new Discipline. It bears mention that an infected character need not have a teacher to learn this new Discipline — the disease manifests itself as it courses through her unliving veins. It is not possible to learn Vicissitude without becoming infected.

The next roll defines how receptive the character's body and mind are to the corruption in her veins. Whenever the character learns a new level of the Discipline, this is the experience cost to do so.

The final roll signifies how destructive to the character's mind the disease is. Whenever the character learns a new level of Vicissitude — even her first — she must make a Willpower roll against the difficulty indicated by the chart. Failure on the roll yields the character a permanent derangement, as decided upon by the Storyteller. Alternately, the Storyteller may

make Dexterity + Dodge rolls to avoid the blood, which must be accomplished by splitting their dice pools. (Obviously, unless an opponent knows the vampire has this power, she's unlikely to split her dice pool on her first attack, which causes many Tzimisce to cackle with glee even as their own vitae sprays out of their bodies and disfigures their foes.)

●●●●● ●● COCOON

The Cainite can form an opaque cocoon from blood and other fluids excreted from her body. The cocoon hardens after a few moments, turning into a tough, white shell shaped vaguely like a rounded coffin. This cocoon provides considerable protection to the vampire, even shielding her from sunlight and, to a limited degree, fire.

System: A vampire may only cocoon herself, and the process takes 10 minutes to perform. Additionally, creating a cocoon costs three blood points. The cocoon offers complete protection from sunlight, and provides a number of dice of soak equal to twice the vampire's normal Stamina (blood augmentation doesn't help) against *all* damage, aggravated or otherwise. It lasts as long as the Cainite wishes, and she may dissolve it into a pulpy, bloody paste at her whim, from which she emerges. A vampire contained within a cocoon may still use mental Disciplines, though they may still require eye contact or other conditions to be met.

●●●●● ●●● BREATH OF THE DRAGON

The Tzimisce becomes like one of the terrible *draculs* of the Old World, able to exhale a deadly gout of flame. This flame does not hurt the vampire himself, though he may become trapped in flames that start if his fire engulfs flammable objects.

System: The flaming cloud affects a six-foot area, doing two dice of aggravated damage to any in the flames' circumference. This fire may cause combustible items to ignite, and it may ignite victims who suffer fire damage as per the fire rules on page 227 of **Vampire: The Masquerade**.

TAINTED BLOOD *CONTINUED...*

rule that a character who fails this roll instead loses a point from a given Virtue, or perhaps Empathy, as the character slides inexorably away from the human she once was and ever more into the thrall of the disease ravaging her body.

Players should roleplay their characters' growing emotional detachment, for maximum effect, as they lose themselves more and more to Vicissitude. This mental degradation is not mania or lunacy, and rarely results in erratic or whimsical behavior. Rather, it is a slow withdrawal from all that is human. Some Tzimisce researchers have hypothesized that the afflicted individual becomes less and less a functional personality, and more of a mindless host for the invasive disease.

VICISSITUDE COST AND DERANGEMENT TABLE

Roll	Initial Cost	Cost per Level	Change of Developing a Derangement
1	10	current rating x 8	difficulty 8
2	10	current rating x7	difficulty 7
3	9	current rating x 7	difficulty 7
4	9	current rating x 7	difficulty 6
5	8	current rating x 6	difficulty 6
6	8	current rating x 6	difficulty 6
7	7	current rating x 6	difficulty 5
8	7	current rating x 5	difficulty 5
9	6	current rating x 5	difficulty 4
10	5	current rating x 4	difficulty 4

The Storyteller (not the player) should roll once on each table entry for a character who contracts Vicissitude, making a note of the result and keeping it secret from the player. Thereafter, each time the character increases her knowledge of the Discipline, the Storyteller may make the appropriate roll in secret, and introduce the result as part of the story.

For example, Darius tastes the blood of his pack priest, a Tzimisce, during the Vaulderie. He later decides that he wants to learn Vicissitude. The Storyteller, ruling that Darius has tasted enough of the Tzimisce's blood to become infected, makes a secret Stamina roll for Darius and fails. Darius may learn Vicissitude without instruction, as the disease slowly spreads through his undead body. The Storyteller also makes three other rolls, to see how much it will cost Darius to learn the Discipline and how likely it is to warp his mind. Rolling a 4, 6, and 3, The Storyteller notes that it costs Darius 9 experience points to learn his first level of Vicissitude, it costs the current rating x 6 to increase thereafter, and Darius must succeed in a Willpower roll against a difficulty of 7 every time he learns a new level of the Discipline or gain a derangement.

●●●●● ●●●● EARTH'S VAST HAVEN

This power, developed in the nights when the Tzimisce were the terrible masters of Eastern Europe, allows the vampire to sink into and disperse himself through the very ground itself. Unlike the Protean power of Earth Meld, however, the vampire actually dissolves his body into the ground; nothing short of a wide-area explosion can affect him, nor may he be dug up bodily. In addition, during the nighttime hours, the vampire may see and hear everything happening in her environment through his mystical connection to the land. The mere fact that this power exists terrifies many Tzimisce, who are secretly unsure of whether or not the diablerie of their Antediluvian was successful.

System: This power costs six blood points to activate, and it lasts as long as the vampire wishes to remain contained within the soil. As per the Cocoon, the vampire may use mental Disciplines that do not require physical solvency or eye contact. He may communicate mentally with anyone who wanders into the area under which he rests.

CHAPTER FIVE: CODES OF THE NIGHT

She'll break a promise as a matter of course
Because she thinks it's fun to have no remorse
— Curve, "Chinese Burn"

The Sabbat practices things a bit differently than do the other vampires with whom they share the night. From their monstrous ethics to the bloody rituals they observe, the Sabbat maintains a few unique conventions.

The Paths of Enlightenment, like the ones presented in the appendix of **Vampire: The Masquerade**, are alternate codes of morality for those hideous vampires who have transcended [*sic*] conventional, mortal morality. These paths exist for those who realize that some form of fortification from the Beast is still necessary.

The *ritae* cover the various ritual and quasi-religious practices of the Sabbat. In the modern nights, the Sabbat practices these obscene observances to unite themselves against their myriad enemies in the Great Jyhad.

PATHS OF ENLIGHTENMENT

In the wake of fire and death left by the Sabbat's passing in their holy war on the Antediluvians, many Cainites find it difficult to uphold the effort and still cling to the ideals that satisfied them as mortals. Nonetheless, completely abandoning morality forfeits one's soul to the Beast, which no Sabbat is willing to do. Steeling themselves against the monstrous aspect of their dual natures, the Sabbat have developed these codes of morality to keep them in touch with the Curse of Caine.

As mentioned before, most vampires of the Sabbat, particularly the young ones, still have Humanity Traits. (Of course, these Traits are likely to drop and degrade over the course of a Sabbat chronicle — see **Vampire: The Masquerade**, page 288 for details on forsaking Humanity to adopt a Path of Enlightenment.) Only those Cainites who have truly abandoned themselves to the dark majesty of vampirism follow paths, and rarely do any turn back.

That said, we offer a word of caution to players and Storytellers. Playing a path-follower is extremely difficult, as it entails looking at existence from the point of view of someone who has explicitly decided that the cultural norm no longer holds any appeal for him. Paths are not intended as opportunities for players to let their characters run rampant. Rather, paths exist to allow characters a greater look into the alien minds of Cainites, the Sabbat in particular. Storytellers, be forewarned: If you believe that a player sets her character on a path to avoid moral issues she plans on having her character face regularly (or, as one Internet pundit put it, adopting "the Path of What I Was Going to Do Anyway"), feel free to restrict the player from that choice. Moral quandary is still as thematic to the Sabbat as it is to the mainstream characters of **Vampire**, and lessening it strips a great deal of accountability and maturity from the game.

The Path of Caine

We are pale shadows of our father, Caine. He exemplifies what we must become.

— Samuel Tremaine, pack priest

Nickname: Noddists

Basic Beliefs: Scholars of nights long past, in seeking keys to the nature of vampiric existence, pursued fragments of knowledge from the *Book of Nod*. Drawing upon the history from that book as well as other esoteric sources, Cainite scholars concluded that only Caine, as the first vampire, is the paragon of vampiric nature. The Noddists seek to become more like Caine, in order to discover the limits and powers of the undead form. By learning from Caine's example, the Noddists claim, one can understand the true nature of vampirism and how vampiric existence differs from one's mortal life.

Noddists seek knowledge and history, recording the experiences of Caine, so that they may learn from his example. To the Noddists, Caine's life reveals the mystery of the vampiric curse; by understanding the undead form, they transcend their mortal weaknesses. They prize any knowledge about the vampiric condition, but the writings and stories of the First Vampire form the core of Noddist lore. As Caine was marked and cast out from mortal society, the Noddists believe that he exemplifies most keenly the differences between vampires and humans. Therefore, this path's adherents cast aside their humanity as inadequate and useless, emulating Caine's exile and seeking new rules to govern their predatory drives.

The heart of the Path of Caine lies in the exemplification of vampiric nature: The questions of existence, the limits of the vampiric form and the changes wrought by the Embrace all drive the Noddists into endless speculation, debate, study and research. Scholarship and historical insight are valuable, but the vampire must simultaneously develop spiritually and physically, to explore the limits of his undead form. Diablerie serves as more than a simple theft of power; it allows the practitioner to learn from the experiences of other undead, thereby developing greater understanding. Other vampires lose themselves in attempts to save lost humanity or find meaning in obscure philosophy. The Path of Caine, instead, finds meaning in the fundamentals of vampirism.

The Path of Caine is demanding and rigorous; few vampires follow its tenets in the modern nights. This path places a high emphasis on scholarship, insight and personal discipline. With the eternal patience attributed to Caine, say the followers of the path, comes the opportunity to slowly refine oneself.

The Ethics of the Path

- Search for the history of Caine. Learn from his actions.
- Develop your willpower and predatory instinct. The Beast, like the rest of the vampiric form, may be mastered.

- Take the vitae of the unworthy so that you may become closer to Caine. Temper this accrual with an understanding of your own potential so that you do not take the Curse for granted.
- Adapt to the needs of your new condition; cast aside your lost humanity.
- Study your abilities and the abilities of Caine to discover what belongs within you. Examine the limits and meanings of vampirism.

VIRTUES

Vampires on the Path of Caine uphold the virtues of Conviction and Instinct.

HISTORY

The Path of Caine developed in the early 16th century as vampires sought new insights into personal enlightenment during the Renaissance. Many vampires felt the need for a system of self-improvement that circumvented the limitations of humanistic beliefs, as human morality conflicted with vampiric nature. This path gained a great following over the next 200 years, as many vampires viewed Caine as an ideal figure. Following the Enlightenment, this path began to decline in favor of newer paths. Few vampires maintained the discipline and studiousness necessary to uphold this path, so it dwindled to a small but respected following. The remaining Noddists maintained a respected place in the Sabbat and continued to recruit from the most intellectual and insightful prospects. As the modern Sabbat selects more fledglings based on their individual potential and achievement, this path has experienced an influx of new followers.

CURRENT PRACTICES

This path appeals to some of the most introspective and reflective of vampires; indeed, all Sabbat subscribe to parts of the theory (if not the practice) of this path. Followers focus on personal growth, but also lead crusades and War Parties to garner hidden knowledge and powerful elder vitae. Additionally, many of this path's students often oversee and participate in rituals and plays celebrating the history of vampirism. Noddists are loath to Embrace randomly during war instead of choosing recruits from promising mortals carefully. Recently, many Noddists have eschewed scholarship in favor of traveling with nomadic packs, experiencing the world and emulating Caine's wanderings. Many of these "adventurous" Noddists travel the globe to chase bits of information and experience vampiric existence in a variety of locations.

PATH OF CAINE HIERARCHY OF SINS

SCORE	MORAL GUIDELINE	RATIONALE
10	Failing to engage in research or study each night, regardless of circumstances	The search for truth requires dedication.
9	Failing to instruct other vampires in the Path of Caine	All vampires must have the opportunity to explore their potential.
8	Befriending or co-existing with mortals	Caine was separated from mortals; as all vampires should be.
7	Showing disrespect to other students of Caine	All of the Children of Caine deserve the respect due their heritage, as long as they strive to understand themselves.
6	Failing to ride the wave in frenzy	Direct the Beast; do not be directed by it.
5	Succumbing to Rötschreck	Master your fear. Terror is for lesser beings.
4	Failing to diablerize a "humane" vampire	Those who do not explore their potential forfeit that potential.
3	Failing to regularly test the limits of abilities and Disciplines	Develop your capabilities to their limits in order to discern your true nature.
2	Failing to pursue lore about vampirism when the opportunity is available	Every scrap of knowledge adds a piece to the puzzle of undead existence.
1	Denying vampiric needs (by refusing to feed, showing compassion or failing to learn about one's vampiric abilities)	To be a vampire, one must satisfy a vampire's needs.

DESCRIPTION OF FOLLOWERS

Noddists are often reserved and educated, with a strong knowledge of history and a drive for self-awareness. Followers of the path are not inquisitive in the sense of seeking deductive answers to problems; rather, they study traditions and historical events in hopes of finding solutions for their questions. Cainites who espouse this path often display a great deal of self-mastery. Additionally, Noddists tend to engage in debate with other vampires, to discern how other Cainites experience the Curse. The Assamite *antitribu*, Serpents of the Light, Toreador *antitribu* and Ventrue *antitribu* who make up the majority of followers tend to assume positions of spiritual authority in the Sabbat, as pack priests or bishops. Many other Cainites find followers of this path haughty and vain.

FOLLOWING THE PATH

Sons and Daughters of Caine should always seek information regarding the vampiric condition, through experience, personal growth and the pursuit of occult lore. Diablerie, development of Disciplines and improvement of self-mastery are all valid means of refining the vampiric form. Noddists rarely engage in Sabbat politics, choosing instead to drive packs to acquire new information and new experiences. They also serve as priests who lead vampires to seek awareness — and development — of their undead condition. Those on this path lead by example, embracing their monstrous natures and striving to attune themselves to their differences from humans, then helping other vampires do the same. Noddists do not hesitate to share their insights, so that all vampires have the opportunity to become closer to Caine; conversely, however, they hoard dangerous secrets to prevent misuse.

Common Abilities: Vampires who adhere to the Path of Caine are studious and philosophical. Followers primarily favor Knowledges — especially Occult and various Lores — but Noddists are expected to be capable of developing the vampiric form to its greatest potential, so Survival, Melee and Athletics are encouraged. Additionally, those who would engage in debate prefer Expression, Subterfuge and Leadership.

Preferred Disciplines: Followers of the Path of Caine prefer those Disciplines considered "natural" to vampires, such as Auspex and Presence. Disciplines that augment the physical form — Celerity, Fortitude, and Potence — are particularly valuable. Some Noddists dislike the use of Disciplines that are not expressly noted in the *Book of Nod*, such as Thaumaturgy and Serpentis, claiming that these Disciplines do not conform to Caine's development. Other followers of the path claim that such Disciplines simply represent a heightened mastery of the vampiric condition. Most Cainites of this path conform to the Disciplines listed by Caine in the early fragments of the *Book of Nod*, simply by way of example.

THE PATH OF CATHARI

Evil comes to this world in many forms. As the harbingers of the Father's Curse, vampires are the pioneers of all of those forms.
— Fabrizia Contreraz, Archbishop of Miami

Nickname: Albigensians

Basic Beliefs: The Path of Cathari sprang from the Catharist heresy of the Middle Ages. A dualistic philosophy, Cathar doctrine holds that the world was created in equal parts by a good ("light") creator responsible for virtue and spirit, and an evil ("dark") creator who acted as the counterpoint, fashioning the material world and its vices. The original Cathars believed the soul to be the root of all that is pure in humanity, while the material body was a shell in the corrupt physical world. Cathars pointed to the noble aspects of the spirit — compassion, sacrifice, honesty and the like — as proof that the only true good lay in the ephemeral. The material world, with its suffering and misery, bore obvious flaws and imperfections. After much persecution, this dualistic doctrine vanished from the mortal world, crushed by papal declarations of heresy. Over the years, the vampires who favored tenets of the philosophy adopted it as their own.

According to the vampires who follow this path, the undead are minions of the evil creator, given eternal existence to tempt others with the lures of the material world. Followers of the path believe that they fulfill a destiny as creatures tied to the physical world through vampiric immortality. Because vampires have been denied the spiritual realms of death, the Albigensians reason that they must serve the vices of the physical realm. Therefore, they seek to spread evil and corruption, seeing iniquity as their natural state.

The Albigensians have perfected a code of evils in which to indulge, however. Theirs is not a path of pointless amorality. Taking the beliefs of the original Cathar priests and twisting them, these vampires deliberately search for means of spreading evil. They pursue sins of greed, lust, pride and the like avidly. Sabbat Cathars seek material wealth and comforts, and they encourage others to do the same. A vampire can serve his proper purpose only by embracing the flaws inherent to his form and to the world, accepting his duties as a purveyor of others' vices. Followers of the Path of Cathari thus ironically find spirituality in depravity.

THE ETHICS OF THE PATH

- Indulge in vice. Wealth, sensuality and material power are hallmarks of the physical world.
- Lead others to temptation. It is your role to promote the depravity of the world.
- Grant the Curse of Caine to those with great passion. Undeath is an evil curse, but those with great conviction can use it well.
- The entire material world is corrupt. Expect betrayal and wickedness because almost everybody is corrupt along with it.

- Your role as a creature of evil is predestined. Accept it and fulfill your purpose.
- Death simply leads to reincarnation. Mortals return after you kill them. However, you should avoid Final Death, since you will return as a mortal if you die.

VIRTUES

The Cathari indulge in vice and depravity, thus necessitating strong Conviction and Instinct.

HISTORY

The Path of Cathari grew out of the aftermath of the Albigensian Crusade in the 13th century. The Manicheanist beliefs in dualism influenced some members of the Church, leading to a 30-year war that many believe led to the creation of the mortal Inquisition. After Albigensian vampires resurfaced following the Crusade, they developed this moral system out of the logical consequences of their philosophy, seeing vampires as tied to the mortal world and therefore purveyors of evil, while the spirits of humans possessed the only potential for good. Soon, many vampires took it upon themselves to fulfill their "duty" as providers of the mortal world's corruption. Over the intervening years, the path changed to include broader philosophies and less formal religious overtones, eventually gaining acceptance in the Sabbat during the formation of the sect. The path weathered the internal struggles of the sect and continued to prove adaptable, keeping the core belief of vampires as traffickers in the vices of the material world. Quite a few Sabbat still find purpose in the business of pleasure — and damnation.

CURRENT PRACTICES

The Albigensians lead others to temptation, despoiling the purity of the spirit. Neonates and elders alike can be found among the Albigensians. Many practitioners see the fast-paced, decaying modern world as a sign of success for the forces of the evil creator, and they seek out ever more challenging converts among mortals and vampires alike.

DESCRIPTION OF FOLLOWERS

Albigensians are hedonistic and impulsive, but they believe that they serve a purpose. The followers of this path are not lazy; rather, they undertake their duties with fanatical abandon. Each Albigensian considers it his duty to embody the vices of the material world and to share those comforts and pleasures with others. Among the Sabbat, the Cathari encourage others to explore their monstrous natures and to spread this hedonism among mortals.

FOLLOWING THE PATH

Cathari are usually quite passionate, devoted to vulgarity and pleasure. They see the mortal world as a vast playground, wherein they may satiate their base urges and encourage others to do likewise. Believing themselves to be agents of

PATH OF CATHARI HIERARCHY OF SINS

SCORE	MORAL GUIDELINE	RATIONALE
10	Exercising restraint	One's purpose is excess, not moderation.
9	Showing trust	Use or be used.
8	Failing to pass on the Curse to the passionately wicked or virtuous	The depraved can serve evil better as vampires; the virtuous can be overcome by the Curse.
7	Failing to ride the wave in frenzy	The Beast, as well as the higher self, must be indulged.
6	Acting against another Albigensian	Those of like purpose should fulfill that purpose, not quarrel among themselves.
5	Impassioned killing	Murder achieves no greater end; dead men cannot sully their souls.
4	Sacrificing gratification for someone else's convenience	Promote physical pleasures, not altruistic achievements.
3	Refraining from indulgence	The material world is a place for the gratification of the flesh.
2	Arbitrary killing	Killing a mortal absolves him of bringing about his own damnation.
1	Encouraging others to exercise restraint	Vampires are creatures of evil; the vampire's purpose is to corrupt, not save.

immorality, the followers of this path are often highly social, befriending and using others to serve their own purposes of spreading debauchery.

Common Abilities: Followers of the Path of Cathari indulge freely in vices and materialism, and they seek to spread these excesses. Thus, Social Abilities like Subterfuge and Streetwise are most useful. Some Albigensians also use Finance and Bureaucracy to make money, so as to make their unlives more comfortable. A few of the more studious followers of the path indulge in Occult knowledge and Academics in order to study the roots of the path.

Preferred Disciplines: Albigensians prefer Disciplines that allow them to fulfill their grim purpose. Dominate and Presence are most valued for the ability to coerce mortals into cooperation. They regard the Discipline of Animalism highly as well, due to its reflection in the powers of Scripture, from which the followers of this path take some of their beliefs.

THE PATH OF DEATH AND THE SOUL

The soul is the only eternal constant. To study the purpose of the soul through its interaction with the mundane is the highest calling of existence.

— Anisa Marianna Lopez, Harbinger of Skulls philosopher

Nickname: Necronomists

Basic Beliefs: As spirits trapped in undying corpses, vampires are creatures caught on the cusp of the physical world and the next plane. Necronomists study the process of death and its logical antecedent — the fate of the soul. While humans are vibrant expressions of the spirit, vampires are caught between life and true death: corpses with an animate form, with supernatural powers and inhuman needs. To understand the purpose of existence, the Necronomists believe, one must develop a comprehension of the soul and its nature, as well as the means by which the soul interacts with the body — especially the means by which the soul is freed from its mortal coil, the passage into death.

By turning their attention toward the pursuit of knowledge, Necronomists deny their unliving Beasts and instead seek enlightenment. As the only eternal constant of existence, the soul contains the key to all life and unlife. Necronomists seek to understand the journeys of the soul and its many attendant forms. Since the soul is eternal, the adherents of this path argue, it must contain the most basic elements of being. From these basic truths, the students of this path hope to extrapolate the reasons for material existence and vampirism. Understanding the universe's mysteries is the most fundamental function of the soul, they claim; conscious awareness is the universe's way of exploring itself, and the followers of this path therefore study the soul, from which self-awareness springs.

Necronomists espouse the view that the heart is the physical seat of the soul and that all power stems from the soul. Thus, the vampiric susceptibility to stakes through the heart stems from the mystical severance of the body and soul by wood, an element at once organic yet unyielding. Similarly, blood, which flows outward from the point of the soul, is the conduit of life and spiritual power; though their unliving bodies cannot produce blood, vampires can draw upon the inherent strength of the blood and merge it with the spiritual abilities of their trapped souls.

THE ETHICS OF THE PATH

- Death is the process by which the soul returns to its unfettered state. Study and understand this transition.
- All of material existence is a reflection of the patterns of spirit. Expose the underpinnings of existence by discovering the workings of the spirit.
- Do not fear Final Death. The soul is immortal.
- Thought and emotion reflect the hidden soul. Analyze consciousness to discover the unique design of each soul.
- Everything contains a piece of the puzzle of existence. Learn of all things to assemble all the pieces.
- In religion and occultism, find the key truths that are pertinent to all existence.

VIRTUES

Necronomists espouse the values of Conviction and Self-Control.

HISTORY

The Path of Death and the Soul is the first of the recognized paths of the Sabbat. Formed by Tzimisce who built on the practices of ancient vampire death-scholars, the path provided an alternate means of viewing existence, one in which conventional morality (as it relates to this path) was simply a construct of lesser souls. Combined with the surge of philosophical thought during the Enlightenment, the path's tenets spread to many spiritual and rational vampires. In the modern night, the path has a small but dedicated following among the Sabbat and even a few other vampires.

CURRENT PRACTICES

Practitioners of the Path of Death and the Soul engage in elaborate rituals designed to bring the architecture of the soul to the fore. Games of torment and endurance are common, as the Necronomists believe that pain and anger are raw and undiluted expressions of the spirit. Necronomists seek to control themselves even in the throes of fasting or agony, exploring their limits of mental endurance. The study of death also ranks highly on the activities of this path's followers, and elaborate sacrifices of humans and vampires alike are valued for the insight they offer. Necronomists deliberately torture their victims to draw out passion and to inspire a lingering imbalance that prompts the dying victim's soul to remain, tied by its own terror and suffering. The transition from flesh to spirit is

PATH OF DEATH AND THE SOUL HIERARCHY OF SINS

SCORE	MORAL GUIDELINE	RATIONALE
10	Attachment to the material world	The material world is ultimately ephemeral and of limited use in garnering understanding.
9	Showing a fear of Final Death	All souls return to the cycle. Final Death is not a death of the soul.
8	Being guided by emotions	Emotions may be studied as expressions of the soul, but they are not useful in cultivating functional understanding.
7	Succumbing to frenzy	The impulses of the Beast do not lead to enlightenment.
6	Failing to kill when useful	Make death a tool. Kill selectively and learn from the victims' passing.
5	Failing to pursue enlightenment	The purpose of the path is to increase knowledge.
4	Showing an aversion to death	Death is the doorway between the material and the eternal. It must be embraced and acknowledged.
3	Showing compassion	Suffering is a step toward inevitable death.
2	Killing without studying the death afterward	Murder offers no opportunity to increase insight.
1	Needlessly preventing a death	All things must die. Do not meddle with the universe's cycle.

ultimately the greatest key to understanding the soul, the Necronomists reason, and they engineer experiments to carefully watch and learn from that transition.

DESCRIPTION OF FOLLOWERS

Necronomists tend to be curious, detached and highly intellectual. Although they do not deny their emotions, they analyze even their own reactions extensively, searching for clues to the nature of the soul. Necronomists are intensely spiritual, yet at the same time distant; emotion, reason and faith are all simple tools in the quest for true understanding. Many possessed a morbidly spiritual streak in life, and continue their explorations even in unlife. Followers of this path rarely form friendships or attachments, but they are staunchly loyal to their allies, with little patience for half-measures and vacillation. The Sabbat of this path come primarily from the Harbingers of Skulls, Tzimisce and Malkavian and Toreador *antitribu*.

FOLLOWING THE PATH

A Necronomist must be open to all forms of intellectual exploration. Emotion clouds proper judgment (and thus is not a means for drawing valid conclusions), but it is a part of self-awareness and as such must be recognized. Followers of this path are focused and determined. There is no room for diffidence or hesitation; unlocking the fundamentals of the soul requires singular dedication. Necronomists must never eschew anything that would lead to greater knowledge of the soul, including death. Advancing one's understanding of the soul is always the first priority; attachment to the material world is attachment to an ephemeral and ultimately flawed existence.

Common Abilities: Obviously, knowledge of death, the afterlife and the fate of the soul is foremost on the minds of this path's followers. They take great pride in their Abilities of Occult, Academics, Research and other intellectual pursuits. Necronomists also study how the condition of the physical form affects the spirit, so they develop their Abilities in Medicine.

Preferred Disciplines: Understanding of the spirit world comes with the Disciplines that allow a vampire to sense and interact with the souls of the dead. Thus, Necronomists often study Auspex, Necromancy and Thaumaturgy. Additionally, one's own suffering can yield tremendous insight (instead of the vicarious knowledge gained through others), and many Necronomists learn Fortitude to push the limits of their own endurance.

THE PATH OF EVIL REVELATIONS

Serve the proper masters, and they will liberate you from your unwanted shackles.

— Saul Joram, Sabbat priest and infernalist

Nickname: Corrupters, Slaves

Basic Beliefs: Vampires are merely one expression of supernatural evil in the world. Although vampires are creatures of great power and depravity, they pale in comparison to the truly ancient beings that reside in Hell beyond the realms of the dead. This, then, is the credo of the Corrupters: All vampires are but pawns to the demons of the Inferno, and the proper place of the vampire is to acknowledge the supremacy of these infernal masters. Some vampires revel in their evil natures and spread their vile ways, but they see themselves as masters of vice. The true masters, whisper the Corrupters, are the creatures formed of the spiritual essence of malevolence, the demons that enslave and devour human souls.

To follow the Path of Evil Revelations, a vampire must believe in the vampire's role as a servant of greater evil, as well as in the place of demons and infernal entities as greater harbingers of the corruption that vampires spread. All Corrupters claim one or more infernal "patrons," spreading the specific brand of vitriol espoused by their demonic lords. The vampires claim to be given great powers and a place in the infernal hierarchy, in exchange for absolute servitude and the sacrifice of their own souls (and the souls of their victims). With such enticements, the Corrupter spreads his own brand of poison among his associates, seeking to turn other vampires to his cause eventually so that they may take their rightful (and subordinate) places in the hierarchy of Hell.

Because the followers of the Path of Evil Revelations give themselves over to various demonic lords, they paradoxically control themselves by serving the interests of their patrons. Obviously, other vampires hate and fear the Corrupters; the Camarilla considers infernalists a threat to security and the Masquerade, while the Sabbat loathes anyone who would willingly enslave himself to some greater unseen power, whether archdemon or Antediluvian. For their part, most devotees of the Path of Evil Revelations consider both organizations foolish and misguided, due to their failure to recognize the infernal lords and their professed "morality," be it in the form of the Camarilla's wayward protection of a Masquerade that preserves both human and vampire or in the shape of the Sabbat's holy crusade to free vampires from the tyranny of the elders. Still, the Corrupters move quietly in both circles, subtly spreading the influence of their masters and arranging the downfall of elders who stand against them.

Ultimately, the Path of Evil Revelations embraces inward evil as a tool for outer darkness. Students of the path come in many forms, but all have bartered their souls for the hope of advancement in a hierarchy predicated on corruption and depravity. Through malicious servitude, the Corrupters seek to be raised above the other vampires — whom they believe will one day be brought to heel by the infernal lords.

Followers of more rigid codes of ethics find Corrupters affected and laughable. Why make such ostentatious shows of adolescent and shallow "evil"?

THE ETHICS OF THE PATH

- You are the servant of greater evil powers. Serve well, and you will be elevated in position.
- You must convince other vampires of the rightness of your cause. Use duplicity and prey upon their weaknesses.
- Fight against vampires who would strive for some semblance of honor or goodness. They are misguided.
- Never reveal your true motives. Others cannot work against you if they do not know the end toward which you work.
- It is acceptable to engage in intrigues with the servants of other demons, but your loyalty to your lord — and to his other retainers — must be absolute.
- Use the Beast as a tool to spread your evil.

VIRTUES

The Path of Evil Revelations emphasizes Conviction and Instinct.

HISTORY

Although many believe that the Path of Evil Revelations was founded by a group of Brujah infernalists in the 1600s, or even as part of a medieval death cult, the truth is that vampires, like humans, have dedicated themselves to infernal powers from time immemorial. However, the actual codification of this path and its philosophies did not occur until the Renaissance. The idea of a philosophy devoted to the service of evil needed the possibility of structured philosophies to exist in the first place. Even so, current Corrupters are far from unified, and a group in service to a particular demon is just as likely to work against a different band of Corrupters as to join forces.

The infernalists of this path suffer at the hands of the Sabbat, which has created its own Inquisition to destroy them. Still, the inhumanity of many Sabbat makes them easier prey for Corrupters than the more reserved and (sometimes) humane members of the Camarilla. With the rapid approach of Gehenna, the Corrupters work harder than ever to gain converts and to spread their influence.

CURRENT PRACTICES

Although the Corrupters have no unified structure, they share some common practices. Most involve themselves in secret debased rituals in which they make sacrifices to their dark lords. Although human sacrifice is common, it's by no means universal — the importance, to these infernalists, lies in the symbolism of the sacrifice itself, so human sacrifice is really the sacrifice of community, morality and free will. Additionally, all Corrupters make a practice of bringing others into the fold, via coercion or compulsion. The lure of power without responsibility to any sort of conscience is a tempting one for many vampires or humans. Indeed, the

PATH OF EVIL REVELATIONS HIERARCHY OF SINS

SCORE	MORAL GUIDELINE	RATIONALE
10	Maintaining any semblance of goodness or honor	Feign goodness but never presume that you are anything more than a servant of greater evil.
9	Missing a nightly devotion	Proper service requires constant affirmation.
8	Helping others when not to your advantage	Compassion and aid are simply tools to bring others into your debt.
7	Passing up an opportunity to acquire temporal power	Power in the material world is the means by which the will of the infernal lords is expressed.
6	Following your own interests	The master's will is more important than one's own.
5	Not working with other followers of your master	The master's goals are best served with unity against one's opponents.
4	Failing to take an opportunity to fulfill your master's goals	Advance the will of your lords whenever possible.
3	Providing infernal secrets to non-converts	Never reveal to outsiders your master's true motives, so that your master cannot be fought.
2	Failing to corrupt or destroy other vampires	All vampires must recognize their proper place as agents of evil or be destroyed.
1	Disobeying your infernal master	You must serve the interests of your superiors in evil.

unification of practices among Corrupters is really only evident inasmuch as many of their infernal masters desire similar devotions. Still, loyal infernalists reaffirm their devotions every night; the dark powers are notoriously fickle with those who show any signs of slackening.

Corrupters are fond of using pawns and intermediaries, especially ill-informed dupes. Followers of this path rarely Embrace others — why make a potential threat to your own power? — but they do make copious use of blood bonds among mortals and vampires alike.

Ultimately, Corrupters can be found among the most depraved aspects of society. The spread of virulent plagues, the kidnapping and torture of families, the engineering of cartels that cater to vice and addiction — each Corrupter has a specialty, a form of malevolence honed and practiced to an exquisitely sublime grotesquerie. Corrupters of the Decani (the lords of disease) encourage the explosive growth of slums like Mexico City's outlying shantytown, where people choke in their own filth and effluvia. Children of Chykas the Riven (a demon of strife) carefully promote emotional confrontations and rifts in friends and associates, until their passions explode into murder and terror. Servants of Nulpheggorath raise cults of ghoulish followers who dine on the decanted brain matter of those who fail the dark masters, promising power and eternal life to those who do not falter. The coming millennium is dark indeed, as the Corrupters plant their seeds in an overripe world set to burst with its own rot.

DESCRIPTION OF FOLLOWERS

The "typical" Corrupter is intelligent, charismatic and relentlessly immoral. These Corrupters use their charm and cleverness to bring less talented (and competitive) but still useful minions into the fold. They usually choose these slaves for their brawn and their tendency to be easily manipulated by promises of power. Both kinds are careful to disguise themselves as vampires of the area's predominant society. Often, a Corrupter leads a "double unlife" in which he acts as an unassuming but loyal member of a vampiric sect, while keeping his private affairs carefully concealed.

FOLLOWING THE PATH

All Corrupters must be ready to place their masters' desires above their own. At any moment, the Corrupter could be called upon to serve as a tool or even a meal for his infernal lord, and he must obey without compunction. This duty never slackens. Every goal, every desire of the follower of the path must bend toward the advancement of his demonic overseer. Corrupters must spread the will and influence of their overlords at all times and bring converts into the fold whenever possible.

Each infernal lord has its own agenda; most are categorized by a particular form of recognized "evil." Thus, a servant of a Lord of Disease is charged with carefully spreading plagues and compromising medical achievements, while the agent of a Duke of Violence pushes others to acts of frenzied destruction and engages in bloody combat whenever feasible. The most effective Corrupters advance their lords' goals subtly and indirectly; a servant of violence who goes on a six-state killing spree will only draw unwanted attention to himself, while the Corrupter who quietly spurs others to acts of violence furthers the work of his master much more — and survives to continue spreading evil.

Common Abilities: The more insightful and cunning adherents of this path develop significant Occult Ability. Subterfuge, Etiquette, Intimidation and Empathy are also useful in drawing converts or hiding one's true nature. The more martial Corrupters study enough Brawl, Dodge and Melee to defend themselves should a physical confrontation result.

Preferred Disciplines: Followers of the Path of Evil Revelations protect themselves by gathering information with Auspex and developing bonds of loyalty with Presence. Many also study Thaumaturgy, as taught by their infernal lords.

The Path of the Feral Heart

I hunt, I kill, I feed. No customs or civilizations bar me in; no walls or traps keep me out. I am a force of nature and the eternal predator.

— Gentha Shale, Sabbat nomad

Nickname: Beasts

Basic Beliefs: Vampires are the ultimate hunters — immortal and invulnerable. The Beast Within is merely the expression of the predator's instinct. To deny one's atavistic attributes is to go against the dictates of nature, or so this path's followers believe. A vampire can only survive by adhering to her inner character and accepting the monstrous drives that accompany the unliving state. Though the Beasts do not revel in their predations, neither do they avoid them. By learning to accept the role of hunter, thereby acknowledging the proper role of the unliving, a vampire becomes like an animal: feral, predatory, but ultimately in her proper place.

A follower of this path feels that the Beast is a natural part of being a vampire and that its needs must be satiated. Still, the vampire is intelligent, and a cunning hunter is a more effective one. Therefore, it is important to strike a balance between Beast and Man — the feral cunning and vicious instincts of the vampire are excellent survival tools, tempered by the reasoning and insight of the mind. By satiating the Beast's urges from time to time, the vampire ironically gains a greater degree of personal control.

Vampires on the Path of the Feral Heart (sometimes called the Path of the Beast) have little use for the trappings of civilization

Cowboys and Indians, also known as Cops and Robbers, is practiced by large packs or by two individual packs. One "team" goes into hiding half an hour before the other goes after them, usually in bad or abandoned parts of town where this sort of hooliganism is overlooked by the locals. The object of Cowboys and Indians is to capture or incapacitate (but not kill) as many members of the other side as possible. Because of vampires' innate resistance to damage, this is easier said than done, and bullets aplenty fly during these games. The best way to capture another vampire, of course, is to stake him. The team that knocks the other out of commission is the winner.

Demolition Derby is usually played in stolen cars, as the vehicles tend not to survive the game. Starting at opposite ends of a street, parking lot or drainage aqueduct, pack members set their cars on fire and charge another team's car. After much bashing and crashing, one team inevitably has to flee their car or burn to death; the first team to exit its vehicle loses. It is legal to fire upon the other car, which is part of the strategy of the game. Drivers may carry only one passenger, or they may sacrifice maneuverability for firepower.

One particularly dangerous game is called Rousing the Beast. This game is a one-on-one challenge, whereby the participant has to release the victim of a failed mass-Embrace. He must choose the grave of a victim who failed to dig himself out of the earth — problematic in and of itself because the mass-grave Embrace is usually performed only in cities under siege or in the midst of a crusade. The Sabbat vampire must dig the completely mad and starving former recruit out from his earthen prison. Once the crazed creature breaks the surface and frenzies, it is up to the game participant to immobilize her and destroy her. The preferred method is by stake; firearms are typically forbidden. Needless to say, this hand-to-hand combat is very dangerous, and the Sabbat does not always win. This game is a trial of will as much as of physical strength, as the vampire must come face to face with his own creation and subsequent inhumanity.

The Rat Race is another popular sport. A human is sealed in a labyrinth of some sort, such as an abandoned factory or part of a sewer system. The human is given weapons that can hurt the vampires, such as handguns, knives, blowtorches or chainsaws. The participating vampires, starting in different locations in the maze, hunt the human, while the human tries desperately to escape the vampires. Whichever vampire captures and drains the human first, wins. Maiming the competition to ensure victory is encouraged, though killing one's opponent is not the object of the game and viewed unfavorably. An alternative to the Rat Race — the Bat Race — involves vampires only. The packmates draw lots; whoever gets the short straw becomes the prey. Obviously, this variant is rarely seen through to the Final Death.

Some insane or powerful packs play a game known as Dogtagging. Packing an off-road vehicle with firearms and tow cables, the vampires rampage into Lupine territory. The object of the game is to capture a werewolf, tag its ear (with tags similar to kind used by cattle ranchers), turn it loose and get the hell out of there before it comes back with friends. A few packs actually hunt Lupines in this manner to kill them — they figure that the werewolf has already been caught, and there's no reason to suffer it to live and possibly come back to even the score another night.

System: Storytellers and players are encouraged to develop their own Games of Instinct; basically, any mayhem works for this *ritus* as long as the pack priest recognizes it and bestows her blessing upon it. Most priests indulge their pack in one Game of Instinct per month or so (if that often); anything more frequent makes this *ritus* less valuable, as it becomes common.

The Games of Instinct allow the Sabbat to hone its skills to the edge. For the duration of one story, the winner(s) of a given Game of Instinct receive one bonus die to the dice pool of the Ability they used the most during the game. For example, if the Corpses Delecti participate in a Game of Instinct, and Walker wins through judicious use of his pistol, Walker gets a one-die bonus to his Firearms dice pool for the next story. A player may not have more than one Skill augmented in this way for any given story.

Storytellers should bear in mind that only the most dangerous (and blatant) of activities are suitable for Games of Instinct — trials of skills in which a pack is already proficient serve little to increase their abilities, and these games tend to draw crowds if not practiced rarely and discretely. If your players insist on having Games of Instinct every night to stock up on bonus dice, feel free to go after their characters with police, Lupines, disdainful elders, et cetera. The games are practiced to build skill and solidarity, not to create super-characters.

MONOMACY

It is inevitable that, among vampires as headstrong and violent as those of the Sabbat, differences of opinion occur. While the vast majority of these conflicts are handled with all the civility and reason a Sabbat can muster, some grievances are so deep as to warrant a more serious solution. When two (or more) Sabbat are unable to come to a resolution, the *ritus* of Monomacy serves to settle the issue.

To the uninitiated observer, Monomacy looks like a simple duel to the death. In truth, however, it is a good deal more. Monomacy serves the Sabbat as the ultimate evolutionary tool: By culling their ranks of those who are incompetent, the sect grows stronger. Monomacy is accorded a sacrosanct status among the vampires of the Sabbat, who recognize that without strong leaders, their struggle against the Antediluvians amounts to nothing. Additionally, the winner of a Monomacy typically diablerizes the loser.

Monomacy is usually practiced by only ranking members of packs. Many young Sabbat are too violent and hotheaded to recognize the gravity of ritual combat to the death, and would resort to it every time a packmate took blood from a vessel they decided they liked. As such, this *ritus* is conducted by the pack priest, to whom a challenge is issued simultaneously with the challenge to the rival. The priest then decides whether or not the grudge is worth Monomacy, and whether or not she chooses to preside over the ritual.

Should the priest deem the cause worthy, the challenged vampire may decline. In theory, there is nothing wrong with declining a challenge, but unless the challenger is of such little consequence as to be below the challengee's notice, declining usually involves a great loss of face (and perhaps an unsanctioned duel afterward). If those who pursue the Monomacy hail from different packs, it may be necessary to involve a neutral third party, such as another pack's priest or even the bishop or archbishop.

The actual practice of Monomacy varies widely — no formal code exists as to the choice of weapons, locations or even terms of victory. Most often, Monomacy duels are fought to Final Death in some ridiculously dangerous or highly inaccessible place like an iron foundry or atop a skyscraper. Whether or not the vampires may use weapons, Disciplines or other assets is typically the decision of the challenged. On the priest's invocation of the *ritus*, the combat begins, and the last vampire standing is declared the winner, usually followed by other *ritae* and celebration. As Monomacy is an *auctoritas ritus*, formal weapons such as swords and daggers are usually used (if any); modern weapons, particularly firearms, are considered inelegant, clumsy and vulgar.

Not every Monomacy is this straightforward, however. Several Lasombra disputes have been settled on life-sized chessboards with living "pieces," and one Tzimisce-Ventrue *antitribu* rivalry resulted in Monomacy that involved shooting each other's ghouls until one competitor had none left standing. (The Tzimisce won.)

Many Sabbat issues are resolved this way, and to the victor usually go the spoils. Pack members who wish to challenge their leader's position, Sabbat who take umbrage with their bishop's leadership and rival pack priests with claims to each other's established areas of influence have all used Monomacy to settle their disputes. Many Sabbat suspect that the regent of the sect attained her position by physically besting her predecessor.

System: The details of Monomacy are best left to the story — troupes should be encouraged to add all the pomp and circumstance they wish to the *ritus* (as it is *auctoritas*, after all), though the exact details differ from pack to pack. Storytellers may wish to play up these differences, highlighting the outlooks of different packs and perhaps even interjecting improprieties and other subtle nuances for flavor ("You can't challenge the pack leader now — it's not three nights after the full moon!").

The challenger decides upon the time and location of the duel. The challenged decides whether or not weapons will be used and what they will be, as well as any other details (until first blood instead of Final Death, no Disciplines,

participants must wear blindfolds, participants must ride the wave of frenzy during the duel, etc.).

The priest administering the *ritus* is an official — the duel begins and ends on her word, and it may be aborted at any time. It is even within the priest's power to declare a Monomacy null and void after the fact, but the priest who does this to favor her own candidate is looked upon with extreme displeasure thereafter by other Sabbat.

PALLA GRANDE

Of the 13 *auctoritas ritae*, the *Palla Grande* is the highlight of any Sabbat coven's ritual year.

The "Grand Ball" takes place on All Hallows Eve, and all Sabbat in the city are expected to attend. Nomadic packs, not wanting to miss the festivities, travel to the closest Sabbat city in order to attend. The highest-ranking Sabbat in the city preside over the affair, and the city's most renowned priest opens the celebration. It is held in a public place such as a civic auditorium or a public park, as long as most of the revels take place in full view of as many humans as possible. In fact, most Sabbat arrange their Grand Balls like raves or public festivals, sometimes even charging mortals admission for the secretly malignant privilege of attendance. The vampires often go the whole nine yards when creating this party atmosphere, hiring bartenders and providing liquor and other refreshments for their guests.

As the *Palla Grande* is a major social event, the Ventrue and Toreador *antitribu*, Lasombra and Tzimisce usually find themselves with the responsibility of planning the affair. In true high-society fashion, many vampires also compete with each other for the most elaborate costumes. Often the most spectacular and unusual displays are by one or two elder Tzimisce skilled in the art of Fleshcraft, but it is not unheard of for a Toreador *antitribu* to exchange favors with a talented Tzimisce "artist" to create a finely fleshcrafted face or costume for the party. Indeed, the regent herself is rumored to have once had 50 mortals fleshcrafted to resemble her at a Grand Ball in the interests of "being everywhere and talking to everyone — and leaving an indelible impression."

Hidden away from the public debauchery, the Sabbat also consecrates a Blood Feast at the *Palla Grande*. The "kinekegger," as the younger Sabbat call it, capitalizes on the public location of the masquerade ball. Victims for the feast are often vampire wannabes, drunken revelers and "witches" out for a good time on Halloween night. These victims are often lured to the feast under the pretense of being invited to attend an exclusive social affair. They have no idea just how fleeting the honor is to be. Other possible sources of vitae for the blood feast include retainers or ghouls selected from the Sabbat covens' own members who may be of no further use to the sect (or are too dangerous to allow to live).

The main event, which kicks off the affair at midnight, is the re-enactment of an event from vampire legend or history. This stage play could be anything from the slaying of

Abel by Caine as told in Biblical terms to the dramatic interpretation of signs and portents of Gehenna. It is completely organized, acted and choreographed by a group of vampires, though "audience participation" in events depicting sacrifice or feeding does occur, with the "guest actors" being whisked away or quietly disposed of after their debut.

After the final act of the historical play, all Sabbat present retire to the Blood Feast for a special version of the Blood Bath. This night the archbishop bathes in the vitae, as a symbol of the sect's power and vitality. The ritual begins with blood from the victims suspended overhead flowing freely into a large, ornate receptacle where the archbishop reclines. Each vampire in the coven adds some of his own vitae to the bath, first bleeding into a ceremonial Vaulderie vessel, then tipping it into the bath. The archbishop performs various rituals and incantations while this process proceeds — details vary city to city. It is rumored that the *Palla Grande* Blood Bath imbues the archbishop with certain powers until the next sunrise, such as the ability to see into the realms of the dead.

At the conclusion of the Blood Bath, all Sabbat at the *Palla Grande* begin a frenetic dance of undeath, dancing to near-deafening music and drinking insatiably from the archbishop's bath, from the hanging vessels and from each other. Many of the participants fall into frenzy, driven on by the violence of the dance and the scent, sight and feel of blood coagulating on the floor, caked on walls and plashing from the carpets as dawn draws near.

Once the night's revels conclude, Sabbat ghouls take care of the clean-up. Any potential loose ends are swiftly dealt with over the next couple nights through death, the Discipline of Dominate or the Embrace, depending on the extent of the problem and potential use of the individuals involved.

System: In addition to the benefits gained from the Blood Feast and Blood Bath, Sabbat vampires who attend the *Palla Grande* completely replenish their Willpower.

Sermons of Caine

Some members of the Sabbat value their knowledge of the *Book of Nod*. Others don't know or care about the book, and they see their role in the Sabbat as one of endless war and violence. Those members who take the story of their origins very seriously often gather to hear sermons on their history to remind them who and what they are. This reminder serves to strengthen their loyalty to the sect and their ideology. Pack members take turns reciting from the *Book of Nod*, while the others sit in a semicircle holding lit candles and meditating on the passages. The sermons are sometimes followed by the Vaulderie, and, among more intellectual packs, intense deliberation. Pack members often discuss the passages read during the *ritus* almost until dawn.

Vampire history, particularly as far back as Cainite legendry is largely an oral tradition — very few copies of the *Book of Nod* actually exist. Few, if any, Sabbat packs can agree unanimously on the exact phraseology of a given passage from

the book. The sect is divided on this matter — some Sabbat believe that as long as the spirit of the *Book of Nod* is preserved, the letter is irrelevant, while others maintain that for all Sabbat to have the same reference, a standard book needs to be decided upon. This schism, of course, results in a wide variety of individual positions on the matter, from violent support on both ends of the spectrum to a profound ambivalence for anything outside one's pack's take on the matter.

System: While this *ritus* does not require a system for a mechanical effect, some Storytellers may wish to award experience points toward the Expert Knowledge: Noddist Lore for participation in this *ritus* (assuming the Storyteller permits Secondary Abilities, as per the **Vampire Storytellers Companion**). Otherwise, this convention is simply an opportunity for Storytelling, roleplaying and revealing bits of the great Cainite mystery.

THE VAULDERIE

The vampires of the Sabbat take their nightly struggle seriously — so seriously that they tolerate no dissent in their ranks. From the lowliest new recruit to the most exalted priscus, the Sabbat ensure loyalty to one another through a bloody *ritus* known as the Vaulderie.

The Vaulderie is similar to a blood bond, though it differs in intent and function. No Sabbat would ever voluntarily succumb to a blood bond, reasoning that such bonds are the tools the elders use to enslave their childer. Rather, the Sabbat swear the Vaulderie to each other, bonding themselves to the pack instead of an individual, and thus, to the Sabbat's greater cause.

Those who are ignorant of the Vaulderie's finer details believe it to be a simple commingling of vampire vitae in a vessel and the subsequent drinking of it. In truth, the matter is far more mystical. To start the ritual, the priest takes a tool used specifically for the Vaulderie *and nothing else* and cuts her wrist. The ritual cutting tool could be a small knife, silver straight razor or awl. To impart more gravity to the *ritus*, many packs use elaborate ritual bloodletters decorated with engraved swirls, spirals or blood droplets. The priest then bleeds into a vessel and passes the cutting device to each Sabbat present, who pierces his own flesh and bleeds into the chalice. The vessel is then passed around the pack again and the priest recites an incantation over it, consecrating it as a terrible sacrament while every member of the pack draws a draught.

Vaulderies take place at any time — before assaults, during important Sabbat gatherings, at the initiation or Creation Rites of new members and almost infallibly at pack esbats. This *ritus* is perhaps the foundation of the sect's *ritae*, and it is afforded the most reverent status.

The result of this *ritus* is known as a *Vinculum*, or blood-tie. These ties connect each member of the pack to one another, engendering a mutual loyalty in addition to bolstering pack morale. Because of the mystical nature of the Vaulderie, however, Vinculi are imperfect — what one pack member feels toward another one night may pale in comparison to what he feels toward her the next. Vinculum ratings may change every time the *ritus* is observed.

Without the Vaulderie, the Sabbat would probably collapse under its own weight and dogma — the chaos and anarchy that follows the sect endemically would erode what little organization it has without the loyalty and sympathy created by the *ritus*. Those who refuse the Vaulderie or oppose it are not viewed favorably by other Sabbat. Vampires who refuse to partake of the Vaulderie at least monthly suffer ostracism from the pack at best — and may become vessels for Blood Feasts or destroyed outright at worst.

System: The first time a character observes the Vaulderie (or during creation of a Sabbat character), roll a die for each character whose vitae is part of the *ritus*. That number reflects the Vinculum the character feels toward the individual whose blood she ingested; see the chart for effects generated by individual Vinculi. Every time a new member participates in the Vaulderie, each player should roll a die and record the score for her Vinculum rating toward that character.

Example: Lucretia, Vaughan and Dezra (characters created by three players) have just partaken of the Vaulderie. Each player rolls a die for the two other players' characters and records this score as their Vinculum to that character. Lucretia's player rolls a 6 for her Vinculum to Dezra and a 4 for her Vinculum to Vaughan. During the course of the game, a new character, Madd Killah, joins the pack, and after her first Vaulderie with him, Lucretia gains a Vinculum of 5 toward him.

Each time the pack partakes of the Vaulderie, each player should roll one die for each of her Vinculi. If the result is higher than the Vinculum score, increase that Vinculum score by one (to a maximum of 10). If the result is a 1, lower the Vinculum score by one (to a minimum of 1).

At times, a character may be at odds with herself over how to react to a given situation because of Vinculi she possesses toward another vampire. In cases such as these, the player should decide which party her character would favor outside the Vinculum. The character then rolls a number of dice for each party equal to her Vinculum score for that individual against a difficulty of 5 (for the party favored regardless of Vinculum) or 7 (for all other parties). The individual who receives the greatest number of successes earns the character's aid. Such is the nature of the Damned and the Vinculum — a character who knows better may sometimes be forced into an obviously bad course of action by following her emotions.

Example: Lucretia has Vinculi toward packmates Dezra and Vaughan. The pack has heard there is a Camarilla Ventrue spy in their city, and its members cannot agree about the best resolution to

Vinculum Ratings

Vinculum	Effect
10	You will readily give your life — or take the life of another — for the individual.
9	You will do practically anything for the individual, including putting yourself in great danger.
8	You will gladly offer resources or influential assistance to the individual.
7	You may put yourself at moderate risk of harm for the individual and, depending on your code of ethics, may kill for him.
6	You feel strongly for the individual and help him even if it inconveniences you. You will gladly fight for the individual.
5	You respect the individual and help him out as long as it's no huge risk or bother.
4	You will aid the individual as long as it doesn't involve risk or anything out of your way.
3	You are loyal to the individual as long as that loyalty doesn't interfere with your own designs.
2	You have a minor sense of kinship toward the individual, but you're not going to go out of your way to help him unless something's in it for you.
1	Fuck 'em. This isn't necessarily hostility, but you don't care about this person on a Vinculum level, though you may on a personal level.

Note: It bears mention that, like the emotions engendered by blood bonds, these feelings are artificial, as they are created through ingestion of blood. It is quite possible for a character to utterly hate someone for whom she would risk her unlife, just as it is possible to have immense love for someone who has little in the way of Vinculum and everything in between. Players are encouraged to explore the full range of these complexities in their packs through roleplaying.

the problem. *Dezra proposes that the pack hunt him down and drink his vitae while Vaughan believes that the best option is to ask around and try to find out information about this so-called spy, believing the confrontation of a vampire of unknown power to be folly. Lucretia thinks Vaughan's option is the wiser of the two, though she must test her Vinculi to see if emotion sways her loyalty to Dezra. She rolls six dice (her Vinculum to Dezra is 6) against difficulty 7 and gains three successes. For Vaughan, she rolls four dice (her Vinculum to Vaughan is 4) against difficulty 5 and gains only one success. Against her better judgment, she sides with Dezra, saying "I'm following Dezra," while flashing Vaughan a defeated look. Dezra smiles and crosses his arms.*

Note: Storytellers should require Vinculum rolls judiciously, and only in matters of dramatic significance. Too much reliance on Vinculum rolls strips free will from the players' characters, and instead of savoring the anguish of their emotional response, players may grow cross at being railroaded by dice rolls.

The Vaulderie can also corrode existing blood bonds. Multiple draughts of the Vaulderie may be required, but sooner or later, the pack's blood will overcome all but the most potent of vampiric vitae. A vampire wishing to break a blood bond via Vaulderie must have no more than one blood point in his blood pool, and must ingest six points of Vaulderie vitae. At that point, the old blood bond fades rapidly, replaced almost as quickly by Vinculi toward those whose blood composed the Vaulderie. A vampire attempting to replace Vinculi with a new blood bond is in for a disappointment — unless her blood is powerfully potent, Vinculi may not be so easily erased.

Unlike normal blood bonds, Vinculi do not fade over time — a Vinculum left after a Vaulderie with a vampire in nights hundreds of years past is still as potent as the night it arose. Indeed, many elder Sabbat have vast webs of Vinculi connecting them to sect members across the world. Some Sabbat whisper guardedly of a ritual that can break the Vinculum outright, though only members of the Nosferatu *antitribu* and the Inquisition are rumored to know this ritual. If these rumors are to be believed, the ritual breaks *every* Vinculum a vampire has, not just select ones. The Inquisition supposedly uses this ritual to break Vinculi toward infernalists, though its obvious other ramifications have many Sabbat worried about the true loyalties of their compatriots.

THE WAR PARTY

The Sabbat thrives on diablerie and the destruction of elders, and this dangerous *ritus* serves to facilitate both of those urges.

War parties consist of multiple packs that vie for the blood of the non-Sabbat elder in question. Hunting the potent elders is not something undertaken lightly, and the Sabbat tries to sway the odds in its favor by sending numerous packs against the enemy. Of course, packs participating in the War Party compete against one another for the privilege

GUESTS AT A WAR PARTY

It was a rowdy gathering, that's for goddamn sure. Chucky and Boy Toy had their faces all painted up like Indian braves, and Jean-Paul did one of his voodoo prayers where he burned a candle and killed a chicken. The vampires from the Blood Hands even dressed like an Old West lynch-posse. The priest told us we were supposed to take down Bruno, some Nosferatu bigshot over in Phoenix. We got pretty out of hand after Gorin gave us the challenge — burned the whole fucking building to the ground, it turns out.

None of that meant shit the next night, though. Gorin told us where Bruno kept his haven, so we hauled ass over there.

Well, as it turns out, "Bruno" was actually Lord Gustaphe Brunnelle, emissary to King Louis the Somethingth of France 500 years ago. It would have been nice to know that beforehand.

Anyway, it was bad. The Harmony Skins got there first, but you wouldn't know it was them unless you checked their dental records or fingerprints. Bruno was weakened, but he still took down Jean-Paul and Ariel. Chucky dove at him, sinking his fangs in Bruno's chest, and Bruno crushed him like a grape.

I unloaded my shotgun into Bruno's chest, which didn't do shit. Boy Toy used my distraction to run him through from behind with a broomstick, staking him with the blunt end (she's fucking strong).

Boy Toy made sure Bruno didn't move while I did the deed. Motherfucker killed half my pack, but I'll be damned if the taste alone wasn't worth it. And now, I'm one step closer to being as bad as Bruno — just not as dead.

of killing and diablerizing the elder, but rarely do the packs come into deadly conflict with each other, reserving their violence for their target.

In preparation for a War Party, the participating packs gather and celebrate. They may also perform the Fire Dance, listen to the Sermons of Caine and participate in a Blood Feast or Vaulderie. The chief of the War Party, usually the most accomplished or highest-ranking priest among the packs (though political War Parties may be called by bishops or other titled officials of the sect), offers the assembled packs the challenge. She stands before the individual packs, each lined up behind their leaders, and asks each of the packs' leaders in turn, "Do you come freely to war, and do you take up this noble cause, never resting until the blood of our enemy is spilled?" The leaders respond with a forceful "We do!" Only after the packs have committed to the hunt does he reveal the identity of their target. A pack suffers great humiliation if it backs out of a challenge after its members have committed themselves to this most dangerous game. For the remainder of the night, the vampires hold a revel, preparing themselves for the hunt the next evening holds in store.

The War Party sets out after its prey on the night following the challenge — the hunt has begun. Sabbat vampires on the warpath stop at nothing to take down their prey. They kill, burn, smash and overturn anyone or anything that stands between them and their target. In fact, once the Sabbat have entered their victim's haven, sometimes they don't even bother to use hallways, doors or passages, instead bursting literally through the walls to find their mark's inner sanctum.

Competition for the elder's blood is fierce during the War Party, but Sabbat almost always recognize the claim of the first vampire to sink his fangs into the victim. (Those who don't usually have their greedy asses beaten into submission by members of the claimant's pack.) Of course, merely biting the elder is no guarantee of victory, as few elders relinquish their blood so willingly. Obviously, once the pack has found the elder, a fight of epic proportions often ensues, unless the elder can somehow escape or convince the slavering, ravenous Sabbat to let him be. It is not unheard of for entire city blocks (under which erstwhile elders made their havens) to be leveled in the fray, as the potent powers of the Damned wreak havoc on the intruding vampires and everything around them.

Camarilla and Sabbat vampires most often come into contact during War Parties, as many of the Sabbat's targets claim membership in the Camarilla. Nothing short of Final Death can stop the packs from achieving their goal, resulting in major property damage, attacks on other Camarilla vampires or anarchs and general brawling. Even sabotage of another pack may occur, but these tactics are generally diversionary; they are rarely intended to do serious damage.

The winning pack is the one whose member consumes the elder's blood first. The target, unliving or dead, or some recognizable portion of the target, must be brought back to the place where the packs accepted the challenge. The Chief of the War Party accepts this trophy and bestows her blessing over the winning pack. Once the chief recognizes the winner, all bets are settled and another celebration is held.

System: The vampire partaking of the diablerie gains the benefits (and sometimes detriments, depending on the potency of the elder's blood) of committing the Amaranth.

Vampires who belong to the winning pack gain a temporary point of Sabbat Status. This point disappears at the end of the next War Party (unless the same pack wins again), or at the *end* of the next grandiose Sabbat affair, such as a *Palla Grande* or *Festivo dello Estinto*. It goes away at the end to allow the characters to reap the benefits of their success. At the Storyteller's option, this Sabbat Status point may be made permanent if the hunted elder was of exceptional power or reputation.

THE WILD HUNT

One of the greatest crimes a Sabbat can commit is to turn traitor, and the sect protects its secrets. If a member reveals a sect secret to the enemy, she is punished severely.

If a Sabbat leaks information of a vital nature, a priest may call for a Wild Hunt. The Wild Hunt is much like the blood hunt, but ends with the eradication of the offending

Sabbat sect member, as well as anyone — Kindred or kine — who may have knowledge of the information. Sabbat from all over the territory are called (and expected) to participate. Nothing stands in the way of a Wild Hunt. Obviously, the gravity of the Wild Hunt depends upon the traitor in question — the packs are expected to police their own ranks, while high-profile turncoats receive the attention of archbishops, prisci, cardinals and all those who serve them.

Necessity dictates that those who have passed on or gained forbidden Sabbat knowledge must be destroyed; it is done in a way that makes it plain that such a breach of trust is intolerable to the Sabbat. The priest assembles the local Sabbat and formally calls them to the hunt, which is sometimes similar to the preface of a War Party.

Once caught, the offending Sabbat is staked and immobilized. The pack takes her before the ductus and priest (or bishop, etc.), who recite her crimes to her packmates. The pack then torments the offender in whatever manner it deems appropriate — hot irons, Vicissitude and mutilation are the least creative forms of vengeance a righteous pack can inflict on a traitor. Finally, the pack destroys the traitor by throwing her (still staked) on a consecrated burning pyre. This action is often accompanied by a recitation from the Chronicle of Caine from the *Book of Nod*, to remind them all that they need unity to overpower their enemies, and mistrust within the sect destroys the Sabbat's foundation.

After the traitor meets her end, the Sabbat pursues those who either learned of the secret or were involved. Sabbat justice is relentless — the sect stops at nothing to ensure their security.

Naturally, the Sabbat cannot know about every little (or even many of the big) secrets that slip through the cracks. Frustration over this fact often makes things doubly bad for those they *do* catch.

System: Sabbat who are subject to the Wild Hunt are no longer Sabbat, and thus, no longer vampires. No amount of groveling (other than a contrition *ritus*) can convince the sect to take back a traitor, though this harsh reality comes more out of security than bullheadedness.

Ignoblis Ritae

Unlike the *auctoritas ritae*, the "low" or "common" rituals vary widely from pack to pack. Several of these *ritae* show up in some form or another in every Sabbat pack, but many of them are unique to regions or even individual packs.

Storytellers and players are encouraged to adapt or create their own *ritae*, to give a sense of camaraderie and significance to the pack.

Acceptance Ritus

This *ritus* welcomes a new member to a particular pack, to recognize the ascension of a recruit, or any time a change in power or membership occurs (such as a new ductus or priest). Each member of the pack must recognize the new position of their fellow Sabbat in a personal manner, be it by

Breaking the Bond

Some suspect that the Sabbat keeps a secret ritual for the breaking of the Vaulderie. It is presumably used for very deep-cover spies, when any contact with the Sabbat would endanger the mission, or in situations in which heretics and infernalists have insinuated themselves in otherwise respectable packs. These rumors usually imply that the breaking of the Vaulderie takes place in the presence of a an archbishop or cardinal, with dispensation from the regent herself. This circumstance occurs only after a very thorough investigation into the nature of the mission, the dedication of the individuals to the Sabbat, and the assurance that there is no possible other way to remedy the situation.

According to one rumor, the *ritus* takes six months to complete, during which the subjects lie staked or starving almost to the point of torpor, and fed a small amount of blood mixed with some vile-smelling liquid.

Prior to participating in the *ritus*, the subjects must sign a parchment declaration in their own fresh blood and verbally declare to the cardinal and any others present that she will resubmit to the Vaulderie (with non-heretic packmates, it is assumed) immediately upon completing the *ritus*. Failure to do so results in the Sabbat being branded a traitor, and the Wild Hunt being called.

sharing blood, the giving of a gift or whatever. The Sabbat being accepted must make an oath of allegiance to each member of the pack, and to the Sabbat cause in general. For example, a new True Sabbat's oath details the gratefulness the recruit has for being allowed into the pack, and his pride in being chosen to serve the pack and the sect. The Acceptance *Ritus* differs from the Creation Rites because it is more social than supernatural. A Sabbat may have received his Creation Rites, but may be snubbed by a pack that refuses to extend him the *ritus* of acceptance.

Allegiance *Ritus*

Before the Acceptance *Ritus* occurs, a vampire already Embraced but not yet Sabbat must go through the Allegiance *Ritus*. This *ritus* is especially important for Camarilla defectors. The Allegiance *Ritus* is long and involved, and it may go on for years before the recruit is permitted the Acceptance *Ritus* and welcomed as a full member of the sect. Part of the process involves the implanting of a secret mark on the body of the defector (a tattoo, scar, brand, etc.) through the use of Vicissitude so it will be permanent. Before receiving this *ritus*, the initiate must sit or stand to the rear of his packmates during *auctoritas ritae*. He must drink last at the Vaulderie, and may not contribute himself. He may not read or discuss passages from the *Book of Nod* aloud. The time involved in confirming the initiate's commitment to the Sabbat makes it all the more difficult for him to leave the sect.

Contrition *Ritus* (also Ablution or Unction *Ritus*)

Even Sabbat commit sins and indiscretions, for which they sometimes need to atone. The Contrition *Ritus* allows for this, much in the same manner a Catholic confession works. This *ritus* is perhaps the most important of the *ignoblis ritae*, as many Inquisitors, Black Hand operatives, priests and ducti offer a choice of contrition or death to Sabbat who have committed wrongs upon the sect. All sensible Sabbat take these *ritae* as seriously as they would any other, for only by the graces of their betters can they continue to exist. Of course, many disingenuous Sabbat may make an insincere act of contrition, but they might not be extended the option next time.

Welcoming *Ritus*

This *ritus* is largely a social convention. Priests invoke it whenever two Sabbat packs meet to spend time together, such as when pilgrim packs stay in a city for a time, or packs unite toward a common short-term goal. The Welcoming *Ritus* reinforces the Sabbat ideology that respects individuality, while requiring unity to achieve the sect's purpose. Most packs carry this *ritus* out quite informally, with the pack leaders sharing blood while their packmates bear witness, but there are two incidents of protocol which typically must be met. At the opening of the *ritus*, all pack members greet each other individually, stating their names and home (if any). This provides the members with a sense of location — where they come from and to where they may travel. At the height of the celebration, a gift is exchanged from pack to pack. It could be a weapon, or a treaty, or the head of an enemy. The gift is presented from a pack's True Sabbat to the other pack's ductus under the priests' supervision. Ducti and priests often use this *ritus* as an opportunity to discuss Sabbat plans.

Ritus of Thanksgiving

This *ritus* is actually less a thanksgiving than a session to boast of one's exploits. The thanksgiving usually comes under the auspices of "I thank Caine for his favor when I..." stories, which usually exaggerate or aggrandize the speaker's prowess. The *Ritus* of Thanksgiving generally precedes esbats or other gatherings of the Sword of Caine.

Martial *Ritus*

In times of war, a Sabbat pack tries to increase its strength in any way possible, often by creating the sense of kinship found only in combat. The Martial *Ritus* serves to whip the Sabbat into a fervor that heralds destruction for its enemies. The *ritus* begins with chanting a mantra such as "strength," "fire," or "muscle and hate." The beating of drums, usually led by the priest, accompanies the chanting. Packs sometimes decorate each others' faces and bodies with blood, paint or henna.

Spilling of Blood

When two or more Sabbat feed together, they sometimes recognize the sharing of their blood meal, saying together, "Hot blood that spurted from Abel at his time of death, sustain us for the will of the Sabbat."

STEALTH *RITUS*

In the interests of maintaining silence, some packs take extra precautions and invoke favorable omens. In the Stealth *Ritus*, all participating vampires bite out each other's tongues and spit them into a fire. Though this causes no health levels of damage, the immediate bleeding and healing consumes one blood point. The priest or ductus usually bows out so he can issue orders, but some packs have developed complex hand signal systems so they may communicate silently while on stealth-intensive activities.

SUN DANCE

The Sun Dance tests Cainites' endurance and bravery. During the *ritus*, vampires writhe and gyrate in a hypnotic dance around a symbolic inscription of a fiery sun from sunset to sunrise without pause, until they collapse in exhausted heaps, covered in blood sweat. The *ritus* always takes place during a full moon, and pack members usually dress for the occasion, wearing frightening masks or red body paint. Pack members prove their courage by seeing who among them, after an exhausting night's dancing, can remain in the open the longest. A Blood Feast sometimes follows the Sun Dance (especially when it is performed at heavily attended sect functions), as the vampires must replenish their spent energy constantly for the duration of the ritual.

TESTS OF PAIN

Sabbat priests use these grueling *ritae* to test how strong of spirit their packmates are. Different packs use the *ritae* in different ways, some for those claiming leadership, others as punishment. One such test is the Indian Stick trial: The pack suspends the subject from a timber forced through his chest at dusk, and he remains immobilized until they release him just before sunrise. (Truly brutal subjects tear their bodies from the pinion before sunrise, and may subject themselves to other tests.) The Trial by Fire involves the ritual singeing of various body parts by the pack priest. The Gauntlet sees Sabbat Cainites line up in two rows while individual vampires run between them, suffering punches, kicks and stabs from the vampires in line. Priest characters and Storytellers are encouraged to create their own Tests of Pain for use in their packs.

THE ASP'S BLESSING

In some accounts, the Sabbat likens itself to a serpent, and many packs practice *ritae* that involve snake-handling. This *ritus*, however, fits with the more traditional and occult ritual of the sect. The priest raises a (usually poisonous) snake before the pack, asks for Caine's watchful eye to preside over the assembled vampires, kisses the snake and holds it before every member of the pack, who must kiss it themselves. If the snake bites an unfortunate vampire, it is believed that Caine holds disfavor for that vampire, and that he has caused the snake to bite her for some past or secret transgression. Some Sabbat even bring humans into this *ritus*, in hopes that the snake will bite them and symbolize Caine's disdain for mortals, the Children of Seth.

Truth Revealed

This *ritus* ensures the honesty of a statement to be revealed (much like the swearing in of a witness at court — it doesn't truly "compel" truth in a mechanical manner). If a priest doubts an individual's statement's veracity, the victim writes her statement on a piece of paper given her by her accuser, in her own blood. The priest then burns the paper, sometimes in a censer. If the smoke burns black, the statement is a lie. If white, it is truth. In truth, the power of the pack's belief in their packmate and his statement determines the outcome of the revelation, and this *ritus* is seldom employed for truly grave matters.

Special Sect Practices

Many lesser rituals other than the *ritae* unite the Sabbat. These practices resemble the trappings of secret societies, and they are useful in identifying another individual as a sect member. Even though younger Sabbat consider these practices antiquated and out of place in modern society, they still find them useful when they meet strange vampires. The greatest problem among these formalities lies in their colloquialism — members of the Tombstonz are unlikely to share the same secret mannerisms as the Köenigen den Ungeheuer. For this reason, many Sabbat contest their use, and more than one Sabbat has met a gruesome (and undeserved) end when unable to provide the accepted regional or pack-specific variation required of him.

Sabbat Oath of Loyalty

Sabbat vampires swear a special creed at sect meetings to profess support of the sect. The oath includes identifying the individual, naming his place in the sect and pledging allegiance to the Sabbat.

Symbol of the Sabbat

The Sabbat has a special symbol any member may wear to identify him as such. It may be in the form of a body piercing, watch, ring, pin, tattoo or a design on a piece of clothing. The symbol is often worn at times of Jyhad to allow other Sabbat to recognize fellow sect members. Unlike other pack secrets, this symbol is universal: an inverted ankh bearing stylized adornments.

Test of Verification

To ensure one is in the presence of another Sabbat, the sect has established a series of questions for identification purposes. The questioning occurs where no outside ears may overhear, and it allows both Sabbat to know it is safe to discuss sect matters. The test is always given to strangers who say they are Sabbat, and sect business is never discussed until after the individuals have passed the Test of Verification.

Localized Signs and Tags

Many young packs (and a few old ones) have adopted the insignia habits of mortal street gangs. These packs have unique hand signals and graffiti symbols used to identify their territory and members. For example, the Young Gods may mark their turf with purple crosses, while the Wulfpak identifies each other by throwing a hand sign that resembles a "W".

Sect Color

In theory, the Sabbat's "color" is purple — members who wish to be identified may merely wear a garment of purple hue (usually hidden, as it's not always healthy to advertise). In practice, this doesn't happen too much. Many sect elders consider the brazen display vulgar or childish, while some young sect members believe it to relegate the sect to gang status, which demeans the holy war they fight each night. The most strict adherents to the purple-garment practice are often young Sabbat who actually enjoy the identification with gang culture or self-indulgent, Victorian Sabbat, who carry on as if they're getting away with some subtle but grandiose ruse.

New Derangements

The Sabbat, prone as it is to frenzy, acts of atrocity and otherwise losing itself to the Beast, is no stranger to the debilitating effects of derangements. Many members of the sect, particularly elders and savage fledglings, have accumulated impressive lists of psychic shortcomings — one can only withstand the sight of so much heinousness before it takes its toll on the mind. Hereafter, then, are several new derangements particularly suited to members of the Sabbat. Of course, any vampire may manifest signs of these mental aberrations, but they are especially poignant in the context of the Sword of Caine.

Bear in mind that a derangement is far more than a simple mechanical penalty to a character — they are the scars left after a character's struggle with the monster he has become. Derangements should have a significant impact on the character's development and behavior, and are excellent opportunities for intense roleplaying. Storytellers may wish to penalize players who neglect their derangements except when the rules absolutely state they must take some action by withholding experience points. Derangements are rarely "on and off" affairs; some degree of the character's emotional erosion should come through in almost every action he takes.

Astute players and Storytellers will note that derangements tend to set the player up for further frenzies, botches and ultimately, more derangements. Such is the nature of the Beast, and such is the inexorable slide into damnation.

Berserk

The berserk individual has tremendous difficulty controlling his feelings of anger and frustration. When confronted with stressful situations, a berserk individual often loses control, lashing out against his transgressors (or whomever he *perceives* to be a transgressor) with blind rage.

Berserk individuals are increasingly common among the Sabbat; the bloodlust and violence of the sect seems to breed this sort of madness. Additionally, a berserk manner often paves the way to other derangements, as the uncontrollable vampire finds himself ever more often in the thrall of the Beast.

Berserk Cainites suffer a +2 difficulty to their rolls to avoid frenzy.

Blood Sweats

In rare cases, a vampire may become so nervous and agitated that his state of mind affects his body. Much as a mortal may exhibit jumpiness and cold sweats, the vampire can become likewise ill at ease. The "sweat" in the case of vampires, however, is composed of blood that works its way to the Cainite's skin. Many other vampires find this particularly disturbing, as the sweat stains clothes and makes the vampire in question a horrid sight to look upon. Obviously, this causes a few uncomfortable situations in which mortals are involved as well.

A vampire with blood sweats excretes and additional blood point worth of vitae over the course of every night he rises from slumber. This blood is almost always very obvious, though by judiciously wiping his brow and changing clothes, he may briefly appear "normal" before displaying beads of collected blood-sweat again. Additionally, the character should act twitchy and unnerved.

Gluttony

Gluttonous vampires have difficulty taking their sustenance in moderation. To the mind of the gluttonous Cainite, why stop when one is merely sated? Why not drink in the heady vitae until one is full as a bloated tick? This derangement is particularly common among elder vampires, who have indulged their vices for so long they lack the ability to control their hunger.

Vampires suffering from gluttony must spend a point of Willpower when they wish to stop feeding from a vessel, unless they have reached their maximum blood pool capacity. Also, a gluttonous character automatically frenzies when confronted with the sight, smell or taste of blood when hungry (at 3 blood pool or less).

Nymphomania/Satyriasis

A notable few vampires have subconsciously denied their undead state, and find themselves "sexually" attracted to mortals, other vampires (and, in particularly severe cases, other paramours). Of course, as vampires lack the ability to procreate due to their undead status, any couplings they may achieve are inevitably frustrating and fruitless.

Such limitations do not hinder the efforts of those who suffer from this derangement, however, and they pursue the carnal act with every ounce of their being. By spending a blood point (see **Vampire: The Masquerade**, page 138-139), the vampire may "function" and even bring a partner to climax, provided they're not dead, too. Vampires under the influence of this derangement often sink into ever more depraved activity, hoping to somehow stimulate the pleasures they have been denied. Indeed, outside of "normal" hetero- and homosexual affairs, these vampires may indulge in bestiality, pedophilia, rape and all manner of other vile acts.

A character afflicted with this derangement is always "on the prowl" and should attempt to consummate as many relationships as he can, according to his orientation (which may well change over the course of the chronicle). This derangement has no mechanical effect; it is included as a curious condition rather than a dice-governed system.

OVERCOMPENSATION

A fear of failure gnaws at some vampires, and this fear colors their every action. Perhaps the character barely passed his Creation Rites, or perhaps he had a close encounter that almost left him with the Final Death. Indeed, the character may harbor a secret lack of self-esteem that causes him to push himself to ever-greater heights in order to find a sense of worth. Whatever the case, the overcompensator always makes sure what he undertakes succeeds spectacularly.

A character with the overcompensation derangement never undertakes anything half-heartedly; nothing is worth doing for its own sake. Every time something of significance arises, the player of the overcompensating Cainite *must* spend a point of Willpower to make sure the action succeeds. This need not happen on every roll, only matters of critical nature require the Willpower expenditure. Storytellers and players are advised to take the Nature of the overcompensating character into account when applying this definition, however. A Bravo may be forced to spend Willpower in a physical fight, while the Chameleon may spend Willpower on Manipulation rolls; the mandatory expenditure does not apply to "generic" stressful situations, only those deemed most vital to the character's personality.

PHOBIA

Sometimes, the Beast leaves the mark of its passage as an irrational, debilitating fear. Although most Sabbat vampires loathe admitting it, some of them have acquired phobias that relate somehow to their loss of control. Indeed, some Sabbat have collected several of these terrors, symbols of their struggle with and loss to their lesser, baser selves. A phobia may take any form, from a simple (and fairly mortal) fear of spiders, to fear of a particular elder, to a fear of automobiles, to a crippling fear of other vampires.

The player and Storyteller should work together to determine which phobia best fits a certain character's circumstances. Any time the character is confronted by the object or person of his phobia, she must make Rötschreck roll against a difficulty of 6 (or spend a point of Willpower before making the roll) or flee the presence of whatever causes her phobia. Of course, this isn't necessarily in response to fire, as Rötschreck suggests, but it serves to simulate the fear as well. If the character botches this roll or has no escape route, the Storyteller may well increase the difficulty of subsequent rolls regarding the given phobia to 8.

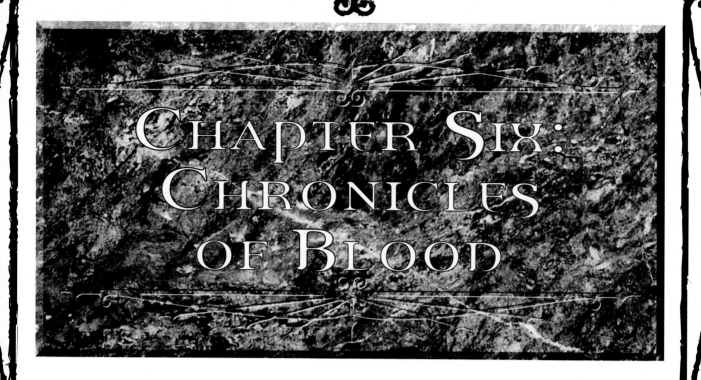

Chapter Six: Chronicles of Blood

*...who kills the sun in order to
install the reign of darkest night.*
— Antonin Artaud

It's a common misconception that the Sabbat is an organization of "bad guys." It's also a common fallacy that a Storyteller can't use the sect as the central focus of a long-term chronicle. Why are these beliefs so strong and so pervasive? Why do they persist and gain momentum? They persist because many of **Vampire: The Masquerade**'s players believe that the Sabbat are the black-and-white villains of the world. Period.

After all, aren't they alien, inhumane monsters from Hell who walk the night; psychotics and murderers who view humankind as game pieces to be used as playthings in their kinky and malicious sport? Come on, don't they use mortals as objects of detached, if amused, study, to further twisted experiments into the dark and alien recesses of their vampire nature? Don't their actions prove that they relegate humans to the status of mere animals under a microscope, equating us with a bovine herd meant for their use — a herd that they can, without guilt or mercy, kill, feed from wantonly, rape, torture, debase and terrorize? Moreover, aren't they simply infernally aligned diablerists who break the largest laws of vampire society by drinking their elders dry? We know that they are, don't we? They are vicious, brutal thugs; mindless killers with no reason and no motivation for what they do or how they act. Right?

Well sure they are — from any other perspective but their own. In a world where most vampires can go decades without ever even seeing another Cainite of their *own* sect, this is what the violence and extremism of the Sabbat leads ignorant onlookers to observe.

Obviously, that's not all the sect is about. The Sabbat, to its way of thinking, is superior to mortals. The vampires of the sect don't believe these beings are worth notice or mention. Vampires, they believe, shouldn't be bothered with the society of humans, viewing mankind contemptuously and derisively, but more often with disinterest and boredom. Members of the sect make little pretense of holding onto the husk of their Humanity, because they don't believe that the human state of being applies to them in the least. For the most part, Sabbat believe that humanity's narrow sense of morality is limiting and beneath their worry. While some vampires within the ranks of the Sabbat become involved in Satanism and many other deviant practices — either as a joke or to show their contempt for the narrow institutions of human faith, that stand against the undead, most specifically the Catholic Church — the more "mature" Sabbat don't, though they do see the value in using depravity as a tool of war (and sometimes, amusement). They see themselves as monsters, not humans, and they fill that role dutifully.

Additionally, and perhaps more importantly, the sect views vampires who try to hold onto the remains of their human essence as weak fools hiding from their true natures. For the most part, Sabbat believe that vampires who don't accept the fact that they're fiends — those who hide behind a cultivated illusion of mortality — are delusional. More seriously, the Sabbat believes that these delusional dupes place the whole of vampiric existence in grave danger.

So they are monsters, yes, but do they have to be villains?

Not at all.

Sabbat aren't simply psychotics who walk the World of Darkness. Troupe members can play a Sabbat character as well and enjoyably as any other **Vampire** character. A Storyteller can lead a Sabbat-focused chronicle with the same ease. Sabbat chronicles can be surprisingly satisfying, poignant and resonant, as long as the Storyteller challenges herself to rethink the misconception that the sect is nothing more than a mob of badly motivated, cardboard thugs. A deep, thoughtful examination of the sect should bring her to the realization that it needn't be relegated to such a static, one-dimensional role within her story. And she'll realize that, if she learns to use the Sabbat effectively, individually and as a group, the sect offers great possibilities to her players and her chronicle for rich, exhilarating drama.

This chapter examines various Storytelling techniques intended to help Storytellers use the Sabbat as the focus of a chronicle. It is written to teach the ways of using the unique qualities, devices and internal dynamics of the sect to color and define a Sabbat story.

THE ETHICS OF THE SABBAT

Would any well-adjusted, mature troupe member find playing a mindless killer attractive? As a Storyteller, have you asked your players how they feel about participating as characters in a Sabbat-focused chronicle? You probably have, or you wouldn't be interested in this book. But, even if you are just thinking about telling a Sabbat story, do you believe that some members of your troupe might be hesitant about participating in it, because they believe that Sabbat characters are unpalatable? Have a few of them told you, wholeheartedly and in a loud, disdainful voice, that Sabbat characters can and should only be used as villains?

Well, maybe, because it's a common prejudice.

If you want this endeavor to work — if you want to tell a Sabbat-focused story and tell it well — you'll have to change their minds. You'll have to guide your players through an understanding of the sect and help them to accept it on its own terms, or (if they can't) to at least give it a chance while skewing their characters to be Sabbat of a different color, those who see the sect from inside it's ranks. Most importantly, you'll have to help them understand that Sabbat characters can be motivated and viable, and that your chronicle about them will be motivated and viable, too. After all, troupe members and Storytellers alike invest a lot of time in a shared vision of the World of Darkness, and if a chronicle is going to work well, it should be enjoyable for everyone involved.

How do you do this? Simple. You help your troupe understand the Sabbat, its teachings, its methods, its unique characteristics and its motivations.

The sect is like any other group of like-minded individuals. Its members have their own ethics, creeds, codes of behavior, joys, wants and hates. The sect and its members have flaws and weaknesses. They just have a different outlook than other groups of vampires do, and this outlook helps to define their behavior.

Logically, all groups and individuals have light and dark aspects. For the most part, stereotyping anyone as "hero" or "villain" doesn't work in **Vampire: The Masquerade** (though sometimes "antihero" fits), and most specifically, it doesn't work for the Sabbat. The World of Darkness is a grand drawing in shades of gray. Show your troupe those nuances by presenting them with difficult story situations, tough choices and scoundrels of ambiguous character.

You'll need to show your troupe, through the plot dimensions presented to them, that the Sabbat is different — brutal, cruel, zealous and yes, even deviant — but that it's not necessarily worse than its antithesis, the Camarilla. All vampires are inhuman by nature, sect notwithstanding. Most do morally questionable things, by human standards. Most vampires can have loyalties to their own kind and to their own ideals, they can all have their own predispositions and their own ways of acting on those predispositions. They can be intractable in their beliefs. Unwavering faith is the mark of any zealot, even if that characteristic proves to be detrimental, even if it causes her to commit acts that are arguably atrocious and horrific. Are these atrocities excusable by standard human ethics? Of course not, but then, your players are not playing humans; they're playing vampires, and the

Sabbat believes that applying human mores to anything vampiric is akin to giving the cows in a slaughterhouse sledgehammers and hanging the butchers upside down. The situations and story hooks you present to your troupe should keep these Sabbat viewpoints at the forefront, but shouldn't rest solely on them. It should show the players how the sect and its ideologies work as a whole through the actions and perceptions of its fanatically loyal and borderline-sociopathic members, its supporters, its detractors, its allies and its enemies.

This is the hardest task any Storyteller has to face when she decides to run with the Sabbat. She may hear loudly and often, "I don't want to play the bad guy! I want to *fight* the bad guy! I want to believe that I'm affecting something positive in this shit-hole of a world you've presented to me!" (Not everyone in her troupe may say this, but those who do may be adamant.) She may hear, "Sweet! I wanna play an Assamite *antitribu* on the Path of Kill Every Fucking Person I Meet! I get to be the bad guy!" The Storyteller's answer to these statements should be more questions. "Well, who *are* the bad guys? Are there really *any* bad guys? What makes for a *good* guy in the World of Darkness?" She'll have to change her troupe's collective mind about the roles of villains and heroes, alike. She can accomplish this goal by showing that the sect, while inhuman, callous and bestial, is not ill-motivated or totally wrong in its suppositions, and that its outlook is perfectly logical *to its genesis and environment*.

Which is difficult, without a doubt, but no one ever promised that Storytelling would be a joyride on the back of a Malkavian *antitribu's* panhead Harley.

The Veracity of Outlook

Many World of Darkness enthusiasts tend to believe that the Sabbat is wrong and the Camarilla is right. Largely, this view stems from the principle that the other vampires try to hold onto their human ethics, and the Sabbat doesn't. Let's examine that.

It's an axiom of Sabbat behavior and teaching that Sabbat do not attempt to suborn the Beast. They embrace it and liberate it. Sabbat philosophy holds that any attempt to hide a vampire's monstrous nature is hypocritical and wrong. The Sabbat wholeheartedly believes that Caine was *cursed* with vampirism, but that he was cursed for a purpose. Sect dogma — a dogma fostered through study of Cainite wisdom — attempts to teach individual Sabbat that ignoring the fact that vampirism is a curse is a betrayal of vampiric nature. Maybe ignoring this fact and reining in the Beast is a betrayal of the divine reasoning for which Caine was created in the first place. Therefore, dodging the Curse and its characteristic monstrousness is hedging, and the sect rarely hedges about anything.

How did the sect arrive at this belief? Many scholars and philosophers of the Sabbat — and they do exist — studied the legends, mythology and lore of the first acknowledged vam-

pire, Caine. The subsequent interpretations of Caine's legends have been used to support the sect's structure and it's dictates for the behavior of its membership. The most striking feature of Caine's mythology that supports the sect's outlook shows him killing his brother Abel and being punished by God for it, then it underlines the fact that he didn't become a vampire directly due to that act of murder. He became a vampire *because he refused God's forgiveness* (several times in fact), and chose to answer only to himself, abiding away from God and outside the protection of Eden. Caine's catechism reinforces the idea that his curse was a punishment for *pride*, not murder. He chose freedom over servitude to God, and he paid the ultimate price for it.

Sabbat vampires view this choice and its subsequent curse as inescapable fact, as a truism that can't be wished away by pretending to be something that they are not — merely human. And the sect, for the most part, defends its progenitor's choice. The Sabbat's zealousness in defending this choice causes them to redefine the Curse of Caine by characterizing it as a *glorious* curse, one meted out for the affront of choosing freedom over safety and subservience.

Is the sect's outlook evil? By human standards, perhaps. But by vampiric standards? In comparison to what? The Camarilla has evil aspects and outlooks, too. Evil, in practice — faith and metaphysics notwithstanding — could be defined as the practice of putting the good of the few before the good of everyone else. Storytellers, ask yourselves if the Sabbat puts the good of the many — the many vampires within its ranks, that is — before the good of the few by acting as soldiers in a war against the eventual dominance of the Antediluvians, the vampires of the Third Generation who will one night rise from torpor and destroy all their childer in a rain of blood and fire? Now, ask yourself if the Camarilla, so often cast as tragic heroes, with its princes and its edicts and its blood bonds, does this? The Sabbat doesn't believe so. The Sabbat believes that its rival sect betrays the whole of vampires, because they believe that the Camarilla has been duped into servitude (knowing or unknowing) to the Antediluvian's cause. And servitude is something that Caine, their father, would never have allowed to happen to himself. So, isn't it an ultimately misinterpreted and pedestrian to view to see the Sabbat simply as the "evil force" in this particular corner of the World of Darkness? In reality, couldn't it be argued that the Sabbat puts the good of the many before the good of the few much more often than the Camarilla does?

So, again, what's evil and what's good?

Vampire: The Masquerade isn't a game that forces ethics into round or square holes like pegs. Defining evil, good and every shade of the median within her chronicle, is up to the individual Storyteller to decide. Still, the exploration of Caine's curse and the ethical questions that surround it, provide an excellent and resonant resource both for story seeds and for background material, because they give the sect a strong *raison d'être*. How can the Storyteller communicate this tenet to the troupe? She can use the catechism of the Curse of Caine to help her Sabbat troupe understand why the sect believes what it does. Then, she can make it's exploration a vehicle for helping them to make sense of how the sect behaves by integrating the choices the Curse creates into the choices the plot presents them.

"Well, that was a mouthful, wasn't it?" you're probably saying. "Okay, then smartass, let's see it in action." Consider:

Pick a plot idea that's appropriate to the Sabbat; say, a skirmish with the Camarilla, and then pick an aspect of the Curse, like "we are not human; we shouldn't try to be." Your troupe is playing a Sabbat pack that's involved in the final aspect of a city siege and is in direct conflict with the Camarilla entrenched therein. The Sabbat have chosen to lay siege because the Camarilla, in its strict adherence to a rigid Masquerade and its belief that vampires should try to hold onto their Humanity, have been lax and inattentive about the threat of mortal hunters in the city and haven't done much to try to curtail their action. Mortal hunters, therefore, have become much more successful in the city's boundaries. The Camarilla prince and her underlings have been too busy using the mortals in their sway, mixing with them, playing with them, vainly courting them even, to protect their own kind from these hunters. In truth, the prince's inattentiveness has left her totally unprepared for any threat against her "Kindred." The Sabbat, in defense of vampiric existence and through its understanding of the Cainite axiom that vampires are inhuman, have carefully executed the siege, which is successful because they've used their inhumanity to fight brutally and well. Then, at the culmination of the siege, the Sabbat victors are left with the decision of having to choose if they will allow the city's leftover anarchs, those who weren't killed in the siege, to remain unmolested, whether they'll drive them off or whether they'll summarily kill them.

Situation, axiom of Caine, application of the axiom through plot, then difficult plot/character choice that conflicts with another axiom. It's really not so difficult after all.

Now, how does a Storyteller make the more inhuman methods and outlooks of the Sabbat enticing to her troupe? After all, most roleplayers aren't social malcontents. Gamers, as a whole, are well-adjusted people who hold down good jobs, share in the community and wish to live positive lives. Doesn't playing a monster fly in the face of that? Absolutely not. Not if the monster has dramatic conflict, flaws and motivations. Not if the monster adheres to its own code of ethics. Not if that monster is presented as an "antihero." Not, for that matter, if the story is presented well and in a mature manner.

CONCEPT: THE SABBAT IS RIGHT AND THOSE OTHER VAMPIRES ARE WRONG.

The Storyteller can make her troupe believe (in the context of the game) that the sect has the absolute right idea. This doesn't even have to be true in her grand scheme or concept, but it's important that she makes the troupe *believe* it's true! She can show her troupe that, by indulging the

Screw All This Crap

Sometimes it's best to run with the mindless brutality.

Not every chronicle needs to be *The Godfather* or *Crime and Punishment*. Every now and then, it's more fun to play *Near Dark* or *Evil Dead* or even —God help us—*Blade*.

So go ahead. Blow shit up. Set things on fire. Gun down mortals in the mall. Rampage up and down the streets of the city, Devil-music blasting out of the car's speakers, swinging baseball bats at pedestrians. Do what you wanna do. It's your game.

This chapter is intended to show you the Sabbat can be used as something other than an adolescent power trip. But sometimes it's fun to indulge in that kind of mayhem.

In the game, of course. If you decide to do any of this kind of stuff for real, check into a hospital. You need help. You are *not* a vampire, and the rest of us don't need boneheads like you making a bad name for us.

bestial aspect of Caine's curse in all its monstrousness, their characters fulfill a role, and at times they may have no other choice than to fulfill it monstrously, because every other possible choice is worse than the one before.

Example: Jackson rarely, if ever, had walked slowly before meeting Jim. His movements were lightning-quick by nature, and his step was quicker. But Jim had never moved quickly, what with his twisted leg — though Jackson never found out how it got twisted or why — but, he liked Jim, so he made the adjustment in his step with only marginal annoyance. Packmates watched each other's backs, after all, and, more than that, Jim had never pissed him off.

The two vampires had been walking the streets, not really looking for anything, and had turned down a silent alley when, suddenly, Jack felt vulnerable, and the slowness of their progress felt even slower than before. The shadows on the bricks of the run-down row of warehouses they'd passed became longer and more alive. "Too alive, too slow, too vulnerable. We're too vulnerable," Jack thought, and then the shit all rained down in slow motion, like a chain saw smiling in a lightning flash. The shadows became two distinct bas-relief shapes which detached themselves from the walls, dropping to the pavement around them with a tiny thud and a flutter of cloth. Their faces were horrible, and as they moved to surround them, close enough so that Jack could smell them, he sucked in an odor like a dog left floating in a sewer drain.

Before Jackson knew it, Jim was on the ground, buried by writhing bodies. They ripped at his chest, his face, his throat with their claws and fangs, and Jackson knew he couldn't to take them both.

But then it stirred. The thing inside Jackson woke, it came out of its cave hungry. And he loosed it. By the time its hunger was sated, a leaf-dead husk lay on the pavement, its bony parchment claws reaching to the sky. He stood in the midst of the other, and nearly unrecognizable shreds of something soaked with vitae clung to his hands and the corners of his mouth. He kicked what was left of it aside with vicious contempt, and looked over to Jim, who slowly climbed to his feet. Jackson watched as Jim moved pains-

takingly to him, and suddenly, he noticed, in the pool of blood gathered at his feet, the glint of a tiny golden ring. "Pretty," Jackson said to himself, and he picked it up, slipping it onto his smallest finger. He waited, patiently, for Jim to reach him, and they walked out of the other end of the alley, as slowly as before.

Interesting, huh? Jackson, who is a monster, has used a monstrous aspect of his vampiric nature to protect Jim. Wasn't Jim weaker than his attackers? What other choice did Jackson have, if any? Within the context of the example, wasn't the attack against Jackson and Jim unmotivated? Sure it was, and perhaps Jackson did the right thing by using his "gifts" to help his packmate.

Plot proofs for the "rightness" of Sabbat action and teaching certainly shouldn't stop at explaining the Beast. The reasons behind the sect's hatred of the Antediluvian threat and its actions against this threat are great plot hooks. The story hooks that arise out the sect's practice of diablerie and why/how they use it as a weapon of war against the Camarilla achieves this end, also, for, aren't the Camarilla vampires just tools used by the Antediluvians, to the Sabbat way of thinking? Any plot device that constrains an individual choice — remember, freedom is a central catechism of Caine — is rife with possibilities for plot twists, danger and conflicts of choice. There are many possibilities. It's up to the individual Storyteller to choose them, define them and incorporate them into the action of her chronicle.

Concept: Antiheroes Have Canons and Follow Them

Most antiheroes follow a code of behavior. The Paths of Enlightenment provide Sabbat characters with these codes, as do the larger laws of the Code of Milan and the *auctoritas* and *ignoblis ritae*. Still, not all Sabbat follow these rules mindlessly. Some do, but others think them through. That's what separates the leaders from the followers, the chiefs from the braves. Some question these codes and refine or redefine them. Some merely go with the flow.

The chronicle best satisfies its players' emotional attachment to ethics — not their true ethics, just their emotional need for a sense of ethical congruity — if it presents the Sabbat as being true to an ideal or a group of them. It needs to illustrate for the troupe that members of the sect are willing to die and kill in defense of these ideals. Storytellers need to show, within story action, how other points of view act in counterpoint to the workings and teachings of the Sabbat, and they should then guide the troupe members in seeing the greater evil in those who have chosen this other path.

Storytellers can create such dichotomy by having troupe members encounter Camarilla rank-and-file who are choking under the yoke of constraint that this sect places on its youngest childer, how these vampires die as front-line soldiers simply to keep a prince and his favorite pets in power. She can show how they are destroyed at a prince's whim, and then contrast it with the freedom of choice and action that the Sabbat offers. She can show how the characters' contacts

and allies have been slaughtered by the opposition for mere rules violations that seem arbitrary and senseless to them. She can illustrate the mindless serfdom of the blood bond, and how it basically robs the vampire under it of self-determined choice and direction. She can even illustrate that the concept of Camarilla vampires clinging to their Humanity is a hypocritical absurdity by showing that they don't treat humans any better than the Sabbat does.

Concept: Beliefs Motivate What Antiheroes Do

Within the structure of their belief system, Sabbat are not all unthinking thugs, bullies and sadists. While there *are* thugs within the sect, and the sect has coarse *tactics*, many Sabbat truly believe that they are soldiers for their way of thinking. They have definite reasons for following the course of existence that they have chosen. Within the chronicle, it's emotionally resonant and works well if the Storyteller shows her troupe that unmotivated actions have consequences and that those consequences are usually much harsher than the initiating action.

Let's say the troupe decides to slaughter a random group of individuals, yet it doesn't have any real reason to do so. Consider that these actions aren't as the result of a city siege, or they're not committed as the result of any of *ritae*, such as a Blood Feast or a peculiar Creation Rite. The characters are just leaving a body count, and they don't care who finds it. Any number of consequences could come out of such actions. Other vampires could take note and come after them. The city's prince — if it's Camarilla held — could call a blood hunt against them. Mortal hunters could come upon the results of the packmates' actions and start hunting them. Their own pack members could punish them for breaking rank and opening the pack up to direct danger and sanctions from higher up within the sect. Bishops, archbishops and other packs may look disfavorably on this kind of blatant violence, which tends to alert police and other parties to the monsters in their midst. There are many possible reprisals.

Storytellers can really drive this point home to the troupe, if they go further and — through their chronicles' interpretation of the teachings of Caine — lead the troupe through an understanding that the mindless actions of Sabbat who *are* merely thugs and bullies are distasteful and no better than the sect's enemies. Even though some members of the Sabbat may be disinterested and unmotivated by the tenets of the sect — because they *are* thugs and bullies, or because they're associated only by lineage or shovelhead origins — a Storyteller's presentation of the chronicle's ethics will be the most effective if she shows that the sect, as a whole, does have ideals, and that wavering from those ideals will bring punishment.

Concept: Actions Have Consequences, Even for the Faithful

Taking the "don't let the mindless go unpunished" proverb one step further, it's an inescapable fact that *all* actions have reactions. If the troupe chooses a course of action, it's not only appropriate but necessary for the Storyteller to follow the evolution of that action to it's natural conclusion, even if the consequences of the characters' choices are detrimental to the continuance of their existence. This is "The Sabbat Storyteller's Rule of Dramatic Relativity." If the she doesn't stay true to it, the chronicle feels arbitrary and falls into unmotivated action faster than she can think of ways to try and stop the descent. It's a good idea for her to try and make these contextual reactions proportionate to the initial troupe action, *unless* the chronicle, as a whole will be better served by the Storyteller using the contextual reaction as a vehicle for illustrating a larger theme.

Concept: Antiheroes Have Flaws

The central postulate of any dramatic literature — and roleplaying is an interactive form of dramatic literature — is that antiheroes have flaws that ultimately become the catalyst of their failure if they don't wise up and do something about them. Remember, flaws are the source of rich dramatic conflict, and an element necessary to a believable and exciting chronicle. Further, flaws are what defines an antihero in the first place.

What are sect's flaws? Does the Sabbat, wholly and individually, want to overcome these flaws? Do Sabbat have *tragic flaws*, those harbingers of dark destiny that dramatic literature puts forth as the final force in an antihero's undoing? Yes, the sect has several exploitable flaws.

Overall, like other groups with strong ideology, the sect can be intractable in its beliefs, and it can be stagnant in its methods of supporting them. Intractability fosters errors in judgment; Sabbat sometimes make poor choices and poor bargains in defense of their belief system. The disorganized "freedom above all else" structure of the sect makes it difficult for the Sabbat to be effective on a large scale and makes it easy for them to be without direction. And they *do* have tragic flaws. They can have any tragic flaws that exists in the nature of emotion, like greed, anger, envy, laziness, pride, obsession, lust for blood, paranoia — the list is endless. Finally, their monstrous natures and the fact that they have embraced the Glorious Curse of Caine with a religious fervor undo them; they know all the while that they can never be fully with God. Understanding

that concept provides the Storyteller with a natural illustration for helping the troupe comprehend the sect's rage and brutality.

How does can the Storyteller show this tragic aspect of Sabbat existence? Communicating emotional and structural flaws will be an easy task for her — she simply shows the flaw and the consequences that result from the flaw. Take pride, for instance.

Epiphany knew that Ashton would be an easy double-cross. He was too pretty, too vain, too stupid, too ignorant of anything but his own importance and his higher rank. He was so proud, in fact, that when she staked his worthless carcass out on the cool, silent earth — after she'd broken most of his bones by driving over him in her pickup; after she had cracked his skull open for the flies ; after she'd removed his eyelids with a razor to ensure his active welcome of the coming sun — he'd been honestly surprised that only laughter answered his beseeching screams….

Communicating metaphysical concepts is a little harder, but can be illustrated with the same scene. The Storyteller just adds the metaphysical reference and it's subsequent resonance.

The pack's laughter grew fainter, less distinct as Ashton's screams became whimpers, then became moans. Precious vitae leaking from dead tear-ducts poured down through his hair pooling on the ground around his head. He could see it now, the hints of pink and purple rising over the hilltops — Epiphany had given him a horrifically attractive view — that heralded his coming extinction, creeping overhead in the colors of a beautiful shroud that she'd sewn for him out of treachery. His fractured skull buzzed with lies and mistakes, and for an instant, through the pain, he thought he saw Caine in the shroud. Caine, his father — no, was this death delirium? And, who was that with him? A man, maybe a woman, but someone with whom Caine was talking, and his father wore a peaceful countenance. For an instant, it seemed as though Caine regarded him with vast regret, turning away, and the irony of his existence struck him like a blow from Epiphany's truck. "Hell awaits; why didn't anyone tell me?" he thought, as his laughter turned to hysteria and the sun's full intensity struck him. His fingertips started to curl and smoke…

CONCEPT: ANTIHEROES OFTEN HAVE ENEMIES OF EQUAL OR SURPASSING EVIL

It's a dirty trick, but it works. There's always another force out there in the World of Darkness that is even nastier, more heartless and less merciful, which uses tactics much more evil than any Sabbat pack can come up with.

A good embodiment of this concept is a vampire who falls to infernal influence and corruption. The attractive Storytelling *shtick* of the infernal is that it really isn't just a threat that captures the souls of the Sabbat's renegade elements alone. Any vampire can make a bargain with the Devil and travel down the road of lies and temptations. But, *any* plot trick of "they're worse than we are" allows reluctant troupe members who are bothered personally by the brutality and callousness of the Sabbat a chance to enjoy the action-heavy and intrigue-heavy Sabbat chronicle and still feel that their characters are fighting for something positive. It may be a hedge, it might be a gimmick, but it's a gimmick that works to allow a Storyteller to be sensitive to the feelings and wants

of all her troupe members, not just those who accept the sect's brutality without being bothered by it.

Other good antagonists that fulfill this role can be drawn from the ranks of the Setites and the Giovanni. Further, those clans that are only loyal to the Camarilla, like the mystical Tremere and the "mainstream" versions of some of the more menacing clans, like the crazily prophetic Malkavians, the secretive and lethal Nosferatu and the regal Ventrue, can offer sound and freakish opponents. So, while **Vampire: The Masquerade** isn't a game that can be slotted into "good guy" and "bad guy," as previously observed, it is a game that can explore darker and lighter shades of gray.

Okay, but how do you communicate this construct in story terms? You construct it through careful choice of chronicle antagonists, and you communicate it by coloring the actions of those antagonists in an interesting manner that's consistent with your chronicle's theme. This characterization can be either a subtle or broad picture — a snap-shot or a Rembrandt — but it should always be thought-provoking and show the troupe that it serves a purpose that is better motivated than that of the antagonist. Let's take a look at this at work, using the dual chronicle themes of the threat of infernal corruption and the shifting sands of power:

Our scene is set in a city currently held by the Camarilla. An ambitious Tremere, one who wanted to rule, but who didn't want to have to deal with the night-to-night administrative humdrum of doing so, has allied with a few Malkavians and Nosferatu. They have effectively put a puppet-prince in charge. The Tremere is a subtle and careful gamesman, one who trucks with a demon and foolishly believes that he controls the fiend, not vice versa. The Malkavians and Nosferatu influence the mortal crime element that abounds in the city. The puppet-prince is a wanton psychotic who applies his own arbitrary vision of the Masquerade to the vampires who use his city as a haven, one who changes the rules arbitrarily, either leaving his subjects alone or slaughtering them as the mood hits him. Recently, a group of anarchs have tried to shift the balance of power, only to be uncovered and exposed by the Tremere through infernal means. The prince has "disposed" of the traitors via a means that is abhorrent to the troupe. He's blood bound them to him and is using the bond to cause them to either act as their own tormentors or not to resist when the prince orders his mortal ghouls to "play" with the captives. What a lesson this will teach those vampires who try to oppose him! Through exposing the anarchs, the Tremere has strengthened the infernal entity's power in the vampiric world.

The Storyteller's troupe enters this situation to act as spies in the early phases of a city siege. The intelligence the sect has gathered so far has brought some of the more salient dynamics of the situation — the presence of Tremere, the murderously arbitrary nature of the prince, and possibly, the taint of infernalism. They now believe that the city is not only ripe for siege, but a necessary target for it because of the Tremere manipulator, his infernal helpmate and, most importantly, the threat to continued vampiric existence the prince poses. The Tremere takes actions that are subtle, malicious and treacherous; the Malkavians and Nosferatu show a self-interested willingness to play all ends against the middle, whatever the cost; the prince gives the characters a glimpse of his twisted nature in broad, alarmingly charismatic brush strokes. The elements of the Tremere's tie to the infernal, the increasing influence of that tie on the city and the tenuous, dangerous power games played by the vampires in question show the chronicle's theme through plot action and situation background.

Can the Sabbat be used in an existing Camarilla chronicle as the antagonists? Can they be further used in such a chronicle as reluctant allies? Sure they can, but the viewpoint of a Storyteller's presentation of the Sabbat shouldn't really be any different than outlined above. Antagonists are best effective when they have sound motivations. Reluctant allies are such because they're completely different in outlook from the protagonists, but they're working with the protagonists because they share a common goal, thus having motivations, too. Neither side fully understands the other's viewpoint, nor should it.

Stereotypically, the Sabbat as antagonists believe that the Camarilla protagonists are simply tools of their own vampiric demise. To borrow the True Sabbat voice for an instant, they define their enemy as "Antediluvian puppets, slaves who don't have the wisdom or the courage to understand our methods, our rites or our purpose." As allies of the moment, Sabbat Storyteller characters might work with a Camarilla coterie under the axiom of, "Well, we need them for now, and we can always double-cross them later." And remember, sect is not really an easily recognizable attribute. Any recognition of sect is up to the Storyteller to make apparent or shadowy, and the two sects may work together much more often than they think they do. Storytellers of Camarilla chronicles can use the Sabbat as warriors of siege to their city, as spies against their sect, as ideological zealots. She can color them as brutal bastards who, through their adherence to freedom above all else and their contempt for the Masquerade, open the Camarilla to the unwanted eyes of mortal hunters. She can make her players see them as enemies motivated by the Beast, a Beast that the Camarilla tries so hard to repress. As reluctant allies, the Sabbat should have a common purpose for working with a Storyteller's troupe, such as a threat that serves to affect both sects — blood plagues, mortal hunters, Lupines, equally threatening clans like the Tremere, infernal taint and corruption — or a purpose that would be mutually beneficial on either a personal or sect level — like ridding a city a of certain prince or ruling council. But, again, the sect of an ally isn't always (hell, or even nearly always) obvious, so she can use them to help her troupe for a while and then use the Sabbat as a vehicle of treachery later on. The most important attribute is consistency. Camarilla-chronicle Storytellers need to approach presenting the Sabbat in their chronicles in much the same way that Sabbat-chronicle Storytellers do, with the greatest storytelling emphasis on keeping the actions of the sect proportionate and consistent with its ideology.

Mixed chronicles can work with careful planning and even more careful execution, as well. Chronicles in which the Storyteller runs with a set of troupe members playing mixed Sabbat/Camarilla characters are a real challenge — it's like trying to carry on two chronicles for the price of one. However, they are by no means unworkable, and they do offer an opportunity for the Storyteller to add direct dimensions of paranoia, treachery, distrust and (heavens forfend!) maybe even hesitant understanding, grudging mutual respect and re-examination of each sect's own dogma to her game.

To accomplish this end, the Storyteller may find that the most effective plots are interesting and resonant to both sets of characters. Then, mechanically, she has distinct choices that she must make about whether she'll run the groups simultaneously and let them react directly to each other, or if she'll run them separately, and let the actions of each group come as a surprise without direct intervention from either side. Lastly, she must decide if she wants to tell stories that put the mixed characters in conflict with each other, if she wants them to have to work together, if she even wants them to be aware of each other's sect or if she believes that any of these elements will work best for her chronicle's theme.

That said, let's put away ethics with one final exploration. What does a Storyteller do when her players just don't "get" the Sabbat, or if they are bothered by the sect's heartlessness?

Sure, there will come a time when a Storyteller finds that she's unable to come up with any good explanation, much less a congruently ethical one, for some of the more evil acts of the Sabbat, like the kidnapping and torture of mortals for fun and games. Some players react negatively to this, some don't, but remember, the players who react negatively do so more loudly than the others. At this point, the Storyteller just has to allow her players to make up their own minds as to how their characters will react to the evil, and let the presented act stand on its own. If this action takes a particular player (or a group of them) in a different direction from "True Sabbat" ideology, she needs to let that happen, because fighting it is fruitless and detrimental to her story and the dynamics of her group. Players have a real distaste for any Storyteller action that they interpret as being deus ex machina.

So, we've now come full circle to this beginning question: Is the Sabbat a viable central point for a chronicle? Yes. The Sabbat characterizes another viewpoint, a different one to be sure, an alien and ghastly one for certain, but a viewpoint that is not unmotivated or necessarily more evil than any other Vampire: The Masquerade character.

Using and Transcending Sabbat Nastiness

Sabbat are heartless and brutal in their tactics. Therefore, any Sabbat chronicle could, and usually does, move naturally toward showcasing action that is brutal and heartless. The unmerciful violence and the depravity of the sect are elements that the Storyteller shouldn't be afraid to use; she can and should keep these elements at the front of her presentation of the sect. They are an absolute characteristic of a large number of Sabbat, from the rank-and-file to the highest sect echelons. While these ingredients are not all that make up the whole of a Sabbat vampire or a Sabbat chronicle — Sabbat can be logical, efficient, intelligent, practical and even courteous — heartless brutality is present

in their actions to whatever degree the Storyteller chooses to use them. We might as well accept it, Sabbat are a study in Social Darwinism, and Sabbat troupe members may, more likely than not, find themselves in situations that tempt or require them to loose their instincts, their brutality and their depravity, because such a loosing is consistent with their freedom, adherence to the tenets of Caine and their genesis as monsters.

Why are most Sabbat so... *inhumane*? Well, they're not human, are they? They understand that fact, they embrace it and they foster it. They don't believe that human values apply to them. While Storytellers need to give them motivations for what they do, how they do it and consequences that arise naturally from their actions, it's not logical for them confuse Sabbat motivations and logical consequences with human morality. Such a confusion will only drive a Storyteller crazy; it serves only to make her presentation of the sect skewed in a manner that's not consistent with its outlook.

What causes some Sabbat to choose the death of opponents over discourse with them? What causes them to play with their mortal prey, like a cat tortures a mouse before it devours it? First, the Sabbat sees itself as a nation of zealots fighting a war, a pitched battle of Armageddon with the Antediluvians. Wars are violent, and the zealots who fight them commit all manner of horrible and atrocious acts against their enemies. Next, they accept the fact that they're monsters, and they don't hold back on proving it. They

simply have no guilt about doing whatever it takes to win the war and about doing what it takes to serve their own natures. Therefore, any vehicle of siege and any act that to displays their heinous superiority is okay — none are really *verboten*, unless they're handled sloppily. Many members of the sect enjoy violence, outright cruelty, torture and malicious sport. They take pleasure in vitae sprayed and consumed by the bucketful, rape and sexual depravity. They toy with human conventions (Church and state alike), and they make mockeries of them, using sacrilegious malice, outright blasphemy against human faith, truck with infernal entities, ruthless treachery, insidious corruption and any other fiendish tactic they believe is true to their purpose and their nature. And they do it with a superior smirk on their faces.

All these plot elements are decidedly mature themes (in that they're not appropriate to the young or underdeveloped. Certainly, more mature ways exist for dealing with problems than shooting a cop in the face and skull-fucking his wife, but it happens, especially in the World of Darkness, and particularly in Sabbat cities), which present a minefield to the Storyteller if they're not handled carefully. Gratuitousness might not be a concept that can easily be applied to the Sabbat, but it can be applied to an audience, and the troupe is that audience. And players have their boundaries.

How much extreme content is too much? Is there such a thing? Yep, there is and one misstep in this area can derail a

Using Ritae

There are thirteen *auctoritas ritae*, and any number of *ignoblis ritae*. Here are some ideas for incorporating them into the chronicle:

The Binding serves as an excellent introduction to the sect, as well as many of the chronicle's key players. Have the pack swear fealty to the sect, then have something odious befall the characters immediately afterward ("Will you hunt down this rogue werewolf for the good of the Sabbat?"), for a dash of irony.

The Blood Bath, which recognizes a Sabbat as having rightful claims to some title, are useful in chronicles of politics and intrigue. This ritual, like many others, is good for introducing the pack priest, whether he is a player's character or a Storyteller character. Make Blood Baths solemn and erotic.

The Blood Feast can be used in conjunction with or around any other ritual. They may occur at any loose or formal gathering of the pack. Make them bloody. Make them kinky. Think of an elegant dinner party, then give it a soundtrack by Trent Reznor and serve the kine up like rare delicacies.

Creation Rites are, of course, best used at the onset of the campaign, but they can be sprinkled in here and there, as a backdrop to esbats. Shovelheading (creating Sabbat in such a violent, sanity-bending way) is vilely disturbing. Use imagery such as abandoned cemeteries with broken granite crosses and rusted iron gates, foreboding stony mausoleums, and screaming kine hoping to die quickly, yet knowing they will not. Throw in a stoic psychotic or two that welcomes the idea, for added flavor.

The *Festivo dello Estinto* (Festival of the Dead) is the Sabbat's answer to Mardi Gras. This festival is a grand Storytelling opportunity because every Sabbat in a given city takes part in it, and such a celebration provides an outstanding backdrop for intrigue-based stories and combat-based stories alike. Inter-pack conflicts are likely to break out. Higher-ups in the Sabbat are going to come into frenzied contact with footsoldiers. Because little effort is made to hide from mortals — within the logical context previously discussed — mortals have a slim chance of becoming aware of the Sabbat, as do hunters and surrounding Lupines. The possibilities for dramatic conflict are numerous. Use the festival as a stage to play out nasty machinations between packs, priests and rivals old and new. Interweave the tension with mundane mortal trappings at night — nightclub crawls, parades, carnivals, convenience stores and churchyards. Turn up the heat by turning up the tension.

Fire Dancing makes for a good background, and it can be used as a landscape against which to run all sorts of stories. Like the illustration given previously, it's a great opportunity with which to underscore tension. It best illustrates major plot points, but it's most effective in conjunction with other *ritae* and as an offshoot of the main plot. Graphically illustrate the horror that happens in counterpoint to it — kine being prepared for feasting, fights between rivals and enemies — and use it to show exactly how dangerous fire is to a vampire.

Games of Instinct are cinematic, and they are really effective if used as a catalyst for an "it went terribly wrong" pack/inter-pack scenario. They are good for illustrating inter-pack rivalries, and they provide kick-starts if the Storyteller just wants to show one night of physical action. Don't be afraid of black comedic touches. Often, these make horrific action more grotesque. Color it with kinky fun, then throw in a truly terrifying image, like a convenience store clerk's blood running through a Slurpee machine.

Monomacy is a ceremonial duel between two Sabbat combatants. These duels are mysterious, majestic and lethal. Duels, in and of themselves, aren't usually extended violent metaphors, but they are either quick and brutal, or slow and teasing. A Storyteller will have her best success if she presents these duels as ritually as possible, steeping them in tradition and mystery. Remembering that Monomacy is an *auctoritas ritus*, the Storyteller can bring about a much creepier feel if she allows the convention to stand on its own merits and plays up the surrounding mystery and liturgy. Throw your troupe's combatant into a hastily accepted duel. Strain her endurance to the breaking point and beyond it. Tell the story around the duel and why it came about. Be creative with your weaponry: knives, clubs, swords, bats, S & M whips, scythes, croziers, shovels, chainsaws and martial arts weapons. Set the fight in a unique location. Define Monomacy with images of savage gallantry and menace.

USING RITAE CONTINUED...

Palla Grande, the Grand Ball, is a masquerade ball held on All Hallows' Eve. It has much the same story potential as the *Festivo dello Estinto*, though it tends to be a more formal event. The ball provides the Storyteller with a chance to outline the "subtext" of the Sabbat for her players, because the *ritus* includes formalized presentation of vampire legends and history through plays and stories. Remember the play within the play in Hamlet? How about having your troupe's characters be the actors in the play, giving them the opportunity to use this convention much as Hamlet does — to disseminate information and to one-up rivals. Use images of majesty combined with in-your-face punk style. Think elegance and perversion.

Sermons of Caine, the gatherings in which Sabbat come together to pass on and debate the legends and stories of Caine, provide the same Storytelling opportunities as the other formal Sabbat gatherings, and their best potential lies in intrigue and "discovery of Cainite fact" storylines. They provide wonderful circumstances for the Storyteller to drop "here's a piece of the mystery" clues to the troupe. Use Sermons of Caine to whip your players into a frenzy or quietly reveal background information.

The Vaulderie, the ritual mingling/sharing of vitae that causes the Vinculum, should happen almost every time Sabbat get together as a group. This *ritus* reaffirms a pack's members' bonds to each other, and it should be engaged in *often*. It's also a sterling chance for the Storyteller to put one over on the pack by using it as a vehicle of harm to them. This device is a core practice; a sacrament that keeps Sabbat loyal to each other. Use it to spread blood plagues, strengthen the pack's bond to each other or as a linchpin in any important event that calls for the Sabbat to act together as a group. Show the players the chalice passed from Sabbat to Sabbat, from wrist to wrist, and employ the senses. Let them smell the blood. Let them taste it. Describe in detail how the blood in the chalice transforms into a miraculous sacrament. Show how the Vinculum transform them, how it makes them feel and how it overtakes them.

War Parties, the ritual hunt of an elder, can function as a central plot device. It works well as an episodic story, and it is a valuable plot catalyst in a crusade chronicle. This ritual hunting of an elder by the Sabbat, is a great opportunity to mix violent, freakishly twisted and insidiously treacherous chronicle content. This *ritus* is a central canon of Sabbat belief, it's holy war against an unholy enemy — the elders who have betrayed their childer to the Methuselahs and the Antediluvians — and the main characteristic of war is violence. So, if used in a Sabbat chronicle, War Party encounters are most effective when presented as massacres. Still, the Storyteller can present the intrigue leading up to the final confrontation of a War Party with terrible subtlety. This mix of styles satisfies the largest number of troupe members, those who prefer intrigue and investigation as well as those who enjoy combat-oriented chronicles.

The Wild Hunt, the Sabbat's ritual pursuit of a Sabbat traitor, is a strong opportunity for absolute chaos. When Sabbat, as ultimate combatants, decry a traitor, they stop at nothing to put an end to them then and there. The targets of a Wild Hunt are lone vampires who have betrayed the sect, their support system of friends and allies and/or anyone who possesses secret knowledge of the Sabbat and its practices because of the initial betrayal. Chase the prey through deserted streets and crowded ones. Make every stumble, every misstep, vibrate with tension.

The esbat had already started. As she stepped through the tangle of dead foliage, Caitlyn could hear the screaming of the pack, the howling of the captives and the ceaseless drumming. She passed already-butchered kine, but they were too cold and desiccated to be enticing. Then she saw Scout. He moved to intercept her, clothed in a cassock and surplice stained with blood. In a voice of gentle authority and menace, he said, "Daughter of Caine, what is your purpose here?"

Caitlyn answered in the form of the liturgy, causing him to smile indulgently at her Southern-style difficulty with the Latin. Satisfied, Scout allowed her to pass. On through the night it went. The tales of brothers and sisters who had performed deeds of honor and glory, punctuated by drumbeats and screams. Scout stepped forward, spreading his arms in praise of Caine, invoking him to guide the pack in the coming assault against the city of Madison.

All bowed their heads in the benediction. It was Festa Luna, one of the pack's ignoblis ritae, and Scout showed its significance to the pack through the ritual sacrifice of a white German Shepherd, an animal moved by the moon, yet loyal to the kine.

Festivals are often ways to distinguish a Sabbat's observance of the *ritae*, and they can vary as much as the individual *ritae*. In our world, different geographical areas often have their own unique festivals; in the World of Darkness, the Sabbat mirrors this variety. Plus, festivals are a great background for Games of Instinct and other *ritae*. In fact, they often serve as a *reason* for them. It's really up to the individual Storyteller to create festivals relevant to her chronicle, and they should always have some greater significance to the whole story. Finally, festivals are great places for the Storyteller to make up some of her own new *ignoblis ritae*.

THE INQUISITION

The Sabbat carries out its own Inquisition. Like the Inquisition under which it was born, the Sabbat uses the techniques of torture and terror to root out heretics to Sabbat ideology, most specifically those beings who follow the Path of Evil Revelations.

The Sabbat Inquisition provides the Storyteller with the chance to present an eldritch, baroque chronicle, because the Inquisition is, always right, it never falsely accuses a Sabbat of being a heretic and it always carries the accusation out to a natural conclusion in foreboding style. The Storyteller can use the Inquisition to best advantage in intrigue/discovery based plotlines and he can punch up such a story's climax with a combat-oriented conclusion. Further, the *auto da fé* (the sentence passed on a heretic Sabbat which brings about Final Death) is most effective when the Storyteller makes it a backdrop or setting for the conclusion of a chronicle installment.

Put the characters on trial. Bring out every questionable motive and wicked act that they've ever committed. Twist each to show how it "proves" that the characters are in service to a demon, then bring on witnesses to support the Inquisition. Build the tension slowly; build proof upon proof.

Shade the trial with outright lies and twisted half-truths. Open the story with an *auto da fé*, and then, just possibly, close it with one.

CITY CRUSADES AND THE GREAT JYHAD

Crusades present Storytelling opportunities that are particularly dramatic. They give the Storyteller a chance to play out a long-term chronicle, they allow her to let the troupe advance in status and recognition in the sect as a whole, they are vehicles for the troupe to affect the whole World of Darkness and they let the Storyteller change the setting and theme of the chronicle. Crusades also provide great transition devices for changing styles (combat to intrigue and vice versa), and they allow the troupe to see the World of Darkness on a global scale, outside the confines of the pack's individual city or area.

Crusades, or the Sabbat sieges of Camarilla-held cities, call for all manner of mature content and presentation. Crusades are righteous, devilish endeavors, and they happen over an extended period of time, so use the opportunity to mix violent and subtle styles which will satisfy the largest groups of players. Color crusades (their spying phase through their culminating coup) with paranoia, intrigue, investigation, deceit and double-cross. Show the troupe what happens to the vampires who get caught up in this — the deaths of the traitors who get caught spying in a Camarilla prince's city, for instance — let them participate in the Final Deaths of traitors to their own cause. Mix these deaths with torturous observance of the *auctoritas* and *ignoblis ritae* of the sect. Paint the mystery, danger and unholy majesty of the culmination of a city crusade with broad strokes and the intrigue and investigation phases with insidious lies, treachery and even internal conflict for individual troupe members.

Play city crusades out over the long term. Taking over a Camarilla city takes time. It can't be done (believably) in a short number of game sessions; therefore, it's probably best for a Storyteller to tell a crusade story as a sweeping epic that incorporates many different themes and styles. It adds to the troupe's enjoyment by giving the players the chance to play the same characters for a long period of time, to develop their motivations and their place within the World of Darkness. Further, establishing the city as a Sabbat stronghold takes a long time. It allows the players to participate in Sabbat politics by their involvement in the birth and implementation of the city's new political structure.

War on the Antediluvians is a much trickier plot prospect. It's highly unlikely that the pack will be able to defeat an ancient vampire. So, use that, and encourage players to participate in the intrigue and investigation that arises around the rumors of where Antediluvians and Methuselahs dwell in torpor. Give them half-truths, secrets garbled from mouth to mouth and mystery. Sprinkle the tension with terrible tales of fallen Sabbat, mere piles of ash and bone, then let the troupe find remains that just possibly fit that profile.

OTHER DEVICES: LUPINES AND DIABLERIE

Sabbat vampires sometimes try to hunt Lupines. Vampires are wary of werewolves with good reason; they know little about them. The Sabbat sometimes hunt them, and while many question the sanity of this practice, it happens. Some Sabbat taunt new recruits, telling them that this is a "rite of passage" among the pack. Other lore has sprung up about powerful Sabbat who have made deals with twisted Lupine terrors, "dancers" who ride a dark and infernal mist of corruption and decay, and that these monsters welcome contact. But investigation of these claims is rare, and pack fun and games that involve Lupines are usually recounted by the few Sabbat involved who actually come back. If your characters are daring enough to try it, present the hunt with an air of murderous danger, and make the endeavor *hurt*. Show them the feral natures of the enemy they face with lonely, elusive settings and ambushes. Show them the ferocious unity of these creatures and the ultimate singular superiority of their combat skills. Use the supernatural nature of Lupines in counterpoint to the twisted depravity of the Sabbat involved as a scare-tactic. After all, shouldn't a "monster" come to be afraid of another monster who could kick the unliving shit out of it with faith and a cause?

Diablerie is a device unique to the Sabbat because the Camarilla so abhors it. Almost for that very reason, diablerie (the draining of an elder vampire to advance in bloodline generation and abilities) is a principle that the Sabbat employs in its war with the Antediluvians. It has become an accepted Sabbat practice.

As a Storytelling device, diablerie frequently comes into play during War Parties and crusades. It could come into the chronicle in inter-pack and intra-Sabbat machinations, but it must be used wisely by the Storyteller to be viable in this way. The Storyteller can use diablerie to punctuate the actions of allies, antagonists and neutrals of the troupe by making it one of the methods that's used against them if their generation/powers warrant it.

Diablerie is a terrible tool of advancement, and it carries a grave price. It is not simply the murder of one vampire by another — the vampire who does the killing steals everything from the victim, including his vampiric soul. This theft stains the murderer with threads that weave the deed around her aura inextricably. It changes her behavior even as it advances her power. Tempt the troupe with the power of it. Place potential victims with enticing qualities in the troupe's past, and make the characters hate these enemies enough to want

to commit the sin in spades. Show them hungry neonates, planning to do the same thing to them.

These plot devices, unique to the Sabbat, offer more than just chances to shoot things with your guns or bite things with your fangs. They provide drama and conflict. They can advance the Storyteller's chronicle or alter it completely. As such, they establish, advance and distinguish a Sabbat chronicle.

Packs

Packs are the Sabbat's answer to the nuclear family, and as such, they fight. They fight with each other, they're loyal to each other, they like, dislike, love and hate each other. Sometimes the loyalties to each other get strained, and these strained loyalties provide dramatic conflict.

The pack, the smallest unit of Sabbat organization, is led by a ductus, and it always includes a priest and a variable number of True Sabbat. Each member has different skills. Each Sabbat has his own place in the pack structure, and members don't always agree with each other. Sabbat have individual allegiances to specific packmates, and different ideas on what it means to be a True Sabbat. Some ways for the Storyteller to use these differences include inter- and intra-pack rivalries, allies and philosophical agreements and disagreements.

Pack interactions vaguely mirror normal life. Some Sabbat like each other, some Sabbat dislike each other. While they're *bound* to each other by the Vinculum, the effect of the Vinculum varies between individual Sabbat. Sometimes it's stronger; sometimes less so. Those who don't "play nice in the sandbox" may try to one-up each other or backstab each other (rivals may even try to cause the other to lose face within the pack). This tension provides the Storyteller with a chance to play out some of the more interpersonal aspects of the Sabbat pack. Such rivalries allow the troupe members to give voice to their characters' personalities by providing them with an antagonist in the plot with which to butt heads.

Further, just like rival political factions, packs of Sabbat often have problems relating to each other. While they all follow the same precepts, they don't always see eye to eye on the way to achieve their larger goals, and each of the factions always wants to be right. Sabbat inter-pack rivalries provide the basic necessary element for Storytelling — dramatic conflict.

Pack members and packs have allies, just as they have rivals and enemies. This dynamic provides Storytellers with a chance to allow the characters to form and nurture allegiances and achieve their objectives through these allegiances. They also provide unique dramatic conflict, because, as the proverb goes, "the enemy of my enemy is my friend." Sabbat packs stay true to *that* proverb in spades.

Differing Philosophies

No two people view the same concept in exactly the same manner. Neither do any two members of the Sabbat, which causes problems for them, as Sabbat are expected to function with unity.

Sabbat ideology, while treasuring freedom, espouses various schools of thought just like mortal ideology does. The Sabbat often argues amongst itself, even down to the least important member, about what that ideology means. If that friction is characterized in plot development, the Storyteller can use it to introduce doctrinal conflict (and the offshoot of doctrinal conflict, armed opposition).

Throw any of the political factions into the stew. Show how friends disagree and how enemies support each other's viewpoints now and then. Punctuate the dialogue with finger-pointing and name-calling. Use imagery that underscores the differences in mundane things, then twist it to be significant to the underlying meaning of the action. Think of Jung's theory of Synchronicity: An elder's timepiece moves too slowly; a neonate's Rolex is way too fast. Then make things happen that use that imagery as foreshadowing.

Theme

Like all chronicles, Sabbat chronicles are guided by themes — the overarching principles that the chronicle illustrates — which give a framework for how alien and terrifying the sect is. These themes can be simple or complex; they can be as easily recognized as the callous power games of a pack priest on the rise, or as subtle as Inquisition informants in the troupe's midst. Themes reveal themselves as subtly as the intrigue surrounding lengthy espionage against the Camarilla, or as overt as the hideous acknowledgment of individual freedom played out in the Games of Instinct. Within every chronicle, theme steers a Storyteller's choice for plot and the actions of supporting cast within that plot.

No chronicle can really survive, or be satisfying dramatically, without a strong theme. If a theme isn't present from the beginning of a chronicle, the action within the story will just occur haphazardly without really *saying* anything at all, which makes for stagnant drama.

What themes work well for the Sabbat? Every story has an endless list of possible themes, but the Sabbat does suggest a few, because of its structure and way of thinking.

Damnation

Vampires are ruthless creatures, but are they truly Damned? Is there any hope for their metaphysical souls? Can they ever attain grace? Chronicles use this existential question as a central theme and showcase the possibility that vampires *are* or *are not* inherently doomed to stand outside conventional spirituality. Demonstrate the hopelessness of the characters' vampiric state by showing them mortal faith. Illustrate how effective such faith really is. Present its beauty and power through the actions of the people that wield it. Force them through this glimpse at the light they believe they can never touch, and make them want it.

Existence

Vampirism is an unnatural means of existence, and continuance of vampiric existence is full of nightly dangers. Further, the warlike nature of the Sabbat (with its crusades and War Parties) poses a real challenge to Sabbat vampires. They have martial skills, yes. They have cunning, surely, but do those attributes always win out? Of course they don't, and a theme on the difficulty of surviving as a Sabbat vampire should be full of those dangers, just waiting for the characters to relax before they strike. Hit your troupe with the dangers of nightly survival. Pack enemies just as fierce, just as ruthless, just as cunning as the pack members themselves lurk in every corner. Show them the bodies or ashes of those Sabbat who don't make it through the night early and often. Take them to a mausoleum full of Sabbat still waiting to crawl out into the night after decades of hunger.

Freedom

Freedom is a central precept to the Sabbat. What threatens that freedom, and what would happen should it be curtailed? What kinds of conflict does the Sabbat meet because of this belief? If a Storyteller chooses freedom and the threats to it as her theme, stories center around facing challenges that serve to diminish it in favor of conformity. Tell stories in which the characters wants to be free of the constraints placed upon it from higher up within the sect, but can't, because the higher-ups are too powerful. Let them act rashly in some endeavor, thinking they are acting for the advancement of the sect by observing such freedom, then slap them down for it. Change the conditions midstream, so that, instead of freedom, they served conformity.

Individualism and the Struggle for Self

Every Sabbat is an individual who personally struggles to identify her own boundaries and choices. Sometimes, these boundaries are antithetical to the group to which she belongs. Any group moves naturally toward conformity, no matter how much it claims to value individualism. Finding her own place within the sect causes a Sabbat vampire to grapple with what is expected of her as a member of a whole. Stories that revolve around this theme put the characters in opposition with their own natures, wants, loves, dreams and ambitions for the good of the Sabbat. Tell a story in which your troupe's characters are forced to uphold an idea that they don't necessarily support, like changing a pack *ritus*, or a city siege that they believe isn't particularly necessary or well-planned. Then, show them the fruits of their labors when the endeavor fails or succeeds.

Infernal Corruption

The Sabbat stands against interference from and allegiance to the infernal, largely because this interference and allegiance constrains freedom. Chronicles use this central theme by involving the characters in story lines that put them face to face with the possibility of that corruption. By allowing the characters to be *tempted* by corruption, and by then letting them see the ultimate failure that it brings about, infernal corruption and the fight against it becomes a compelling chronicle focus. Place your characters in situations where the infernal comes creeping in. Tease and torment them with promises and lies and dreams of the impossible fulfilled easily. Let them bargain, then tangle them up in their own promises by showing how deceitful the entities they bargain with really are. Conversely, give them good reasons to stand against infernal corruption, such as the threat of the Inquisition, and stories and rumors of the *auto-da-fé*.

Intrigue

Unlife in the Sabbat and in its dealings with its enemies, is full of potential intrigue. It's full of paranoia and danger. Sabbat politics twist and turn like a web woven by thousands of drunken spiders, and all have the spiders have their own ambitions. Worse, they all have fangs poised at your neck. Players in the political game will smile in an opponent's face while sharpening the stake destined for his heart. The theme of intrigue puts the characters right in the center of all these machinations and brings the innate distrust, fear and suspicion of such an endeavor into sharp focus.

Mercy

Sabbat ideology believes that it's weak to show mercy. Do any of the Sabbat ever stand against this idea? Can they survive within the sect if they do believe that its not only right but *necessary* to be merciful at times? Show how the Sabbat is inhumane, and let your troupe decide how inhumane its characters will be. Counterpoint this decision with the actions of an individual Sabbat who is merciful to a mortal victim, putting it out of its misery quickly, so another can't torture it further. Let the players see the consequences of this action, and let them decide if they want to be merciful, too. Give them good reasons to be merciful — victims that were their friends in life, struggling against their ropes as they are hoisted into the trees, and then put the knife of their friend's intended destruction in their hands.

Power

Power is a corrupting force. Sabbat vampires, being powerful creatures, are always at risk from the temptations that arise out of a wish to be in control of something. Cainites are corrupted through their adherence to ideas that are no longer relevant to their existence — for instance, failing to recognize that they are no longer human — or conversely, by using this fact to further their own gain at all costs, without any thought to how their actions affect the whole of the Sabbat. Sabbat vampires play politics, an activity fraught with compromise and shaky alliances. How does the Cainite traverse the halls of Sabbat power without having some of its inherent taint rub off on her?

Storytellers can play all sorts of power games. Stand the characters as allies of a political up-and-comer. Make her a formidable upstart, one who has risen through deeds and Monomacy. Put the Status Quo faction soundly in her way;

THE DEVIL, YOU SAY?

Do we really need to say this again? You are *not* a vampire. The Devil is *not* your unholy master. You are a player. Perhaps your game involves some infernal presence in the context of the story, but when that's done, leave it at the table.

make other factions think she is useful to their causes. Make it evident that her problems are the characters' problems. Then, make it evident that she is using the pack for her own ends; that she cares about it and its ideas as much as she cares about kine.

MOOD

Mood denotes atmosphere. A Storyteller needs to pick a mood, or series of them, that underscores her theme. Doing so allows the players to employ as many of their five senses as possible, and goes a long way toward aiding the Storyteller in fostering the troupe's understanding of her theme, and it makes the chronicle much more resonant by presenting it viscerally.

Matching the atmosphere to the action is important. For instance, a meeting of Sabbat spies who have infiltrated a Camarilla city for the purposes of siege will be tense and paranoid. An esbat throbs with an overwhelming feeling of mystery, excitement and anticipation. Games of Instinct are playfully macabre, and the emotions derived from the mood should bring this dark fun to the foreground. Mood should be relevant to the plot, and it should showcase what is happening.

Remember those short ideas, and you've got mood down cold.

But what sort of moods are appropriate to a Sabbat chronicle? Here's a sampling:

Fear

Fear is what the Sabbat is about. Use it to motivate the troupe by playing on their character's fears, then contrast it with the fear they evoke in their prey. Fear of the infernal, fear

of reprisal for mistakes, fear of Gehenna — all of these concepts are good mood motivators.

Lust

Erotic hunger for vitae, lust for power, perverse cravings for excitement are also good motivators, because they are so deeply tied to how abominable Sabbat Cainites truly are.

Paranoia

Running with the Sabbat is rife with danger. Enemies lurk everywhere, and many situations are fraught with tension. Remember this tension and display it in your chronicle by showing the knife in the hands of an enemy or friend (literally or figuratively) that's poised for the small of your players' characters' backs.

Anger

Sabbat vampires have an edge of anger because of how they were created. Wouldn't you be pissed if someone tortured you, drained you of your blood, then buried you, all on the slim chance that you *might* claw your way out of the grave?

Black Comedy

The Storyteller can use comedic subtext to drive home the violence and depravity of what her players' characters do, and their actions became doubly horrific because of the joke. Give some of the nastier deeds of the Sabbat black comedic touches — witty comments made during torture of kine, victims killed in ironic ways (remember the clerk and her mishap with Slurpee machine, mentioned earlier?) and other odd and quirky imagery.

WRAPPING IT UP

So now it's done. The planning is over, the kine are drained and the Sabbat slumber in their havens, smug in the knowledge that they'll get up tomorrow night and do it all again. Likewise, we're done discussing how a Storyteller can use the sect to scare her troupe out of their collective minds. So have, fun, sleep well, and remember: Where the Sabbat is concerned, sleeping well is sleeping lightly.

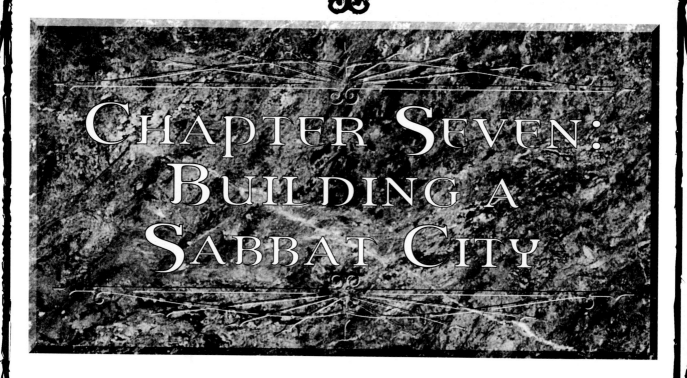

CHAPTER SEVEN: BUILDING A SABBAT CITY

"Will you walk into my parlour?" said a spider to a fly...
— Mary Howitt, "The Spider and the Fly"
If that fly just walked on in, he deserved whatever he had comin'. Dumb motherfucker.
— Kim Wylie, pack priest

Through a combination of intimidation tactics, murder and some limited influence, the Sabbat extends a brutal hold over its conquered territories. Young Sabbat exercise their freedoms in bloody fashions unknown among the "Kindred" of the Camarilla; the elders of the sect rely on their innate powers more than they use any sort of influence among humans. Obviously, lacking the dreary strictures placed on vampires by more domineering rulers, cities of the Sabbat are *exciting* places... if you're a vampire.

For the Storyteller constructing a Sabbat-held city, the Sabbat's peculiar perspective toward mortals is paramount. After all, the teeming hordes of humans must be kept unaware of the vampires living in their midst (even if those vampires believe themselves the true and rightful rulers of humanity), and with young and rebellious Sabbat engaged in pastimes such as "Mossberg Madness" and car-chasing (with Celerity and Potence), the Sabbat is forced to adopt some sort of policy regarding mortal influence. In theory, the Sabbat disdains mortals as little more than food and fodder, but in practice, the elders and the Sabbat's revenant families exert control over those areas that are crucial to the sect's security and prosperity. Similarly, the appalling lack of human morality among Sabbat leads to disturbing trends in the mortal societies they manipulate. Without consideration for their herds, the vampires of the Sabbat often allow execrable conditions that would never be tolerated in cities of the Camarilla — or in cities bereft of vampiric influence (if such places exist). Indeed, Sabbat cities are hellish, even when one fails to realize that vampires lurk behind the scenes.

Relationships between Sabbat and Camarilla also color the development of a Sabbat city. The Sabbat sees itself as an army at war; as such, its cities are assets, military striking points and zones of control. While the decadent vampires of the Camarilla may be content to use their mortal lackeys to gather money, art and blood, the Sabbat always keeps an eye toward internal security and external expansion. As a result of this policy, the Sabbat keeps multiple auxiliary havens (for defense as well as the hosting of nomadic packs) and often has an "open border" policy allowing vampires to enter the city easily — something many Camarilla princes eschew, but that the Sabbat feels comfortable with given their use of recognition signs and *ritae*. These and other differences should be readily noticeable to anyone familiar with conditions in cities dominated by sects other than the Sabbat. Indeed, a Sabbat city can often be evaluated by its adherence to some of the sect's more common policies.

As with any chronicle, presenting a Sabbat city is a matter of preparation. However, the presentation differs from that of Camarilla or independent cities. The Storyteller needs to be careful to set up the proper mood and locations. After all, once the players start asking about communal haven locations and ritual cemeteries, the Storyteller needs the requisite information at hand. Following the guidelines in this chapter is a good way to set up interesting, complete and *believable* cities.

(This chapter is intended for Storyteller use only.)

On Semantics

A word often associated with vampire influence in a city is *control*, which bears some investigation. Vampires are rarely feudal lords in the modern nights, commanding peasants from their gilded thrones (though some Tzimisce in the Old Country…). Modern vampires exert subtle influence over (or otherwise dominate) aspects of mortal culture — they are unchanging predators who follow societal trends, not make them.

Indeed, it is unlikely that any vampire, no matter how powerful, could truly *control* a modern city. Her enemies would besiege her and bring her down within a matter of nights, were she to be so obvious. Rather, vampires occlude their presence under numerous layers of secrecy and misdirection.

This technique may seem strange for the Sabbat, as raucous and blatant as it is. For all the sect's faults, however, its leaders are not stupid. If they rampaged through the streets every night, blowing heads off bank tellers and crushing political institutions, they wouldn't have lasted long enough to achieve the success they have. In fact, once past the *ritae* and open depravity, little distinguishes the Sabbat from vampires of other sects at all. As in the mortal world — how different is an average person's life in Canada than it is in the United States when matters come down to brass tacks? — ideology almost always takes a back seat to the basic requisites of life… or unlife. Vampires all suffer the Curse of Caine first and foremost; all other matters are secondary at best.

Sabbat Cities

Suspended in various stages of perpetual confederated anarchy, the cities of the Sabbat teem with the elements that the sect sees as useful and valuable. While the Camarilla avoids open shaping of human society, the Sabbat has no compunctions about directly — albeit judiciously — encouraging the elements that ease its means of existence. As such, Sabbat-controlled cities often evidence high incidences of violent crime, drug trade, population overflow and corruption. Feeding among squalid masses of homeless and skimming money from the underworld, members of the Sabbat turn barrens and slums into their own personal (and pack) domin-

ions. The upper echelons of human society become the grounds for the most affluent and subtle among the Sabbat, glutting the jaded and esoteric tastes of the sect's more influential members.

Each Sabbat city is an exercise in barely controlled chaos (though some are more controlled than others). Nominally overseen by an archbishop or council of bishops, the city's Sabbat strive against one another for power and prestige with ferocious abandon, held in check only by the bonds of the Vaulderie. Authority trickles down to lesser leaders and ducti, who advance the causes of the sect (and themselves) in their own individualistic fashions. Instead of loyalty along strict clan lines, the Sabbat thus works in mixed groups; the separation of packs, and the fact that the Vaulderie is shared only rarely between rival packs, means that Sabbat vampires are quite likely to engage in internecine warfare. When combined with the Loyalist movement (which advocates personal freedom and disobedience) and the fractiousness of young, modern and deranged Sabbat, this means that outbreaks of vampiric violence (against either mortals or other vampires) are fairly prevalent. Only common cause and the power of the Vaulderie keep Sabbat vampires working together — which shows in the fact that Sabbat cities are more likely to have slip-ups wherein humans learn of the existence of vampires and are brutally dispatched (or otherwise dealt with) before they can become problematic. One tale from the bizarre streets of New York concerns a rash of "Vampires Are Real!" news stories from a sensationalist writer who was found three days after his last story saw print, drunk, dazed and high on the steps of the *New York Times* offices wearing only greasepaint and a clapboard sign that read, "Yes, we're real. Stay out of the East Village."

Mortal Influence

Disdaining mortal influence causes the Sabbat multiple problems in its sway over cities. The Sabbat refuses to recognize mortals as a threat, and few of its members treat humans as anything more than ambulatory meals. This is a dangerous oversight on the part of the sect, for it means that mortal agencies can be used easily against the Sabbat.

The worst problem with the Sabbat's lack of influence, of course, is the possibility of mass exposure to mortals through the actions of rash, frenzied, insane or just hyperactive Sabbat. Unless the vampire in question has subtle and pervasive influence in the media — and few newly Embraced Sabbat do — the sect relies on terrorism and blunt uses of Disciplines to address problem mortals. This course of action backfires, of course, if a particularly talented mortal escapes and manages to acquire competent aid (say, from the Inquisition). The Sabbat counters this potential liability by fostering high crime rates in its cities, so that the occasional odd murder or disappearance goes unnoticed, but this tactic creates problems of its own. Savvy Sabbat leaders recognize the usefulness of the media, but in general, the media remains unexploited by the Sabbat.

The Sabbat's lack of financial investment in mortal society means that the sect as a whole has little sway over industry, politics or transportation. Although any vampire can get a small amount of cash simply by waylaying a hapless mortal, the ability to move large quantities of money around — exerting control over businesses and industries — eludes most Sabbat vampires, who see mortal business as a waste of time. After all, running a business requires *paperwork*, and it doesn't directly provide a source of food or entertainment. Elder Sabbat recognize, though, that interest in mortal industry and politics is necessary in order to develop staging grounds for attack and to support the herds necessary for vampires. A look at the sad economic state of many Sabbat cities shows that mortals often flee oppressive conditions, and the Sabbat has had the majority of its cities turned into burned-out economic wrecks through the efforts of other vampires — or even mortal industries. Some Sabbat leaders advocate more direct control of mortal financial and political institutions, but many younger Sabbat shout that the leaders are acting just like the Camarilla.

Crime-rates in Sabbat-controlled cities border on the appalling. Without recourse to media or police control, the Sabbat stimulates crime to cover its activities. After all, a few more missing people won't be noticed when hundreds die or disappear every year. Additionally, the vampires of the Sabbat find underworld traffic a good way to acquire money, drugs and guns, all of which are useful in fighting a war, be it against adversaries in the sect or versus enemies in neighboring cities. In particular,

the Serpents of the Light, the Lasombra and the Ventrue *antitribu* tend to engage in more criminal activities than any of their compatriots, which leads to the higher incidence of violent activity among mortals that the Sabbat needs in order to cover up its own tracks. Additionally, the use of smuggling rings to transport vampires is not lost on the Sabbat, and many a racket previously devoted to smuggling cigarettes or weapons had found itself commandeered to transport unliving cargoes across terrain that would typically be dangerous for a vampire. A few enterprising Nosferatu *antitribu* even ran an "Underground Railroad" for vampires during the early 1980s, but rumors indicate that this venture is now defunct.

SABBAT NUMBERS

Because of their casual policies toward feeding and tendency to create new vampires in wartime, Sabbat cities usually support more Cainites per capita than most other cities. A typical Sabbat city may host up to twice the usual number of vampires — one Cainite per 50,000 mortals — though such overpopulation is misleading, as excess vampires meet Final Death in combat or simply leave with nomadic packs. Combined with the lack of an *enforced* Masquerade, this overpopulation means that Sabbat members are more likely to be discovered as vampires, although their use of direct means to rectify the situation means that they are no more likely to be completely exposed (and, indeed, the elders among the Sabbat recognize the need to keep humans in the dark — for now).

CONTESTED CITIES

Perpetual warfare occupies the nights of the Sabbat. Whether overthrowing the oppressive grip of the Camarilla, waging war against the cannibalistic Ancients, hunting down hostile Lupines or crushing enigmatic prodigals like wizards and ghosts, the Sabbat has its collective Black Hands full in trying to maintain control over its cities while expanding its reach. Packs contest against one another in ritual combat in order to hone their skills, while archbishops and other luminaries of the sect plan long-term stratagems to fight the war against the Antediluvians.

From the Sabbat perspective, the Antediluvians lurk behind the actions of everyone and everything outside the sect. It is little wonder, then, that the sect has no patience for anyone who doesn't join the cause. This, in turn, means that the Sabbat is always at war — one is either with the sect or against it, and the Sabbat cannot allow others to stand against it. As a result, the sect strives to spread its influence into as many cities as possible. The leaders of the Sabbat wage crusades (wars of territory) against the cities of the enemies so that the pawns of the Antediluvians get no respite. Just about any city within striking distance of the Sabbat has felt the effects of a crusade.

STARTING THE REVOLUTION

Acquiring good information is the first step in taking over a city. To this end, the Sabbat makes extensive use of scouts in enemy territory. The exceptional selection of Disciplines among Sabbat vampires allows for a great deal of flexibility in espionage agents. Combining the powers of Vicissitude with the loyalty of the Vinculum means that the Sabbat is capable of activating highly effective spies. As long as covert agents avoid detection by paranoid individuals skilled in mind-reading, there is almost no way to ferret out Sabbat agents. These spies gather vital information about the allegiances of the city's vampires and the locations of havens and bases, as well as the strengths of the city. For delicate operations, the Sabbat even uses heavily Dominated moles or nearly undetectable revenant ghouls to infiltrate important places in the city's infrastructure.

Sabbat spies aren't Embraced as warriors. They generally operate independently or in pairs, with specific mission objectives. ("Discover the location of the Tremere chantry and return.") Assassination isn't a common goal for spies; the benefits of removing a particular scion of the city are usually outweighed by the fact that such tactics cause the rest of the city's vampires to draw together. Even when presented with the opportunity, a spy is unwilling to compromise her cover by killing an adversary.

The Sword of Caine

Once Sabbat spies have determined important information about the city, the crusade begins in earnest. In the past, the Sabbat would attempt to recruit anarchs or independents to their side. However, experience has shown that failure while attempting to recruit immediately alerts the targets to the impending Sabbat attack. Instead of announcing its presence, therefore, the Sabbat often strikes immediately.

The first casualty in a Sabbat crusade is the Masquerade. Since the Camarilla expends a great deal of its energy and resources in maintaining the Masquerade, the Sabbat works to force the Camarilla's hand. By selectively indulging in violence, the Sabbat can force the Camarilla to use its influence to cover up provocative incidents. This, in turn, allows the Sabbat to uncover areas of Camarilla influence in mortal society, and also keeps the Camarilla busy. Of course, the Sabbat is careful in just how much of a show it creates; nobody wants to fight the kind of two-front war that would result if hunters (especially the Society of Leopold) descended on the city as a result of blatant supernatural actions. Thus, the Sabbat usually limits the number of witnesses to its attacks and leaves a means of explaining them. For instance, a Sabbat vampire is unlikely to run through a mall in the evening at Celerity speeds, cutting up people with razor blades. It's simply too conspicuous, and it brings mortal investigators and hunters too quickly. However, if a half-dozen people are kidnapped by "a crazed psychotic who claimed that he is a vampire," the Camarilla can be forced to debunk the sighting while simultaneously trying to uncover the perpetrator, all of which allows the Sabbat to locate the Camarilla's pawns in the media.

Once the Sabbat has galvanized the local vampire community by forcing it to exercise its mortal influence, the attackers strike at those areas of influence. The horribly recessionary economics of many Sabbat cities are a grave testament to the efficiency of Camarilla influence in fighting the Sabbat, and the sect now does its best to undermine such counterstrikes. It has members buy off mortal agents, kill ghouls and rob or vandalize businesses. Some Sabbat, particularly Lasombra, even take pleasure in matching influence for influence, fighting against the Camarilla's political and economic moves in a chess game of mortal pawns and intermediaries. Here, the Sabbat's revenants come into play. Fiercely loyal and skilled beyond the capacities of "normal" ghouls, revenants can infiltrate mortal society almost invisibly and still match the Camarilla's servitors.

With pawns in place to fight battles of influence, the Sabbat makes a double strike against the city's vampires. Tremere chantries almost always become primary targets, and large quantities of recruits inevitably sacrifice themselves to destroy the mystical might of the Camarilla. Simultaneously, the Sabbat strikes at the prince and primogen of the city, undermining the leadership structure by playing up past injustices and rekindling rivalries. Once the elders of the city have fallen to bickering among themselves, the remaining younger vampires are (theoretically) easily rounded up or frightened off.

Often, the Sabbat strikes directly at Elysium, demoralizing the vampires of the city by attacking on their neutral ground with overwhelming force. (Look at the cover of this book, for example. It's the same location as the **Guide to the Camarilla**, after the Sabbat has chased away those poncey bastards.)

RECRUITMENT

Due to the heavy losses involved in taking a city, the Sabbat often needs to recruit new "talent" in order to complete its crusades. Once the attack begins, anarchs or independents are sometimes offered positions in the sect (though experienced Sabbat keep careful eyes on them). Such converts are often given difficult jobs and assignments to kill their own allies, both as a test of loyalty and as a means to get rid of troublesome adversaries. Those who fail are summarily executed.

Because the Sabbat cannot count on the conversion of existing vampires to swell its ranks, multiple-Embraces are the most common tactic for recruiting *en masse*. A pack may initiate a score of individuals in one fell swoop, throwing the whelps against the enemies in a frenzied horde. Survivors among the converts are rounded up, then added to new groups and once again directed at the enemy. Obviously, this makes for high mortality rates among new (and not yet True) Sabbat, as might be expected of groups of untrained and berserk vampires thrown against Tremere chantries and princely domains. Still, some do survive, and in recognition of their survival (and for weakening their targets), such converts receive the Creation Rites, to become True Sabbat after they have proven themselves or attained several years of existence.

CRUSHING RESISTANCE

Even in cities that have fallen to the Sword of Caine, partisan resistance remains a problem. While most Camarilla vampires flee to safer territory when a city falls to a crusade, some stubbornly refuse to leave their homes, and they continue to harry the Sabbat. The Gangrel and the Nosferatu are the most ubiquitous among these pests, but a properly prepared and entrenched vampire of any clan can be troublesome.

Given the use of expendable troops in combat, the Sabbat's tactics for dealing with such interlopers are obvious. Typically, once partisan activity manifests, the Sabbat uses a few rank neonates to "feel out" the enemy, by presenting an easy target. Once these sacrificial lambs have gotten a "bite," the sect's packs strike on the now-revealed enemy. Simple. Unless….

Crafty vampires avoid striking the Sabbat directly. After all, the sect's major strength lies in its frontal combat capability and its willingness to use raw numbers. A hiding enemy may avoid all contact, picking and choosing his own targets. Such an opponent can't be drawn out. For these situations, the Sabbat must rely on Assamite *antitribu* and City Gangrel: The urban hunters take over, attempting to track the opponent down. Likely places are watched (old havens, possible resources, exit and entry points for the city) and double agents are called into play. Heavily Dominated converts are used to attempt to establish contact with the resistance under the pretense of assistance — and, of course, the Sabbat springs the trap once a meeting is arranged.

THE AGONY OF DEFEAT

Of course, the Sabbat does not always win its crusades. The loss of a few small cities to the Camarilla amply demonstrates some of the weaknesses of the Sabbat's war effort, and the Camarilla is increasingly forced to fight the Sabbat on home turf — hidden wars of influence, instead of street-to-street combat.

The lack of front-line fighting ability in the Camarilla, and the unwillingness to meet the enemy head-on for fear of destroying the Masquerade, means that the Camarilla fights circumspectly. However, the Sabbat has little experience with or patience for such conflicts, and continually tries to drag the battle back to its area of expertise — raw combat. Brujah and Gangrel *antitribu* are dispatched in numbers, to tear the enemy to bloody tatters; Assamite *antitribu* hunt down individuals while members of the other clans counter the Camarilla's advantages (Ventrue *antitribu* countering the Camarilla's use of Dominate and Presence, Salubri *antitribu* and Harbingers of Skulls using their occult knowledge to neutralize the Tremere, and so on).

In order to fight against the Sabbat and win, the Camarilla must play to its own strengths, which means avoiding direct combat with the Sabbat's vampires while nullifying them through influence. Police forces are beefed up and mobilized to deal with the "gang threat." Auxiliary havens are activated as primary havens are abandoned to slow the Sabbat advance. Nosferatu and Malkavian spies funnel information about Sabbat whereabouts, and Brujah strike and fade, leaving confused and injured Sabbat to be rounded up by mortal lackeys and ghouls. Most importantly, the Tremere use their decisive advantage of Thaumaturgy to counter many of the Sabbat's unique Disciplines and to gather information or even strike at Sabbat leaders from a distance. Once the architects of the assault are isolated, they are picked off individually, leaving disorganized groups of recently created Sabbat with little instruction or experience to be dealt with expediently.

The Camarilla also has an advantage in that it maintains influence in geographically large sections of territory, where several powerful vampires make their havens. Once a city is under siege from the Sabbat, the Camarilla calls in assistance from the justicar and archons. Many of the Sabbat's shock troops are fledglings. A dozen hungry Sabbat may be able to pull down a single elder, but against an organized coterie of experienced and well-equipped archons, complete with powerful Disciplines and the benefits of age and generation, the Sabbat's young Licks tend to fall like paper tigers without reasonable tactics. Even when archons cannot be counted on for assistance, neighboring cities lend aid indirectly. Sabbat traveling to a siege site may find themselves waylaid en route by the actions of a neighboring city's Camarilla prince, exerting influence

over the highways and transportation of the area. Bishops leading the attack on the front lines suddenly find themselves flanked as their own home cities are besieged by Camarilla forces from other locations. Blood bound, Dominated or Entranced agents arrive and stir up mortal unrest, causing difficulty among the Sabbat's own herds.

Deep Cover

When gathering information about enemy groups, the Sabbat makes great use of intelligence operations. After all, with the Vaulderie backing up loyalty and the sect's use of multiple specialized Disciplines, infiltration work is almost second nature. Given such circumstances, it's no surprise that the Sabbat has agents in many, many Camarilla cities throughout the world — arguably all of them (though such claims are generally made by the Sabbat itself and may not be wholly objective). Undercover work is dangerous and unglamorous, but a successful Sabbat agent gains a great deal of prestige in the sect for cunning and daring.

Manchurians

With extensive use of the Dominate Discipline, it's possible to rebuild someone's memory and personality, even to the point where the individual is not aware of her own true loyalties. The Sabbat makes use of this tactic to send in agents who are honestly unaware of their Sabbat ties. Nicknamed "Manchurians" (after the film *The Manchurian Candidate*), these agents are provided with a false set of memories and a few subconscious commands (post-hypnotic suggestions to make regular reports, usually), ensuring that they cannot give away their allegiances.

Sabbat Manchurians are often drawn from among the ranks of young, newly Embraced members hoping for quick fame. Most often, the subjects are Dominated by older Lasombra in the sect, who are meticulous in rebuilding the target's personality and memory. Some of these "programmers" even possess enough mastery of the Discipline to ensure that others have a difficult time penetrating the layers of false memory when attempting to undo the psychological work. Once the programmer has completely rebuilt the persona of the Manchurian, the agent is taken to a likely spot, instilled with a memory of traveling to the area or escaping from attackers, and released to find her way into Camarilla territory, there to be accepted into society (hopefully). Subconscious triggers force the target to report through dead-letter drops or surreptitious phone calls, promptly forgetting the event thereafter.

In a few rare cases, the Sabbat has made use of captured Camarilla vampires, altering their memories slightly and implanting commands to demand information and reports. These hapless Manchurians often have no idea of the fate to which they have been resigned until they are caught and executed by their own sect. This tactic is risky, though, since the victim's allies (if any) may be ferocious in their retribution.

DOUBLE AGENTS

Far more dangerous than working under mental conditioning is working with full knowledge of Sabbat connections. Since any paranoid Cainite with sufficient mastery of Auspex or Dominate can uncover hidden loyalties, Sabbat who pose as Camarilla or independents must step very carefully.

The most common double agents among the Sabbat are Brujah *antitribu*, since Brujah tend to spout revolutionary rhetoric anyway. The clan's loose structure makes it easy to join up with any Brujah gang or anarch front and work to benefit the sect while pretending to be a simple rebellious punk. Nosferatu *antitribu* are sometimes dispatched, but in many cases, the Nosferatu of an area are tightly knit enough to know of Sabbat loyalties of their brethren, and they may well sell such information to the highest bidder — if they care at all.

Another option is to infiltrate the upper echelons of vampiric society by claiming to be a powerful Toreador or Lasombra *antitribu*. This tactic is very risky because the credentials of such individuals are often surreptitiously "checked" by gentrified vampires who would prefer to find all of the skeletons in a potential rival's closet. To counter this investigation, the Sabbat sometimes creates a new vampire of early generation, and spends several months in specialized training and indoctrination to turn the subject into a shadowy pretender who has "apparently escaped notice" but now turns up seeking a place among the elders.

Other times, a Sabbat vampire may pose as a member of another clan, learning the Disciplines necessary to carry off the charade and then claiming a little-known branch of lineage. Obviously, this feat is nigh-impossible among strictly hierarchical clans like the Tremere, but a Lasombra might claim to be a wayward Ventrue, while a Tzimisce could pass herself off as a Nosferatu (and some take delight in doing so). Of course, any Lick who takes this course had better steer clear of the Warlocks; the blood-magic of the Tremere makes it too easy to detect such forgeries.

REPLACEMENT VAMPIRES

Considering the fleshcrafting predilections of the Tzimisce, rebuilding an individual to look like someone else is a simple matter. With this in mind, the Sabbat occasionally engages in kidnapping particular vampires, then replacing them with fleshcrafted duplicates. This job is exacting and demanding, but ultimately one of the most effective forms of infiltration — it is rumored that the dreaded Dracula himself (should he exist) made use of this tactic to confound his political enemies.

To successfully pull off impersonation, the Sabbat spy must be able to watch the victim carefully for quite some time. The victim's habits and mannerisms must be studied, her friends and allies must be discovered, even her deepest secrets must be uncovered. Any failure on the part of the spy could break cover, warning the other vampires to the Sabbat presence. Adding to the difficulty, the spy must learn all of the victim's Disciplines, in order to fully duplicate the powers and limitations of the subject.

The use of powerful Disciplines other than Vicissitude often accompanies impersonation. High proficiency in telepathic contact, through Auspex, is essential in stealing the personality as well as in developing a complete template of the victim's behavior. The Dominate Discipline, used as with a Manchurian, ensures that the spy has no confusion about who he really is (by making him think about and remember himself as the victim). In some cases, Thaumaturgy conceals the victim's aura, but the lack of blood magic's accessibility due to the recent disappearance of the Tremere *antitribu* makes this tactic difficult; now, the agents must often rely on extreme proficiency with Obfuscate.

SOUL-SWAPPING

A very recent tactic among the Sabbat involves the capture of a Camarilla vampire or anarch and the intervention of an experienced Harbinger of Skulls. Using the powers of Necromancy (specifically the Bone Path), the Harbinger exchanges the soul of the victim with that of a loyal Sabbat. Followed with a ritual or magical item to mask his aura, the new agent becomes almost undetectable. Again, the agent must learn some of the victim's Disciplines and mannerisms, but the body is obviously perfect and the spy need only worry about the possibility of mental detection.

DEEP COVER AGENTS AND THE VAULDERIE

Deep cover agents must work behind enemy lines without much contact with the Sabbat, and the power of the Vinculum sometimes inexplicably weakens over time. Without the enforcement of the Vaulderie, some Sabbat may find themselves questioning their motives and methods.

The first possible solution to such a problem is to arrange for surreptitious meetings in which the agent can partake of the Vaulderie with his fellow Sabbat. Such is preferable because it allows the agent to maintain his original loyalties. However, doing so is dangerous, because if the agent is followed and his activities are noticed, the entire point of the exercise is ruined. Instead of meeting up with a pack, therefore, a few agents are taught the Vaulderie, and they have mixed blood shipped to them so they can maintain the Vinculum themselves. The risk here is the possibility that the agent may decide to forego the ritual, weakening his own loyalty to the sect, or that he does not know the proper *ritus*.

The second solution to loyalty problems is to blood bond the agent. This prevents the Sabbat from escaping from his loyalty to a member of the sect. Most often, a local bishop or archbishop becomes the focus of such a bond, though due to the possibility of Thaumaturgical detection the subject may instead be a ductus. This method is frowned on because of the Sabbat's distaste for the blood bond, but sometimes there is no other viable option (for instance, if the agent must penetrate deep into Camarilla territory where meetings are impossible). In any case, the bond is broken with the Vaulderie once the agent returns from duty.

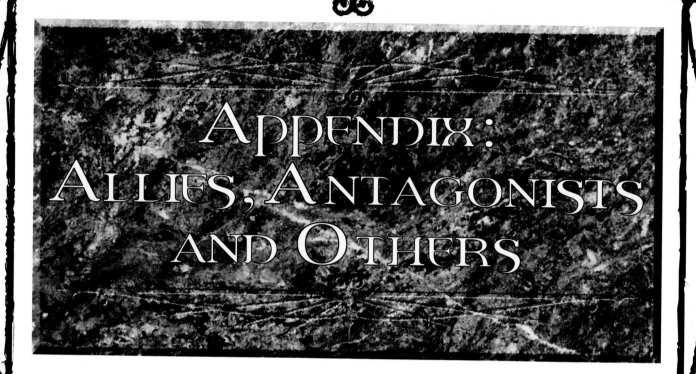

Appendix: Allies, Antagonists and Others

There will be no pleading for forgiveness.
They are rubbish, they are criminal scum. They
are different from us. There is now no fear in us.
They are weak.
— Irvine Welsh, Filth

Sabbat Templates

This section provides stock Sabbat members for use in your chronicles. Although the idea of an "average" vampire is fatuous at best, these templates are extremely useful for Storytellers who need to introduce a character yet do not have the time to create one. They also provide a good starting point for Storytellers who wish to create their own unique characters. It is impossible to pigeonhole each Sabbat member into a stereotype, but with a little modification, the following stereotypes present a host of characters who make up the variety and fuel the intrigue behind the Sabbat.

It is also important to note that there is much more to a character than a simple collection of dots. Power, even among Sabbat, does not necessarily equate to long lists of Disciplines or martial abilities. Characters can attain responsibility and prestige with driving personalities as easily as do they can with brute force. A bishop need not be even as potent as presented here — other vampires' *perception* of her is all that truly matters, which is an aspect that goes far beyond the numbers.

Bishop

Background: The bishops of a city have attained their position through cagey politicking or merit. Shrewd and savvy, bishops administrate the nightly affairs of the Sabbat, and they may answer directly to an archbishop if the city has one. Because Sabbat cities usually have multiple bishops, these vampires must hone their wits to keep their compatriots' talons away from their throats. It is unwise to cross a bishop.

Image: The bishop's nightly struggle with paranoia has etched deep lines in her face, and her bestial grin attests to the ferocity under the surface. Her fine clothes lend her a distinguished air, like an ornate scabbard hiding a deadly sword.

Roleplaying Hints: You consider yourself to be superior to everyone else (except the archbishop and regent, of course.) You don't take chances, citing precedent and protocol as the reason you let others do the dirty work. After all, your true enemies will come to *you*.

Clan: Tzimisce

Nature: Perfectionist

Demeanor: Traditionalist

Generation: 8th

Physical: Strength 4, Dexterity 4, Stamina 5

Social: Charisma 4, Manipulation 4, Appearance 5

Mental: Perception 5, Intelligence 4, Wits 4

Talents: Alertness 2, Brawl 3, Empathy 2, Expression 2, Intimidation 3, Leadership 3 , Streetwise 2, Style 1, Subterfuge 3

Skills: Drive 1, Etiquette 3, Firearms 2, Fire Dancing 3, Melee 2, Performance 2, Stealth 1

Knowledges: Academics 2, Bureaucracy 3, Camarilla Lore 1, Enigmas 2, Finance 2, Investigation 2, Linguistics 1, Occult 3, Politics 3, Sabbat Lore 3

Disciplines: Animalism 2, Auspex 3, Celerity 2, Dominate 3, Fortitude 2, Obfuscate 2, Presence 2, Thaumaturgy 2, Vicissitude 4

Thaumaturgical Paths: Path of Blood 2

Backgrounds: Contacts 4, Herd 1, Influence 3, Resources 3, Retainers 1, Rituals 4, Sabbat Status 3

Virtues: Conviction 3, Instinct 3, Courage 3

Path of Enlightenment: Path of Power and the Inner Voice 6

Willpower: 8

Templar/Paladin

Background: Mysterious and secretive, templars are personal guards for archbishops, prisci, cardinals and other important sect leaders. They serve the desires of those they protect, to the point of assassinating their opposition — even if the opposition is another Sabbat. For this reason, paladins are held in contempt by many, especially the members of the Black Hand. Templars may take any form, from a quasi-medieval knight, to a ninja, to a modern hitman and everything in between.

Image: The paladin's impressive appearance wins many fights before they begin. She wears her hair cropped short, so as to provide no handhold for an opponent. Her large frame belies a surprising and deadly quickness.

Roleplaying Hints: Detail-oriented, you notice every nuance and innuendo. You are brave, loyal and fearless. Your charge's safety is more important than your own. You are also more than just a brute — dumb brawlers don't make it among the paladins, as they are too dense to see potential threats coming. You are quick with a cutting remark, and just as quick to defend it.

Clan: Lasombra

Nature: Masochist

Demeanor: Conformist

Generation: 9th

Physical: Strength 5, Dexterity 5, Stamina 5

Social: Charisma 2, Manipulation 2, Appearance 2

Mental: Perception 3, Intelligence 3, Wits 3

Talents: Alertness 3, Athletics 3, Brawl 5, Dodge 4, Empathy 2, Grace 3, Intimidation 4, Streetwise 3, Subterfuge 2

Skills: Crafts 1, Drive 2, Etiquette 2, Firearms 1, Melee 5 (broadsword), Performance 2, Stealth 4, Survival 2

Knowledge: Academics 2, Black Hand Lore 1, Camarilla Lore 1, Investigation 4, Politics 3, Sabbat Lore 3, Underworld Lore 1

Disciplines: Auspex 2, Celerity 2, Dominate 2, Obtenebration 4, Potence 4, Presence 1

Backgrounds: Resources 2, Rituals 2, Sabbat Status 3

Virtues: Conscience 5, Self-Control 4, Courage 5
Path of Enlightenment: The Path of Honorable Accord 7
Willpower: 8

ARCHBISHOP

Background: Seldom encountered by non-Sabbat — or even many lesser Sabbat — archbishops oversee all Sabbat activity in a given city. This manipulative overseer is a megalomaniac. Chances are that he has diablerized, backstabbed and otherwise murdered his way to the top. He has many contacts, and many owe him favors.

Image: Sunken eyes, a perpetual snarl and a domineering presence attest to the archbishop's great age and utter lack of human emotion. The archbishop wears the robes of a priest, in open mockery of the offices of the Church and its promises of redemption.

Roleplaying Hints: You rankle at the idea of anyone challenging your "advice," and you have to be the center of attention. Others encourage your behavior in hopes of currying favor. Brook no misconduct and punish the behavior of those who fail to afford you the respect you know you are due.

Clan: Lasombra

Nature: Autocrat

Demeanor: Director

Generation: 7th

Physical: Strength 3, Dexterity 4, Stamina 6

Social: Charisma 5, Manipulation 6, Appearance 4

Mental: Perception 5, Intelligence 5, Wits 4

Talents: Alertness 2, Brawl 1, Dodge 2, Empathy 2, Expression 2, Grace 2, Intimidation 4, Intuition 2, Leadership 4, Streetwise 1, Style 3, Subterfuge 5

Skills: Archery 1, Crafts 1, Drive 1, Etiquette 3, Firearms 2, Fire Dancing 2, Melee 4 (fencing), Performance 2, Security 1, Stealth 2

Knowledges: Academics 2, Black Hand Lore 1, Bureaucracy 3, Camarilla Lore 1, City Secrets 2, Finance 2, Investigation 3, Law 1, Linguistics 2, Occult 3, Politics 4, Sabbat Lore 4

Disciplines: Auspex 4, Celerity 1, Dominate 5, Fortitude 2, Obfuscate 2, Obtenebration 5, Potence 2, Presence 4

Backgrounds: Contacts 5, Herd 2, Influence 4, Resources 4, Retainers 1, Rituals 4, Sabbat Status 4
Virtues: Conscience 3, Self-Control 3, Courage 5
Path of Enlightenment: Path of Honorable Accord 7
Willpower: 9

PRISCUS

Background: Masters of manipulation, prisci serve the Sabbat by advising archbishops and cardinals, though many detractors of the prisci say that they use their political power and influence to serve only themselves. The position of pricus is more honorary than functional — prisci possess great insight but little "official" power. Nevertheless, prisci move among powerful circles and often possess a respectable personal prowess as well. One does not earn a consultory position if he is weak or foolish. Prisci rarely avail themselves to other Sabbat, let alone other vampires.

Image: The priscus is a modern chamberlain, his robes of office having given way to his tasteful three-piece suit. He is a strong argument for the fact that not all Sabbat are cackling punks in leather biker jackets. The priscus bears a stern, impassive face, and he does not hesitate to turn up his nose at incompetence or failure.

Roleplaying Hints: You have a knack for taking control of a situation — even if it's it something you know nothing about. Implacable confidence and self-assuredness draws others to you, and you always take advantage of those others — usually without their knowledge. You harbor no fools in your midst, and you are loath to forgive or accept apologies.

Clan: Toreador *antitribu*

Nature: Conniver

Demeanor: Perfectionist

Generation: 7th

Physical: Strength 4, Dexterity 4, Stamina 4

Social: Charisma 5, Manipulation 6, Appearance 6

Mental: Perception 6, Intelligence 3, Wits 4

Talents: Alertness 3, Brawl 1, Dodge 1, Empathy 5, Expression 5, Grace 4, Intimidation 5, Leadership 3, Streetwise 3, Style 4 (glamorous), Subterfuge 5

Skills: Crafts 4, Etiquette 5, Firearms 2, Fire Dancing 2, Lip-Reading 2, Melee 4 (fencing), Performance 5, Security 5, Stealth 2

Knowledges: Academics 4 (Classical), Black Hand Lore 1, Bureaucracy 4, Camarilla Lore 2, Finance 3, Investigation 4, Linguistics 3, Occult 2, Politics 5, Sabbat Lore 4, Underworld Lore 2

Disciplines: Auspex 4, Celerity 2, Dominate 3, Fortitude 4, Obfuscate 1, Obtenebration 2, Presence 6, Potence 1, Thaumaturgy 2, Vicissitude 2

Thaumaturgical Paths: Path of Blood 2, Hands of Destruction 1

Backgrounds: Contacts 5, Influence 5, Herd 2, Resources 5, Retainers 4, Rituals 3, Sabbat Status 5

Virtues: Conviction 2, Self-Control 4, Courage 4

Path of Enlightenment: Path of Death and the Soul 6

Willpower: 9

CARDINAL

Background: Cardinals oversee vast areas of Sabbat influence — archbishops answer to them on matters of their individual cities. Cardinals are old, powerful and deadly, having spent centuries or more amassing their personal and political power. Many young Sabbat wonder why vampires of this age oppose the Antediluvians at all, as they are closer to the Ancients than young vampires like themselves. For whatever reason, cardinals support and guide the sect in the Great Jyhad with terrifying efficiency.

Image: The cardinal is quite old and set in his ways. His clothes are anachronistic, hinting at nights spent in the courts of kings long ago. His face has become a perpetual scowl — centuries of brooding, plotting and looking over his shoulder have taken their toll.

Roleplaying Hints: You no longer think like a human being — having been undead for hundreds of years has muted any compassion, sympathy or understanding you may have once mustered. In place of emotion, you have cultivated cunning and ruthlessness. The bottom line is all that matters to you, and that bottom line is the destruction of the Antediluvians. At least, that's what you tell younger members of the sect....

Clan: Lasombra

Nature: Rogue

Demeanor: Director

Generation: 6th

Physical: Strength 5, Dexterity 5, Stamina 5

Social: Charisma 4, Manipulation 7, Appearance 5

Mental: Perception 6, Intelligence 5, Wits 5

Talents: Alertness 1, Brawl 1, Dodge 3, Grace 5, Intimidation 5, Intuition 5, Style 4, Subterfuge 6

Skills: Archery 3, Crafts 4, Firearms 1, Melee 3, Performance 5, Survival 3

Knowledges: Academics 5 (history), Black Hand Lore 2, Bureaucracy 4, Camarilla Lore 2, Finance 4, Investigation 4, Law 2, Linguistics 3, Occult 3, Politics 6, Research 3, Sabbat Lore 5

Disciplines: Auspex 3, Dementation 3, Dominate 7, Fortitude 3, Obfuscate 2, Obtenebration 5, Potence 5, Presence 5

Backgrounds: Allies 3, Contacts 5, Influence 6, Herd 4, Resources 6, Retainers 4, Sabbat Status 5

Virtues: Conviction 3, Instinct 3, Courage 4

Path of Enlightenment: Path of Power and the Inner Voice 5

Willpower: 10

BLACK HAND AGENT

Background: The rank-and-file of the Black Hand is made up of specialized soldiers and spies. The Black Hand agent is such a person, existing either to unearth secrets or eliminate the threat they represent. Black Hand agents offer little information about themselves — in fact, one may never know a vampire belongs to the Hand until faced with the fact overtly....

Image: The Black Hand agent is all business — unreadable eyes hide a steely resolve, and she never smiles unless it's part of her cover to do so. She also dresses in a no-nonsense style, preferring loose clothes in which she may move — and kill — with ease.

Roleplaying Hints: "Kill first, ask questions later," is your motto, and you prefer to kill from seclusion rather than fight an open battle. You have an uncanny knack for always coming out on top when the chips are down. Everything and everyone around you is a tool or an asset, so be aware of how they may be best used, should your situation demand it.

Clan: Assamite *antitribu*

Nature: Chameleon

Demeanor: Survivor

Generation: 10th

Physical: Strength 5, Dexterity 5, Stamina 5

Social: Charisma 3, Manipulation 3, Appearance 3

Mental: Perception 4, Intelligence 3, Wits 5

Talents: Alertness 3, Athletics 2, Brawl 4, Dodge 3, Intimidation 3, Mimicry 2, Streetwise 4

Skills: Demolitions 1, Disguise 2, Drive 2, Firearms 5, Melee 4, Performance 2, Security 4, Stealth 3, Survival 3

Knowledges: Black Hand Lore 3, Camarilla Lore 1, Investigation 2, Sabbat Lore 2

Disciplines: Celerity 2, Obfuscate 3, Potence 2, Quietus 3

Backgrounds: Black Hand Status 2, Contacts 5, Mentor 3, Resources 2

Virtues: Conviction 4, Instinct 4, Courage 5

Path of Enlightenment: The Path of Caine 7

Willpower: 7

BLACK HAND REMOVER

Background: These vampires devote themselves solely to the art of killing. Remorseless and brutal, the Black Hand's removers take their prey efficiently — it is said that victims of the removers may not even realize they are in danger until they see the assassin's face. That is, if they see a face at all.

Image: The remover's cold eyes are impassive and distant. Life and unlife alike mean nothing to this vampire; he takes both with equal aplomb. The remover bears a scar that he wears as a badge of honor, given to him by a particularly cunning target.

Roleplaying Hints: You don't say much. Pay close attention to fine details and subtle nuances, and always be aware of your surroundings. Let no emotion slip from beneath your façade, for that way lies weakness.

Clan: (Country) Gangrel *antitribu*

Nature: Competitor

Demeanor: Monster

Generation: 9th

Physical: Strength 5, Dexterity 5, Stamina 5

Social: Charisma 3, Manipulation 3, Appearance 3

Mental: Perception 5, Intelligence 4, Wits 5

Talents: Alertness 4, Athletics 2, Brawl 5, Dodge 4, Intimidation 3, Leadership 1, Streetwise 4, Throwing 3

Skills: Animal Ken 2, Disguise 3, Drive 2, Firearms 5, Fire Dancing 1, Melee 5, Performance 2, Security 4, Stealth 4, Survival 4

Knowledges: Black Hand Lore 3, Camarilla Lore 1, Computer 2, Investigation 3, Sabbat Lore 3

Disciplines: Animalism 3, Celerity 1, Fortitude 3, Obfuscate 2, Potence 2, Protean 5

Backgrounds: Black Hand Status 3, Contacts 5, Pack Recognition 2, Resources 5

Virtues: Conviction 4, Instinct 5, Courage 5

Path of Enlightenment: Path of Power and the Inner Voice 7

Willpower: 8

BLACK HAND DOMINION

Background: The dominions call the shots for the Black Hand, though the seraphim supersede them. Of course, few vampires have ever seen a dominion, let a lone a seraph, so the distinction is fairly moot to the casual observer. Dominions are cool and collected — brilliant, ruthless and bloodthirsty. Formidable in political and physical power, only a fool challenges a dominion in anything but an assured victory.

Image: The dominion speaks little, but his haughty demeanor exudes an aura of indomitability. He has witnessed massive bloodshed, and his gaze suggests that he is sizing up everyone he meets. His fine features have darkened in his great age.

Roleplaying Hints: There is only one purpose: serving the Hand. You ask your underlings nothing that you would not ask of yourself. You would gladly meet the teeming throngs of the Camarilla head on, but you know that little can be gained from such a blatant assault. Think before acting and consider all your options — acting rashly is acting foolishly.

Clan: Assamite *antitribu*
Nature: Director
Demeanor: Fanatic
Generation: 7th
Physical: Strength 5, Dexterity 5, Stamina 6
Social: Charisma 3, Manipulation 5, Appearance 3
Mental: Perception 5, Intelligence 4, Wits 5
Talents: Athletics 3, Brawl 4, Dodge 2, Expression 1, Grace 2, Intimidation 5, Leadership 4, Streetwise 3, Subterfuge 3
Skills: Archery 3, Drive 2, Etiquette 1, Firearms 3, Herbalism 2, Meditation 2, Melee 6, Professional Skill: Poisons 2, Security 4, Stealth 4, Survival 4
Knowledges: Academics 2, Black Hand Lore 4, Camarilla Lore 2, Enigmas 2, Expert Knowledge: Tactics 2, Investigation 4, Linguistics 2, Medicine 2, Occult 1, Politics 2, Sabbat Lore 3
Disciplines: Auspex 2, Celerity 3, Dominate 3, Fortitude 2, Obfuscate 3, Potence 2, Protean 2, Quietus 6
Backgrounds: Allies 3, Black Hand Status 5, Contacts 5, Herd 1, Resources 5, Retainers 2, Rituals 1, Sabbat Status 4
Virtues: Conviction 3, Instinct 4, Courage 5
Path of Enlightenment: Path of Caine 7
Willpower: 9

NEW COVEN MEMBER

Background: Ambitious and green, these vampires are still learning about unlife in a Sabbat City. They may be True Sabbat or rank neonates, depending on whether or not they have tested their mettle in battle. Novitiates have much to prove, yet often possess great ambition.

Image: The new recruit fits the archetypal "punk" image, if only for show. He's as tough as nails and ready to demonstrate it. Adorned with tattoos, piercings and other scars (ritual and otherwise), the neonate makes his rowdy nature obvious to all who see him.

Roleplaying Hints: Even when you're scared, you never let anyone know it. Your daring personality and brutality make you popular with your packmates. Your burglary skills make obtaining money a breeze, which also earns you respect from the pack. You have an independent streak, though, and that might get you in trouble if you're not careful.

Clan: Brujah *antitribu*
Nature: Rebel
Demeanor: Bravo
Generation: 12th
Physical: Strength 4, Dexterity 3, Stamina 3
Social: Charisma 3, Manipulation 2, Appearance 3
Mental: Perception 2, Intelligence 2, Wits 2
Talents: Alertness 2, Athletics 1, Brawl 2, Dodge 2, Intimidation 2, Streetwise 3, Subterfuge 2
Skills: Drive 2, Firearms 2, Performance 1, Security 2, Stealth 2
Knowledges: Computer 1, Investigation 2, Law 1, Medicine 1
Disciplines: Celerity 1, Potence 2, Presence 1
Backgrounds: Mentor 1, Resources 3
Virtues: Conscience 2, Self-Control 2, Courage 3
Humanity: 4
Willpower: 4

EXPERIENCED COVEN MEMBER

Background: Experience, cunning and connections give these Sabbat members a competitive edge. They have drive and a sense of the proper pecking order of the pack. As they continue to gain trust and status within the pack, they do their fair share of ass-kissing in order to further their support with pack elders.

Image: The experienced Sabbat knows her place and seeks to better it — which one must be noticed to do. She wears shocking clothes and obvious body jewelry. The experienced Sabbat is loud, obnoxious and starved for attention, just as her appearance suggests.

Roleplaying Hints: It's amazing how things just sort of "happen" around you. You always manage to survive, pulling yourself up by your boot straps. Because of your calm composure in the midst of chaos, your growing manipulative abilities and your readiness to lend others a hand, no one ever suspects you to be the cause of the problems. Make a spectacle, but do it so that you gain attention rather than rouse suspicion.

Clan: Nosferatu *antitribu*
Nature: Eye of the Storm

Demeanor: Survivor

Generation: 10th

Physical: Strength 3, Dexterity 4, Stamina 4

Social: Charisma 2, Manipulation 3, Appearance 0

Mental: Perception 2, Intelligence 3, Wits 4

Talents: Alertness 2, Brawl 4, Dodge 2, Expression 1, Intimidation 3, Streetwise 2, Subterfuge 3

Skills: Drive 1, Firearms 3, Fire Dancing 1, Melee 2, Performance 1, Security 2, Stealth 3, Survival 1

Knowledge: Academics 1, City Secrets 2, Computer 1, Investigation 3, Occult 1, Sewer Lore 2

Disciplines: Animalism 2, Dominate 1, Obfuscate 3, Potence 1

Backgrounds: Contacts 1, Mentor 2, Resources 2, Sabbat Status 1

Virtues: Conscience 2, Self-Control 3, Courage 3

Humanity: 3

Willpower: 6

VETERAN COVEN MEMBER

Background: Veteran Sabbat know the ropes. Having fought numerous battles in the Great Jyhad, these vampires are tough, clever and mean as hell. Although they may not lead their pack, veteran Sabbat are truly accomplished, and not to be taken lightly, whether they have earned recognition or not.

Image: The veteran has seen her share of fights, and she's got the thousand-yard-stare to prove it. She's been scarred in battle, but that only serves to accentuate the predatory image she cultivates. She's older than most of her packmates, and she eschews modern body piercings for good, old-fashioned tattoos.

Roleplaying Hints: If anyone gives you any lip, kick his ass. You know you're true to the sect, and you may even put your unlife on the line for it again, as you have so many times in the past. You don't rest on former glory, though — you're ready to jump into action right now, as long as someone has a plan. Or not. Whatever.

Clan: Lasombra

Nature: Fanatic

Demeanor: Traditionalist

Generation: 9th

Physical: Strength 4, Dexterity 5, Stamina 5

Social: Charisma 2, Manipulation 4, Appearance 4

Mental: Perception 3, Intelligence 2, Wits 4

Talents: Alertness 2, Brawl 4, Dodge 4, Expression 2, Intimidation 3, Intuition 2, Streetwise 3, Style 2, Subterfuge 3

Skills: Drive 2, Firearms 4, Fire Dancing 2, Melee 4, Performance 2, Security 1, Stealth 3, Survival 2

Knowledges: Academics 1, Area Knowledge 2, Investigation 2, Politics 2, Occult 1, Sabbat Lore 1

Disciplines: Dominate 3, Fortitude 2, Obtenebration 3, Potence 2

Backgrounds: Contacts 3, Herd 2, Influence 1, Resources 3, Retainers 1, Rituals 1, Sabbat Status 2

Virtues: Conviction 4, Instinct 4, Courage 4

Path Enlightenment: The Path of Power and the Inner Voice 5

Willpower: 7

SABBAT INQUISITOR

Background: These vampires are among the most driven of the Sabbat. They exist to purge the Sabbat of infernal influence. Inquisitors devote themselves utterly to their cause, believing that infernalism serves only to place the sect under the yoke of demons rather than the Antediluvians. Inquisitors make dangerous opponents, not only because of their personal powers, but because of their political ones as well.

Image: The Inquisitor affects the regalia of a medieval knight, albeit with a very modern twist. His armor is kevlar, and his horse is a souped-up motorcycle. His sword is still a sword, however, as one does not purge the Devil's taint with vulgar modern weapons. The Inquisitor's stoic face serves as a notice to others of how seriously he takes his responsibilities.

Roleplaying Hints: Seek out those who would sell their souls and relieve them of the option. Some accuse you of having no sense of humor. They're right. This is no laughing matter.

Clan: Ventrue *antitribu*

Nature: Penitent

Demeanor: Judge

Generation: 8th

Physical: Strength 4, Dexterity 4, Stamina 5

Social: Charisma 3, Manipulation 5, Appearance 4

Mental: Perception 5, Intelligence 3, Wits 4

Talents: Alertness 3, Brawl 1, Dodge 2, Empathy 4, Expression 1, Interrogation 3, Intimidation 3, Intuition 3, Leadership 3, Streetwise 1, Style 2, Subterfuge 4

Skills: Animal Ken 2, Drive 2, Etiquette 3, Firearms 2, Fire Dancing 2, Melee 4

Knowledge: Academics 2, Camarilla Lore 1, Enigmas 2, Investigation 5, Law 1, Linguistics 2, Occult 4, Politics 3, Research 1, Sabbat Lore 2

Disciplines: Auspex 2, Dominate 5, Fortitude 2, Presence 4, Thaumaturgy 2

Thaumaturgical Paths: Path of Blood 1, Spirit Manipulation 2

Backgrounds: Contacts 5, Influence 3, Mentor 4, Resources 3, Retainers 2, Sabbat Status 5

Virtues: Conscience 5, Self-Control 3, Courage 5

Path of Enlightenment: Path of Honorable Accord 8

Willpower: 9

New Pilgrim/Nomadic Sabbat

Background: Traveling the road as one of the Damned is difficult for the newly sired Sabbat. The road is a harsh reality, especially for those who are considered expendable. Nonetheless, new nomadic recruits have many opportunities to prove their worth to the pack. After all, if they don't, they end up Lupine chow or greeting the sun in podunk jail cells.

Image: Part Lestat, part Mad Max, the nomadic neonate wears a combination of leather and road grit. Her eyes scan the horizon warily, always alert for marauding werewolves or other threats. Her features are sunken and sallow, as the right to feed goes to the proven members of the pack first.

Roleplaying Hints: You did not make it through the Creation Rites with your wits intact. Your bizarre and unpredictable actions cause others to distance themselves from you. You're not very popular, but once you demonstrate your worth, your lot should improve. At least, you hope so. But if you don't succeed, you'll meet Final Death trying.

Clan: Malkavian *antitribu*

Nature: Enigma

Demeanor: Loner

Generation: 13th

Physical: Strength 3, Dexterity 3, Stamina 4

Social: Charisma 2, Manipulation 2, Appearance 2

Mental: Perception 3, Intelligence 2, Wits 3

Talents: Alertness 2, Brawl 3, Intimidation 1, Streetwise 2, Style 1, Throwing 1

Skills: Crafts 1, Drive 2, Firearms 2, Melee 2, Panhandling 2, Security 2, Sleight of Hand 2, Stealth 1, Survival 2

Knowledges: Investigation 2, Law 1, Linguistics 1, Medicine 1

Disciplines: Auspex 2, Fortitude 1, Obfuscate 2

Backgrounds: Resources 1, Contacts 1

Virtues: Conscience 1, Self-Control 2, Courage 4

Humanity: 3

Willpower: 5

Experienced Pilgrim/Nomadic Sabbat

Background: Adaptable pioneers, hunters and warriors, these vampires know how to survive even in "Lupine alleys" or Camarilla territories. Whether alone or with a pack, they know how to stay focused on their goals and kick a little — or a lot of — ass while they're at it. Experienced nomads have been hardened by the night roads and years, if not decades, of violence on the road. Tread with caution around these individuals, or you may not survive to meet them again.

Image: The experienced nomad has the "cowboy scowl" caused by many years of squinting into the dark distance. He wears weather-beaten leathers adorned with a few of his trophies — fingerbones, ribs, teeth and the like. The nomad's hair is long and dusty, pulled back into a ponytail.

Roleplaying Hints: You're good in a fight, and always ready for one. You sometimes think before you act, which would have been the end of you multiple times if it weren't for your packmates. You meet everyone with an air of hostility or disdain, and you despise those who appear soft or squeamish.

Clan: Tzimisce

Nature: Survivor

Demeanor: Thrill-Seeker

Generation: 11th

Physical: Strength 4, Dexterity 3, Stamina 5

Social: Charisma 2, Manipulation 2, Appearance 4

Mental: Perception 4, Intelligence 2, Wits 4

Talents: Alertness 3, Brawl 4, Dodge 2, Intimidation 2, Streetwise 2, Style 2, Subterfuge 2

Skills: Animal Ken 2, Drive 3, Crafts 3, Firearms 3, Fire Dancing 2, Melee 3, Security 1, Stealth 2, Survival 4

Knowledges: Enigmas 2, Investigation 2, Linguistics 3, Politics 2, Sabbat Lore 1

Disciplines: Animalism 2, Auspex 2, Fortitude 2, Vicissitude 2

Backgrounds: Contacts 3, Resources 1, Rituals 2, Sabbat Status 1

Virtues: Conviction 3, Instinct 3, Courage 5

Path of Enlightenment: Path of Lilith 6

Willpower: 6

VETERAN PILGRIM/NOMADIC SABBAT

Background: Soldiers of fortune, these vampires are welcome and respected in any Sabbat-held city because of their legendary acts of bravery and monstrosity. They eschew the politics and hierarchy of city unlife for the road, which has turned them into hardy horrors, if a bit coarse. Veteran pilgrims have seen it all — Lupines, sieges, anarch warbands and elder politics in the cities they pass through. They have also learned to deal with everything they've seen....

Image: The veteran nomad resembles nothing so much as the "pale rider" of western American lore. His skin has become weather-beaten, his gaze a slit-eyed squint and his smile a fanged snarl.

Roleplaying Hints: If it becomes a problem, kill it. If it's not a problem, you may want to kill it for kicks. You serve the Sabbat in thought and deed unquestioningly, and it is your first priority in any situation. You have little patience, however, for the soft schemers and aristocrats who would "guide" the sect from their laps of luxury. The sect as you see it is devoted to freedom, and the price of freedom is eternal vigilance (or so you've heard).

Clan: Ravnos *antitribu*

Nature: Monster

Demeanor: Rebel

Generation: 9th

Physical: Strength 5, Dexterity 5, Stamina 5

Social: Charisma 3, Manipulation 3, Appearance 3

Mental: Perception 5, Intelligence 2, Wits 4

Talents: Alertness 4, Athletics 1, Brawl 5, Dodge 3, Intimidation 3, Intuition 3, Leadership 1, Streetwise 3, Subterfuge 2, Throwing 1

Skills: Animal Ken 2, Crafts 4 (Motorcycle Maintenance), Drive 4, Etiquette 1, Firearms 5, Fire Dancing 2, Melee 4, Performance 2, Security 4, Stealth 4, Survival 3

Knowledges: Academics 1, Enigmas 1, Investigation 3, Linguistics 2, Sabbat Lore 2, Underworld Lore 1

Disciplines: Animalism 2, Auspex 1, Celerity 2, Chimerstry 4, Fortitude 4

Backgrounds: Contacts 5, Resources 2, Sabbat Status 2

Virtues: Conviction 3, Instinct 4, Courage 5

Path of Enlightenment: Path of Power and the Inner Voice 7

Willpower: 7

NOVICE SCOUT

Background: Novice scouts make up the majority of the Sabbat's spies. Scouts typically operate alone or with one partner. Unlike Sabbat packs that act as reconnaissance parties, these Sabbat actually "join" the Camarilla or anarchs of another city. Some Sabbat actually experience depression and intense feelings of isolation accentuated by the absence of the Vaulderie.

Image: The scout poses as an entertainer in his adopted city, working as a DJ at a club popular among the anarchs and neonates (as well as the kine…). He wears flashy designer clothes and keeps his hair short so the odor of smoke from the club doesn't stick to it. Everything about him exudes an air of cool calm, except his eyes, which reveal his inner fear of having his cover blown.

Roleplaying Hints: Sometimes your performances are so good that even you forget you're a spy. Your love for music

consumes you, and at times you have to remind yourself of your primary objective. You have to balance the unlifestyle you enjoy so much with your responsibility to the Sabbat.

Clan: Toreador *antitribu*
Nature: Bon Vivant
Demeanor: Gallant
Generation: 12th
Physical: Strength 2, Dexterity 2, Stamina 2
Social: Charisma 4, Manipulation 3, Appearance 3
Mental: Perception 2, Intelligence 4, Wits 2
Talents: Alertness 3, Brawl 1, Dodge 2, Empathy 2, Expression 2, Grace 2, Streetwise 3, Style 3, Subterfuge 1
Skills: Drive 2, Etiquette 1, Firearms 1, Melee 1, Performance 4, Stealth 3, Survival 1
Knowledges: Academics 2, Computer 2, Linguistics 1
Disciplines: Auspex 2, Celerity 1, Presence 2
Backgrounds: Alternate Identity 2, Contacts 2, Herd 1, Resources 2
Virtues: Conscience 2, Self-Control 3, Courage 3
Humanity: 5
Willpower: 5

EXPERT SCOUT

Background: Senior scouts handle more sensitive Sabbat reconnaissance efforts, to the point of impersonating key elders and ancillae in Camarilla cities. Most experienced scouts, however, continue their covert work, gathering information nightly and reporting back to their superiors at established intervals. They could have retired from these dangerous assignments years ago, but the thrill and the desire to aid the Sabbat keeps them in enemy territories. Occasionally, they may be paired with novices for training purposes.

Image: The expert scout has an unassuming aspect, and many who see her forget what she looks like altogether. She wears fine — but never flashy (unless her role requires it) — clothing and keeps herself well-groomed. The scout keeps her hair long, but cuts it when it is required of her. After all, it grows back each night....

Roleplaying Hints: You have maintained your Humanity to better hide among the Camarilla idiots, but you are Sabbat through and through. Give yourself wholly over to the false identity you assume, even to the point of denying your true self. Think like your "new" personality would and never let your true nature emerge from underneath that façade.

Clan: Malkavian *antitribu*
Nature: Deviant
Demeanor: Chameleon
Generation: 9th
Physical: Strength 4, Dexterity 3, Stamina 4
Social: Charisma 3, Manipulation 4, Appearance 3
Mental: Perception 4, Intelligence 4, Wits 4
Talents: Alertness 3, Brawl 3, Dodge 2, Empathy 3, Expression 3, Grace 2, Intimidation 3, Intuition 2, Streetwise 4, Style 4, Subterfuge 3
Skills: Drive 2, Etiquette 3, Firearms 2, Melee 3, Performance 5, Security 2, Stealth 2, Survival 3
Knowledges: Academics 2, Camarilla Lore 3, Computers 1, Investigation 4, Sabbat Lore 1
Disciplines: Auspex 3, Dementation 3, Fortitude 3, Obfuscate 4
Backgrounds: Allies 1, Alternate Identity 3, Contacts 3, Resources 3
Virtues: Conscience 3, Self-Control 2, Courage 4
Humanity: 5
Willpower: 7

INTERROGATOR

Background: The fiendish interrogators of the Sabbat are second to none when matters of extracting information arise. Using their Vicissitude, these vampires have perfected the art of torture to its immortal depths. They can draw all useful information from prisoners brought before them, regardless of how tough the victim believes himself to be. After all, they have an eternity to keep trying.

Image: The interrogator may have started his torture practice on himself, judging from all the piercings, tattoos and ritual mutilations that adorn him. He keeps his head shaved (so no blood or gore gets on it) and wears leather,

rubber or PVC clothing because it's easier to clean after a particularly vigorous session of interrogation.

Roleplaying Hints: This is a good line of work for you because you're one sick fuck. Nothing delights you so much as causing others pain, and you even enjoy pain yourself. Sometimes, after you've taken everything you need from your subject they tend to suffer "accidents." Funny how that happens. Others have expressed concern that you grow more cruel by the night, but hey, that's part of your responsibility.

Clan: Tzimisce

Nature: Sadist

Demeanor: Creep Show

Generation: 10th

Physical: Strength 2, Dexterity 4, Stamina 3

Social: Charisma 1, Manipulation 5, Appearance 5

Mental: Perception 3, Intelligence 2, Wits 3

Talents: Alertness 3, Empathy 5, Interrogation 4, Intimidation 4, Streetwise 3, Style 3, Subterfuge 3

Skills: Crafts 4 (Body Crafts), Drive 1, Etiquette 2, Fire Dancing 2,

Knowledges: Academics 2, Camarilla Lore 3, Sabbat Lore 3

Disciplines: Auspex 2, Dominate 2, Thaumaturgy 3, Vicissitude 3

Thaumaturgical Paths: Lure of Flames 1, Path of Blood 3, Spirit Manipulation 2

Backgrounds: Herd 2, Resources 3, Sabbat Status 2

Virtues: Conviction 2, Self-Control 3, Courage 2

Path of Enlightenment: Path of Death and the Soul 5

Willpower: 6

DIABLERIE ADDICT

Background: Drinking Cainite blood is one of the most euphoric experiences imaginable. The diablerie addict knows this all too well, and he can't stop himself. Whether committing the amaranth on packmates or enemies, the vampire loses himself in the heady rush of power and bloodlust.

Image: The diablerie addict is smooth, graceful and gregarious. He dresses well, relying on a "kid brother" or "successful associate" image to get other vampires to trust

him. His smile is both genuine and false — it's a lure, but he truly does relish the *essence* of his compatriots' company.

Roleplaying Hints: You go out of your way to shock and intimidate people with your bizarre behavior. Most of your friends know you have a habit, but they think it's street drugs, not friends and acquaintances. Who cares about Gehenna? Unlife is for the here and now. Besides, others in position of prestige and rank have lunched their way to the top; why shouldn't you?

Clan: Panders

Nature: Rogue

Demeanor: Bon Vivant

Generation: 8th

Physical: Strength 2, Dexterity 2, Stamina 2

Social: Charisma 4, Manipulation 3, Appearance 3

Mental: Perception 2, Intelligence 3, Wits 3

Talents: Brawl 1, Empathy 3, Expression 3, Grace 2, Streetwise 3, Style 2, Subterfuge 3

Skills: Drive 2, Etiquette 2, Firearms 2, Fire Dancing 1, Melee 1, Performance 1, Sleight of Hand 1

Knowledges: Academics 2, Computer 1, Finance 1, Politics 1

Disciplines: Auspex 1, Celerity 1, Dominate 1, Fortitude 1, Obfuscate 2, Obtenebration 1, Protean 1, Quietus 1, Serpentis 1, Vicissitude 1

Backgrounds: Resources 2

Virtues: Conscience 2, Self-Control 1, Courage 3

Humanity: 4

Willpower: 5

GHOULS

Reluctantly, the Sabbat sometimes makes use of ghouls to interact with mortal society and protect communal havens during daylight hours. Since the Sabbat tends to dislike and distrust humans, vampires of the sect prefer ghouls that are animals. Regardless, there are times when human ghouls become necessary, and the Sabbat goes to extraordinary lengths to ensure loyalty, to the point of using Vicissitude and the blood bond to bind servant to master. (Of course, a Sabbat would never bond another Sabbat, but what the hell, these are mere humans....) Ghouls also serve as food, cannon fodder and companions (i.e., pets).

For the most part, the sect treats its ghouls with utter disdain. It is not uncommon for ghouls to be used as bait during Lupine hunts, and many Sabbat make a practice of killing the bearer of bad news, who is most often a ghoul. Ghouls are also responsible for much of the scout work of the sect — cleaning havens, driving communal vehicles, kidnapping vessels, mopping up after esbats and the like. Certainly, the life of a Sabbat ghoul is precarious and abysmal. At any moment, the masters may decide the ghoul makes better food

than help, and most of what the ghoul is assigned to do is dangerous, illegal or both.

Needless to say, few mortals actually seek to become involved with the sect (assuming they know about it at all, which is unlikely unless they're already ghouls, and quite knowledgeable at that). Most mortal ghouls are conscripts, offered a "serve and *maybe* die or just die outright" proposition. Ghouls become pack property, rarely acknowledging a single master and serving whomever yells at them the loudest or most recently. A few individuals actually enjoy the submissive aspect of these relationships, but they rarely live long, suffering the twisted whims of their masters or dying to alleviate their domitors' boredom.

Animal ghouls, ironically, generally receive better treatment than their human counterparts. This isn't to say that animal ghouls have it easy; rather, their masters often twist them into monstrous shapes, starve them of normal food, send them to fight foes and kick them when they're upset. Most Sabbat are wise enough to realize, however, that animals are utterly dependent upon their masters, and they treat them as they would a new recruit or a favored pet.

The Sabbat looks down on the practice of ghouling, but accepts it as a necessary evil. Packs are usually "allowed" one or two ghouls — not that there's any formal complaint lodged against them if they keep more, but other packs may view them as weak or dependent and develop antagonism toward them. For the most part, packs keep a ghoul or two for perhaps a few months or years and then replace him. Obviously, few ghouls survive replacement.

FAMILY TIES: THE TZIMISCE REVENANT HOUSES

For untold centuries, the Tzimisce have practiced the art of selective breeding on their most trusted (or at least most useful) servants. In the early Middle Ages, certain elders of the clan undertook a long-term experiment studying the effects of regular vitae infusion into the blood of several Eastern European noble families. The eventual result, a handful of generations later, was the creation of revenants: humans with vastly extended natural life spans and hereditary affinities for certain vampiric Disciplines, which they can develop much as Kindred can. Revenants also naturally produce a less powerful version of vampiric vitae, making them something of self-sustaining ghouls. Conservative voices among the Fiends suggest that there is more to the creation of revenants than simple vampire blood, however, and attribute part of the effect to the natural magic of the lands of Eastern Europe.

A millennium ago, over a dozen distinct revenant lines served the Tzimisce. However, several were exterminated during the Inquisition and the Anarch Revolt, two (the Narov and the Ruthvenski) were absorbed into surviving families through intermarriage, and it is rumored that two others (the Ducheski and the Rustovitch) have broken away from the Tzimisce and now serve other masters — a distinctly dangerous proposition, given the Fiends' penchant for extended, exquisite vengeance. Other rumors state that the Assamites, Setites, Giovanni, or Tremere have followed in the footsteps of the Tzimisce and cultivated their own lines of revenant servants.

The four Sabbat revenant families that have survived to the modern nights are universally wretched and disturbing specimens by any "normal" standard. Incest, pedophilia, cannibalism, bestiality, substance abuse, and fringe-movement political activism are among the more tame hobbies practiced by the revenant families — and such behavior endears them all the more to their masters, who watch these depraved antics with a twisted glee. Revenants often follow Sabbat Paths of Enlightenment in place of human codes of morality; indeed, many of the older revenants have accepted their Paths more fully than have Cainites of comparable age, having been born into households that look askance at mainstream morality and view "ordinary" mortals as distinctly inferior beings. A revenant is able to casually pass for human more easily than low-Humanity vampire simply by virtue of having a pulse and being in the habit of breathing, but don't expect her to succeed in a college ethics course unless she's been trained to make a deliberate effort to fit in.

Revenants are like other ghouls, with the following exceptions:

• A revenant produces one blood point of vitae per night. This is not considered Cainite blood, and it cannot be used to create other ghouls, Embrace a drained corpse, or create blood bonds. A revenant has a maximum blood pool of 10 blood points, plus one blood point for every century he's existed.

• In addition to family Disciplines, a revenant also inherits a family weakness in much the same manner as a vampire acquires a clan weakness.

For more information on revenants in the modern nights, see Ghouls: Fatal Addiction. Players and Storytellers seeking data on historical revenants should consult Libellus Sanguinis I: Masters of the State.

BRATOVITCH

The most bestial of the four families, the Bratovitches mainly keep to their isolated rural estates, breeding hellhounds and other unsavory fauna and emerging only to hunt Lupines and other beast of the night, to kidnap brides and studs, or to serve as trackers for nomadic Sabbat packs. Members of this family are, as a general rule, more subhuman than most other revenants, and they delight in their perversity and savagery. Most Sabbat tend to avoid Bratovitch estates unless they are truly desperate. This is not out of fear — Bratovitches look up to Sabbat Cainites as "big, nasty uncles" of a sort — but rather out of disgust. Cross a stereotypical back-country hill clan with a Tzimisce and season with a liberal amount of pure Neanderthal hunt-kill-mate mentality and you'll have a good representation of a Bratovitch. The family primarily lairs in the North American wilderness, though a handful of outposts can be found in South America and the family's ancestral estate in Poland is still a respectably sized holding.

Members of the Bratovitch line do not follow Humanity; it's too alien to them. Curiously, many Sabbat Paths of Enlightenment are spread fairly equally through the family, and the handful of Bratovitches with scholarly pretensions have actually preserved some antiquated codes of morality that even most vampires have forgotten.

Disciplines: Animalism, Potence, Vicissitude

Weakness: Bratovitches are easily annoyed — some would say psychotic. They make all rolls to resist frenzy at +2 difficulty, and do not play well with normal mortals.

GRIMALDI

Once merchants in the Italian city-states of the 12th century, the Grimaldis still enjoy a profitable position of go-between for the Sabbat's dealings with mortal society. They are probably the most "normal" of the four families, though some would argue that extreme wealth sets one apart as much as their vampire blood does. Grimaldis are usually groomed for positions of power, and it is not uncommon for a member of this family to hold a high political office or a corporate leadership role in his home city. Starting at birth, Grimaldis enjoy every luxury that life has to offer, from private schools and tutors to decadent vacations at the most exclusive resorts to the most *wonderful* toys....

In addition to furthering the political agendas of their masters, the Grimaldis have a second, more personal goal that is kept secret from all but the leaders of the family. Grimaldi elders believe that their continued existence hinges on their utility to the Sabbat, and their destruction will be swift and total should the Tzimisce ever withdraw their aegis. Accordingly, the Grimaldi have begun to formulate contingency plans for a transfer of family loyalty to the Ventrue of the Camarilla or, alternately, to the Giovanni, should the Sabbat ever decide that the Grimaldis have outlived their usefulness. Needless to say, this information *would* ensure the family's total obliteration should it ever come to light, so the privileged few who know of these treasonous thoughts make certain to stay well away from their nominal masters.

The majority of Grimaldis follow the Path of Honorable Accord or the Path of Power and the Inner Voice. Some, however, are known to walk the Path of Caine (with appropriate allowances for their inability to commit diablerie). More and more younger Grimaldi have taken to rejecting their forebears' "antiquated" moral codes and staying with Humanity, a development that distresses the few Tzimisce who have observed it.

Disciplines: Celerity, Dominate, Fortitude

Weakness: All Grimaldis past puberty are blood bound to Sabbat members of bishop rank or above. This began as a safety measure to ensure that the Grimaldis did not betray the Sabbat in the course of their extensive mingling with mortal society, but has devolved to little more than a formal rite of passage and sign of majority in modern nights. Most Sabbat rarely call upon their thralls; those unlucky Grimaldi whose regnants frequently impose their will upon the revenants will most likely be written off as "acceptable losses" if and when the family decides to shift its allegiance.

OBERTUS

Reclusive scholars, the Obertuses have managed to maintain their continued existence by avoiding the Sabbat's notice and by feeding their Tzimisce patrons a steady trickle of research data. Originally librarians and clerics for the Tzimisce lords of the Byzantine Empire, the Obertus family moved first to the clan's ancestral homelands in Eastern Europe, then to the New World during the first waves of Sabbat colonization. They still maintain a strong presence in the New England states and the eastern Canadian provinces. The Obertuses can best be characterized as chthonic, both in their reclusive small-town nature and in their constant search for knowledge that they may not necessarily want. Obertus research tends toward the paranormal: "ghoulies, ghosties, long-leggity beasties, and things that go bump in the night," among other subjects.

Like the Grimaldis, the Obertuses have a secret objective that might well lead to their destruction should the Sabbat discover it. The Obertus family elders have come to believe that revenant existence is the key to the next logical step in human evolution: *Homo obertus* is destined to replace *Homo sapiens*, just as modern humans exterminated the Neanderthal. To this end, the family conducts experiments with various permutations on the Embrace and the ghouling process, using vitae from several captured Camarilla "Kindred" and one Tzimisce elder who was foolish enough to enter voluntary torpor in an Obertus-controlled fishing village outside Boston. No definite results have appeared yet, but the Obertuses believe they may be close to discovering the secret of perpetuating "ghoul" existence without a source of vampiric vitae.

Most Obertuses prefer to follow the Path of Death and the Soul, the Path of Harmony, or the Path of Honorable Accord. Recently, some have begun studying the Path of Metamorphosis with an eye toward adapting it to their "new man."

Disciplines: Auspex, Obfuscate, Vicissitude

Weakness: The Obertuses were bred for intellectual ability, sometimes at the expense of stability, and are thus prone to monomania and similar psychological disorders. The vast majority of Obertus revenants suffer from the Obsessive/Compulsive derangement (see **Vampire: The Masquerade**, p. 222). At the Storyteller's discretion, an Obertus may suffer another intellectual-style derangement for the "default" derangement — but *all* Obertuses exhibit some derangement.

ZANTOSA

The Zantosas don't really seem to have a reason for continued existence; in fact, if asked her opinion of them, the average Sabbat vampire — assuming she had even heard of revenant families — would reply with a blank look. The Zantosa family appears to have outlived its usefulness, and exists primarily to continue its members' decadent, self-indulgent lifestyles and to provide entertainment for the Toreador *antitribu*, Serpents of the Light, and Tzimisce. Once the cream of Eastern Europe's social elite, the Zantosas have curdled and withdrawn, forsaking long-term sociopolitical manipulation for short-term gratification. The primary family pursuits these nights include petty crime, vice, black marketeering, and pushing the boundaries of pleasure, pain, and other sensations. Indeed, the only ostensible reason the Zantosas haven't been wiped out by a Black Hand-led pogrom already is that the end results wouldn't be worth the effort expended to cleanse their penthouses, nightclubs, and movie studios.

Recently, an internal purge rocked the Zantosa family estate in New York. No less than two dozen family members, most with previously impeccable reputations (as Zantosa reputations go), were put to death in sudden and grisly fashion by household elders. Sabbat inquiries were notably cursory ("let them kill themselves off" seems to have been the general attitude) and were met with responses that the destroyed parties had been caught dabbling in dark sorcery — a response that, curiously enough, did *not* warrant an Inquisition investigation. The truth, known only to the Zantosa family's uppermost echelon, is far more ominous. For the past several centuries, the Zantosa family has guarded a torporous form believed to be a Tzimisce vampire of great age. One night in mid-1997, the crypt in which the body in question lay was found empty with no prior warning and no evidence . No explanation has yet been forthcoming.

Most Zantosas study the Path of Cathari with an enthusiasm bordering on fanaticism, and some observers have commented that this family is more suited to following the Toreador *antitribu* than to serving the Tzimisce. A few dedicated individuals pursue the Path of Death and the Soul, and one rural enclave with close contact with the Bratovitches follows the Path of Death and the Soul. Persistent rumors state that there is a secret Noddist society within the family, but no Zantosa has openly admitted to following the Path of Caine.

Disciplines: Auspex, Presence, Vicissitude

Weakness: Zantosas are rather weak-willed when it comes to resisting temptation — *any* temptation. Accordingly, whenever a Zantosa is exposed to a particularly pleasurable experience, she must make a Willpower roll (difficulty determined by the Storyteller, depending on the experience in question). Failure indicates that the Zantosa is now obsessed with or addicted to that particular sensation (which can be anything from doing a new drug to performing a particular sexual position to enjoying a sumptuous wine to the act of being fed upon) and will do damn near anything to experience it again. Zantosas are also unable to spend Willpower to resist any supernatural power that entices them toward a new source of pleasure, and many have met untimely ends at the hands and other appendages of Cainites, fae, and stranger creatures.

The following three types of ghouls are those most commonly found among Sabbat havens. **Ghouls: Fatal Addiction** also offers a vast array of ghouls who could serve the Sabbat effectively, as well as more insight into the sect's attitude on the matter.

HELL HOUND

The hell hound is a warped dog. Tzimisce use their powers of Vicissitude to horribly disfigure the poor animal, making it even more terrifying to view. Tzimisce prefer large hounds like mastiffs, rottweilers and wolfhounds, but any canine will do.

Physical: Strength 4, Dexterity 3, Stamina 4
Social: Not applicable
Mental: Perception 3, Intelligence 1, Wits 3
Talents: Alertness 3, Athletics 2, Brawl 4, Dodge 3, Empathy 1, Intimidation 4, Stealth 2
Disciplines: Potence 2
Willpower: 6
Blood Pool: 4
Attack: Bite/5 dice, Claw/3 dice
Health Levels: OK, OK, -1, -1, -2, -2, -5, Incapacitated

TOADY

Few human ghouls serve the Sabbat for any length of time. Those who do primarily protect or provide for the needs of communal pack havens. These ghouls are often horribly altered through Vicissitude which binds them to their Sabbat master since mortal society would reject such a visual freak. Toadies may generally do as they please, provided they serve their masters faithfully. In the end, however, these minions are mere mortals, and they often meet gruesome demises at the hands of their cruel keepers, if not in combat.

The following entry represents a guardian ghoul altered through Vicissitude. Most ghouls of this type are… unique… in appearance.

Physical: Strength 5, Dexterity 4, Stamina 5
Social: Charisma 1, Manipulation 1, Appearance 0
Mental: Perception 2, Intelligence 2, Wits 4
Talents: Alertness 2, Interrogation 1, Brawl 4, Dodge 2, Intimidation 2
Skills: Animal Ken 1, Firearms 3, Melee 2, Stealth 3
Knowledges: Computer 1, Investigation 2, Occult 2

Disciplines: Fortitude 1, Potence 2
Virtues: Conscience 1, Self-Control 2, Courage 5
Humanity: 3
Willpower: 4
Attack: Vicissitude-enhanced bone spur/6 dice

FACE

Despite their disdain for the mortal world, many Sabbat still deal with humankind to some degree or another. Obviously, their nocturnal unlifestyles make this difficult, so some Cainites employ the aid of ghouls to speak and act for them. These ghouls often live skittish, tenuous lives, always looking over their shoulder for their twisted masters, or suffering the ire of other vampires. Paranoia often overtakes even those who do not suffer the stings of their masters' whips as they slowly sink into a world of intrigue and sanguinary treachery.

The following entry is for a "mouthpiece" ghoul, a manservant who has duties other than violence and haven-guarding.

Physical: Strength 2, Dexterity 2, Stamina 2
Social: Charisma 3, Manipulation 3, Appearance 3
Mental: Perception 2, Intelligence 2, Wits 2
Talents: Alertness 2, Empathy 2, Subterfuge 1
Skills: Drive 2, Etiquette 2, Firearms 1, Stealth 1
Knowledges: Computer 1, Investigation 2, Politics 1
Disciplines: Dominate 1, Fortitude 1
Virtues: Conscience 3, Self-Control 3, Courage 3
Humanity: 6
Willpower: 4

NEW CLOSE COMBAT MANEUVER

• **Chainsaw Gouge:** This devastating maneuver almost always results in death to the victim, or at least a crippling wound.

The attacker must first "impale" his victim with a chainsaw (though this may be performed with any cutting-and-impaling weapon, such as a sword or knife) by scoring three or more successes on his attack roll, which damages the victim normally. The victim must then succeed in a Dexterity roll (difficulty 6) or be "trapped" by the blade. The following turn, the attacker pulls the chainsaw up *through* the victim's body, spraying blood everywhere and inflicting brutal damage. As the chainsaw is already lodged in the victim's body, no roll is required to see if the attacker actually "hits." Fiendishness of this caliber requires a Conscience roll (difficulty 6) for anyone possessed of Humanity 3 or greater who performs such an act (though followers of some paths might not suffer such qualms).

Ability: Dexterity + Melee	**Difficulty:** None
Accuracy: None	**Damage:** Weapon type+2

NEW RANGED COMBAT MANEUVERS

• **Hollywood Shooting:** Some would-be shootist will always insist on holding his gun sideways like the gangsters and tough guys in the movies. Maybe it looks cool, but it ruins the accuracy of the shot and often causes the gun to jam as the ejected shell casing catches between the slide and barrel (a "stovepipe"). To be sure, nothing positive can come of shooting like this, but some onlookers seem to think it's nifty. This style of shooting may also be appropriate for someone with no Firearms skill who's seen too many movies, or for a gun-wielding thug whose experience comes from the streets instead of the gun range.

If the assailant botches on his Firearms roll while Hollywood shooting an automatic, not only does his gun jam, but the gun jerks his arm away (as the gun literally catches the casing and follows it), resulting in a –1 to all dice pools on the following turn (and any other actions taken during the same turn). Botching with a revolver carries no unique penalty — perhaps the cylinder explodes or refuses to spin, as per a normal botch.

Ability: Dexterity + Firearms   **Difficulty:** +1
Accuracy: -1   **Damage:** Weapon type

• **Spray:** Flamethrowers issues forth a "spray" of flame instead of a physical projectile. The weapon emits a steady stream of flame, not unlike a fire hose, which sweeps over an area. This spray functions like strafing, adding 10 dice to a standard attack roll, with a +1 difficulty for each meter in area of effect covered beyond the first.

Successes are divided up just as in strafing and do not apply to the damage effect; each success on the roll yields one automatic health level of burning damage, which may be soaked as described in **Vampire: The Masquerade**, page 227.

Dodge rolls against fire spray are at +1 difficulty.

Ability: Dexterity + Firearms   **Difficulty:** 5
Accuracy: +10   **Damage:** Special

Weapons

The Sabbat, taking into account its members fanaticism and fledgling fiendishness has been known to make use of some unconventional weapons when violence becomes an issue. Whether charging a Camarilla prince with a flamethrower or gutting a rowdy biker with a broken bottle, the Sabbat is unafraid to hurt itself, as long as it hurts its opposition more.

Firearms

Firearm Traits

Caliber: The diameter of the bullet fired by the gun in question. Caliber is given in either a fraction of an inch (e.g. .45 caliber is 45/100 of an inch across) or millimeters (e.g. 9mm). None of the weapons here have a true caliber, however; the Trait is included merely for consistency.

Damage: The base number of dice rolled for damage after a successful strike. All firearms do lethal damage against mortal targets. Against vampires, firearms do merely bashing damage, unless the head is targeted (which adds 2 to attack difficulties and one die to damage pools, as per **Vampire: The Masquerade**, page 209), in which case the damage is considered lethal.

Range: This is the practical shot range in yards. Weapons may be fired at twice this distance, but the attacks are considered long range (difficulty 8).

Rate: The gun's maximum cyclic rate, or the number of shots it may fire per combat turn.

Clip: The number of shots that the weapon holds.

Conceal: P = Can be carried in the pocket; J = Can be hidden in a jacket; T = Can be hidden in a trenchcoat; N = Cannot be concealed on the person at all.

Zip Gun: Simple, homemade affairs, zip guns are hastily assembled mechanisms for firing bullets in the general direction of the gunman's enemy. Anything resembling accuracy is impossible with such low-tech methods, but these guns' disposable nature and low cost (they can be made from parts stolen from cars parked on the street) make them a viable option in a pinch.

Caliber: None, really; varies by whatever bullet you fire out of it

Damage: 3 (some models have no chamber to aid compression, and may cause only 2 dice of damage)

   Range: 5 to 15
   Rate: 1
   Clip: 1
   Conceal: P, and if a cop finds it, you're in serious trouble

Flamethrower: A vampire carrying a canister of volatile liquid on his back is unlikely to last long, but some Sabbat are so devout (or insane) that they'll take the chance if it means smiting enough enemies. A flamethrower "shoots" a high-pressure spray of combustible liquid at its target, igniting the liquid as it leaves the weapon. Needless to say, getting a hold of one of these is quite difficult, and ludicrously illegal. **Note:** If a bullet strikes the tank, the Storyteller should roll a die. On a 7 or less, the tank explodes, doing 12 dice of aggravated damage to the wearer, reduced by 2 dice for every yard of distance from the blast for anyone else caught in the conflagration. Aiming for the tank increases the difficulty of a given shot by 3.

   Caliber: N/A
   Damage: Varies by amount of target's body covered. See **Vampire: The Masquerade**, page 227
   Range: 3 to 10
   Rate: N/A
   Clip: 20 turns of fuel
   Conceal: N (the rig weighs between 30 and 60 pounds)

Melee Weapons

Melee Weapon Traits

Damage: The base number of damage dice rolled after a successful strike. For melee weapons, this is based on the character's Strength Trait (and Potence, if any) plus a number of dice determined by the size, mass and design of the weapon in question.

Conceal: The amount of clothing under which the weapon may be hidden. P = in a pocket, J = under a jacket, T = under a trench coat, and N = the weapon is too large to carry concealed.

Minimum Strength: The minimum Strength (Potence applies to this total) that a character must have in order to wield the weapon in combat.

Blunt Weapons

Bottle: Ubiquitous and conveniently sized, bottles make passable improvised clubs. If the bottle is broken, it becomes an edged weapon that does lethal damage. Breaking a bottle so that it is a *functional* edged weapon and not a handful of shattered glass is difficult, and subject to Storyteller discretion.

Damage: Strength
Conceal: J
Minimum Strength: 1

Sledgehammer: This refers to a construction-grade sledgehammer, used primarily for breaking concrete and other masonry. In the arms of even an average man or vampire, the sledgehammer is capable of splitting heads like ripe melons. Being caught walking around with one is a good way to spend an hour or two in the back seat of a police car, with a possible bonus stop at the county lockup.

Damage: Strength +3
Conceal: T
Minimum Strength: 3

Edged Weapons

Edged weapons do lethal damage unless otherwise indicated.

Board with a Nail: The archetypal thug weapon, boards with nails are cheap, menacing and dangerously effective. Police take dim views of those who arm themselves with such obvious implements of destruction. The board with a nail may be soaked as if it was a blunt weapon, but leftover damage is considered lethal (and thus not halved by vampires).

Damage: Strength +2
Conceal: T
Minimum Strength: 2

Chainsaw: A chainsaw is a gas- or electric-powered sawblade used to cut down trees. It is merciless when used as a weapon, as it passes through soft flesh like a hot knife through butter. It is also quite awkward, and attempts to use it as a weapon are at +1 difficulty.

Damage: Strength +4
Conceal: N
Minimum Strength: 2

Cleaver: A heavy, oblong kitchen knife, the cleaver is surprisingly quick. They're used to dress chickens and dice vegetables, and have similar effects when used on human anatomy.

Damage: Strength +1
Conceal: J
Minimum Strength: 1

Machete: A heavy, broad swordlike knife used for hacking one's way through jungle undergrowth, the machete becomes brutal and intimidating when used as a weapon. Many Sabbat packs in Mexico have adopted the machete as their weapon of choice.

Damage: Strength +2
Conceal: T
Minimum Strength: 1

Meathook: Meathooks are used in slaughterhouses and meat-packing plants to drag or hang hundred-pound animal carcasses. While of questionable effectiveness as a weapon — their curved shape tends to stick *in* the victim — they nonetheless cause a significant amount of impaling trauma. Additionally, their wicked look makes quite an impression on would-be enemies.

Damage: Strength +1
Conceal: J
Minimum Strength: 1

Straight Razor: The straight razor does little damage, as its fine blade causes minimal trauma in and of itself. However, the precise cuts they make can cause havoc when applied to important blood vessels, or they may be used to open the skin in preparation for stripping it all away by hand.

Damage: Strength -1
Conceal: P
Minimum Strength: 1

INDEX

INDEX

Index